ROGUE ELEPHANT

ROGUE ELEPHANT

*Harnessing the Power of
India's Unruly Democracy*

SIMON DENYER

BLOOMSBURY PRESS
NEW YORK · LONDON · NEW DELHI · SYDNEY

Copyright © 2014 by Simon Denyer

All rights reserved. No part of this book may be used or reproduced
in any manner whatsoever without written permission from the publisher
except in the case of brief quotations embodied in critical articles or reviews.
For information address Bloomsbury Press, 1385 Broadway, New York, NY 10018.

Every reasonable effort has been made to trace copyright holders
of material reproduced in this book, but if any have been inadvertently
overlooked the publishers would be glad to hear from them.

Published by Bloomsbury Press, New York
Bloomsbury is a trademark of Bloomsbury Publishing Plc

All papers used by Bloomsbury Press are natural, recyclable products made
from wood grown in well-managed forests. The manufacturing processes
conform to the environmental regulations of the country of origin.

LIBRARY OF CONGRESS CATALOGING-IN-PUBLICATION DATA HAS BEEN APPLIED FOR

ISBN: 978-1-62040-608-3

First published in Great Britain in 2014
First U.S. Edition 2014

1 3 5 7 9 10 8 6 4 2

Typeset by Hewer Text UK Ltd, Edinburgh
Printed and bound in the U.S.A. by Thomson-Shore Inc., Dexter, Michigan

Bloomsbury Press books may be purchased for business or promotional use.
For information on bulk purchases please contact Macmillan Corporate
and Premium Sales Department at specialmarkets@macmillan.com.

To my girls, Sarah and Molly, and in memory of my
mum and dad, for all their love and support

Contents

Introduction

When I arrived in India in February 2004, the country stood on the cusp of an exciting new era. The government led by the Hindu nationalist Bharatiya Janata Party (BJP) proclaimed that India was 'shining', the tourism ministry declared it was 'incredible', and the nation's self-confidence seemed irrepressible. The economic reforms begun more than two decades before had pushed aside the suffocating red tape of India's quasi-socialist controlled economy, and unleashed the country's formidable entrepreneurial spirit.

India was changing in front of my eyes, as gleaming shopping malls selling the latest Western brands sprang up across its major cities. The streets of New Delhi were packed full of cars, and a growing middle class was gorging itself on luxury imported goods unimaginable in the old days of Indian 'self-reliance'. Mobile phones were flying off the shelves and reaching into some of the remotest rural corners of the country. The economy was growing at more than 8 per cent a year, foreign investors were flocking to its shores, and the boom had given the nation a huge dose of self-confidence. India was being talked about in the same breath as China, not just as an unmissable emerging market opportunity but as a potential superpower in the making.

Ironically, the 'India Shining' slogan was credited by some for losing the BJP the election in April and May of 2004, because it had left hundreds of millions of rural poor feeling excluded. Yet the idea behind it lived on. A coalition led by India's grand old party, Congress, came to power. The party's choice of prime minister was the man who had started the ball rolling as finance minister back in 1991, the 'father' of India's economic reforms, Manmohan Singh. The promise of a golden era beckoned. For several years, economic growth continued to impress, and when the Western world reeled under its worst financial crisis since the Great Depression, India merely shrugged off the bad news and kept on going.

The narrative was powerful. For the international media, it became distinctly unfashionable to report on the 'old India' of child brides and malnutrition, of caste and slums. Foreign journalists flocked to India, unearthing stories about India's fast-growing middle class and changing lifestyles, subjects far more appealing to foreign editors eager to 'capture the change'. In India, one leading newspaper proclaimed that India was officially no longer a poor country, not because poverty was falling, but because it boasted four of the world's ten richest billionaires.[1] Around the world, newspapers, commentators and politicians scrambled to proclaim the dawn of 'India's Century'.

In 2006, George W. Bush arrived in New Delhi to sign a landmark deal between the world's two largest democracies, developing nuclear power for civilian use, proclaiming that 'the partnership between our free nations has the power to transform the world'. Four years later, Obama called that accord 'one of the defining partnerships of the twenty-first century'.

And so India re-entered the Western consciousness, and not just for its supposed mysticism, poverty and snake charmers. At Reuters, the global news agency where I ran the India bureau at the time, we hired dozens of new reporters to satisfy the demand for business news. When *Slumdog Millionaire* won eight Oscars, friends in Washington threw a Bollywood party. At Reuters we launched an Indian website and hired a Bollywood reporter.

In 2009, Singh won a second term in office, at the head of another coalition government. Then, just as India started to preen itself, just as its self-confidence took on a distinct edge of cockiness,[2] the dream fell apart.

Where Beijing had wowed, charmed and slightly scared the world with its ruthlessly efficient Olympics in 2008, two years later India invoked scorn and not a little pity with its chaotic preparations for the Commonwealth Games. These games, a smaller version of the Olympics, invite fifty-four countries to compete in twenty-one different sports, ranging from athletics to lawn bowls, from swimming to rugby. Yet instead of advertising India's rise, the Commonwealth Games in New Delhi proved a public-relations disaster. Just days before its opening, child labourers were photographed installing seats in the Games' flagship Jawaharlal Nehru stadium, while outside the stadium a footbridge collapsed injuring thirty people. But it was the filth and lack of hygiene in the apartments at the athletes' villages that most shocked the outside world. Building grime and debris littered the bathrooms even as officials arrived to inspect the accommodation, with pools of water in bathrooms and human excrement reportedly found in one sink. Stray dogs foraged freely in piles of rubbish outside the athletes' apartments. The Scottish team proclaimed their accommodation 'unfit for human habitation', while one British newspaper summed it up bluntly: 'India's games stink'.[3]

Yet it was the stench of corruption that really sickened many Indians. A twelve-day event that had been hailed as India's opportunity to showcase its arrival on the world stage served instead to uncover its politicians' supreme ability to steal. Government auditors were to conclude that more than $400 million was wasted from a total budget of some $2 billion.[4] The accounts also revealed a trail of rigged tenders and vastly inflated bills that ranged from $80 for individual rolls of toilet paper to $514,000 for a bandstand that was never even built.

Then, a few months after the Commonwealth Games in 2010, an even more damaging scam broke over the nation, striking at one of the most emblematic industries of the new India.

In the decade from 2002 to 2012, the number of mobile phones in India had grown from 6.5 million to 900 million. Today far more Indians own mobile phones than have access to toilets. But, as it turned out, government licences to operate telecommunications' bandwidths had allegedly been given away at rock-bottom prices in return for hundreds of millions of dollars of bribes. When the government's independent auditor investigated, he concluded that the episode had cost the exchequer tens of billions of dollars in lost revenue.[5] The telecom industry was supposed to be a prime example of the rich pickings found in India's vast and expanding consumer market. Instead it became a prime example of how the government's almost insatiable greed could tarnish even the most shining of success stories, and a caution to foreign investors of the perils of doing business here.

These scams, eagerly gobbled up by India's now-dominant television news channels, seemed to do more than damage India's image abroad. They seemed also to undermine India's self-belief. The government froze. Its inability to make decisions was magnified only by the fear of making the wrong one, or of being associated with corruption. If graft could not be eradicated, the system's only defence against these allegations was to seize up completely. Partly as a result, long-overdue reforms to liberalize the Indian economy further – to sort out labour relations and regulate the way that farmland is acquired for industry, to allow in more foreign investment, and to expand India's overloaded infrastructure with more roads, power plants and ports – were delayed or derailed.

The reforms enacted by Singh in 1991 had not just unleashed two decades of economic growth, they had also generated a consumer and information revolution. They had led, in other words, to what some economists call 'a revolution of rising expectations', as India's people sought to throw off the narrow confines of class and caste and take their place in the modern economy. But economic progress had also placed huge new demands on the Indian state to deliver. It was no longer enough for India's government to get out of the way of the private sector, as it had started to do in 1991; it now needed to build the physical infrastructure and nourish the human capital, as well as provide the governance and regulatory framework, required to support that economy.

In that task, the Indian government has largely failed. Today, the Indian state seems stuck decades in the past, while the private sector strives to remain on the cutting edge of twenty-first-century progress. As the second decade of that century opened, India's economic miracle began to fade. Growth slowed and foreign investors began to re-evaluate their initial enthusiasm.

As the gap began to yawn wider between the Indian people's aspirations and its politicians' ability to deliver, frustration gathered. In 2011 a nationwide movement against corruption brought hundreds of thousands of people, many of them members of the traditionally politically apathetic middle class, onto the streets. They were organized through Facebook and Twitter and encouraged by television anchors who began to see themselves as crusaders for change. As the Arab world rose against its dictators and military rulers that year, so the youth of India experienced their own collective epiphany: that they could demand more from their rulers, and that tolerating corruption with a shrug and a grumble was no longer enough.

But that movement, and beyond it the general mood, also contained a deep sense of despair about the nature of democracy. The leaders of the India Against Corruption movement asked whether parliament, made up of India's elected politicians, could any longer be trusted to make the nation's laws. Many ordinary citizens asked the same question. Could a democracy that was so corrupted really satisfy the fast-growing aspirations of its people?

Polls showed that a majority of middle-class Indians felt that democracy itself was an obstacle to the country's economic progress,[6] and some even looked enviously towards the apparent certainties of China's one-party, pro-growth dictatorship.

I had arrived in India from a previous posting in Pakistan, a country feeling its way in the post-9/11 world under the military dictatorship of General Pervez Musharraf, and been immediately intrigued by India's insanely complex democracy. I had interviewed the BJP's deputy leader Lal Krishna Advani on board his orange campaign bus as he toured southern India, I had met Congress leader Sonia Gandhi, as well as her children Rahul and Priyanka, as they campaigned in their traditional strongholds in Uttar Pradesh. I had watched, enthralled, as the world's largest exercise in democracy unfolded in the spring of 2004, in four phases, across 700,000 polling stations and four weeks.

In the years that followed, I'd had plenty of time to ponder India's unique democracy. I had visited the insurgency-racked states of Kashmir, on the country's northwest border with Pakistan, and of Manipur, on its eastern border with Myanmar, and I saw first-hand what happens when democracy is mangled and manipulated. Strangely, those trips gave me a greater respect for the benefits democracy brings to the heart of India. I had seen politicians failing to honour their promises, but I had also seen voters getting their revenge, mostly at the ballot box.

In 2007, on the sixtieth anniversary of India's Independence from Britain, I'd thought long and hard about the nature of democracy here, as I talked with a charming elderly gentleman about the horrors of Partition.

His name was Ranbir Rai Handa, and he had been just fourteen years old when he was pitched into the madness of Partition, forced to flee his hometown of Lahore on a train travelling from newly independent Pakistan to India. What he saw when he arrived in Amritsar on 14 August 1947 still kept him awake at night. Thousands of Muslims, men, women and children, all waiting to take a train in the opposite direction, slaughtered before his eyes, killed, stabbed and beheaded. Three or four trains full of Muslims were due to leave for Pakistan that day. None of them did. 'I saw Muslims being burnt alive, thrown onto bonfires, I saw bodies, I saw blood, I saw many things,' he told me over a cup of tea at his New Delhi home. 'The madness that very first day could have finished everybody.'

About 12 million people, Muslims, Sikhs and Hindus, fled for their lives during Partition. Almost a million died. Entire trainloads of dead bodies crossed the border in both directions. In 1931, Winston

Churchill had warned that if the British left India, majority Hindus would gain 'the armed ascendancy', public services would collapse and the country would fall back rapidly 'into the barbarism and privations of the Middle Ages'. Introducing democracy to a country as poor, diverse and divided as India was described by one sceptical newspaper editor as 'the biggest gamble in history'. At the time, it must have seemed a particularly bad bet.

And yet, those dire warnings had not been borne out. Despite the violent orgy of its birth, India had survived and even begun to prosper, as the world's largest democracy and a broadly secular state. The historian Bipan Chandra had summed up for me neatly at the time. 'Despite the country being partitioned, and so much bloodshed, India became a secular, democratic country,' he told me. 'I think that is one of the greatest achievements of modern times.'

India is a nation of almost unimaginable diversity, whose Hindu majority is stratified and divided into a thousand castes and sub-castes that were supposed to define every person's identity and place in society. But it is also home to the world's third-largest Muslim population, as well as Sikhs, Christians, Jains and Buddhists. It boasts twenty-two official languages and many more dialects, many with mutually unintelligible scripts, and myriads of peoples with different traditions, value systems and outlooks. In its cities, beggars bang their withered limbs on the windows of luxury imported cars, while densely packed slums lurk within sight of modern office blocks. It is a land whose IT industry stands at the forefront of the twenty-first century, but whose villages sometimes seem stuck in a far-distant past. To put it another way, there are many forces that divide India, from caste to class and economic inequality, from language to religion. All have caused conflict, sometimes brutal slaughter, and yet none have changed the map of India that had been drawn – in haste by the rapidly departing British – in 1947.

Aside from my reporting, I owe much of my understanding of India's democratic achievements to Ramachandra Guha's magisterial history *India After Gandhi*. Guha, a historian and political commentator, is the leading chronicler of Independent India. As he points out in his book, the real success of modern India is political, not economic. It remains to be seen if India can transform its software success story into more general prosperity, he wrote. 'But that India is still a single nation after a testing 60 years of independence, and that it is still largely democratic – these are the facts that should compel our deeper attention.'

For all its faults, democracy has provided a crucial pressure valve during the past six-and-a-half decades that has preserved a broader peace. Indeed, India's very diversity, where people of different religions, castes and even languages are thrown together in its vast cities, may have been a source of strength. There was, in a sense, no other way to live in peace. Compromise is a way of life in a nation where no one sect or group could reign supreme.

Democracy has also given voice to the voiceless of India: the media may still be captured by the elites, but political power has increasingly been grabbed by representatives of the underprivileged, allowing one of those treated as 'untouchable' – a member of the lowest rung of the caste system, and a woman too – to be elected as a chief minister of the country's largest state. Politicians may not always have delivered much to their electorates, but the poor at least had the chance to turf them out of office every five years – an opportunity they often embraced enthusiastically. Nor should we forget the freedom of speech that Indians cherish, one of this nation's greatest strengths that seems to sustain its vigour.

Today, a pan-Indian feeling has grown even as regions have reasserted their own identity, while the exuberant cinema of Bollywood and the national obsession with cricket have become strong cultural glues.

Over that cup of tea, Handa had told me that he still remembered the Muslim and Sikh families who helped his parents during the Lahore riots of 1947, including his family's Muslim driver who returned unbidden to risk his life by driving their car and belongings across the border to India. Today his daughter is married to a

Muslim, a fact that Handa delights in, just as he takes deep pride in secular India.

If Indian democracy is a miracle, much of the credit has to go to India's first batch of post-colonial leaders, especially Prime Minister Jawaharlal Nehru,[7] the upper-class and urbane British-educated lawyer who devoted his life to the Indian nationalist struggle, was a close friend of Mahatma Gandhi although a very different character, and ended up becoming the newly independent nation's first prime minister. People like Nehru, his much more down-to-earth deputy Vallabhbahi Patel and B. R. Ambedkar, the Dalit leader who chaired the immense effort to draw up a new constitution for India, will be remembered as the giants of Indian democracy, the men who built and defended the institutions upon which a nation was founded.

The British had left behind not a unified nation, but a patchwork of territories, some ruled directly by the Raj, others indirectly through a variety of chiefs and princes. There were more than 500 so-called 'princely states', ranging from the size of a European country or American state to just a collection of villages, and many of the Maharajas, Nawabs, Nizams and other potentates who ruled them began to dream of their own independence from New Delhi. Patel was ably backed by his sharp secretary V. P. Menon, and the pair somehow convinced the collected 'princes' to come on board in the building of a new nation that would see their privileged roles dismantled. True, the Hindu ruler of the Muslim-majority Jammu and Kashmir vacillated, only joining India after tribal raiders from Pakistan invaded and backed him into a corner, while the Muslim ruler of Hindu-majority Hyderabad in the south held out until Indian troops invaded in 1948. Yet from this patchwork rose a new united nation of India.[8]

The crafting of India's constitution was a scarcely less formidable obstacle to overcome. Nehru supplied and stoutly defended his idea of a secular nation where every citizen would be entitled to vote and minorities would feel secure and protected, a powerful vision that has been central to the preservation of India's nationhood ever since.

Ambedkar presided over a three-year drafting process and a constituent assembly that contained more than 300 members. The members were almost as diverse as the nation itself, but somehow they gave birth to a document of 395 articles and 8 schedules, probably, according to Guha, the longest constitution in the world. The assembly resisted a temptation to replace the English of the erstwhile colonial rulers with Hindi as the national language of administration, a move that would have threatened the smooth absorption of India's non-Hindi-speaking east and south. It also resisted a call to introduce reserved seats for Muslims, a move that again would almost certainly have cemented divisions rather than removed them. But Dalits or untouchables, the victims of thousands of years of discrimination at the foot of India's powerful caste system, were to have reserved seats set aside for them in legislatures and jobs reserved for them in government.[9]

The India that grew out of this phenomenal effort was proud and progressive, with the state at the helm of a new industrialization policy. Its economy stuttered along for decades, at a modest pace of expansion that became dismissively known as the 'Hindu rate of growth', yet arguably it still did more to dignify its people and advance their literacy and health than any government operating on this soil had ever done before. Thanks to Nehru, it drew together other developing nations into a position of 'non-alignment' between the antagonistic blocs of the Cold War world. It was a nation that went to war three times with its arch-rival Pakistan, twice over Kashmir, which had been divided and a source of tremendous friction ever since that Pakistani incursion was repulsed. It went to war once with China, and subsequently has never lived comfortably with its northern neighbour. Yet it kept its own army firmly out of politics, setting itself apart from Pakistan.

Nehru and his cohorts were immensely popular in the years that followed Independence, yet they resisted the temptation to allow broad popularity to slide into one-party rule or to undermine the checks and balances of a democratic system. It was a temptation that other post-colonial leaders from Ghana to Zimbabwe, Sri Lanka to South Korea and Indonesia, all succumbed to.

Such was the aura surrounding Nehru that his family have come to dominate Indian politics in the five decades since his death. But if Nehru helped to build and defend the institutions of democratic India, the same cannot be said for his daughter and ultimate successor, Indira Gandhi (whose husband Feroz was, incidentally, no relation to the Mahatma). She had been selected by Nehru's Indian National Congress party to become prime minister two years after her father's death in 1964, because senior leaders thought she would be would be weak, a 'mute doll' in the words of one senior figure, who would be easy to manipulate.[10]

She proved exactly the opposite, the ultimate Iron Lady of Indian politics who ruled ruthlessly and centralized power remorselessly, effectively dismantling intra-party democracy within Congress in the process. She had tremendous charisma and a natural connection with the poor, and is remembered with affection and awe by many Indians to this day, but her socialist economic policies were far from a success.

In 1975, faced with a judicial challenge to her rule, and a popular nationwide protest against her government, Indira Gandhi showed her authoritarian teeth, suspending democracy, jailing opposition leaders, curbing free speech and imposing emergency rule. It remains Indian democracy's darkest hour.

Yet even by then, less than three decades after Independence, democracy had taken root in India, and Indira's attempt to uproot it proved futile. Two years after the start of the Emergency, as the period is now best known, Indira was forced to back down, and was thrashed at the polls.

Indira, with her signature shock of grey hair nestled among the black, was to be voted back into office three years later, and then assassinated by her own Sikh bodyguards in 1984, in the midst of a Sikh insurgency, and after ordering Indian troops to clear out the insurgents from their religion's holiest shrine, the Golden Temple in Amritsar.

The story of the Gandhi dynasty, of Indira's son Rajiv, prime

minister from 1984 to 1989 and also assassinated in 1991, his Italian-born widow Sonia, who overcame her reluctance to get involved
to become, today, the most powerful figure in Indian politics, and
their son Rahul, the dynasty's crown prince, will be told in more
detail later in this book. Together, the family has ruled India for
more than half of its post-Independence history, and their tale is
intimately entwined with the story of Indian democracy, for good
and for ill.

India has changed dramatically since the days of Nehru and Indira,
even if its villages sometimes still seem to be mired in the Middle
Ages. Gone are the socialist strictures that held it back, even if the
bureaucracy is still infuriatingly overexacting; gone is the old-fashioned distaste for business, even if its politicians still make a show of
wearing modest handspun cotton. Today's India is characterized by a
scramble for wealth and a desire to flaunt it. But the debate over
Nehru's legacy remains alive: what remains of his ambitious vision for
the world's largest democracy?

Those who see the glass half-full argue that India's credentials as a
secular democracy have been challenged at every stage of its post-
Independence history and passed the test. Mahatma Gandhi's
assassination in 1948 at the hands of a Hindu nationalist extremist
robbed the nation of its father and its conscience, yet India survived.
Indira Gandhi's assassination in 1984 triggered vicious anti-Sikh riots
that killed 2,700 people in violence that was said to be aided and
abetted by local Congress politicians and even the police. The nation's
secular fabric was sorely tested again by the rise of the Hindu right in
the 1990s and communal riots in Gujarat in 2002 that killed 2,500
people, most of them Muslims. Yet two years later the Hindu right
was thrown out of power and into retreat after the 2004 elections in
which 400 million people took part. Democracy and the nation
survived, and peace was largely regained.

Those who see it half-empty argue that merely keeping India
together is no longer nearly enough. Under democracy, corruption
and cronyism have flourished, criminality has entered politics, and

caste divisions have become important political markers. The institutions meant to support a modern, lawful democracy have been seriously undermined, from parliament to the police force, from the judiciary to the bureaucracy. In their place has grown up a vast network of patronage and vested interests, of corruption and nepotism. The gap between rich and poor is yawning ever wider, and hundreds of millions of people scrape out lives of terrible poverty and deprivation, even if they bear their suffering with incredible strength. A Maoist insurgency in central and eastern India is pulling poor, tribal Indians away from democracy and towards a violent resolution of their problems. At the same time, gulfs are growing between politicians and the business elite, politicians and the middle class, politicians and the growing mass of young people.

These pessimists see a state responding to its people's anger and scrutiny in ways that remain rooted in the past: cracking down on protests, censoring social media, and sometimes just shutting down. With bureaucrats now scared to make decisions, lest later they be called upon to justify them, they see a state that has frozen like a deer in headlights.

Those who see the glass half-empty see middle-class Indians withdrawing from India's broader society, focusing narrowly on themselves and their own families. They see them seeking private education for their children, private health care for their families, travelling privately in their own cars, and living in gated, guarded communities. They see the self-exile of a growing middle class that is unprecedented in global history.

But those who see the glass half-full see an unprecedented awakening of India, enabled by an Information Revolution. They see young people who care about the future of their country, and activists who are fighting bravely – using the tools and institutions of democracy – to forge a better nation. They note that India's people are now demanding transparency, accountability and efficiency – and the extension of opportunity to more than just the exalted few. They see India's more and more powerful private sector also demanding coherent decision-making, the rule of law and a complete overhaul of the country's overburdened infrastructure. They see voters demanding more from their elected politicians, and rewarding those who respond. This is the story of that awakening.

The present era feels like a pivotal moment in India's modern history, a time of change when the old ways have broken down. It is time to ask whether democracy will deliver. Will India emerge, like China, as an economic and diplomatic powerhouse? Will India come even close?

By the summer of 2013, the power unleashed by the economic reforms of Manmohan Singh two decades before had completely dissipated. Economic growth was sinking below 5 per cent a year, and inflation rising towards 10 per cent. Exports were contracting, the current account deficit widening and foreign investors scrambling for the exit. The rupee fell by more than 20 per cent in just the first four months to a new all-time low against the dollar in August 2013, and talk of crisis rent the air. The *New York Times* proclaimed that the Indian economy stood 'in disarray', with worse still to come.[11] Singh's own reputation was in tatters.

In the course of this book, I will trace not just Manmohan Singh's fall from grace, but democracy's broader malaise, as corruption and nepotism seemed to gnaw at its very soul. But I will also trace India's awakening from that democratic slumber, as the power of television, information technology and good old-fashioned grassroots activism try to harness the power of popular frustration and turn it to good use. We will meet people all over India fighting for change, sometimes in the glare of the national spotlight, sometimes in the shadows. We will ask what lies in store for the world's largest democracy, who might lead it, and in which direction.

I

Asking For It

Gang-rape provokes unprecedented outcry

'Incredible India, where women are not safe in the womb or outside it.'
'Just because I show my legs, doesn't mean I spread my legs.'
Banners at Delhi's gang-rape protests, December 2012

'The victim is as guilty as her rapists . . . She should have taken God's name
and could have held the hand of one of the men and said "I consider you
my brother," and she should have said to the other two "Brother I am
helpless, you are my brother, my religious brother." This could have saved
her dignity and life. Can one hand clap? I don't think so.'
71-year-old Hindu spiritual leader Asaram Bapu,
speaking to followers in Faridabad, January 2013

Twenty-three years old at her death, J was a physiotherapy student by day and a call-centre worker by night. The eldest of three children, she was born to a mother and father who thirty years earlier had moved from a hard-scrabble existence in a poor village to the capital in search of a better life.

Her dreams were modest, according to family members and friends: she wanted to do a job where she could help other people, and to earn enough to enable her brothers to follow in her footsteps. She wanted a smartphone for herself, and the chance to live abroad. Having done well at school, she had even earned the family some extra money by tutoring younger kids as a teenager. She spoke English well, and liked to read. She had particularly enjoyed a novel by Chetan Bhagat, *One Night @ the Call Center*, a huge best-seller that spoke directly to her generation and their aspirations. But she liked movies too, especially those from Hollywood, and she loved visiting new places in India with her male friend Awindra Pandey, a 28-year-old, bespectacled and slightly round-faced software engineer. She was fun to be around, a joker who always had her brothers in stitches at the dinner table, someone who was 'very inclined to spontaneity', said Awindra. J was a typical young woman who enjoyed the popular TV show *Big Boss*, an Indian version of *Big Brother*, liked shopping for bargains and, when she could, would treat herself to a new pair of high heels.[1]

J had wanted to become a doctor, but the studies cost too much. Instead, she settled for a cheaper physiotherapy course at a college 150 miles north in a town called Dehradun. Still the fees were a struggle, and the family sold their land in their village to finance her studies, 'to help her become what she wanted to be', as her father B told me. She had brought in extra money by working at a call centre at night, advising Canadians on their mortgages, while for many years her father was also pulling a double shift, most recently as a baggage handler at Delhi's modern new airport. 'Both of us were doing double duties,' B said, 'both of us together, pulling things through.' Together, their lives held the promise of a new India, a transformation from rural penury to urban plenty in a single generation.

J had returned to New Delhi from Dehradun for her internship. She had known Awindra for a couple of years, and they often went away for the weekend together, he told me. On the day that she was raped, she had called Awindra, who was feeling down. To cheer him up, she convinced him to meet her at the Select Citywalk shopping centre in south Delhi, one of the gleaming air-conditioned malls that act like a magnet for India's aspirational middle class. There they did some window-shopping, had an ice cream, and then caught an early evening showing of *The Life of Pi*. With coupons he had received from Citibank, they bought some popcorn and soft drinks. Afterwards, J's mother called, asking her not to stay out late.

Meanwhile Awindra was still feeling subdued – 'just one of those days when I wasn't talking too much,' he recalled – so they decided to head back towards J's home on the outskirts of the city. But none of the drivers of the three-wheeler auto-rickshaws outside the mall wanted to take them so far from town; instead the pair took a shorter ride to a nearby bus stop. A private bus passed, a young man hanging from the door calling out the very destination they wanted in the 'sing-song' voice that he used to attract customers. They were unsure about whether to board, but J was in such a hurry to get home, Awindra told me later, that against their better judgement they boarded.

What followed is by now well known. There were six men on board, including the driver and the young man who had called them in. Otherwise the bus was empty. J and Awindra were first verbally abused and then physically attacked by the six men on board. Awindra was knocked down and held on the floor. J was overpowered, repeatedly raped and bitten by her attackers. They were both beaten with an iron bar, which was then used to destroy her insides, an act of pure sadism that was ultimately to kill her. The pair were then dumped, naked and bleeding, by the side of the road, on a patch of dried grass near a strip of budget hotels not far from Delhi's airport. J had lost consciousness and was presumed dead, the bus driver later confessed, but still he tried to run them over before speeding away. There they lay for twenty-five minutes, helpless, crying out. 'A lot of cars passed us by,' Awindra said. 'I tried to stop them but nobody would stop. They slowed down to see what was happening, and then drove away.' Eventually some passersby stopped, and one called the police. A crowd gathered and gawped. As they stood about talking, policemen from different stations argued about whose jurisdiction the case fell under, because nobody wanted to take responsibility. Awindra, still naked, lifted J's body into a police car himself and they made their way to hospital.

I met with J's father just over a month after her death, in the family's impossibly cramped two-room basement apartment, where he and his wife live with their two remaining children, in the narrow lanes of a poor residential area just beyond Delhi's airport. Sitting in a plastic chair in one of the plain, whitewashed rooms, B remembered how J used to cry as a small child if she was not allowed to go to school, and how she always got her own way, especially with him. 'She was very stubborn, very headstrong,' he told me. 'Whatever she wanted she had to have it, and I always had to get it for her. Suppose every child in class had a particular book, but I was not in a position to buy it. She would insist she needed it, and I would have to find a way to give it to her.' He remembered how she had dreamt of living outside India, and how she used to love eating food from her father's plate. 'She would barge into the house, and if it was dinner time, she would come right up and say "Papa, can you give me a morsel, can you give me a bite in my mouth?"'

For two weeks J had battled for her life, even though doctors gave her no real chance of survival, such was the damage to her intestines. The government had moved her to Singapore, ostensibly in search of better treatment – but also, one suspects, partly so that she did not die on Indian soil. As she lay in her hospital bed, J had several times asked her father for food. But this time, B had been unable to grant his daughter's wish.

Nearly two weeks after the attack, father and daughter spoke for the last time. 'Even then, she was worried about me,' he said. 'She asked "Papa, have you had dinner? You should rest." I put my hand on her forehead, and said "Beta [daughter], now you also go to sleep." She took my hand and put it to her lips, and gave it a kiss. Then she went off into such a sleep that she has still not woken up from it.'

If J once represented the Indian dream, the seventeen-year-old boy who beckoned them on board the bus symbolizes its antithesis. His story is one of child-trafficking and child labour, of abuse and the denial of opportunity, of exclusion from India's bright future, and the alienation that can breed. His story is one that many middle-class Indians often choose to ignore, or accept as the way things are and always have been.

He belonged to a poor family in a rural village in the vast northern state of Uttar Pradesh, a state run by a dysfunctional government that is home to 200 million people and boasts some of India's most gruelling poverty. He was the first-born son of five children in a poor Muslim family, whose father had mental health problems and whose mother struggled to earn enough to feed them. His nickname was 'Bhura', or brown.

When I visited his home village of Bhawanipur, a five-hour drive from Delhi on the plains, I found his 35-year-old mother, Anisha, lying on a straw bed under a torn piece of black tarpaulin that served as her makeshift roof. She was too weak to get up, she said, because the family did not have enough money for food. Neighbours reported that she had been lying there in a state of near-collapse since hearing what her son had done. A teenage daughter appeared and sat by her mother, flies settling on their feet and hands as they chatted. The daughter had never been to school and did not know her own age. She and her sister worked in the fields a few days each month for just $1 a day. This is what the family lived on. As we talked, a crowd of onlookers gathered to listen in. Around the village, a few people worked in the fields of mustard and wheat, and boys eked out a miserable existence in the brick kilns that dotted the countryside. Hundreds of cowpats, stacked up in pyramids, dried in the midday sun, eventually to be recycled as fuel.

'He was a normal child, just like other children. He played around like other children,' Anisha told me. But after a year in a government school, the young boy gave up. Schooling was a luxury the family could not afford, and according to some accounts he had left after being beaten by a teacher. At the age of eleven Bhura was then trafficked to Delhi, one of half a dozen boys from the village sent away supposedly to look for a better life and a brighter future. 'It's my fault he left,' Anisha said. 'But we were all dying of hunger, he had no choice.'

In Delhi, Bhura ended up in a dhaba, a roadside restaurant, in a poor part of the capital. The restaurant owner, a genial Muslim with a long grey-streaked black beard, told me that Bhura had served customers and washed plates, claiming to have started him on 700 rupees ($14) a month. Bhura slept on a wooden bench in the open-fronted one-room restaurant, ate his food there, and had his clothes bought for him. 'He was never any trouble for all the time he worked here,' said the 42-year-old owner, Islamuddin Ansari, sitting on a rope charpoy as a large bowl of fatty meat curry cooked on a low heat beside him. 'He never once turned around and answered me back.'

For the first three or four months after he left, Anisha said the restaurant owner had sent her 300 rupees ($6) a month on behalf of her son. Then, nothing. 'I thought he had died,' she said. But just before the police came to her village claiming her son was a rapist and murderer, she says she started worrying about him again. She had even visited a local Hindu holy man, to ask what had become of Bhura. 'He said my son was alive, but caught in a trap,' she said.

Meanwhile in Delhi, Bhura had spent a few years working in road-side restaurants, before moving on to a bus station where he washed the buses, ran errands for drivers and worked as an assistant on the roads, calling out to customers with the same sing-song voice he had used to lure J and Awindra aboard.[2]

It's a common story. Every year, hundreds of thousands of Indian children are trafficked and forced to work in farms, factories and homes, or sold for sex and marriage. Many are kidnapped, but most are lured away from home with false promises made to their parents that their children will be looked after, and given the chance to lead a better life. Sadly, it is the traffickers, not the children, who profit, and the employers who find a steady stream of obedient, cowed children to slave for them almost every waking hour, for little to no money. Many of these children are sexually abused, often as a means of instilling fear and reinforcing control.

The fortitude of India's poor never ceases to amaze me; the deprivation and oppression that they cope with is a constant reminder of the strength of the human spirit. But can such suffering and abuse be inflicted on so many young people, so routinely, without any consequences?

At the bus station, Bhura seemed to fall in with a hard-drinking, bad-tempered 36-year-old bus driver called Ram Singh. On the night of the attack, Bhura had gone to Ram Singh's house in a crowded and dirty Delhi slum to ask for the return of some money that the older man had borrowed. He ended up staying for dinner, drinking alcohol and being invited on a 'joyride' with Singh's friends. Ram Singh drove a fifty-seater white coach that was licensed to carry children to school during the day, but such was the lax enforcement of New Delhi's traffic rules that the group would have no problem operating it on established bus routes at night.

Singh, in a confession recorded by police, said the men fully intended to pick up a female passenger 'to have sex and make merry'.

In 1991, one of the most significant reforms initiated by the then-prime minister Narasimha Rao and his finance minister, Manmohan Singh, was the liberalization of the Indian television industry, granting both private and foreign broadcasters a foothold in a previously closed market. This last decade has seen an explosion in the number of television news channels and a concomitant increase in their power to shape the national debate. Today, there are more than 450 news channels in the country, in languages from Hindi and English to Tamil, Telugu and Assamese, reaching into 143 million of the country's 233 million homes. Their reporting is sensational, often inaccurate, frequently polemical, but there is no doubt that they have played a major role in reinvigorating India's democracy and calling its politicians to account. Increasingly, they campaign for change, and actively promote issues that will resonate with viewers in the search for ratings. Times Now's brash young anchor and editor Arnab Goswami has become the master of the journalism of outrage. Goswami had been a rising star in Indian television before he convinced the nation's largest media company, the Times Group, to let him front their new channel in 2006 as a relatively raw

32-year-old. His relentless pursuit of ratings has had a profound effect on India's media industry, to both good and ill effect. But there is no doubting the energy he brings to the television screen.

And so, as the news of J's rape broke, it was the television channels that led the charge. Banner headlines flashed up screaming 'India betrays her daughters', 'Nation outraged', 'Raped and left to die', 'No more talk, time for action'.

Reporters were dispatched to record people's reactions, and to loop it back to the nation. A few small knots of protesters emerged in New Delhi, while young people were collared by television cameras to give their thoughts. But that did not quite capture the anger that the channel editors could see beginning to break on Facebook and Twitter, so reporters in other parts of the country were sent out to record the nation's 'outrage', and explicitly told to gather a crowd when they did. At least one journalist had to break the news of the incident, before filming a group's furious responses. Gradually, the spark spread on social media, onto the streets and by Tuesday, two days after J's rape, into parliament.

At every stage, it was the authorities' apathy and heavy-handed response that fuelled the fire. An early turning-point came that Tuesday, when a smallish crowd of students and older activists had protested outside a police station in south Delhi, according to Ranjana Kumari, director of the Centre for Social Research, an advocacy group that resists violence against women. The police started pushing the students around, she recalled, behaving with their usual contempt towards protesters. 'Everybody had a phone in their hand, and I saw the students SMSing and tweeting immediately,' she said. 'One student typed, "If it takes numbers for them to listen to us, let's be there in large numbers."'[3]

By the weekend, after the government had singularly failed to address the mounting anger, that anonymous student's promise began to take shape. Their every step trailed by the television cameras, thousands of young people, mostly students with a few older activists showing solidarity, now streamed into New Delhi and took their anger right to the heart of government. They first massed near India Gate, the sandstone war memorial built by the British in 1931 and modelled on the Arc de Triomphe, now an important Indian national symbol and landmark. Then they marched west down the wide ceremonial boulevard of Raj Path towards the small rise at its western end known as Raisina Hill. On the brow of this hill, facing each other across the road, the sandstone buildings of North Block and South Block house the government's most important ministries; on the summit stands what was once the British Governor-General's house and is now the presidential palace. The protesters were determined to be heard. To them, perhaps, it seemed entirely natural to be marching and protesting in a public space, letting the government know that the young people of India wanted justice, action, and protection for women. Yet the authorities interpreted these marches as a direct challenge. This is, after all, the heart of VIP Delhi, once the centre of British colonial power and now a district where cars with red flashing lights bear very important passengers to their very important business, and the general public is tolerated only if it shows appropriate respect.

A weekend of violence followed, with protests met by barricades, water cannon and hundreds of tear-gas shells. But the protesters grew more violent too as the weekend wore on, their numbers amplified by troublemakers. Stones were thrown, police and civilian vehicles damaged and overturned, bus windows smashed. Protesters burned wooden posts which had been erected for the 26 January Republic Day parade, a celebration of the day in 1950 when India's constitution came into force. Police closed down nine Metro stations, barricaded approach roads and imposed 'Section 144', an emergency law supposed to prohibit gatherings of more than four people. Order was gradually restored, but not before more than 100 police officers, and a similar number of protesters, had been injured.[4]

But the flame had been lit. Protests spread across the nation, in marches and candlelit vigils, from Chennai and Bengaluru in the south to Mumbai in the west and Kolkata in the east, in an outpouring of grief and anger. Once again, social media played an important role – nineteen-year-old Sambhavi Saxena continued to tweet as she was bundled into a police van in Delhi on Christmas Day 2012, and her appeal for help from Parliament Street Police Station was retweeted 1,700 times, and was estimated to have reached 200,000 people.[5] Then, on 29 December, news that J had finally lost her life in Singapore prompted more anguish and yet more protests.

The following week I walked to Jantar Mantar, that unique space in the Indian capital where dissent is herded, in a way that poses absolutely no threat to anyone in power. This street, barricaded at both ends, is named after the neighbouring park that houses the strangely shaped red-painted buildings of an eighteenth-century astronomical observatory. Almost every day of the year Jantar Mantar is home to some protest or other; its railings adorned with sets of banners proclaiming some cause, from Tibetan monks demanding freedom from Chinese rule to communist trade unions demanding freedom from capitalist oppression. This was where the rape protests had ended up, contained behind barricades but under the sweeping booms of a host of television cameras, peaceful but certainly no less powerful. Candles fluttered on the tarmac, small knots of young people chanted slogans, others gathered cross-legged on the ground and listened to a succession of speakers.

There was a thirst for vengeance. Drawings on the roads showed the silhouettes of six men hanging from a gibbet; others advocated castration; one kindly looking eighteen-year-old woman, Kajal Singh, told me in graphic detail how the rapists deserved to have their every bone broken before being burnt alive in a vat of boiling oil, 'so they could *really* experience pain'. But there was a lot more to this protest than just anger, or a demand for more generous application of India's laws on capital punishment; the chants of 'We want justice' were consistently more strongly backed than 'Hang the rapists'. What really struck me, what really set this protest apart, were the thoroughly modern slogans on the homemade billboards.

'Don't teach us how to dress, teach your sons not to rape,' read one.

'Let's envisage a society where women can roam around wherever they want, where they want, wearing what they want,' read another, held by a 21-year-old man studying Russian. 'Just because I show my legs, doesn't mean I spread my legs,' read a third, held by that same eighteen-year-old who had demanded such minutely imagined punishment for the rapists.

This, my colleague Rama Lakshmi later told me, was SlutWalk resurrected. The original idea, born in Toronto after a Canadian policeman had warned women not to dress like 'sluts' if they wanted to be safe from sexual assault, had been watered down in India, the Hindi translation preferring a word meaning 'shamelessness' to the more confrontational 'slut'. Rama, an experienced reporter for the *Washington Post* who had become a friend, teammate and an invaluable sounding board, had covered Delhi's version of that global protest in July 2011, just seventeen months before, and had reported on how uncomfortable it had made India's older generation of feminists.[6] Gone, she reported, was the provocative clothing that the marchers elsewhere employed to challenge the stereotypes. Women in Delhi marched in their regular clothes. Attendance had been relatively sparse. Ranjana Kumari, a prominent author and activist who has spent a lifetime on a crusade to protect the rights of women in India, had advised the organizers not to 'ape the West', arguing that local reaction to America's so-called 'bra-burning' campaign had set the Indian feminist movement back decades. Yet the ideas behind Slut-Walk had struck a chord among the students of New Delhi, and their slogans were beginning to permeate social consciousness.

The anger was certainly understandable, given the abject failure of the legal system to protect Indians in general and women in particular. Roughly two-thirds of Delhi police are not even involved in what might be described as regular police work, but are deployed instead to protect the elite from their citizens, acting as armed bodyguards to politicians, senior bureaucrats, diplomats and other 'Very Important People'. The rest often seem more interested in running protection rackets or shaking down motorists. Indeed, the bus that had picked up J and her boyfriend that night had no permit to use public bus stops to pick up passengers; but such is the failure of the public transport system, and the lack of legal enforcement, that violations are rife.

Then there is the shortage of female police officers, whose absence often discourages women from reporting rapes, and allows their misogynistic or apathetic male police colleagues to dismiss a rape victim's account. Until it was finally outlawed by the Supreme Court in 2013, there was the invasive, degrading and unscientific 'finger test', to which many rape survivors were subjected, supposedly to determine whether the hymen is broken and measure the 'laxity' of the vagina; the implication being that a survivor's 'habituation to sexual intercourse' (even if the test could measure such a thing) is somehow relevant in a rape trial. There is the huge backlog of cases that have built up in India's appallingly overburdened court system, and a depressingly low rate of conviction when cases do at last reach trial. India has around fifteen judges for every million people; China has 159. One Delhi judge estimates it would take 466 years to clear the legal backlog in the capital alone.[7] There was, until recently, the lacuna in the legal code that failed to admit a rape charge unless penetration had occurred, and dismissed anything that falls short as a much lesser offence. All this had combined to create a culture of impunity that allowed rapists to believe they could escape scot-free; indeed, it is hard to imagine that this recklessly public rape would have been a first for the men on that bus.

But the deeper reason for J's death, and for the rape of tens of thousands of Indian women every year, is the incredibly low status of females in Indian society; where domestic violence is socially acceptable; where victims of rape and sexual assault are often blamed for having invited their attacks, and are socially stigmatized afterwards. This is a society where nearly half of India's young women marry before the age of eighteen and too many are treated as slaves by their in-laws; where more than half of young boys and girls between the ages of fifteen and nineteen think that wife-beating is justified.[8] This is a country with one of the lowest female-to-male population ratios in the world, thanks to the selective abortion of around half a million female foetuses every year, and one of the lowest ratios of women's participation in the workforce.

All of this has long been broadly acknowledged and shrugged off. In a nation of more than a billion people, it is tempting to think of such problems as insurmountable. Politicians are corrupt and useless, so don't vote for them. Police do not provide security, and public transport is rotten, so live in a gated compound and employ a driver. The city is unsafe, so never venture out alone. The poor are so numerous that they cannot be helped, so ignore them knocking at your car window and drive on. This is, of course, a generalization. Many Indians do care deeply about those less fortunate, and many devote large parts of their lives to helping them. But the fact remains that Indian society as a whole has not found an answer, and people have had to find their own ways around them. Often that means concentrating on their own extended families.

Somehow, J broke through the nation's indifference. She was, after all, a 'person like us', to whom many young middle-class Indians could relate. Any young woman who had suffered sexual harassment – what this country dismissively refers to as 'eve-teasing' – could relate to J's fate; and that means pretty much every young woman in the capital city today, so routine is this crime. Similarly any young man who has been forced to pretend that he can protect his girlfriend or a female friend on a dark and dangerous journey home, to live up to the Bollywood stereotype of the male hero able to bash any baddie who threatens 'his woman', could relate to Awindra's inability to protect her. The media named her 'India's daughter', and in a sense she was, if by India one means the nation that belongs to the aspiring, English-speaking middle class.

Unsurprisingly, there was anger towards India's police and politicians, including the Gandhi family. Sonia Gandhi is the president of the Congress Party and chairperson of the ruling United Progressive

Alliance coalition government, but the bigger disappointment was with her son Rahul, the 42-year-old expected to reinvigorate Indian politics and reconnect it to the nation's youth. Rahul had not said a word, nor ventured once outside his privileged cocoon to meet the protesters; nor indeed had any of the 'young turks' who are Rahul's closest friends in politics, and rising Congress party stars. 'We expected Rahul Gandhi to be here,' one young female student of English said. 'He is nowhere, hiding in his house.'

In truth, India's politicians and religious leaders had alienated the protesters right from the start, proving themselves far closer in outlook to the Canadian policeman who originally provoked the SlutWalk movement than to the citizens. Just two days after the rape, the opposition parliamentary leader Sushma Swaraj, a 59-year-old saree-clad traditionalist from the Bharatiya Janata Party (BJP), had argued that J would 'live her whole life as a living corpse if she survives'. Why battle the stigma that surrounds rape victims in India, when one can reinforce it?

The BJP is a conservative Hindu nationalist party, taking its ideological cues from a nationwide volunteer group, the Rashtriya Swayamsevak Sangh, an organization that runs schools, charities and clubs aimed at reviving what they see as India's essentially Hindu culture. Its leader, Mohan Bhagwat, blamed the tragedy on the adoption of Western values in Indian cities, arguing that crimes against women do not happen in traditional, rural India. As if that myopia was not enough, a controversial 71-year-old 'godman', or Hindu spiritual leader, Asaram Bapu, was reported as laying equal blame on the 23-year-old J: she should have called the attackers her religious 'brothers' and pleaded with them to stop. Not to be outdone, a prominent Islamist preacher blamed the whole mess on co-education.

But it was not just the usual cultural and religious conservatives who blundered into the debate. One Congress politician wrote a letter recommending that girls be banned from wearing skirts to school. Another said women should not roam around at night.

Mumbai's police chief blamed sex education in India's schools for rising crime against women.[9] Abhijit Mukherjee, the son of the President of India and himself a Congress politician, then invited widespread scorn by dismissing the protesters as 'highly dented-painted' women who go 'from discos to demonstrations'. Abhijit Mukherjee, I was told, was making an obscure reference to the dents removed from second-hand cars before they are resprayed and then resold.

Not for the first time, the Congress party's leaders also showed themselves as supremely out of touch. While the bureaucrats and politicians scuttled out of the back entrances of government offices to avoid the protesters, Sonia Gandhi and Manmohan Singh gave the issue their usual silent treatment. When they finally did speak to the nation, it was too late and remarkably poorly handled. Gandhi's televised address to the nation seemed the more heartfelt, but by staring at an autocue to the camera's right, she failed to look India squarely in the eye. Singh was by some margin even less convincing, bleating woodenly from a prepared text, his eyes fixed on the piece of paper in his hands, glancing up momentarily at the end of each paragraph but never quite raising them high enough to meet the camera's gaze.

At the end of his recording, Singh looked up to check he was done, mumbling 'Theek hai?' – Hindi for 'Is that OK?' – into the camera. Unfortunately, his question to the producers was far from OK. The recording was made a week after the rape, but Singh's media adviser, the supposedly experienced television professional Pankaj Pachauri, was in a panic to get the message out, authorizing its immediate broadcast without realizing that the final two words had not been edited out. Pachauri had let his boss down badly. Within minutes, the #TheekHai hashtag was going viral on Twitter and the PM was being savaged. Somehow, these innocuous two words from India's silent prime minister had more impact than his carefully prepared text. 'Sorry, but PM's speech was without feeling, wooden and totally unequal to the situation. The "theek ha" at the end revealed it as theatre!' tweeted the television presenter Sagarika Ghose (@sagarikaghose).

Social media then magnified the government's blundering and belated efforts to catch up. Consisting largely of men in their sixties, seventies and eighties, the current administration still remembers the decades when Congress ruled India almost unchallenged. In the previous two years, periodic attempts to close down Twitter accounts or to order satirical cartoons mocking Sonia Gandhi or Manmohan Singh to be removed from Facebook only underlined how out of touch they were.

'The government is completely disconnected with the reality of the twenty-first-century urban India,' said Reema Ganguly, a 44-year-old woman who posted photographs and messages from the Delhi protest on Facebook. 'They can't keep talking down to us, but they must engage with us. Facebook is not just about making friends,' she told my *Washington Post* colleague, Rama.[10] 'After the gang-rape incident, we aired our grievances, shared stories of our experiences of facing sexual violence in this city and signed petitions. Word spread like wildfire on social media. Does the government even understand this anger?'

The government began wondering how it could react to what it had cluelessly started calling 'flash mobs', rather missing the point that the rape protests were spontaneous acts of political protest rather than premeditated demonstrations. The gap between what the young Indians at Jantar Mantar expected and what their leaders were delivering was gaping ever wider.

After leaving Jantar Mantar, I travelled just a few hours outside Delhi, to the feudal, conservative and largely rural state of Haryana, through plains of wheat and rice fields and thorny scrubland, to test out Mohan Bhagwat's thesis that rape was somehow only an urban phenomenon associated with evil 'Western values'. I had also wanted to experience first-hand the values to which those clumsy, misogynistic Indian politicians still clung. Indeed, were they quite as clumsy and out of touch as the media was making them out to be, or were they simply ignoring the liberal elite and speaking to a much larger, and electorally more important, mass of rural, patriarchal Indians? And how deeply entrenched was the culture that these optimistic young Delhi-ites were determined to overturn?

In a sense, I already knew. My first major trip to rural Haryana had been in 2008, when I had visited a small village called Balla, just a two-hour drive from the capital, where a young couple had been strangled to death for daring to fall in love, in defiance of a local custom that prohibits relationships between members of the same village. The woman was called Sunita, twenty-one years old and twenty-two weeks pregnant. Her father had confessed to killing her himself; an uncle and two cousins had also been arrested. But what was so striking about that particular murder, what still shocks me today as I think back, was how everyone I spoke to in that village stood united behind the act, publicly proud of what had happened. What I found was a deeply conservative society striking back in a brutal and despicable way at such supposedly evil Western ideas as love and freedom of choice. 'The people who have done this should get an award for it,' 48-year-old Satvir Singh, a member of the village council or panchayat told me. 'This was a murder of morality.'[11]

My second trip, in the first few days of 2013, was a chilling reminder of the ruthlessness with which traditional rural society deals with confrontation. I was travelling with Suhasini Raj, my part-time assistant and translator, who was also an accomplished journalist in her own right and had a formidable contacts book, and together we tracked down victim after victim of horrific sexual violence.

Rapes are common in Haryana, steadily rising and rarely reported, activists told us, and the perpetrators even more rarely convicted. Here, you don't even have to fall in love with the wrong person, for any woman who shows a flicker of independent thought is especially vulnerable – even to own a mobile phone, or to visit a local market after dark, can be a challenge to traditional male authority.

The first rape survivor we met had done nothing except be young and pretty, and be left at home alone while visiting her parents, just three months after getting married. A female neighbour, who was

apparently in league with a gang of men, had lured the seventeen-
year-old girl out of her home by claiming that her husband had called,
and was waiting to pick her up at a nearby railway crossing. There she
was overpowered by four men (one was the neighbour's cousin) and
bundled into a car. For five days she was imprisoned, naked, in a
windowless outhouse on nearby farmland, and repeatedly raped.
Then, with her family desperately searching for her, she was dumped
back at the same railway crossing, her precious gold earrings stripped
from her ears, her rings and anklet stolen too. Her discovery provoked
no national outrage, no protests, no sympathy, just a few lines in a
domestic news agency story about a string of such crimes. The headline merely read: 'Four more rape cases in Haryana'.

The rapists were swiftly found, but no one called for their hanging
or castration. A medical report confirmed rape, but in the village of
Banwasa, society's only reaction was to pressure the girl to drop the
charges. Such was the pull of tradition – of patriarchy, of caste and
acceptance – that the girl's father was planning to bow to society's
demands. 'So many people have been coming and urging us to
compromise, saying "They are young lads, you should think about
their future, their lives should not get spoiled,"' he told us. 'When
respected people in the community ask for forgiveness, how can I be
above that? We don't want to do anything wrong in the eyes of society, and lose our place.'

The father, a tall man with white stubble and a grey shawl thrown
over one shoulder, said he had been offered around $7,500 by the
rapists' families, but refused to take it. That would be like selling his
daughter, he said. Instead, he would agree to drop the charges for free.
He seemed like a gentle, honourable man, and without being asked,
left us alone to interview his daughter for several minutes so that she
could speak more easily. It soon emerged that although she was going
to go along with her father's decision, she didn't feel quite so magnan-
imous. 'I want them to be punished by whatever the law permits,
whether that is life imprisonment or hanging,' she said, sitting
huddled on a simple bed, her shawl partly covering her mouth. 'The

environment is very bad here. Boys won't listen to anything; they just do whatever they have to do. Boys think that if rapists get away with it, they will also do it with impunity.'[12]

Impunity was a word we had encountered many times in rural Haryana, alongside the tremendous social pressure brought to bear on the women and their families not to report rapes and not to punish the perpetrators. In short, society protects the rapists and ostracizes the victims. In one case, in late 2012 in the village of Sacha Khera, a sixteen-year-old girl had poured kerosene on herself and burned herself to death because she could not bear the shame of having been gang-raped by five men. The young woman from Banwasa had come under mounting pressure in the weeks that followed our visit, threats made directly to her as well as to her parents and her in-laws. She was called a nymphomaniac and a prostitute because she had run away briefly with a mechanic from a neighbouring village before she had been married. Village elders told her father that the entire family would receive no work on any farm in the area unless she retracted her statement. Back with her in-laws, while she waited six months for the court to convene, it was clear she was getting little sympathy from her mother-in-law. 'There was a threat to my son's life,' the mother-in-law told *Open Magazine*. 'We were anyway ready to take her back even after such a big blot on her character. Tell me, who accepts such a girl back into the family? And then you want us to help her fight the case too?'

Trapped at home, contemplating suicide but never let out alone, the young woman eventually gave in, telling a judge in April 2013 that she had been at her in-laws' house during the period of her rape, and that she had only had sex with her husband. She was charged with perjury, sentenced to ten days' imprisonment, and fined 500 rupees ($9). 'This is an unequal society. Boys can do what they want,' said Jagmati Sangwan of the All India Democratic Women's Association. 'Honour is for girls only, and they pay such a high price for that.'

I have often wondered about the fate of that spirited young woman from Banwasa who tried, unsuccessfully, to fight against society's rules that punish the raped and forgive the rapists. If she had a daughter, would she teach her to be meek and submissive because she knew too well the risks of stepping out of line? If she had a daughter-in-law, would she treat her with the same contempt with which many daughters-in-law were treated? I hoped not. I hoped that she would not be broken, but would keep the spirit of that young, defiant woman burning inside her. But who could blame her if she gave in to the oppressive demands of Indian rural society?

Government statistics show that the number of rapes reported nationwide rose nine times to 24,923 since the authorities first started collecting data on the crime in 1971. (Over the same period, the number of recorded murders has roughly doubled.) In the past decade, rapes recorded nationwide are up by just over a half. In the same span of time in Haryana, a state of 25 million people, the figure rose over 85 per cent to 668.

Those numbers represent a tiny fraction of the actual number of rapes taking place, say activists, but the rise reveals two things: not only that women are starting to come forward in greater numbers to report incidents, but also that more such attacks are taking place.

Such is the premium on males in India that sex-selective abortions are common. Haryana has the lowest female-to-male ratio in all India: just 830 girls to every 1,000 boys aged six years old and under – the national ratio is 914 to 1,000. With jobs scarce, the state is home to a small army of idle young men. Not only is rape on the increase, but gang-rape is emerging as a major new trend, said Suneeta Tyagi, an activist and zoology professor from the town of Gohana who welcomed us into her house. 'Women have no respect in the home here, they are basically treated as doormats,' she said. 'Now, there is a growing tribe of young men who have no jobs or education. Nobody wants to marry their daughters off to them. Their frustration results in such heinous crimes.'

The police are not much help either, with officers at the local level especially coming from the same patriarchal background as the rest of society. Often, they stand at the forefront of efforts to protect the rapists, encouraging the victim's family to compromise, especially when the perpetrators come from a higher caste. In October 2012 a senior police officer from the town of Gohana had shown his reactionary hand, informing the Indian magazine *Tehelka* that rapes were on the rise because girls and women were 'easily influenced' and wore Western clothes.[13] That is a common lament, from members of an entrenched patriarchal society deeply threatened by social change and modernization and by the slightest hint of women's emancipation. Women are, in this sense, 'asking for it' by daring to exist as independent, thinking human beings.

In many cases, upper-caste boys prey on Dalit girls, knowing that the victims can often be threatened into silence. Dalits were traditionally condemned to occupations seen as polluting or degrading for other Indians, from cleaning latrines or collecting rubbish to leather-work. Today, they still suffer widespread and sometimes violent discrimination, and make up the bulk of India's bonded labour force. We met a fifteen-year-old Dalit from the village of Dabra, a shy, bespectacled girl who told us how she had been kidnapped by two upper-caste men in September 2012, drugged and driven to a dry riverbed. There she was raped for several hours by at least half a dozen men. The perpetrators even took a video and pictures on their mobile phones, and the girl was told the video would be circulated and her family killed if she dared speak out. But the boys could not bottle up their perverse pride in what they had done. The video began to be shared within the village anyway, and the girl's father eventually saw a copy. That night, he committed suicide by drinking pesticide.

The girl's family and their lawyer allege that the police deliberately transcribed the girl's statement to suggest that she had given her consent, and that the perpetrators were landless Dalits rather than the upper-caste, landowning Jats who dominate government, police and the rural economy here. This 'error' was only discovered by a Dalit rights activist who later read the statement. Not surprisingly, the girl's relatives had little faith in the authorities – after all, the families of eight other local Dalit girls, who they knew had also been raped by Jat men, never went to the police. 'We are Dalit families,' said the girl. 'We are working on lands owned by the Jats. Where will we go after complaining?'

But then, something extraordinary happened, something that gave me hope, because it suggested that the kind of outrage that surrounded the New Delhi incident had been slowly gaining ground in rural areas. First, the family refused to collect the father's body from the hospital unless the police took the case seriously. Then, activists and local television channels drew attention to the case, and hundreds of people staged a candlelight vigil in the nearby town of Hisar. Spurred into action, the police properly recorded the girl's statement, and six men were put behind bars to face rape charges. Four have been convicted of rape and sentenced to life imprisonment, while two others are still out on bail.

Such is the stigma surrounding the *victim* of rape that even married women who suffer sexual attacks are often cast out by their husbands. Girls are sometimes made to marry their rapists in a perverse attempt to preserve their honour. Many, perhaps most, rape survivors remain silent rather than denounce their attackers. The girl from Dabra said she was proud that her family had stood by her and insisted that justice be done. 'There have been twenty-five rape cases after my incident, where they have all gone and filed [police complaints] after seeing me do it,' she said. Also proud of her performance at school, she added that she wanted to become a journalist so she can 'speak out' against the government.

While I was in Haryana, Rama tracked down one of the protesters she had met at Raisina Hill. Avantika Shukla is a twenty-year-old political science graduate who had braved the water cannon and the tear gas, who lit candles and distributed handbills, and who screamed her lungs out, chanting 'No silence about violence.'

Rama received permission to follow Avantika for an entire day, on her journey to and from college, observing the challenges and choices she made, to understand the experiences that had brought her out onto the streets to mourn J. I don't think even Rama expected quite so eventful a day.

The moment Shukla leaves her home, safety is her only concern. She can't take the shortest route to meet the classmate who gives her a daily ride to college on a scooter – for a man often lurks behind the trees in the narrow byways near her home and exposes himself when he sees young women. Instead, she takes a longer, twenty-five-minute route, which, as Rama wrote, is not entirely safe either:[14]

As she steps through the gate of her apartment block, wearing light-blue jeans and a red fleece jacket, two vegetable vendors leer at her, crack a joke and laugh. Shukla ignores them. A few yards ahead, a young boy turns on a lewd song from a new Bollywood movie on his cellphone. She walks on as if she doesn't hear it.

As she walks through the neighbourhood market, a group of men sipping tea crane their necks to stare at her. She looks down and passes by. When she walks along the busy main road, a motorcyclist slows down and deliberately brushes past her. She ignores him and walks on.

'It was as if my built-up anger and frustration at suffering sexual harassment silently over the years just boiled over,' Shukla said, recalling her participation in the protests. 'But even after all the outpouring of anger in Delhi, the men have not improved, even now.'

As she reaches her women-only college, she points to a police jeep. 'Some of these policemen stare at the students all day,' she said. 'It made us uncomfortable. So the college principal had to request the police to park farther away from the gate.'

Shukla, who lives in middle-class, government-owned housing with her family, wants to be a corporate lawyer and has begun taking a short course on corporate compliance after college hours. But that means she has to take a bus and the Metro to another part of the city each day to attend evening classes.

Last week, the class discussed the inappropriate remarks made by some Indian political leaders in the aftermath of the gang-rape. 'It is always a woman's fault somehow,' Shukla said. 'The woman should have been more careful, she shouldn't have worn that, she shouldn't have gone out at that time, she shouldn't have drawn attention to herself. When will all this change?'

Shukla and her sisters rein themselves in all the time. Their mother tells them not to confront or shout back at the men on the street for fear of reprisals. They don't venture out for an after-dinner walk or ice cream in their neighbourhood, they don't wear sleeveless shirts or short skirts, they don't go to evening movies, and they don't go out for dinner with friends.

Since the gang-rape, her freedom has shrunk further. She now texts and calls her sister or father when she leaves college, when she boards the Metro, when she has boarded the bus and when she has managed to find a seat on the bus. Her father waits for her every night at the bus stop so she doesn't have to walk home alone.

'Earlier, I would plug my headphones in and listen to music when I was in a public place or transport,' she said. 'Not any more. Now I try to stay extra alert to the people around me. Music can wait until I reach home.' Riding the Metro is safest, she said, because of surveillance cameras and women-only coaches. But the Metro does not serve every neighbourhood. She dreads public buses most of all.

'If the bus is crowded, it is as if my body becomes public property. Men take advantage of the crowd to touch, push or grope,' she said, waiting for the bus in the evening. 'Letting the crowded bus go means I get late. Then there is a problem of empty buses, too. I now check if enough women are sitting in a bus before boarding.'

A crowded bus crawls in. Shukla looks at the time. It is late. She decides to board. She pushes to find standing room among the passengers, packed like sardines.

'What are you doing?' she shouts at a man who begins to run his hand over her arms. Nobody around her registers her protest. The man melts away in the crush. Shukla's phone rings. Her father wants to know how far she is from her destination.

'The day isn't complete in Delhi for a woman without hearing a cheap comment, or getting leered at or groped,' Shukla said, getting off the bus. 'Just like our families teach children that they should touch elders' feet and lower their head in a temple, why can't they teach their sons to respect women, too?'

When I first asked B what his daughter's death should stand for, he offered an understandably bleak assessment: that 'her life should serve as an example for women of future generations: that they should not expect anyone to come to their rescue or help; that they must be strong enough to protect themselves'. But later in our conversation he offered a little more: that her death had already empowered women to speak up when they are raped. 'I read news reports saying complaints have been going up,' he said. 'Girls used to be forced to hide their faces, but not any more. They are coming forward to tell the world what has happened to them.'

Two hundred and fifty million young Indians are due to enter the workforce by 2030, according to demographers. The nation's future depends on those young people finding jobs and adding value to the economy. Idle and unemployed, they could become a magnet for crime and drugs, a drag on the country's future, a demographic disaster. But educated, trained and given the chance to work, they could give India what is known as a demographic dividend, a sustained boost to the country's gross domestic product growth of the type that powered the East Asian economies forward in the 1970s.

But I believe they could do even more than that – they could also offer India a *democratic dividend*. For the young middle-class Indians of today are growing up in a world where the media is freer than ever before, and where social media is giving voice to their frustrations, hopes and demands. They are a generation who will demand accountability and transparency, some of whom will demand equal rights for women too. There is no doubt that the system they confront is deeply entrenched, both in the patriarchal villages of Haryana and the preening corridors of power. But they could be on the cusp of unleashing an unstoppable force.

So far Indian politicians have conspicuously failed to address the new young nation that confronts them. But at the tail end of 2012, a friend sent me an email from the New Delhi protests that made me stop for a second. In it, an elderly white-haired man, his back to the camera, holds up a placard.[15]

In block capitals, it reads: 'THIS IS THE FIRST TIME I'VE FELT HOPEFUL IN A VERY LONG TIME.'

2

Man Out of Time

The silent fall of Manmohan Singh

*'It has been my general practice not to respond to motivated criticism
directed personally at me. My general attitude has been, "My silence is
better than a thousand answers; it keeps intact the honour of innumerable
questions."'*
Indian Prime Minister Manmohan Singh, to reporters outside
parliament, after a speech defending his record in the 'Coalgate'
scam was drowned out by opposition catcalls, August 2012

As soon as I saw the caller ID, I knew I was in trouble.

Just as my profile of India's Prime Minister Manmohan Singh was
published in the *Washington Post*,[1] his media adviser was on the phone.
This was September 2012, eight years after Singh had assumed the
leadership of more than a billion people. Singh, I had written, was in
danger of going down in history as a failure, as a silent, tragic figure[2]
who probably should have resigned at the end of his first term. I knew
this call meant trouble.

Singh was seventy-nine, a shy, soft-spoken professor and career
bureaucrat credited with designing the 1991 economic reforms that
had propelled India into two decades of rapid growth. Bearded, with
large, thick glasses and a pale-blue turban, Singh had run India's
central bank and served as finance minister before being catapulted
into the top job in 2004. An immensely shy man, he spoke in a barely
audible monotone and was certainly no politician, but was very well
respected outside India. George W. Bush had called him 'one of the
really true gentlemen in the international arena'; Barack Obama saw

Singh as one of his closest friends on the world stage, 'a wonder-ful, . . . very wise and decent man'. Everyone agreed that Singh was honest – except that personal honesty, I had written, was not enough, when his intellectual dishonesty was impossible to ignore.

The phone kept ringing.

I had described Manmohan Singh as a dithering, ineffectual bureaucrat in charge of a deeply corrupt government; a man who had looked the other way and remained silent as his colleagues filled their pockets; a deep disappointment to foreign investors, in the words of a leading banker. I had also mentioned the jokes that had circulated for months: about officials going into meetings with their phones on 'Manmohan Singh mode', and the cartoon dentist who pleads with the PM to 'please open your mouth here'.

So when I saw that caller ID, I thought about letting the phone ring out, taking the time to collect my thoughts and calling back a little later. But there didn't seem much point. Stepping out into my garden, I took a deep breath and answered.

What followed seems slightly surreal. The Prime Minister's commu-nications adviser, Pankaj Pachauri, was shouting at me. He was furious because I had apparently not given their side of the story; furious, above all else, because I had called his boss 'silent'. He was furious with me, and someone was obviously furious with him.

I learnt later that Manmohan Singh was angry, or more probably hurt. Yes, Singh's reputation at home might have been tarnished, but he was still widely respected on the world stage and he clearly valued this standing and his friendship with Obama. Yet just three months before, in July 2012, *Time* magazine had taken a swipe, labelling Singh 'The Underachiever' on the cover of their Asian edition. So was my offence to make Singh lose face with the Americans?

As the government vented its fury, so my criticism of the Prime Minister became the top national news story of the following forty-eight hours, dominating prime-time TV debates on every major channel. I was used to being on camera, but this was the first time that I had been the story. I was forced to defend my piece on television. In interview after interview I insisted that my criticism was mild compared with that of the Indian press, and that I had been careful to list the Prime Minister's achievements. But that seemed only to inflame tempers. India's Information and Broadcast Minister threatened to make a formal complaint to the American government. 'Yellow journalism,' she said, indignant.[3] An interview I had scheduled with the Commerce Minister was abruptly cancelled. One by one, my sources were challenged. One denied ever having spoken to me, only to retract when I offered email transcripts and phone records. Another said our conversation was supposed to have been off the record, though no such agreement had ever been suggested. Word came back that my phones were being tapped.

But if the government was exploring every avenue to attack me, the popular mood was very different. My story went viral, dominating debate on Twitter and recording nearly 8,000 Facebook recommendations on the newspaper's website. It was read voraciously on every university campus in Delhi and probably across the nation. Guards at the American Club, where I swam with my family throughout Delhi's long, hot summers, could barely contain their pride at knowing me. A friend's driver came up to shake my hand and tell me I was expressing 'the voice of the common people'. A taxi driver, transporting a colleague nearly 2,000 miles away in southern India, stopped the car and doffed his cap at her in appreciation of the *Washington Post*. At a party in Brooklyn, an American of Indian descent told my sister-in-law that the whole country was behind me. A senior magazine editor described me in a column as a 'pesky foreign correspondent' whom the government had tried but failed to cow.[4] The opposition even used my story in parliament to renew its call for Singh to resign, saying his position had become untenable.

When he took office as Prime Minister back in 2004, Singh seemed to represent the best of Indian politics. Honest as the day is long, intellectually head-and-shoulders above your average politician, he embodied the hope that India might write a new chapter in its democratic history. Those hopes were, in the long run, cruelly dashed. During the next nine years, Singh struggled and failed to impose his will on a government and a system that seemed irredeemably corrupt.

The story of Singh's dramatic fall from grace and the slow but steady tarnishing of his reputation played out in parallel with his country's decline on his watch. As the economy slowed, and as India's reputation for corruption reasserted itself, the idea that this nation was on an inexorable road to becoming a global power came increasingly into question. The irony is that Singh's greatest selling points – his incorruptibility and economic experience – became the mirror image of his government's greatest failings.

This is the story of how an honest economist came to be running a corrupt government that threatened to ruin India's economy. It is the story of how Singh's humility and his loyalty, the very qualities for which he was chosen by Congress party leader Sonia Gandhi to lead the government, proved to be the undoing of his reputation and of his record as a leader. It is the story of how an honourable man was dragged down by the twin evils of corrupt campaign financing and dynastic rule lurking at the heart of India's dysfunctional democracy: twin evils we examine in much more detail in the two chapters that follow.

The tragedy of Manmohan Singh is that, on one level, he undoubtedly cares about the poor and less fortunate than himself, and is dedicated to his work and to his country. Unlike most Indian politicians, he seems to have an aversion to using his office to personally enrich himself. He is hard-working to the point of obsession – Daman, one of his three daughters, told *Caravan* magazine's Vinod K. Jose in 2011[5] that she had only seen him take one vacation in her lifetime, and that was a three-day family trip to a hill station just outside Delhi. And he desperately wants to achieve a lasting peace with India's nuclear-armed arch-rival Pakistan.

But in those qualities also lie the seeds of his downfall, for greatness will ultimately be denied Manmohan Singh. His humility was bound up in an immense shyness, which prevented him asserting himself when it really mattered for the future of his country. His loyalty to Sonia Gandhi was so strong that, in the words of Ramachandra Guha, it bordered on 'obsequiousness'.[6] It also prevented him doing anything to rock the boat – even when that boat of government was already sinking fast.

Manmohan Singh's beginnings were certainly humble. He was born in 1932 in what is now Pakistan, in a drought-prone village, he later recalled, 'with no drinking water supply, no electricity, no hospital, no roads and nothing that we today associate with modern living'. His father was a dry fruits trader and the family was not well off. But Singh's ambition and appetite for hard work was apparent even then: he walked miles to school every day and studied by the light of a kerosene lamp.[7]

The family moved to India shortly before the violent Partition of the subcontinent in 1947. The poor refugee boy won a series of scholarships that allowed him to continue those studies in India, then at Cambridge, where he took a first-class honours degree in Economics, and finally at Oxford, where he completed a PhD. His sense of public duty, perhaps, propelled him into the Indian bureaucracy, where his intellect and dedication marked him as a rising star. Singh went on to run India's central bank, and later its Planning Commission, the government department reporting directly to the Prime Minister that is supposed to coordinate policy and set long-term goals.

It may be that Singh was perfectly suited to a lifetime in India's bureaucracy, and in many ways he remains a bureaucrat at heart. But India needed him elsewhere. In 1991, he was dragged into politics by Prime Minister Narasimha Rao, and entrusted with the role of Finance Minister at a time of a deep crisis in the Indian economy. It was Singh's moment, the one he later (modestly) hoped might earn him 'a footnote in India's long history'.[8]

Private-sector business in India had been tied down by a complex set of bureaucratic rules that restricted their operations, their investments and their imports, known as the Licence-Permit Raj, but by 1991 the experiment in a centrally planned economy had run its course, as India ran out of foreign exchange. With his back to the wall, and with the encouragement and support of Prime Minister Rao, Singh abolished many of the vestiges of India's socialist past, freeing up the economy from direct state control, pulling down many of the formidable barriers to starting a business, and cautiously welcoming in foreign investment. It was controversial at the time, but it was to prove to be gloriously successful, with profound and irreversible consequences.

Presenting the budget to parliament in July 1991, Singh quoted Victor Hugo to argue: 'No power on earth can stop an idea whose time has come.' The idea he had in mind was 'the emergence of India as a major economic power'. India, he declared confidently, was 'now wide awake'. As India embarked on a journey towards the centre of the world stage, those words came to symbolize a nation's rise.

But the man who was dragged into the cut-throat world of Indian politics was never quite at home there. In 1999 his one attempt to run for a parliamentary seat in the middle-class district of South Delhi ended in ignominious defeat. On paper, he was defeated by the BJP, who had held the seat for a decade, but in many ways Singh was defeated by his own party workers, who failed to mobilize the support, including the Muslim votes, that he needed.

His campaign, one media report concluded,[9] had been deliberately sabotaged by senior members of his own Congress party, ironically because they were jealous of Singh's closeness to Sonia Gandhi and feared – correctly as it turned out – that she might one day nominate him to the Prime Minister's chair in her place. His wings, in other words, needed to be clipped, and so they were.

In the end, Singh lost by 30,000 votes, a margin of more than 10 per cent. It was a devastating blow to his political self-confidence, and one that was to haunt him many years later when he became Prime Minister. In this episode, perhaps, lie the seeds of his later failings as a political leader. His lack of political self-confidence was a major factor in his inability to impose his will on his own cabinet. Nor, as his career unfolded, was it the last time that Singh's rise was to incur jealous retribution from within the Congress Party. Nothing, perhaps, invites resentment quite like success.

Still, he remained an important figure within the party, serving for six years as its leader in opposition in India's upper house of parliament, the Rajya Sabha. When Congress won a surprise victory in the 2004 elections, Sonia Gandhi followed her 'inner voice', rejected her party's pleadings and renounced the Prime Minister's role. Instead she nominated Singh, a loyal servant who would serve as a perfect figurehead for her new government. He became, in his words, an 'accidental prime minister'.

Yet there was a pleasant symmetry in Singh as PM. The architect of economic reforms that had laid the foundations for a sustained boom was now in the perfect place to carry that legacy forward.

Sonia, born to a working-class family in Italy in December 1946 as Edvige Antonia Albina Maino, had been a reluctant entrant into the world of politics, but the pull of the Nehru–Gandhi dynasty had proved hard to resist. She had met husband Rajiv Gandhi while he was studying at Trinity College, Cambridge and she was at a language school. The couple married and settled in India; he took a job as an airline pilot and they largely avoided the limelight, leaving the politics to his mother, Prime Minister Indira Gandhi, and his younger brother Sanjay, Indira's anointed successor.

When Sanjay died in a plane crash in 1980 at the age of thirty-three, Sonia had, in her words, 'fought like a tigress' to prevent Rajiv being sucked into politics to replace him.[10] It was a battle she lost. Rajiv was swept to power as prime minister when Indira was assassinated in 1984, only to be assassinated himself in 1991. There was no one left in the family but Sonia to keep the dynasty alive and unite the Congress Party; still, she resisted appeals to take over the Congress Party presidency for a further six years.

In 2004, when she turned down the job of prime minister, there was a certain amount of sycophantic hype about Sonia's classically

Indian qualities of self-sacrifice and renunciation. But this was only part of the story; in reality, Sonia had no intention of completely surrendering the reins of power. Instead, she was to maintain a regal distance from the dirty and demanding world of politics, with Manmohan Singh the convenient mask to hide behind.

From the start, it was obvious that Singh knew who was boss. In public, his instinct was always to walk behind Sonia Gandhi, so meek that she would often have to shoo him forward. In parliament, at the end of an important debate, it was Singh who would walk up to Gandhi to pay his respects, with palms pressed together in an obedient and respectful namaste. Loyalty, timidity and exaggerated deference: these were consistently to prevent Singh from asserting himself with Gandhi in the years that followed.

Indeed, watching them together in parliament during important debates was revealing – Sonia was regal but always engaged, shepherding her Congress troops like a commander, dispatching ministers like lieutenants with messages for unruly backbenchers or coalition partners. Singh, by contrast, sat there like a cardboard cut-out, not even cracking a smile when the cut and thrust of parliamentary debate had everyone around him laughing. Many politicians sit in the House with headphones around their ears, which provide simultaneous translation of debates in Hindi and English. During one crucial debate late in his second term, when the future of his government seemed to be on the line, I wondered if Singh had switched the audio feed and was listening to some particularly relaxing music. His eyes were open, but it did not look like anyone was at home.

My own first engagement with Singh typified the man. It was 2004, and dozens of foreign correspondents waited expectantly in the plush confines of his official residence. Singh's media adviser, Sanjaya Baru, a suave, articulate and self-confident former newspaper editor, emerged to greet us. The Prime Minister, he said, had requested that our questions be directed solely towards foreign policy issues. Singh, he added, did not want to speak about domestic politics. Oh, and yes, everything would be off the record anyway.

A few minutes later, Singh himself walked in, an elderly figure with a neatly combed white beard, immaculately dressed in his trademark light-blue turban, and wearing glasses. Nervously clearing his throat into the microphone, Singh began with a barely audible apology for having a sore throat.

'I have been told,' he said, 'that I should only talk about foreign policy issues, and not about domestic politics.' I had not long moved from Pakistan, where President General Pervez Musharraf only ever admitted to being 'told' to do one thing and by one person – that he should run the country, by God – because he was the only person suitable. Singh, it seemed, was not even master of his own press conference.

What followed was no less disappointing: more than an hour of foreign policy platitudes, which consisted of a declaration of friendship and partnership with almost every nation under the sun. All uttered in Singh's dull monotone. Even if it had been on the record, there would have been precious little here to report.

In a world of self-promoting, self-satisfied and self-interested politicians, Singh's meek and humble nature had seemed like an asset at the time. In the end, it was to prove more of a handicap.

For a while, though, the Gandhi–Singh double act seemed to work, and the India success story seemed destined to continue as before. She was the glue that kept the Congress Party together; he kept the sun off her face. The economy surfed the waves of a global boom, and then deftly avoided the subsequent crash in 2008. World leaders flocked to Delhi to meet Singh and court business deals in what promised to be the new China. The cardboard-cut-out prime minister was trotted out to smile meekly next to everyone from Bush to Putin, from Hu Jintao to Sarkozy, in a long string of photo opportunities.

Meanwhile, Singh cultivated his image as a humble man, telling American talk show host and journalist Charlie Rose that he was merely doing his duty by fulfilling the task that had been allotted to him. 'I'm a small person put in this big chair,' he famously said, in an ostentatious display of humility.[11] He got away with it; his humility served as a useful foil, deflecting some of the criticism that might otherwise have come his way. That is, until the wheels started coming off, and some leadership was required.

One of the main complaints against Singh is that he failed to build on his own legacy, or indeed undermined it, by failing to force through the reforms India needed so as to underpin its economic resurgence. By the time he took office, and in stark contrast to China, India's infrastructure was seriously struggling to keep up with the growing demands the economy had placed on it. Power supplies were shaky, ports were clogged, roads were choked and potholed, bureaucratic decision-making was sluggish, land for industrial development was increasingly hard to obtain, and laws governing labour relations were stuck in the country's socialist past. Instead of reforms to unleash India's world-beating private sector, Singh presided over a massive expansion in the government's subsidy and welfare bill that was eventually to help sow the seeds of the economy's demise. Leading Indian economist Surjit Bhalla argued in 2013 that Congress-led government had not initiated a single policy that was positive for the economy in nine years of rule – although he argued the blame for such muddle-headedness bears the unmistakable stamp of Sonia Gandhi rather than Manmohan Singh.[12]

In his first term, Singh had a reasonable excuse for the lack of progress, forced as he was to govern with the support of India's main communist party. But in 2009 that excuse evaporated, when Congress swept back into power, and this time was able to govern in a coalition that no longer included the left. It seemed like another God-given opportunity for Manmohan Singh, a personal mandate to realize his vision for India.

Three years later, as the economy slowed, as investors started to look elsewhere and shine started to come off India's economic miracle, foreign investors and bankers were to tell me of their shock and surprise at the way Singh completely failed to grasp that mandate, astonished by what they saw as his lack of leadership, boldness and will. The leading TV journalist Barkha Dutt wrote that Singh had abruptly tumbled from being a middle-class hero to becoming a symbol of middle-class exasperation.[13] Part of the reason may be that Congress misread the mandate it was granted in 2009, interpreting it as approval for 'pro-poor' policies like a massive waiver of farmers' loans and its rural employment guarantee scheme, instead of a middle-class swing behind high rates of economic growth that allowed it to sweep the country's cities.

But there was a sense also that Singh had allowed his timidity to get the better of him, unable to articulate the policies he believed in, or to act as though he had any electoral mandate behind his own leadership. By 2012 he was so cowed that he was often silent at his own cabinet meetings, I was told, even to the point of not speaking up for the sort of reforms he ought to have been championing: to ease the acquisition of farmland for industry, to open up the Indian economy to more foreign investment or cut bureaucratic red tape. For a time, his deferential nature, insiders say, left him apparently unable to contradict or overrule his own finance minister, the veteran Pranab Mukherjee, whose mismanagement of the economy, mishandling of foreign investors and fiscal profligacy had caused many of the problems of Singh's second term.

There were two famous occasions when Singh did stand up and fight for what he believed in. Ironically, both came at the behest of the United States, to fulfil promises he had made, first to George W. Bush and then to Barack Obama. Increasingly ridiculed and ignored at home, Singh was still widely listened to and respected abroad. It obviously matters to Singh that he is able to hold his head up on the global stage as a man of his word. This, it seems, is why my critical piece in the *Washington Post* had stung so sharply. Singh, as one leading Congress politician cattily observed to me, cared more for his constituents in Manhattan than for those in Mumbai. Unfortunately, the victories he won on both occasions proved hollow.

The first performance came in 2008, with Singh's obstinate championing of a landmark civil nuclear cooperation deal with the United States. The accord was supposed to unleash billions of dollars of

American investment to develop India's nuclear power sector, but it was also supposed to herald a new dawn in relations between the world's largest democracies. The United States had imposed sanctions on India after it conducted nuclear tests in 1974 and 1998; this deal offered New Delhi a way in from the cold, and, in effect, an entry card into the club of nuclear powers. Singh and Bush had staked real political capital on the deal and pushed hard to overcome the obstacles during years of painstaking negotiations; so when India's parliament baulked at approving the agreement, the Prime Minister refused to buckle. Indeed, so firm was his determination that it almost toppled his government, and made him consider his own resignation.

After two days of bitter and bad-tempered parliamentary debate, with Singh's own speech drowned out by catcalls from the opposition, India's prime minister got his way. The government won a no-confidence vote by a relatively comfortable nineteen-vote margin. Which foreign head of government, Singh later asked party leaders, would have taken the Prime Minister seriously if he could not stick to his word?

Two years, later, however, the deal began to unravel when parliament passed another Bill that saddled suppliers of nuclear equipment with potentially ruinous liabilities in the event of an accident, even if they were not actually operating the plant in question. Partly as a result of that law, no single watt of electricity nor dollar of foreign investment has yet flowed from the nuclear deal.

The second occasion for Singh to perform came in 2012, when he pushed his reluctant cabinet colleagues to allow foreign investment in supermarkets and department stores, fulfilling a promise he had made to Obama some years earlier, that companies like Wal-Mart would be allowed to invest in India. When the opposition demanded a parliamentary debate on the measure, and a non-binding vote, Singh actually overcame his shyness for long enough to convince a few reluctant lawmakers to back him. Again he won. For a while, business leaders looked for the dawn of a new era of reforms, but progress was slow. Ultimately, and tragically, the decision came too late to save the economy or boost Singh's standing in any significant way.

But the second major complaint against Singh, and perhaps the most toxic to his eventual reputation, is that he turned a blind eye to corruption within his own government. There had always been a strong feeling that it was cash and not conviction that kept the cabinet together, and it was apparent that Singh had little say in the allocation of portfolios in either of his terms. Instead, according to the leading editor Bharat Bhushan, writing in the *Mail Today* newspaper, coalition partners 'chose portfolios where everybody knew you could make money, where discretion was involved and massive investment was taking place'. But it was not until 2010 that this cosy conspiracy began to unravel, with dramatic consequences for Singh's government and, in a sense, for the Prime Minister himself.

There are many people who can claim a role in Singh's fall from grace, from the editor and anchor of the Times Now television news channel, Arnab Goswami, to the campaigners who led a nationwide movement against corruption, Anna Hazare and Arvind Kejriwal. All three have played important roles in exposing the canker at the heart of Singh's government. Hazare and Kejriwal brought India's middle classes out on the streets in their tens of thousands, to demand that the government act decisively against the graft eating deep into its core. Goswami relentlessly championed their cause on twenty-four-hour cable news, keeping the issue at the heart of the national debate.

But perhaps the two leading architects of Singh's demise were two men who were as different from each other as one could imagine, one of them called Rai, the other Raja. One was a career bureaucrat, a tall, slender, silver-haired man from a privileged upper-caste background, educated at Harvard and usually seen in a jacket and tie. The other was a politician through and through, with a sharp eye for the main chance and a sharply populist instinct, a small, moustachioed mobilizer of India's lower castes who dressed in a safari suit. One fills me with hope for India's future; the other brings only a weary despair.

One showed courage in rooting out corruption that Singh conspicuously lacked; the other exposed his Achilles heel, his lack of political nous. One was effectively appointed by Singh, the other was part of his cabinet.

Vinod Rai was what is known as the Comptroller and Auditor General (known in India as the CAG), a man appointed by the President on the recommendation of Singh himself to cast an independent eye over the government's accounts. He was supposed to be a faceless bureaucrat, but became a household name, a major player in the battle against corruption in India.

Andimuthu Raja was a political leader from the southern India state of Tamil Nadu, a junior but key partner in Singh's coalition government. As Minister for Communication and Information Technology from 2007 to 2010, he was an important member of Singh's cabinet, but he became deeply embroiled in the largest corruption scandal in Indian history, and ended up spending fifteen months in jail.

The scandal, known as the 2G spectrum scam, started to break around the time of Singh's re-election in 2009, striking at one of the emblematic industries of the new India, telecommunications. Running that industry had been entrusted to Raja not because he knew the slightest thing about it but because his party, the Dravida Munnetra Kazhagam (DMK), was a relatively important member of the coalition, from the southern state of Tamil Nadu. Everyone understood that it was a lucrative portfolio, offering Raja the chance to gather money – in the form of bribes – to contribute to his party's campaign coffers back in the southern city of Chennai. But no one realized quite how lucrative – and how damaging – its mismanagement would be until it was too late.

It was Raja's ministry's job to decide how licences to operate slices of spectrum or bandwidth – the radio frequencies that companies use to transmit data – were to be allotted to individual companies. Around the world, some countries favour a transparent auction process where licences are granted to the highest bidder. That has the benefit of transparency, and of raising significant amounts of revenue for the government. Other countries, including India, had decided that this method burdened the telecom suppliers with excessive costs, and left companies holding too little cash to invest in critical infrastructure like phone towers. To keep telephone call rates low, they sold off the licences more cheaply, either on a first-come-first-served basis, or via what is known as a 'beauty contest', to companies that seemed most qualified and supplied the best business plans.

It was a perfectly reasonable policy to follow. The problem was that it was much more open to abuse, especially because India's archaic governance had failed to keep up with the economy's march into the twenty-first century. Instead of devolving the issue to a strong, independent regulator, huge discretionary power was deliberately vested in the Department of Telecommunications and the minister who headed it – effectively allowing him both to set the rules of the game and to decide the winners.

The way Raja's ministry allegedly abused that power bears explaining in some detail, for what it reveals about the links between politics, business and corrupt campaign finance in India. Valuable licences were allocated at rock-bottom prices in an opaque and arbitrary manner, allegedly in return for significant bribes. Such was the scale of the financial losses involved that *Time* magazine was later to list it as one of the top ten 'abuses of power' in modern history, just behind the Watergate affair.

Out of the blue, on 23 September 2007, with the Indian telecom market booming and demand for operating licences skyrocketing, Raja's ministry had invited applications from interested companies, giving them until the end of the month, just eight days, to submit expressions of interest.[14] A few companies, including some real estate companies with no prior experience in the industry, seemed mysteriously well prepared for the announcement, and filed their applications within twenty-four hours. Others, obviously not forewarned, took longer, but still met the deadline.

Then, on 10 January 2008, in the words of a later Supreme Court ruling, Raja's ministry changed the rules of the game, 'after the game had begun'.[15] Only those applications that had been filed by 25 September would be accepted, he announced. Several companies with experience in the industry, which had met the original deadline, would now be excluded.

Since that clearly was still not enough to fix the result of the game, he then tipped the entire playing field on its head. Short-listed companies were given just forty-five minutes to collect 'letters of intent' from the Department of Telecommunications, after which they were supposed to submit bank drafts for the stipulated fees and deposits, and finalize the paperwork. Priority would be given, not to those companies who had experience in the industry, or even to those who had applied first, but to those who won the bizarre sprint to fulfil these last-minute conditions.

Stranger still, thirteen of the sixteen short-listed companies had apparently been tipped off in advance by the ministry, and so had been able to prepare the bank drafts several days ahead of time. Thus favoured, these companies jumped straight to the head of the queue. Raja, it is alleged, won favours in return.

The whiff of possible wrongdoing had begun to surface at the tail end of 2008, when the maverick politician Subramanian Swamy wrote to Singh demanding Raja be arrested, and the Centre for Public Interest Litigation, a non-governmental organization, filed a legal petition. But what really blew the whole conspiracy wide open was Vinod Rai's decision to order his office to carry out an independent investigation.

Many of his predecessors in the CAG's chair would probably have left this particular hot potato well alone – the office's 63,000 employees around the country are kept pretty busy doing their routine and fairly low-profile audits of government projects and finances. But Rai was not that kind of man. Deeply principled, determined to do his job to the best of his abilities, keen on making a mark, he was clearly not afraid of offending the establishment.

In March 2010, with the entire credibility of the CAG's office behind him, Rai's office produced an explosive report into the auction process that simply could not be brushed aside.[16] It was to deepen the cracks opening up under Singh, and has permanently blotted his copybook. The report mapped in excruciating detail the trail of arbitrary decisions that Raja's ministry was alleged to have made, and the way the bidding rules had been manipulated to favour certain companies. Looking at various estimates of what the government could have raised had it conducted a competitive auction for the licences, it controversially concluded that the country had lost the equivalent of somewhere between $13 and $39 billion dollars in revenue.

The vast majority of the licences were granted to companies that 'did not satisfy the basic eligibility conditions . . . and had suppressed facts, disclosed incomplete information and submitted fictitious documents,' the CAG's report said. Some of them made immediate windfall gains by selling stakes in the licences to foreign companies. But just as revealing as the scandal itself was the way Raja was apparently allowed to steamroller his plans through the cabinet despite deep misgivings among some of his colleagues, and how he ran rings around the Prime Minister.

Advice from both the finance ministry and the law ministry to reconsider the way spectrum licences were being granted was brushed aside, the report showed. A letter from the Prime Minister himself, suggesting that Raja might consider switching to an auction to ensure 'fairness and transparency', also appears to have been ignored. At the time the Indian media, led by Goswami, had a field day, relentlessly taunting Singh and Congress over the affair. Perfectly valid arguments against conducting a competitive auction got lost in the furore; the highest number in the CAG's report – $39 billion – became the eyeball-grabbing headline of the nation's most sensational corruption case.

Raja, meanwhile, has always claimed that the Prime Minister was kept fully informed of his decisions, and insists he met Singh during the first week of January 2008 to secure his agreement with the

minister's proposed course of action.[17] Indeed, *The Hindu* newspaper
says it is in possession of files that largely confirm that assessment.[18]
Two weeks after the licences were allocated, however, and as criticism
started to mount, the Prime Minister requested that his office be kept
'at arm's length' from the whole process. Raja, it seemed, was to carry
the can alone.

It was not the first time that a minister in charge of India's telecommunications revolution had been caught with his hands in the
till. In 1995, then Telecoms Minister Sukh Ram was accused of
favouring a private firm in the purchase of communications equipment; 'the mother of all scandals' as it was then known brought
parliament to a standstill for several weeks.[19] But it was not until his
Congress government lost power the following year that the Central
Bureau of Investigation raided Sukh Ram's two homes and found
hundreds of thousands of dollars' (3.6 crore) worth of cash stuffed
in suitcases, trunks and pillow cases and hidden everywhere from
the prayer room to toilet tanks. There were also diaries meticulously
listing the bribe-givers. After a series of court cases, and several
convictions for corruption, he was finally sentenced to five years'
imprisonment in 2011.

Raja's case though was different in two key respects: first because of
the staggering amounts of money involved, and second because his
fall from grace happened when he was still a minister. Both factors say
something about how modern India is changing, how the fruits of
corruption are growing with the economy, and how pressure is rising
on government to become more transparent.

Raja was finally arrested in February 2011 and sent to jail for fifteen
months, before finally being released on bail. He is charged with
accepting bribes that could have approached $650 million, although
much of that would presumably have been destined for his political
party's coffers rather than his own. Two senior bureaucrats and more
than a dozen business leaders have followed him into jail or onto the
charge sheet.

The Supreme Court later ruled that the way the auction process unfolded 'leaves no room for doubt that everything was stage managed' to favour certain companies. It ordered all the licences that Raja's ministry had granted be revoked, in the process penalizing foreign companies like Norway's Telenor, which was not accused of any wrongdoing and had subsequently invested more than $3 billion in the Indian market. In this action, the court has been widely criticized for overreaching its powers and for veering into policy matters best left to an elected government. Yet, of course, it would not have been able to assume such powers if the government had functioned in a transparent manner.

The whole affair served not only to tarnish one of India's greatest economic success stories,[20] but also to demonstrate how little authority Singh had over his own cabinet, and how, in the final analysis, his personal honesty cut no ice when corruption is so deeply ingrained in the system.

A cartoon published in early 2011 seemed to sum up the popular mood. The first frame showed Singh holding up his hands and declaring, 'I'm above all this.' The next frame zoomed out to show India's premier perched on the bow of the sinking ship of his government, in shark-infested waters representing the corruption scandals.

But the final, tragic irony of this whole affair was the way that Andimuthu Raja seems to have bounced back. Released from Delhi's Tihar jail in the summer of 2012, he returned home to a hero's welcome in the southern state of Tamil Nadu.[21] Indeed, as he was to confide to a friend of a friend later, the whole episode seemed to mysteriously raise his prestige within his own party: people looked at him with new respect after they knew how many billions of dollars he was supposed to have embezzled. Singh, the man who stole not a penny and did nothing worse than fail to stand in Raja's way, lost respect in everyone's eyes. In the world of Indian politics, better a strong and daring thief than a weak man of integrity.

I met Raja in May 2013, my request for an interview granted on the day before I was due to leave India. Over tea and a South Indian dish of sambar vada, he chatted happily about the whole affair. His rationale was simple, and superficially appealing, especially to his electorate. (Whether it will find favour with a judge is another matter.) When he took office, he said he discovered that a few big players in the telecom industry were colluding with bureaucrats to form a cartel and exclude everyone else: all he had tried to do was to open the market to all-comers. He tossed out statistics like confetti, although they seemed to change every few minutes, but said he should be judged by one thing only: his performance.

Glossing over the details of his alleged manipulation of the bidding process, he simplified his argument into one central point: that by selling off spectrum licences cheaply, he had introduced more competition and forced down prices. He seemed baffled that anyone should need more details. 'I am a victim of cartel forces,' he said, sitting at his desk, with me to one side, dressed in a white shirt, grey pinstripe trousers and white socks. 'They managed the media to put up a wrong story, which was then endorsed by the CAG and the Supreme Court.

'There were three crimes I committed. I raised the number of mobile phones from 30 crore to 90 crore [300 to 900 million]. I brought call rates down from one rupee to 25 paise, and I brought rural tele-density up from single digits to more than 40 per cent. For these three crimes I committed, I spent one and a half years in jail.' So Raja, in fact, was the victim of crony capitalists? 'That is my case,' he said.

He argued that the Prime Minister knew everything and was 'very happy' with the auction process, but then went on to suggest that he, as the Telecoms Minister, was the ultimate decision-maker anyway, especially because he was following a policy (which he repeatedly called First Come-First Come) that had been agreed by cabinet and endorsed by parliament. Singh, he said, was merely the 'minister prime', only one member of that cabinet, someone who was account-able to parliament, 'and not vice versa'.

Raja said that he and his entire family had been investigated by the Central Bureau of Investigation, and not a single paise of ill-gotten wealth found. If they found any money at all that he shouldn't have, he promised to not even contest the case, but plead guilty and go to prison 'for life'.

As 2012 began and corruption came to dominate the headlines, Singh's government, with the veteran politician Pranab Mukherjee heading the finance ministry, did its best to discourage foreign investors and dismay the domestic corporate world. It had lost a court battle over a huge tax claim against Britain's Vodafone, so decided to change the law in its favour with retrospective effect – a move that provoked howls of protest from foreign governments representing investors who could no longer trust the ground beneath their feet. Meanwhile, inflation was approaching double digits, the economy was slowing, and a massive rise in subsidies was pushing the fiscal deficit into dangerous territory. 'How India is losing its magic,' *The Economist* promised to explain on its front cover story in March 2012, arguing inside that the country's 'desperate politics' was preventing it fulfilling its vast potential.[22]

The following month, the ratings agency Standard and Poor's warned it might downgrade India's credit rating to junk status, blaming divided and ineffective leadership at the very top. 'It would be ironic,' it concluded, 'if a government under the economist who spurred much of the liberalization of India's economy and helped unleash such gains were to preside over their potential erosion.'[23]

Shortly afterwards the CAG again exposed Singh's government, in a report that was perhaps even more damaging than the previous one. Again, the country's valuable natural resources had been given away – in this case valuable blocks of coal-rich land – for throwaway prices, in a process that the CAG said 'lacked transparency and objectivity'.[24]

It quoted the most senior bureaucrat in the coal ministry, Coal Secretary P. C. Parakh, as having warned that private companies were walking away with 'windfall' gains because of the giveaways, and it calculated that the sum of those private sector gains – and government losses – since 2004 was something approaching $40 billion.

It was all horribly reminiscent of the telecom scandal, except this time it was even closer to home: for three years during the audit period, the man in charge of the coal ministry was none other than the PM himself.

There has never been any suggestion that Singh benefited personally from the scandal that became known as 'Coalgate'. Indeed, he was again on record, early in his tenure, as having approved, in principle, Parakh's idea of auctioning the coal blocks instead of giving them away on the cheap.

Coal is such a lucrative source of kickbacks that the idea of public auctions inevitably ran foul of members of Singh's own government, as well as from state governments across India with congenital aversions to transparency. Predictably, documents showed that Singh appeared to cave in without a fight, showed no urgency in pressing for a change in policy and allowed the rapid sale of coal blocks to continue. The file kept bouncing from one ministry to another without a decision being taken, Parakh recalled, speaking in the documentary film *The Curse of Coal*. 'To my mind, the whole objective was to keep the whole process in suspended animation until all the good blocks had been allocated through this system, and then do it perhaps when nothing is really left to put up for bidding,' he said.

As with the telecom sector, many of the blocks went to companies with little or no mining experience, whose only interest appeared to be in making a quick rupee from a skewed auction process. Most of the blocks allocated since 2004 remain idle to this day.

'Corruption By Weakness' proclaimed the headline of the investigative magazine *Tehelka*,[25] one of a series of headlines that saw Singh's reputation besmirched by Coalgate. The opposition had a field day, disrupting almost an entire session of parliament with a call for Singh to resign.

A few months after that scandal erupted, towards the end of 2012, I caught up with Vinod Rai for a chat in his office. He came across as a principled, thoughtful and intelligent man, who declared himself very satisfied with his work as Comptroller and Auditor General. A tennis player from the southern state of Kerala, Rai has a relaxed manner and an easy charm. The credit, he said, had to go to his staff, a sprawling network that includes accountants in every state capital of India, and who do a 'tremendous job' with the highest standards of professional integrity. His role had only been to point them in the right direction.

As we chatted, he first laughingly admitted and then diplomatically denied that the government might regret having appointed him, before finally concluding that 'Yes, probably they are surprised in some ways' by the way he has gone about his job.

After a lifetime in India's bureaucracy, the then 64-year-old Rai himself admits to a few surprises since being plucked from the finance ministry to take over at the CAG's modern office in the heart of Delhi. 'The lack of integrity at the highest level of government . . .' he starts to say, before diplomatically correcting himself: '. . . at high levels of government, certainly it has come as a surprise to me.' It is clear, from his reports if nothing else, that Singh himself does not escape the CAG's disapproval. There is more than a hint of bad feeling between these two bureaucrats who have interpreted their mandates so differently, one so cautious, the other so aggressive.

Rai, whose term as CAG ended in May 2013, said the amounts of money involved in the scams were mind-boggling. 'The man in the street talks about it but does not have first- or second-hand knowledge of it,' he said. 'Today, what's happened is citizen groups have come centre stage and are seeking a certain level of public accountability, and I think we all owe it to them to bring these things centre stage.'

Rai was not the first auditor-general in Indian history to bring a government to its knees – a CAG report into massive kickbacks in the purchase of army field howitzers from a Swedish company contributed to the 1989 election defeat of Rajiv Gandhi's government. But he has undoubtedly interpreted his mandate more aggressively than his predecessors, going beyond narrow financial audits to examine how government policies have performed. It is a move, in his own words, 'from pointing out individual irregularities' to uncovering 'systemic irregularities'. That is a role that other auditors around the world often undertake, but not one that many of his more cautious predecessors have chosen to adopt, and one where India's constitution and law offers little guidance.

Rai subsequently came under serious criticism from Singh for over-stepping his constitutional mandate, 'going into issues' that were not the concern of his office, including policy issues. 'We are now a permissive society,' Singh lamented. 'I think if the media can get away with murder so can the CAG.'[26] One senior Congress leader even accused Rai of having political ambitions of his own.[27]

Rai had shrugged off most of the barbs as a reflex defence mech-anism from the government, one that just showed he was doing his job, but the personal nature of some of the attacks clearly irri-tated him. 'If we call them names, they have every right to call us names,' he told me. 'The only thing different now is the stridency of the personal attack, which attributes motives and quite often political aspirations.'

Fortunately, India's Comptrollers and Auditors General enjoy constitutional protection from dismissal, except through a process of impeachment – and Rai used that quasi-immunity to devastating effect. Along with a vibrant media, an activist Supreme Court and a more and more vociferous civil society, his supporters say Rai made his office into a powerful force for accountability in modern India. 'This heralds the start of a completely new era of government being forced to become more transparent,' said the independent MP Rajeev Chandrasekhar, who argues that the auditor and the judiciary provide important checks and balances in a democracy where parliamentary scrutiny of the executive is weak.

Rai is not scared of creating headlines, complaining at the World Economic Forum a few weeks before we met about the appalling 'brazenness' with which government decisions were taken. Perhaps that is why his style is not to everyone's taste. Some have accused him of blurring the lines between exposing corruption and criticizing government policy. More damagingly, independent economists have raised some valid questions about certain of the assumptions upon which the CAG has based his estimates of losses to the government (I share some of those doubts). There is a suspicion that, in its eagerness to attract attention, the CAG's office has on occasion been careless or even perhaps sensationalist in its calculations.

Unfortunately, Rai did not respond to those criticisms directly during our meeting – he said he did not want to comment on the details of individual audits. However, he did order a global peer review of thirty-five of his audits, including the 2G spectrum report, which supported them as 'conceptually sound'.[28] In any case, though, to criticize the CAG on the basis of his figures is to miss the broader point, in the view of commentators like Pratap Bhanu Mehta, president of the Centre for Policy Research, who believes that Rai has played an important role in India's great information revolution and awakening.

'The CAG's reports are part of the great churning now under way. In the medium- to long-run these will make the government stronger, not weaker, because it will be forced to ask the right questions,' Mehta wrote in the *Indian Express* after the coal report was tabled in parliament in August 2012. 'You can contest the CAG's numbers. But the reports, even if they do not say it, leave us in no doubt the government is a rotting ancient regime.' The truth is that the government would be in a much better position to discuss and contest the details of the CAG reports if its actions were not so riddled with corruption and rent-seeking. Perhaps the CAG is occasionally vested with a little too much of the moral high ground, but that is partly because there is so little high ground elsewhere.

Under the unforgiving gaze of this new transparency, India's bureaucracy and government have sometimes seemed paralysed, with even senior officers reluctant to take responsibility or make decisions. But Rai, quite correctly in my view, dismissed this paralysis as 'an alibi for non-performance', and said the government would eventually learn to make decisions that withstand public scrutiny.

'We were all aware of what was happening, but the silent majority was suffering silently. When the middle class realizes it has a voice of its own, it will assert itself,' he said, adding that the new era of public scrutiny of government was a major step forward for India. 'It's quite a watershed. I am very upbeat, very bullish on this. This was a churning which was necessary in society, and it has come.'

In the course of exploring for my profile of Singh over the spring of 2012,[29] I had spoken to several friends and colleagues, along with senior officials in the government and the Congress Party, and asked what had gone wrong. Together, they painted a picture of a man let down by his own party, whose character prevented him asserting himself, and who, despite his party's victory in 2009, eventually sank into a mood of depression and self-pity.

In a stunning re-emergence of the jealousy that had undermined Singh's first stab at politics in 1999, Congress never accepted that their second election victory was a mandate for Singh, and resented the idea that this man could be seen to be anywhere near as important as the Gandhi family to whom they all bowed down in a deeply sycophantic way. Rahul, Sonia's son, was being groomed to take over from Singh, and plenty of other people were vying for power; once again, his rivals decided that Manmohan Singh needed to be cut down to size.

His 1999 election defeat came back to haunt him in another way, so thoroughly destroying his confidence that he refused entreaties from well-wishers to contest a parliamentary seat in both 2004 and again in 2009. The only Indian prime minister never to have won a direct election, Singh's standing was fatally weakened in the eyes of the party, the cabinet, the coalition, and indeed in the eyes of the opposition.

Increasingly ignored or bypassed by his own cabinet, Singh turned once again to one area where he felt he could make a difference: foreign policy, and specifically relations with Pakistan.[30] Once again, a well-meaning man found himself on the wrong side of history, first missing a once-in-a-lifetime chance to make peace with Pakistan and then stubbornly refusing to accept that the chance had gone. In the end, his belated efforts at rapprochement proved to be spectacularly mistimed, and simply handed his opponents in Congress another stick with which to beat him.

The Muslim-majority region of Kashmir lies at the heart of India and Pakistan's enmity. Divided between the two countries, it is claimed by both, and has been the direct cause of two of their three wars. Since 1989, Pakistan has backed an Islamist and separatist insurgency against Indian rule in the Kashmir Valley, the heart of the region, which has cost tens of thousands of lives. The issue remains a tinder-box constantly primed to explode.

That is exactly what happened in December 2002, just three months after the 9/11 attacks in the United States. Five gunmen wearing police uniforms drove into the compound surrounding India's parliament, in a car apparently showing the relevant home ministry and parliament security tags. Once there, they opened fire. Four policemen, a security guard and a gardener were killed in the attack: all five militants also died. India swiftly blamed Pakistan for the attack, and said the militants belonged to the Islamist terrorist outfits Lashkar-e-Taiba (the Army of the Righteous) and Jaish-e-Mohammed (Mohammed's Army). The two groups, which have long enjoyed close links with Pakistan's military intelligence agency, are made up of fanatical jihadis with a deep hatred of India. Intent on winning back Indian Kashmir for Pakistan, they have carried out frequent and indiscriminate attacks on the security forces and civilians.

After the attack on parliament, tensions soared between the nuclear-armed rivals, and were further fuelled by a subsequent attack on an Indian army base in Kashmir. By the summer of 2003 the two countries were on the brink of war, with hundreds of thousands of troops said to be confronting each other 'eyeball-to-eyeball' across their heavily fortified frontier in Kashmir.

But when the United States convinced India not to retaliate, Pakistan's leader Musharraf began to explore the opportunities for a different relationship. His country, he told me in an hour-long interview in December 2003, was prepared to meet India 'halfway' on the question of Kashmir, the Muslim-majority Himalayan region divided between the rivals but claimed by both. Crucially, Musharraf told me, Pakistan was prepared to drop its decades-long insistence on a referendum in Kashmir, an idea backed by the United Nations that would have allowed its people to choose which country to join.[31]

Learning that I was soon to be posted to India, Musharraf extended our discussion by a second hour to stress his desire for a legacy of peace on the subcontinent. Pakistan's military leader, it turned out, was pushing for a deal that would leave the region's heart, the all-important Kashmir Valley, in Indian hands, provided New Delhi dropped its claim to territory held by Pakistan and agreed to create a soft border between the two sides of Kashmir. It was a huge and historic climbdown, discarding decades of Pakistani propaganda about Kashmir, its right to rule the entire region, and the Indian army's systematic human rights abuses there. He had taken a position that would have seemed unimaginable just a year earlier, and forced many Pakistanis to confront a reality that had been staring them hard in the face but that they would never have admitted before: they were never going to regain control of the Kashmir Valley from India.

Indeed, I remember vividly how Musharraf's climbdown affected middle-class thinking within Pakistan. When I arrived in 2002, it was almost heretical to argue that Kashmir should be divided with India; by the time I left in 2004, many people had accepted this was ultimately inevitable. Meanwhile, Musharraf, I believe, had his eye on a place in history, and wanted a legacy not as a military ruler who had seized power in a coup, but as a peacemaker.

With the same conciliatory message being conveyed behind the scenes, the prospects for peace suddenly brightened. Singh's predecessor, the Hindu Nationalist Prime Minister Atal Bihari Vajpayee of the BJP, visited Islamabad in January 2004 and seemed to strike up a rare rapport with Musharraf. A deal between India's right wing and Pakistan's army, impossible as that may sound, was not completely out of the question – until, that is, Vajpayee lost power.

It was clear at once, however, that a government with the Italian-born Sonia Gandhi as its de facto leader was always going to find it harder to reach territorial concessions with Pakistan than a right-wing government would have done. Vajpayee's rabidly nationalistic party might – and I stress might – have been dragged towards peace when they were in power, but they were certainly not going to accept a peace made in Italy.

In what was perhaps an attempt to shore up the government's credentials, the Prime Minister appointed K. Natwar Singh as his Foreign Minister – a short, dapper, self-satisfied man in his seventies with a small white moustache. It proved to be a spectacularly unimaginative appointment, for although Natwar Singh was a man with a long career in the foreign service and the Congress party, he soon earned the nickname 'Nitwit Singh' for his clumsy approach to diplomacy.

I sat next to Natwar Singh on a plane ride back from Nepal shortly after he took office in 2004, and it was clear straight away that this old-fashioned man simply lacked the imagination to grasp the historic opportunity that was on offer. Barely acknowledging Musharraf's change of tack, he talked about pushing the Kashmir question onto the back burner – for decades if necessary – while the neighbours tried to improve trade relations. It was a model that was working with China, he explained, as I sat there silently shaking my head in disbelief.

I could understand that it was intensely hard to trust Musharraf given some duplicitous dealings with India in the past, and hard to negotiate with Pakistan while it continued to sponsor Islamist militants to attack India. But surely Musharraf's offer deserved to be explored? It seemed not. India's hawkish and conservative bureaucracy – headed by the obstinate figure of Natwar Singh – were determined to look the other way.

* * *

As I was later to realize, Natwar Singh's attitude towards Pakistan was deeply entrenched in India's foreign service. A foreign diplomat once asked why the Indians were dragging their feet so frustratingly over the simplest request, when it came to moving forward in negotiations with Pakistan over relatively uncontentious issues. One answer, as Indian bureaucrats freely admit, is that New Delhi sees itself as the 'status quo power', as holding the Kashmir Valley, and therefore having little fundamental interest in change – especially when it comes to negotiating with an untrustworthy foe.

In 2005, Musharraf visited New Delhi for a cricket match between India and Pakistan. While there, he spelled out his ideas in more detail and seemed to strike up a rapport with Manmohan Singh. By then, I have no doubt Singh grasped what was on offer; that is when, colleagues say, he began dreaming of a Nobel Peace Prize. Tragically, though, the window of opportunity was already beginning to close. Although negotiations were far advanced behind the scenes, Indian bureaucratic and popular opinion was not primed for any kind of deal. The peace process, which could have taken root under Vajpayee, had grown feeble under Singh, disconnected from the nation at large, and a peace deal was, I believe, now a more distant prospect than has sometimes been suggested. There were, as there always are in India, elections in some state or other looming on the calendar, and the Indian government dragged its feet. In the meantime, Musharraf's popularity began to wane at home, and protests erupted against his rule. If there had ever been a chance for progress, that chance was lost.

In August 2008, Musharrraf was finally forced to step down as President of Pakistan. In November of the same year, Pakistani terrorists landed on the shores of India's commercial capital Mumbai and embarked on a three-day killing and hostage-taking spree that left 166 innocent people dead and the entire Indian nation in a state of outrage and shock. Pakistan, in short, had reverted to violent and devious type, allowing the organization and training for the attack to be carried out under the noses of its intelligence services – by militant groups with whom those same intelligence agencies enjoy a close relationship – and then blatantly dragging their feet when it came to bringing the instigators of the attack to justice. Whether or not one believes that Musharraf was ever genuine, there could now be little doubt that the window for peace had slammed shut.

Singh, of course, shared the intense shock and anger that everyone in India felt at that time, including myself. But, having seen the idea of peace move tantalizingly close, I believe he never quite accepted that it had definitely gone away again. Making peace with Pakistan remained, one colleague told me, the topic he appeared to care most about; a Nobel Peace Prize, the chance to truly cement his legacy as a foreign-policy, as well as an economic, visionary, remained his cherished dream. In July 2009, just eight months after the Mumbai attacks, he met his Pakistani counterpart Yousuf Raza Gilani on the sidelines of an international summit in Sharm-el-Sheikh in Egypt and pledged to resume peace talks with Pakistan. It was a spectacular misjudgement, for Singh came under immediate fire at home and was soon contradicted by his own party. The Prime Minister went into what one Congress leader called 'a huge sulk'.

'He has the big picture intellect, and yet a self-pitying side too,' Shekhar Gupta, editor of the *Indian Express* newspaper, told me. 'After Sharm-el-Sheikh, the Congress Party admonished him, and he hasn't been the same since. His character being what it is, he just withdrew.'

By that stage it had been clear to many people that Singh should have resigned years earlier. But that, friends and colleagues stressed, was not in his nature. This was not, after all, a man who would do anything that might be seen as disruptive or might rock the boat. It is not in his nature to break ranks, or to embarrass the party or his party leader. 'He really sees his role as working from within – that is the bureaucrat's role,' Columbia University Professor Jagdish Bhagwati, who has been close friends with Singh since their Cambridge University days, told me. 'He has an inability to go out and fight – that's not his style.'

But if Singh was determined not to rock the boat, others would rock it for him. Together, the media, civil society and the CAG's office aroused India's slumbering democracy and fuelled a powerful new demand for accountable and transparent government. I believe the state's response to this awakening will determine India's future. Singh's response to the challenge is instructive, if not particularly encouraging. It constitutes the final complaint against Singh.

By 2004, Singh had been out of government for eight years, and the information and societal revolution that India underwent in that time had seemingly passed him by. He was already seventy-six years old by the time he won a second term in 2009, and an intensely loyal member of the Gandhi family's sycophantic entourage. As later became apparent, his honesty and integrity was accompanied by rather old-school attitudes about power and accountability.

His first instinct in the face of the criticism he faced was to say nothing. He had never been good at dealing with the media, and came across as terribly wooden and wimpy as a public speaker. The party seemed content to let others do the talking. The problem was that Sonia Gandhi did not enjoy the limelight or trust the press either, and nor did her son Rahul. Effectively, the three most important voices in the party had muted themselves, while the media and the opposition had a field day. It clearly was not an ideal strategy, and by the start of 2011 the vultures were beginning to circle.

It was around this time that I returned to India, after a twenty-month stay in Washington, D.C., where I had been running the Reuters bureau and managing a large team of people. An opportunity had come up to return to writing and reporting, to join the *Washington Post* as their India bureau chief, and I jumped at the chance. But when I returned, it was to a very different India to the one I had left behind. Everywhere I went, people seemed sunk in gloom. The bubble had well and truly burst while I had been away.[32] Rajeev Chandrasekhar, the IT billionaire turned parliamentarian who appears throughout this book and is someone who thinks and cares deeply about Indian democracy, told me the country was undergoing a 'psychological crisis of confidence'. Chetan Bhagat, an author of trendy books about the lives of young, aspirational Indians, told me the idea that India was on an automatic path to becoming a developed capitalist economy had been 'delusional'. He went on: 'It doesn't just happen. It needs systemic changes, structural changes, cultural changes. And the biggest roadblock is corruption.'

So I remember vividly the moment that Singh, or his advisers, decided that lofty abandon was no longer a sustainable tactic. It was time to tear down the walls of silence. Promises were made about regular, even weekly, interactions with the media, starting with an hour-long grilling by several senior television news editors in February. I also remember my disappointment. Singh, sounding hesitant and defensive, lamely asserted that his was not a 'lame-duck government' and he was not a 'lame duck prime minister'.[33]

In fact, it was largely the media's fault, he implied, for doing the country down. As usual, the instinctive response to criticism was to blame the messenger. 'An impression has gone round that we are a scam-driven country and that nothing good is happening in our country. In the process, I think we are weakening the self-confidence of the people of India. I don't think that it is in the interest of anybody in our country.' He blithely batted off a question about whether he might have thought of resigning – 'Things are not entirely the way I would like them to be, but frankly, I have never thought of resigning, because I have a job to do' – then went on to advise the media how to do their jobs: 'in reporting the affairs of our nation, we mustn't focus excessively on the negative features'.

Not surprisingly, little changed. The media took aim. Singh ducked. Four months passed, and finally it was the turn of newspaper editors to meet the Prime Minister. Again, the assembled media was berated, for becoming, 'in many cases . . . the accuser, the prosecutor and the judge'.[34] At every stage, Singh's defence was to blame the realities of coalition politics, or the tactlessness of other people for daring to mention how recklessly and blatantly corrupt his government had become, what he called 'a mindless atmosphere of negativity and pessimism' over corruption that was undermining the morale of the government.[35]

There were some very valid criticisms of how the media and the CAG were operating, and there were certainly some genuine limitations imposed on the leader of a coalition government in modern India. There was also a concern that government servants were scared to make decisions lest they be forced to answer for them later. But Singh's indignant attacks on the people who were exposing corruption – while at the same time the corrupt were being shielded – seemed to strike the wrong chord.

What grated more was that Singh's attacks seemed to send a signal to the party that the attack dogs could be unleashed. The media was constantly berated and threatened with regulation if it didn't behave, while social media was blatantly censored, with Facebook ordered to remove posts deemed to have insulted Singh or Sonia Gandhi, and several Twitter accounts blocked.

The government's response to my piece in the *Washington Post* is a case in point. Another good example came in Singh's rather peevish reaction in 2012 to a protest by fishermen and farmers about the construction of a nuclear plant near a seaside village called Kudankulam in the south of the country. In a rare interview with *Science* magazine, Singh dismissed the protests as part of an international conspiracy to block India's development, blaming non-governmental groups 'mostly I think from the United States, [which] don't appreciate the need for our country to increase the energy supply'. But progress was being impeded because India, he rather ruefully concluded, is a democracy, 'not like China'.[36]

His comments sounded dangerously close to the Cold War era fears of a 'foreign hand', a phrase used by Indira Gandhi to tar her opponents when she pushed democracy aside and declared her infamous State of Emergency in 1975. Singh offered no objection to the charging of thousands of Kudankulam protesters with sedition, a dangerous precedent in a country supposed to value freedom of speech; instead, his government later tightened the rules on foreign funding for non-governmental organizations, a move activists denounced as an attempt to curb 'our democratic right to dissent and disagree'.[37]

Despite the inexorable decline in his reputation, Manmohan Singh decided not to resign. My story about him ran on 4 September 2012. Just ten days later, he finally woke from his long slumber.

A decision to allow foreign investment in supermarkets and department stores had long been mooted; it was announced in 2011 only to be withdrawn as the government's coalition allies kicked up a stink about the impact it could have on India's legion of small shopkeepers. Then, on 14 September 2012, Manmohan Singh told a cabinet committee that the decision could no longer be delayed. 'We have to bite the bullet,' he was quoted as saying. 'If we have to go down, let us go down fighting.'[38] Foreign investment from the likes of Wal-Mart and Britain's Tesco would be allowed, albeit under strict conditions. The nation's diesel prices, long heavily subsidized, were now also raised, and foreign investors were invited into India's airline industry. A few weeks later, with the wind in its sails – with business leaders and to some extent the media swinging behind it – the government announced a revival of long-shelved plans to invite foreign investment into the insurance and pensions sectors.

Suddenly, wherever I went, whomever I spoke to, I was being congratulated for having helped to goad Singh into action, for helping to unleash a new round of reforms that would save India's economy. Indian-American businessmen in California, academics in New York and Washington and senior editors thanked me for my supposed role. Everyone, that is, except the small store owners and their activist leaders, who worried that Wal-Mart would put them out of business. For them, the *Washington Post* was now part of an evil conspiracy with the American empire.

Eventually, as the economic gloom lifted marginally, even the government seemed to thaw. When I captained the Foreign Correspondents' Cricket Club to a noble defeat against an Indian foreign ministry team, we received a consolation prize from an affable foreign secretary. The 72-year-old Power Minister then agreed to meet me for an interview, still finding time as I was leaving to complain about that terrible article about the PM. 'The Independent, wasn't it?' he asked. 'No, The Times, that's it,' he concluded, in a mumble. Smiling nervously, I beat a hasty retreat.

Yet in parliament, the opposition lawmakers continued to taunt Manmohan Singh, suggesting that he thank the Washington Post for the alarm call. But in truth, my article probably had little effect on finally waking the Prime Minister. The writing had been on the wall ever since Standard and Poor's had warned a few months earlier that Indian debt was facing a possible downgrade to 'junk' status. The government was running out of money, and had had no choice but to act.[39]

Yet Singh's valiant attempt to save his legacy was to prove ineffective. Wal-Mart has yet to open a single supermarket in India, deterred by the strict conditions attached to the foreign investment in multibrand retail (although it continues to operate twenty wholesale cash-and-carry stores under the Best Price Modern Wholesale brand). Global investor confidence continues to ebb. By the summer of 2013, Indian economic growth was slowing dramatically, the rupee was in free fall, and no one seemed to have a good word to say about the Prime Minister.

Manmohan Singh will go down in history as India's first Sikh prime minister and the country's third-longest-serving premier, as the man who designed India's economic reforms, and yet, in historian Ramachandra Guha's words, also as something of a 'tragic figure'. For me, that tragedy lies in his inability to live up to the hope that was vested in him, and his inability to overcome the dysfunctional nature of the democracy over which he presided. His attempts to portray himself as divorced from the conspiracy of corruption at the heart of his government, and above the dirty politics of coalition formation that had placed him in a position of power, ultimately failed to convince many Indians. If his cabinet was corrupt, and that corruption was dragging the economy down, the Prime Minister must take a large share of the blame.

Throughout India, dedicated men and women with far less power at their command are struggling to invigorate Indian democracy, to clean up its politics and make its bureaucracy more accountable. As Prime Minister, Manmohan Singh had more power than any of them, yet seemed reluctant to act, unwilling to stick his own neck out to take on the vested interests at the heart of his government. At times, as we shall see in the story of the Right to Information Act in chapter 5, he behaved more like an obstacle to progress.

Singh was on the right side of history when he launched the economic reforms of 1991. Two decades later, those economic reforms have led to rising aspirations among the Indian people, and rising demands on what the state needs to provide – demands that have so far been met by paralysis and peevishness. Singh now seems like a man on the wrong side of history, in the words of an old Elvis Costello song, 'A Man Out of Time'.

3

Money (That's What I Want)

The battle to rid Indian democracy of criminality and corruption

'If you work hard you can steal a little, but you cannot behave like dacoits [bandits].'
Shivpal Yadav, minister in the state government
of Uttar Pradesh in northern India, speaking to officials

In India's democracy, crime really can pay.

Bhagwan Sharma faces thirteen criminal cases and has forty-three charges against his name, ranging from rape to extortion and from rioting to causing grievous bodily harm.[1] There are nine separate charges of criminal intimidation, and one of trying to take a second wife without informing her that he was already married. But Sharma is not behind bars. Instead, he is a member of the state parliament, known as the legislative assembly, in India's northern state of Uttar Pradesh, and he keeps on winning elections.

He is not alone. All across India, hundreds of men facing serious criminal charges have enjoyed long and successful careers as politicians, both at the national and state level. This is the story of how criminals became so deeply embedded in India's political life, and of why they keep getting elected. It is also the story of how corruption entrenched itself in India through the illegal financing of election campaigns, and how this led to the damaging corruption scandals that so badly undermined Manmohan Singh's legacy.

For India's prime minister is in some sense a victim of a much larger malaise that runs through the heart of Indian democracy: a victim of the corruption, crime and cronyism that have eaten away at the soul of Nehru's dream.

The numbers tell a worrying tale. In India's last national elections in 2009, voters elected 162 politicians who were facing criminal charges to the country's 545-member parliament, almost 30 per cent of the total.[2] Of them, seventy-six were facing charges for murder, rape and what is known as 'dacoity', crimes ranging from kidnapping to robbery and extortion. Even more worryingly, the numbers are rising: in the previous national elections in 2004, 128 members of parliament facing criminal charges had been elected, of whom 58 were charged with so-called 'heinous offences'.

In March 2012, my research assistant Suhasini and I travelled to India's largest and one of its most crime-ridden states, Uttar Pradesh, to cover state elections there. Bordering the capital, it stretches across northern India over the broad, fertile plains of the Ganges. UP, as it is known, is home to 200 million people; one in every six Indians, one in every thirty-five people in the world, lives here. If it were a country, it would be the fifth most populous in the world. Politically and economically, it holds many of the keys to India's future – most of the country's prime ministers have come from UP – but it is one of the nation's poorest states, with a reputation for lawlessness and bitter caste divisions. Its countryside is beautiful at harvest time but its traditions are deeply rooted in the past; buffaloes cavort in village ponds, but women hide their faces. Its towns are bustling, but ugly and congested, tangles of electrical wires dangle across the street, and every imaginable form of transport struggles for space at ground level.

Despite a nationwide outcry against corruption the previous year, little seemed to have changed in UP politics. Of 2,000 candidates contesting these elections, a third were facing criminal charges, and thirty were running for office from jail. I caught the tail end of Bhagwan Sharma's campaign in the constituency of Debai, some 80 miles' drive southeast of New Delhi. As we caught up with him in the villages around the town, the crowds started to swell, his convoy pursued by supporters in cars and on motorbikes festooned with the party's red and green flag. As we entered Debai itself, everything slowed to a standstill, and the streets thronged with people. Sharma, better known here by his nickname Guddu Pandit, clambered on top of his vehicle, where he sat cross-legged acknowledging the cheers, garlanded in marigolds. At times he stood up, red and green Gandhi cap on his head, and pressed his palms together in the Indian namaste salutation. I ran alongside taking photographs, conscious that my very presence here could be seen to be adding imperceptibly to the mystique surrounding this man.

But there was no doubting his appeal. 'He is a muscle man, he is a powerful man,' Anshul Yadav, a 21-year-old shopkeeper, told me with undisguised glee. 'Guddu Pandit stands up for poor people,' said 55-year-old farmer Nanak Chand. 'He goes out of his way to help people, he sorts out disputes, and if someone is sick he is there to help.' Om Vir Deshwal, a local secretary for the All India Farmers Union, agreed. 'He arranged for electricity supplies to our area,' he said. 'And he helped get jobs for poor families.'[3]

A few days before, in New Delhi, I had asked the then Chief Election Commissioner of India, S. Y. Quraishi, what the appeal of strongmen like Sharma was. 'I call it the Robin Hood syndrome,' he told me. 'They take care to use their corrupt money, money that they get through illegal means, to give to the poor.'

If Sharma appears an unlikely Robin Hood, it may be because there is something more than money at play. In a country where the state can often be arbitrary in the way it deals with ordinary citizens, where bureaucrats and officials have enormous discretion, where the social safety net is weak and not universally available, where castes and communities compete fiercely for resources, the advantage of having a strongman like Sharma in your corner is undeniable.

Milan Vaishnav at the Center for the Advanced Study of India at the University of Pennsylvania spends his time thinking deeply about how the nation's democracy functions. Strongmen are particularly attractive where the state is weakest and caste divisions are fiercest, he says, and are often seen by voters as the most credible protectors of their community's interests. 'Voters are not ignorant or uninformed,' he wrote in an analysis on the UPenn website in early 2012. 'They are simply looking for candidates who can best fill a perceived representational vacuum.'[4]

Bhagwan Sharma's story is an unlikely rags-to-riches tale. The former bicycle repairman was first hired as a driver for a powerful politician who was a minister in the Uttar Pradesh government. When the minister, Amarmani Tripathi, was jailed – for allegedly murdering his mistress – Sharma rose swiftly to become a property dealer in the fast-growing New Delhi suburb of Noida, and then a politician in his own right.

But the recurring charge against Sharma is that he used his power and influence to bully and cheat whoever might stand in his way. In 2006 he married an Agra University research scholar, Sheetal Birla, allegedly without informing her he was already married with two children. When Birla found out, and refused to become his mistress, she claims he threatened to kill her, and subsequently raped her.[5]

In 2007 he was first elected to represent Debai on behalf of the Bahujan Samaj Party (BSP), an outfit that draws the foundation of its support from India's Dalits, the former untouchables. The BSP ended up winning those 2007 elections, but Sharma eventually became something of an embarrassment in the state capital Lucknow. Twice thrown into jail, he was eventually thrown out of the BSP as the party tried to clean up its battered image. Nevertheless, he still had standing in Debai; he soon joined the BSP's main rival, the socialist Samajwadi Party, and stood for re-election for the same constituency.

As his campaign drew to a close, I had a few minutes to quiz Sharma, in a crowded alley by the side of a building surrounded by his supporters. Gruff-voiced, moustachioed and thuggish-looking, he said the charges against him had been trumped up by his opponents to discredit him. He was expelled from the BSP, he said, not because of his criminality, but because he fought hard for his constituents and refused to play politics with caste divisions. Then, his bodyguards brushed the crowds aside, and Sharma roared off on his favourite black motorbike.

To be fair, the breakdown of the criminal justice system in India means that an innocent person's name can potentially be tarnished by a politically motivated charge that might take years or even decades to be resolved by the sluggish and overburdened court system. But it is equally true that politicians guilty of terrible crimes routinely escape conviction, abusing the power that comes with office to derail the legal process. Whistleblowers within the bureaucracy are often transferred in an attempt to silence them; witnesses routinely disappear or mysteriously change their evidence; prosecutors are transferred and investigating bodies are quietly swayed to back down.

But in Sharma's case, what seemed remarkable was that his supporters scarcely seemed to care one way or the other. 'He is a social worker, he works for the poor, so it doesn't matter if he has a thousand cases against him,' said 38-year-old Subash Balmiki.

Of course, not everyone in Debai is comfortable electing a man facing charges of violence, corruption and rape. Suhasini and I passed by the local headquarters of the India Against Corruption movement. There, in a concrete-floored room adorned with the face of the movement's figurehead Anna Hazare, 49-year-old businessman Hari Om Dubey said he had been fighting against graft for twenty-five years and had taken several carloads of people to New Delhi for one of Hazare's rallies in 2011. Now, he was advising people to vote for the most honest candidate. The trouble, he said with a resigned air, is that 'not a single candidate is spotlessly clean'.

A discussion in that office about the options facing voters in Debai drew out the frustration that many Indians felt with the political system and the elite who had cornered power. 'I won't vote for anyone,' said 31-year-old electrician Dinesh Kumar. 'Fifteen per cent of this country's population is ruling over the other 85 per cent. It angers me so much that I wait for the day the 85 per cent wake up to roar and trample that 15 per cent.'

For India's politicians, campaigning is an expensive business. A typical Indian constituency at the national level might have more than a million voters spread out over 6,000 square km. In rural areas, those voters could be dispersed in 1,000 villages, and, on election day, be casting their votes in 1,000 polling stations. Any serious candidate needs an extensive network of paid workers just to man those booths on election day. With campaign finance limits until recently as low as $45,000 per constituency, that has forced candidates to raise funds in ways that do not have to be accounted for. 'Who has access to unaccounted funds? Criminal elements. This forces you into bed with criminal elements,' said M. R. Madhavan, one of the founders of PRS Legislative Research, a non-profit organization dedicated to helping India's parliament function more effectively, and a group that I have visited several times in my efforts to understand democracy in this country.

In the end, money is the root of much of the evil in Indian politics.

While many Americans lament the role of big business in funding political campaigns in their country, the corruption and criminalization of Indian politics ironically stem from the opaque nature of its campaign funding. The political analyst and columnist Prem Shankar Jha was one of the first people I had met on arriving in India in 2004, and we had met and talked many times since. Jha had written a perceptive and persuasive piece for the investigative magazine *Tehelka* in 2011 in which he argued that the rot set in when Prime Minister Indira Gandhi outlawed corporate contributions to political parties, after Congress had come closer than ever before to its first general election defeat in 1967.[6] Indira's aim, he said, was to cripple a nascent right-wing opposition movement by depriving it of funds.

Ever since, in order to cover the huge cost of running election campaigns in this vast country, India's political parties have been forced to find other sources of money. In practice, this has meant that bribes, patronage and trading favours have become the only way that politicians can survive in modern India. 'The ban on company donations closed the only honest, open and transparent avenue of raising funds to fight elections,' Jha had written. 'The harm it has done is beyond measure.' In other words, it is practically impossible to be completely honest as an Indian politician – even if one is personally not corrupt, one has no choice but to accept campaign donations off the books and under the table.

The only alternative to funding from large corporate donors was to establish a network of patronage and favour-swapping from small donors at the constituency level that soon became entrenched – the origin, he argued, of India's 'clientelist politics'. Ironically, the move also led to a dramatic power shift from the central leadership of the Congress Party to its local chieftains, reducing the government's capacity to take hard decisions in the national interest. In order to reclaim some of that lost power, the central command of the Congress Party realized it too needed to raise more money: it was soon demanding massive illegal kickbacks from business deals, mostly on defence and infrastructure contracts. This, said Jha, was the road that led to the Bofors scandal, the major corruption scandal involving the purchase of howitzers from the Swedish company Bofors, which was behind the defeat of Rajiv Gandhi's government in 1989.

Vinod Jose's profile of Manmohan Singh in *The Caravan* magazine contains a fascinating anecdote that reveals how even the supposedly cleanest man in the nation's politics could not stand against this tide.[7] During his ill-fated campaign for a Lok Sabha seat in 1999, Singh had resolutely refused to meet a series of industrialists who had been queueing up to hand over illegal campaign contributions in cash: until, that is, his campaign ran out of money. Finally, even Singh buckled, according to his campaign manager Harcharan Singh Josh, and a compromise was worked out: industrialists would ask what they could do to help, Singh would say he only wanted their best wishes, and the contributions would be handed over to his wife in another room.

The ban on corporate donations was lifted in 2003, but by then the cancer was too well entrenched to save the body politic. Instead of funding political parties, big industrialists have found a cheaper way to influence decisions: buy the decision-maker. That is the source of the 2G scandal and the allegations against the former Telecoms Minister A. Raja.

There were, of course, other factors behind the corruption of India's body politic, including the weakness of the police and criminal justice system. In the 1970s, a phenomenon known as 'booth-capturing' began to emerge in the politics of northern India, especially in densely populated and poorly policed states like UP, Bihar and West Bengal. Gangs of thugs, paid by politicians, would take over polling booths on election day and openly stuff ballot boxes with votes in favour of their candidate. Local police officers were either intimidated or bribed into standing aside, and genuine voters turned away. So successful was the tactic that the gang leaders gradually came to wonder why they were doing it on someone else's behalf. If criminals could get other people elected, why not just get elected themselves?

Bhagwan Sharma, though, was not just accused of criminality, he was also a property dealer, and this is equally revealing in today's India. A study of leading Indian corporates by the auditors KPMG in 2001[8] found the real estate and construction industry was perceived as easily the most corrupt sector of the economy. It is also the one where politicians have the most discretion to make arbitrary decisions on granting land or permission to build. In 2013 the World Bank ranked India at 182 out of 185 countries around the world in dealing with the construction permits required to build a warehouse, scraping in just ahead of Ukraine, Albania and Eritrea (and just one place behind China).[9]

Indeed, the links between the property business and illicit campaign financing in India have grown so strong that they can actually be measured, according to a research study conducted by Vaishnav, again, and Devesh Kapur for the Center for Global Development in Washington, D.C.[10]

Politicians often park their wealth in building and real estate, investing in a fast-growing sector of the economy that does not attract too much scrutiny. At the same time, they use their power to dole out favours for their developer friends. Then, at election time, the favours pay off. Huge sums of money flow the other way, back to the politicians to finance their campaigns, strangling liquidity from the construction sector. The effect is so marked that cement production actually declines by around 15 per cent when state election campaigning is in full swing, and by up to 38 per cent when national and state elections coincide.

From the corruption of India's politicians, all else flows. How, indeed, can one expect a bureaucracy to function honestly when it reports to a kleptocrat elite? When politics becomes only about money, how can one blame large sections of the Indian population for becoming alienated from the whole process?

Against these mighty forces of crime and corruption, India's impressive Election Commission survives as the beating heart of the country's democracy. Established as a constitutionally independent body shortly after Independence, it has a credibility and authority as an institution that are unmatched in modern India.

Every five years, it administers the world's largest exercise in democracy, employing helicopters, tractors and bullock carts – as well as donkeys, camels and elephants – to ferry polling materials to every remote corner of India, from the highest Himalayas to the driest deserts and the remote islands of the Indian Ocean. Five million polling staff and police officers operate under its command during national elections; its electoral roll comprises 670 million people.

Much of the credit for the high regard in which the Election Commissioner is held belongs to T. N. Seshan, who led it in a hugely successful campaign in the 1990s against the booth-capturing and fraud that had so blighted elections in northern India for more than two decades.[11] His successors have carried on his work in impressive manner. Today, India employs innovative electronic voting machines that will only record a maximum of five votes a minute – slowing down the process of ballot-box stuffing that had occurred in the past, and giving police more time to send reinforcements. Police from outside the state are also brought in, since they are less susceptible to political influence, and polls are staggered in the most lawless states to give the forces of law and order time to provide fuller coverage.

Videographing of polls as well as a computerized photographic database of electors, backed by individual election cards, further reduces the scope for fraud.

The Commission also pored over voting records, demographic data and crime records to identify polling booths where booth-capturing might have occurred or might in the future, so that policing can be stepped up. Known criminals in vulnerable areas are identified; in some cases, preventative arrests are made over the election period, while security deposits are demanded from other people, deposits that will be forfeited if they commit a crime during the elections. Police are also pressed to step up efforts to seek out 'absconding' criminals, who have warrants against their names for serious offences but have so far evaded arrest.

Thanks to these measures, booth-capturing has become a thing of the past in India. However, the flow of illegal or 'black' money is not so easy to stem. While elections in Uttar Pradesh exemplify the role of crime and intimidation in this country, democracy in the southern state of Tamil Nadu stands out as perhaps the most influenced by bribery. The state, home to India's fourth-largest city, Chennai, boasts above-average levels of education and health, a reasonably efficient bureaucracy and buoyant economic growth, but is blighted by large-scale cronyism and corruption.

There had long been a tradition of giving out freebies like sarees and lungis to convince people to vote for particular parties in Tamil Nadu, but as the economy grew and ambitions rose, bribe inflation set in. In 2006, the DMK, the party of India's former Telecom Minister A. Raja, was in opposition and all set to lose an election to its rival, the All India Anna Dravida Munnetra Kazhagam (AIADMK). But the DMK came up with the idea of promising not just cheap rice but also free TV sets to the poor if it came to power. Much to its own surprise, it won the election. Over the following five years some 15 million television sets were distributed to low- and middle-income households, all marked with the emblem of the government of Tamil Nadu.[12] The scheme was neat, since the money for the television sets came out of state government funds, but some flowed back neatly to the party bigwigs, who dominated the cable network industry in the state.

But it was not just government money that was used. At the same time that Raja was accused of pocketing huge sums of money from telecommunications companies, all the parties in his home state of Tamil Nadu were distributing cash to voters. It was a direct violation of the electoral laws, but it was so blatant that party leaders were openly admitting it to Frederick Kaplan, Acting Principal Officer of the US Consulate-General in Tamil Nadu's capital Chennai. Bribes, he wrote in a revealing diplomatic cable subsequently released by WikiLeaks, are a regular feature of elections in southern India.[13] 'Poor voters expect bribes from political candidates, and candidates find various ways to satisfy voters expectations,' he wrote. Some politicians built wells for villages, or gave money for temples and community halls; others simply handed out cash. 'The money required to pay bribes comes from a variety of sources, primarily from the proceeds of corruption and from the funds the parties raise from businesses. Although the precise impact of bribery on voter behaviour is hard to measure, it no doubt swings at least some elections, especially the close races.'

In the slums of Chennai, agents from the DMK and AIADMK would turn up between two and four in the morning, Kaplan was told, 'when the Election Commission is asleep', carrying rice sacks filled with cash. Every family on the voter list received 500 rupees ($10).

Bribe inflation was fuelled after a by-election run by M. K. Azhagiri, the son of DMK boss and Chief Minister Muthuvel Karunanidhi, in 2009. Azhagiri had a reputation for 'political thuggery', Kaplan wrote, noting his controversial acquittal on charges of murdering a political rival some years before, and the 2007 burning down of a newspaper office by his supporters, a fire in which three people died, after the paper published a poll showing that Azhagiri was considerably less popular than his brother, M. K. Stalin (who was, incidentally, named after Joseph).

In January 2009, Azhagiri was so determined to win the race in the town of Thirumangalam that he handed out ten times the usual amount, 5,000 rupees or $100, to every voter. Nor did he bother to sneak around in the middle of the night; instead, the money was distributed to voters in an envelope inserted into their morning newspaper, together with instructions on whom to vote for. As a brazen attempt to buy support, it took some beating.

How well the bribery worked was a subject of debate, Kaplan concluded, especially with bribe inflation raising expectations. Some middle-class people felt insulted by the bribes, he was told, while others clearly voted according to the quality of the candidate, the strength of the party and the issues. 'Anil Ambani [one of India's richest men] can't win an election just by paying people – it doesn't work that way,' one politician told Kaplan, admitting at the same time that 'bribes can help put you over the top'.

But no one in Tamil Nadu, it seemed, could avoid them. By the time of state elections in 2011, the gifts and sops had grown even further. Sarees were no longer enough. Free medical insurance for the elderly, gold for poor brides, and, in aspirational India, even free laptops were on the menu for Tamil Nadu's voters.

At the Election Commission, there is a renewed sense of vigour about the battle to expose money power in politics. Cars, helicopters and planes are searched during elections in case they are transporting illegal stacks of cash: even ambulances are searched – only after, Quraishi stressed, they have dropped patients off at hospital. In Tamil Nadu, the Election Commission seized more than $12 million in cash during the 2011 elections, including one haul of $1 million hidden in sacks on the roof of a bus. 'We are making phenomenal progress,' Quraishi told me, perhaps a little more enthusiastically than was warranted.

But if the Election Commission has yet to turn back the tide, it would be wrong to be defeatist about efforts to limit the power of money and corruption in Indian politics, or to bring a little more transparency to the system. Indeed the battle to rid Indian politics of crime and corruption exploded into the open in the summer of 2013, and looks set to continue for years to come. It is going to be a crucial battle in the war to reinvigorate Indian democracy.

The story begins in early 1999, when two professors from the Indian Institute of Management in the western city of Ahmedabad, Trilochan Sastri and Jagdeep Chhokar, decided they were fed up with the criminalization of Indian politics and wanted to do something about it. They discovered that the nomination papers for election candidates called for only four pieces of information – the candidate's name, father or husband's name, address and voter registration number. In a country that requires long and complicated forms to be filled out for the most routine of requests, this seemed all too easy.

One of the most powerful features of the Indian legal system is what is known as a Public Interest Litigation (PIL), in which anyone can invite the courts to rule on almost anything that is in the public interest. Brushing aside the scepticism of their friends and colleagues, the professors filed a PIL in the Delhi High Court demanding that candidates in Indian elections be required to disclose any criminal cases pending against them. In order to bolster the credibility of their case, and on the advice of their lawyer, they also formed the Association for Democratic Reforms (ADR) with a few fellow professors and alumni.

Their lawyer took up the case, and the two professors got on with their jobs. Then, two years later, a colleague came up to Chhokar. 'He told me the judgement on our case was on television,' Chhokar recalled. 'I watched at eight o'clock that night, and sure enough it had top billing. The next day all the newspapers had it. No one even knew who ADR was.'

The High Court had ordered not only that candidates declare criminal convictions and pending cases against them, but also their financial assets and liabilities and educational qualifications. 'We were elated,' Chhokar said. 'We thought our job was done.' Chhokar says Sastri was really the driving force, and he was only going along 'for a lark'. Nevertheless, what followed was to suck them deeply into a years-long battle with the government, and convert Chhokar from a casual observer into a passionate crusader for democratic transparency.

First, the government appealed against the decision to the Supreme Court, arguing this was a matter for parliament and not the judiciary to decide. They lost, but did not give up. With the Election Commission of India eventually swinging behind the ADR, and preparing to implement the new rules, drastic action was required. An all-party meeting was convened and an emergency law, or ordinance, drawn up and quickly passed – in secret – that would have overruled the Supreme Court order.

Hearing rumours that the order had been sent to the President to sign into law, the ADR professors and other civil society representatives sought an audience with President A. P. J. Abdul Kalam and made their case. A few days later the President, whose role was largely ceremonial, refused to sanction the law, and returned it to the cabinet. But the cabinet stood firm, re-submitted the law to the President, and this time he was forced, by the rules of the constitution, to sign it.

The Supreme Court, however, was not done. In response to another appeal, it declared the government's actions 'unconstitutional' and the law invalid. The government had lost. On 27 March, more than three years after the original litigation was filed, the Election Commission put the new criminal and financial disclosure rules into action.

Chhokar said the episode showed him two things: that the government can work quickly and efficiently when it needs to, and that politicians can be unanimous if they want to be, or when their interests are threatened. But it also taught him something fundamental about the nature of politics. 'There is no limit to their shamelessness,' he told me. 'I haven't recovered from the shock yet.'

Today, ADR works hand-in-hand with the Election Commission, collating and compiling the information in those affidavits and disseminating it to the voting public. Running its day-to-day operations is Anil Bairwal, a former software engineer, who worked in the United States for close to a decade. Returning to India, he ran the Indian operations of a large multinational for a while, before starting his own business in Bengaluru. 'I got sick of running a business, so I quit,' he said. 'I wanted to do social work.' Still only forty-two, he has been ADR's National Coordinator since 2008, joining at first for just six months before he was convinced to stay on. 'Whichever problems our country faces, the root cause was our unaccountable and non-transparent political system,' he told me. 'If we can make a little improvement in the political system, it will have a cascading effect on other issues.'

Bairwal really comes alive when he talks about his work, and the progress ADR is making. Although the number of elected MPs with charges against them has risen, a closer look at the data shows the proportion of *candidates* facing criminal charges actually fell, from 25 per cent in the 2004 elections to 14 per cent in 2009.

What is happening, Bairwal says, is that criminals are finding it harder to enter the political process these days, because parties are more cautious about taking them on, given the new disclosure rules and the bad publicity it attracts. But those who already have a foothold in the system, and who have built up their own support bases in their constituencies, are still getting tickets and still winning elections.

When J was raped, the issue of the criminalization of politics was once again back on the agenda. The high-level panel set up to look into ways of preventing violence against women in the wake of her gang-rape and murder concluded that political reform was essential if the weakest members of society were to be protected.

'If murderers and rapists are deciding what kind of laws should relate to women, it's very obvious – they won't do anything against their vested interests,' the head of the committee, retired Justice J. S. Verma, told the CNN-IBN news channel.

Even before the committee completed its deliberations, ADR had put out a report[14] showing that political parties had given tickets to six people accused of rape in the 2009 elections, and to twenty-seven people contesting state elections in the past five years, six of whom, including Bhagwan Sharma, had won their elections and were sitting in state legislative assemblies. (Four of the six, incidentally, are from Uttar Pradesh.) That, said Bairwal, left the parties struggling to explain themselves.

'Five years back, no party would ever accept they have criminals in their ranks. Now, they acknowledge there are these elements,' he said. 'Clearly today, political parties are on the back foot when it comes to the criminalization of politics.'

India's landmark Right to Information Act – the subject of chapter 5 in this book – has become 'a very, very powerful tool' in the organization's attempts to prise open the black box of Indian politics, Bairwal said, and a central part of its work. ADR is engaged in a constant process of filing applications, and appealing to the Act's adjudication body, the Central Information Commission, for assistance when critical information is withheld. Each application might trigger multiple responses from different departments, so that, on any given day, forty letters might arrive at the reception desk concerning different requests. It is a constant process of detective work, pushing deeper and deeper into the data until discrepancies leap out, trying to spot, for example, when candidates have declared income tax returns to the Election Commission but not actually filed them with the government.

ADR is expanding, with some thirty permanent staff in New Delhi, a small office in Bengaluru, a national network of volunteers and partnerships with 1,200 other charitable organizations around the country, building pressure 'from the ground up' on political parties to clean up their acts.

The nature of criminality is also changing. These days, the proportion of politicians facing charges relating to violent crime is falling, Bairwal says, while the proportion charged with 'white-collar offences' like financial crimes, property swindles or lying under oath is rising.

ADR's efforts to expose the role of 'black money' – money that circulates outside the legal system and away from the tax authorities – have also begun to bite harder in recent years. It has been using the RTI Act to try to force political parties to declare their sources of funding, and to force candidates to reveal their tax returns.

In 2012, ADR was able to reveal that eighteen political parties, including many significant regional parties, had not filed reports into their sources of funding since at least 2004 – reports that are required by law to be sent to the Election Commission and the Income Tax Department.[15]

Parties are also required to list donations of more than 20,000 rupees ($370): one major regional party, the Bahujan Samaj Party from Uttar Pradesh (the same party that had kicked out Bhagwan Sharma), claimed that it had not received a single donation above that amount in the entire 2009–10 and 2010–11 tax years, despite having a total declared income of 1.72 billion rupees ($31 million).

Indeed, the party revelled in its wealth, showering its leader Mayawati with gifts and money to demonstrate its power and largesse. In 2010, a massive garland made of thousand-rupee ($20) notes was draped around Mayawati's shoulders – a ring of money so thick and so large it dwarfed the recipient and attracted the income tax department's attention. It was estimated to have been worth hundreds of thousands of dollars.

At first, ADR and the nation's political parties waged a low-level guerrilla war. The parties were uncooperative, Bairwal and his colleagues say, and the Income Tax Department was no more helpful in disclosing information. Even the Ethics Committee of the upper house of parliament refused a request to make a register of members' interests publicly available, until it was ordered to do so by law.

But the battle really exploded into the open in June 2013, when the Central Information Commission (CIC) ruled in ADR's favour in a crucial decision under the RTI Act. It found that political parties were 'public bodies', came under the purview of the RTI Act, and therefore must by law respond to ADR's requests to open up their books. It seemed like a significant step forward in the battle for transparency in India – until the government proposed to amend the RTI Act specifically to overturn that CIC ruling, and exclude political parties from its purview. It was a brazen decision that shocked and dismayed many activists in India, striking at the heart of a cherished piece of legislation and the fundamental principle of transparency.

There was, however, an extraordinary public outcry. Members of parliament were bombarded with petitions, emails and phone calls. People expressed their feelings on social media, and at protests and meetings across India. Twenty-five BJP MPs came out against the amendment, and they were joined by a handful of others. The government blinked, and referred the amendment to a standing committee, where it now rests.

Then in July 2013, the Supreme Court dropped another bombshell. In a landmark ruling, it declared that politicians convicted of serious crimes should lose their seats instantly. In the past, politicians had avoided this fate simply by filing an appeal, shamelessly exploiting a loophole in the law; this tactic would no longer save them from disqualification. Although the ruling was prospective rather than retrospective, it was hailed as another major step forward in cleaning up Indian democracy. But once again, the Indian government went on the offensive. The ruling Congress party tabled a bill in parliament that would partially overturn the Supreme Court order, by allowing convicted politicians to continue to take part in debates but not actually vote, pending their appeal.

Then, in September 2013, it went a step further, using a special provision that allows cabinet to pass emergency laws when parliament is not in session, to ram the measure through as an executive order (or ordinance), at least until parliament got time to pass the bill. Their haste was apparently motivated by two important verdicts that were looming in India's courts, affecting a Congress member of the upper house or Rajya Sabha, and a key ally in the Lok Sabha, Lalu Prasad Yadav. The latter was officially outside the coalition government, but was a long-time Congress ally and had backed it at important times.

What happened next was truly historic. Once again, the Indian people were outraged by the brazenness of the move. Public pressure mounted. *The Times of India* organized a campaign against the ordinance that drew 700,000 supporters in just four days; the global advocacy group Avaaz gathered another 114,000 signatures for its petition, and organized an online campaign that saw more than 13,000 messages sent to Indian politicians in just a week. Avaaz also organized an opinion poll and claimed that 98 per cent of Indians wanted criminals out of politics. The campaign swiftly got the backing of some of India's more enlightened politicians, including the independent Rajya Sabha MP Rajeev Chandrasekhar.[16]

The opposition BJP saw its chance to embarrass the government. It asked President Pranab Mukherjee not to sign the ordinance into law, and, shamed by the outcry, even the Congress Party began to get cold feet. Milind Deora, a Congress MP and junior minister in the government, tweeted that the ordinance could 'endanger already-eroding public faith in democracy' and President Mukherjee, a veteran Congress Party politician, also sought a clarification on the ordinance, quietly signalling that he would not be happy to sign it into law.

Finally, in a dramatic gesture, Sonia Gandhi's son Rahul, a Congress member of parliament and leading figure in the party, made a short but explosive statement at the Press Club of India, calling the ordinance that had been passed by his own government 'complete nonsense'. 'It should be torn up and thrown out,' he said. 'This is the time to stop this nonsense. If we want to actually fight corruption in this country, whether it is my party or the BJP, we can't continue making these small compromises.' With elections looming in 2014, Gandhi was widely tipped as possible prime minister if Congress were to win another term, and his intervention proved crucial.[17]

A few days before Rahul's outburst, Congress politician and Rajya Sabha MP Rasheed Masood was sentenced to four years in jail in a corruption case involving nominations for medical colleges when he was health minister in 1990. Then, immediately afterwards, Lalu Prasad Yadav was found guilty of embezzling 9.5 billion rupees, supposedly to pay for livestock fodder that turned out not to exist, while he was chief minister of the state of Bihar in the mid-1990s. Both men faced losing their seats under the Supreme Court's new rules. Even so, the government backed down: on 2 October it announced that, by a unanimous decision of the cabinet, it had withdrawn both the ordinance and the parliamentary bill. On the following day, Lalu was sentenced to five years in jail. Although he swiftly announced his intention to appeal, he stood disqualified from parliament.

'The educated urban middle class has traditionally felt marginalized by India's vote-bank politics of caste, community, region and other special interest pressure groups,' the *Times of India* said in an editorial. '"Our voice is rarely heard," is an oft-repeated lament . . . But that's changing. The backlash against the ordinance, as evidenced in the massive response to the *Times* Campaign symbolizes an emerging middle class voice. The fact that Rahul Gandhi chose to listen to it shows he is aware of the power it now carries.

'One man who knew how to move the levers of moral power was [Mahatma] Gandhi-ji, and he did so to stunning effect against a great empire. India's middle class must realise that it has access to new levers of power, and that these levers can and should be used as a force for good.'[18]

A year earlier, Bhagwan Sharma had comfortably won re-election in Debai in 2012 with 34 per cent of the vote, but thanks to ADR, the charges against him are out in the open, as is the fact that he has declared net assets of 18 million rupees ($330,000) in 2012, and just 250,000 ($46,000) in 2007. Thanks to the Supreme Court, the possibility that conviction on any of the serious charges he faces could see him disqualified from parliament must now loom over his entire political career.

Looking further forward, there is no shortage of suggestions for more extensive legislation to clean up Indian democracy. Some people have suggested the government fund political parties. This is probably unrealistic in a country the size of India, but there is no doubt that transparency in the financing of political parties is one of the most important changes this country could make to straighten out its dysfunctional democracy.

To bolster popular faith in democracy, the Election Commission has been pushing a series of reforms for many years, and Quraishi has repeatedly expressed his disappointment with the government for failing to table legislation. To reduce the role of criminals, it has proposed going even further than the Supreme Court's latest judgement, arguing that anyone charged with any offence punishable by five years' imprisonment should be excluded from the elections. The fact that a district court would have to frame such charges would go a long way to prevent fraudulent accusations being brought, but as an added safeguard only cases filed six months or more before an election would be covered by this rule, to avoid last-minute attempts to derail an opponent's campaign. At the same time, a special authority would be established to audit candidates' assets, and the limits on election expenditure regularly reviewed.

To encourage greater choice, the Supreme Court ruled in September 2013 that voters would be allowed to reject all candidates on a ballot by selecting 'none of the above', in an attempt to force parties to field better candidates. It did not go as far as some had hoped: even if a majority of voters reject all the candidates, there will be no repeat of the vote – the candidate with the most votes, however few, will still win. Nevertheless, Quraishi said the verdict represented progress. 'It's time for government and Parliament to take the comprehensive electoral reforms forward, for the health of our democracy,' he wrote. 'If they don't, the current momentum will peter out.'[19]

A similar set of suggestions for reform is enshrined in a draft bill proposed by ADR.[20] Bairwal says politicians agree, in public and in private, that the bill is a good idea, but says the conversation seldom goes any further.

The government's overt attempts to overturn both the Central Information Commission decision and the Supreme Court order in 2013 show how reluctant the political establishment is to endorse anything that might legislate away its impunity and inject transparency into the murky world of campaign finance. But the way that extraordinary public pressure actually forced the government to backtrack on both moves was a stunning example of the power of democracy in India, a signal that popular will can bring about change.

Joining the bandwagon at the last minute, and helping to tip the scales against the ordinance, was Rahul Gandhi, the great-grandson of Jawaharlal Nehru and the latest generation of a family that has dominated politics in this country since Independence. The crown prince of Indian politics, Gandhi says he wants to clean up the nation's political system. Yet he, more than anyone, represents one of Indian democracy's greatest weaknesses: the replacement of meritocracy in politics with dynastic rule. What the 43-year-old Gandhi makes of that contradiction could be one of the most important questions facing India in the coming decade.

4

It's a Family Affair

How dynastic politics is stifling Indian democracy

*As a child, 'if I had ever come up with the notion that I would be
prime minister, my father would have given me one across the face,
no questions asked.'*
Rahul Gandhi to the author, July 2004

It started as soon as Rahul Gandhi left his constituency home in
northern India in July 2004, with hundreds of men and women
crowding forward for a few seconds to press their demands through
his open car window. An old man with an enormous handlebar moustache wanted help for his family's medical costs; a shifty young man
wanted a job; another wanted Gandhi to help his son, who he said
had been unfairly failed on a school exam.

Gandhi listened patiently to each supplicant. Letter after letter was
passed through the window, and placed in a large canvas bag in the
back.

At the age of thirty-four, Gandhi was just three months into
his new job as a member of India's parliament, and was already
being widely tipped as a future prime minister, just as his father
had been, and his grandmother and great-grandfather before
that.[1] But he was also discovering for himself the enormous expectations his entry into politics had generated, and the limits to
what he could do.

'It's a free for all,' he said, sitting with me in his white Ambassador car, the regulation mode of transport for Indian politicians,
modelled on the old Morris Oxford. 'When my father was here, he

was prime minister, we did a hell of a lot for this place, so they expect that.'[2]

The burden of expectation, and the burden of living up to his assassinated father (a man he clearly still worships), is never far from the surface in Rahul Gandhi. As a bespectacled and tousle-haired twenty-year-old carried his father's body to its funeral pyre in May 1991, journalists were already asking the question: When will this boy take on the mantle of his family's tradition? Ever since then, Waiting For Rahul has become a national pastime.

As we saw in the introduction to this book, Rahul's great-grand-father, Jawaharlal Nehru, had, along with Mahatma Gandhi, led India's struggle to throw off British colonial rule, and was the chief architect of India's secular democracy. His legacy, however, was undermined by the political dynasty he spawned. His own daughter Indira was to jail tens of thousands of opponents during a State of Emergency in 1975–7, as well as muzzle the press. Within Congress, too, she was immensely retrogressive, her fear of challengers leading to the abandonment of internal elections for party posts and encouraging a culture of sycophancy that persists to this day. That same sycophantic culture propelled her son Rajiv to the prime ministership, and then, after his assassination, her daughter-in-law Sonia to the top of the party. It has now thrust Rajiv and Sonia's son – Indira's grandson – Rahul into the spotlight.

Today, Rahul is styled by Congress as the hope for India's young voters, a man who can restore the dream of clean, secular and sincere politics that his great-grandfather had envisioned. But the great contradiction of Rahul Gandhi is that he has risen to prominence only because of his position as the crown prince of India's political royal family. The question that faces India is whether the product of a dynastic and sycophantic political culture can breathe new life into its politics.

In attempting to answer that question, we must begin with Indira Gandhi's assassination by her Sikh bodyguards in October 1984, and the riots that followed in which an estimated 3,000 Sikhs died at the hands of mobs often led by senior members of the Congress Party.[3] At a time of personal and national shock, Rajiv Gandhi had seemed indifferent to the mass slaughter when he observed: 'For some days people thought that India was shaking. But there are always great tremors when a big tree falls.'

Rajiv had been a reluctant entrant into politics, his Italian wife Sonia even more protective of the family and its privacy, but he swept to power in the elections that followed Indira's death. He is credited with starting the process of modernizing India's economy and sowing the first seeds of its IT revolution, but his administration was marred by a massive corruption scandal over the import of howitzers, when Bofors was accused of paying millions of dollars in bribes to senior government officials to secure the arms deal.

Rajiv set out to reform the Congress, promising to reinstate internal elections but never delivering, and in the end is remembered only for surrounding himself with friends and cronies rather than for any party reforms. Perhaps most damaging to his reputation was how he swung back and forth in an attempt to appease distinctly unmodern religious sentiments.

First, he backed demands from conservative Muslims to overturn a Supreme Court verdict in favour of a divorced woman called Shah Bano. The court verdict would have forced Muslim men to provide regular financial support for their ex-wives, a ruling that many reasonable Muslims accepted. Then he caved into pressure from the other extreme, by allowing Hindu devotees to gain entry to a mosque in the northern town of Ayodhya where one of their idols had mysteriously been placed. Emboldened by this decision, a Hindu mob was to tear down the mosque, which they believed to have been built on the site of the birthplace of Lord Ram, triggering years of tension and violence between the two religious communities.[4]

The decisions failed to appease the fundamentalists on either side, while alienating moderates. In 1989, beset by the Bofors scandal, Congress won less than half the number of seats it had won five years before, and Rajiv lost power.

At home, Rahul and Priyanka had both idolized their grandmother, and been deeply affected by her death. Pulled out of school for security reasons, they were tutored together at home. This, and their shared suffering, may have helped build the bond between brother and sister that is obvious when they interact in public, according to Rahul's biographer Aarthi Ramachandran in *Decoding Rahul Gandhi.*[5]

As a father, Rajiv was 'loving and approachable but strict', Sonia wrote in *Rajiv*, an account of their life together. 'He could not tolerate any symptoms of what he considered "spoilt brat" behaviour, such as fussing over food or wasting it,' she wrote.[6] 'He had a strong aversion to rudeness or bad manners, and would revert to the old school of punishment – for instance, make the children write 100 times, "I will not bang the door".'

That Rajiv might occasionally have resorted to some more old-school methods of discipline was hinted at by Rahul when I asked him whether he had ever thought, as a boy, about following in his father's footsteps to become prime minister. 'My father would have slapped me . . . as would my grandmother, as would my mother, so no,' he said, adding a little later: 'Literally, if I ever came up with the notion that I would be prime minister, my father would give me one across the face, no questions asked.'

According to Sonia, Rahul had been 'consumed with anxiety' about his father's safety after he lost the prime minister's job.[7] When his father died while on the campaign trial, assassinated by a Sri Lankan ethnic Tamil suicide bomber in 1991, Rahul accompanied his father's ashes back by train to the family's ancestral home in Allahabad in Uttar Pradesh. That, he told me, was when 'something clicked inside' and he decided to go into politics. 'When we entered UP, there was a huge crowd running with the train, very emotional and upset,' he said. 'I felt then that I had a certain responsibility towards these people.'

There is always a sense with Rahul that he feels his father got a raw deal, that his legacy to India has never been properly understood. That is entirely natural in a son whose father died a violent death when he was still a young man. But it can lead to some ambitious leaps of political logic, especially when he claims the credit on his father's behalf for India's mobile phone revolution or idolizes him for keeping the forces of fundamentalism at bay. More generally, I can't escape the feeling that Rahul's uncritical examination of his family's record means he may not be learning the right lessons from history.

Yet it is true that Rajiv Gandhi does deserve some credit for his vision of computers being integral to India's future. Rahul remembered being sat down in front of a computer as a boy, struggling with the complexities of the old MS-DOS operating system, at a time when his father was 'the only person [in India] who knew what a computer was'. Rajiv did play a role in nurturing India's hi-tech industry by reducing import duties on certain electronics goods and parts, and was the driving force behind a network of state-sector public call offices, or PCOs, throughout rural India. But the mobile phone revolution came much later, and Rajiv's mistakes in allowing corruption to flourish or appeasing religious conservatives do not feature in his son's account.

'My father, if he had not been killed in 1991, he would have been prime minister for the next ten years, fifteen years, without a problem,' he said. 'That is the unfortunate thing for my dad, that he didn't get that chance. I truly believe he would have changed this country, and we wouldn't have had to deal with ten years of fundamentalists making a racket.'

Perhaps this criticism sounds uncharitable, but there is a sense running through Rahul's telling of history that his family could do no wrong, or indeed that they did no wrong. It leads to some disturbing dissonance, as we will see later. Some would call it hypocrisy. His politics becomes a slightly uncomfortable mix of his entire family's tradition, as it is filtered through his rose-coloured spectacles. Secularism runs through it, of course, and a strong 'pro-poor bias', as well as anger at the 'fanaticism' that, at that time, he saw as on the rise in India. 'Of course I have always had my family breathing down my neck,' he said, when I asked about his influences. 'My grandmother actively had disdain for rich people,' he said, especially rich landlords who treated their tenants like dirt. 'She didn't have much respect for them, and I think the same is true of my great-grandfather.'

'In my family we have this thing for the underdog,' he said. 'If I see a person in a position of strength and they are abusing that, it makes my blood boil.'

Rahul spent a year at Delhi's elite St Stephen's College, where a classmate remembered him as a quiet student who sat at the back of the class, but also as 'a regular kind of a guy' rather than a stuck-up brat. He was always accompanied by safari-clad security guards, and often missed classes because his security guards would not let him leave home. He went to Harvard in 1991, but withdrew after his father died, apparently because of further security concerns. Eventually he was to complete a B.A. at Rollins College in Florida and an MPhil in Development Studies from Trinity College, Cambridge in 1995. There were three years with a management consultancy in London, followed by a brief stint back in India running a company called Backops that specialized in engineering design outsourcing before his entry into politics.[8]

Shortly after that political debut, I had been invited to Amethi to meet Rahul; it was an informal get-together in his constituency home in July 2004 for around thirty journalists who had covered his campaign. The following day, I had found myself in his car, touring his constituency and visiting education projects that Rahul was supporting. As we travelled, we talked.

Many of the supplicants who had crowded around his car window were 'opportunistic types', he explained. 'They want a government job so they can sit on their backside doing nothing. Basically a hand-out. So we hardly give any government jobs.' In villages, demands tended to be more realistic, he added, for a road or a hand pump.

When Rajiv Gandhi was prime minister and member of parliament for Amethi, he had showered this constituency with money, development and jobs, working through a state government also controlled by his own Congress Party. But the largesse yielded little lasting benefit. When Rajiv lost power in 1989, Congress was also routed in the vast and densely populated northern state of Uttar Pradesh in which Amethi was situated, a defeat from which the party had never recovered. Amethi was no longer the favourite child of the state government.

By 2004, Congress was back in power in New Delhi, but the party was still out in the cold in UP. Rahul said he was allotted just $430,000 a year for development in Amethi by the state government, enough to build just six miles of roads in a 230-square-mile constituency. 'I am elected to bring development, but I am not empowered,' he said. 'My hands are tied.'

I had secured my interview with Rahul because I had expressed an interest in the education projects he was sponsoring in his constituency. Working through a local charity, and drawing on party workers as volunteers, he was giving children who could not read extra tuition outside school. 'It's quite pleasing when you see these little kids, you know,' he said, as we toured. 'You can see on their faces. Three months ago, they used to be the laggards in the class, they didn't know how to read. Now if you put them with somebody who used to be a good student, the guys from our programmes beat the pants off the other ones, and they've got a big smile on their faces when they are doing it.'

Rahul Gandhi's pleasure in seeing those children's faces appeared genuine, and I believe that he does care about the poor. But the dissonance is never far from the surface. At the news conference in Amethi, he talked about the links between politics and crime, and the way that members of a Congress-led coalition government were themselves facing charges ranging from corruption to murder.

'If there were Congress ministers who were tainted, I'd be having something to say about it,' he said. 'But the ministers are part of a coalition government, and obviously there are compromises that need to be made.' Which is all well and good, except for the blinding reality of widespread crime and corruption within Congress too. I felt, quite honestly, that here was a young man struggling with the realities of the world around him, and who was coping by willing himself to believe that he and his family had the highest principles.

He was frustrated, he said, not just about how little he could help his constituents, but also how little anybody around him in politics cared. 'It is in our power as politicians to help people on a reasonably large scale,' he said. 'But a hell of a lot of people are not interested . . . sometimes you want to do something and you realize you're alone, or very limited.'

When his constituents asked for electricity, he could only appeal to the state government. They were not helping, he said. 'Why should they?' So if Congress was in power in the state government, it would also decline to help constituencies run by rival parties? I asked at the news conference. 'Absolutely,' he said, with a wry smile.

In the summer of 2004, Rahul's reluctance to be rushed into taking more political responsibility had seemed to make a great deal of sense. There was already pressure for him to take a cabinet berth, as well as a sense that Manmohan Singh was simply keeping the prime minister's job warm for him. 'If I go by people's expectations, I will go mad,' he told me, later ending the interview by saying: 'I am thirty-four years old, you know. I need to be in a phase of understanding as opposed to a phase of executing.'

But that considered approach eventually began to look laboured. As the years went by, and Rahul continued to reject offers of a place in Manmohan Singh's cabinet, that caution began to look less like wisdom, and more like a character flaw. By 2005 his reluctance to even ask questions in parliament was already being noticed. His response, in an interview with the investigative magazine *Tehelka*, was particularly revealing, and not just of his unhurried approach. 'I don't ask questions in Parliament because I like to think things through,' he said. 'Just look around at the questions that are asked in Parliament and you'll know why I don't ask questions. I mean look at them. Is that the kind of stuff you want me to ask?'[9]

* * *

Such is Rahul's apparent disregard for parliamentary proceedings that
he seldom even bothers to attend. His record shows he attended 63
per cent of parliament's sittings in his first term in office but only
contributed to five debates, asked just three questions and tabled no
private member bills. His record in his second term (up to the end of
March 2013) was even worse: he attended just 43 per cent of the time
that parliament was in session (compared with an average for all MPs
of 80 per cent), took part in just one debate (compared with an average of 32.9 per MP), asked no questions (compared with an average
of 255 questions per MP), and brought no private member's bills
(compared with an average of 0.8). His great-grandfather had fought
hard to establish India's multi-party democracy and parliamentary
system of government, against considerable opposition. Rahul either
holds parliament in contempt, or feels he can better make his presence felt through more direct access to power.[10]

Nor does Rahul appear to think that interacting with the media is
part of his role, but whether that is because he does not trust journalists, wants to dodge tough questions, or thinks he is above having to
explain his views is not entirely clear to me. Aides say his fingers were
burned with that *Tehelka* interview, when Rahul was reported as
having said: 'I could have been prime minister at the age of twenty-
five if I had wanted to.' Gandhi claimed the comments had been
made in the course of a 'casual chat' rather than an on-the-record
interview, and *Tehelka* was forced to withdraw the remark from its
online transcript of the interaction. Since then, he has not granted a
single interview.

Perhaps nowhere else in the democratic world could someone be so
widely tipped to become a future prime minister yet remain so aloof
from the press, or so uninterested in setting out their credentials for
the job. But that, perhaps, is the privilege of dynasty, for Rahul never
has to labour for power. It is there, whenever he deigns to embrace it.
He has also taken a leaf out of his mother's book, and perhaps his
grandmother's before that. Indira Gandhi consolidated her power
through silencing rivals, squashing dissent, and granting real access

only to the trusted few. Sonia has turned aloofness into an art form, setting herself in what the columnist Santosh Desai aptly describes as a quasi-royal position above the fray, where access is controlled, a sense of mystery is created and explicit responsibility avoided.[11] For nearly a decade she has presided over the world's largest democracy, as its most powerful figure, without holding a single press conference. Aarthi Ramachandran was not only denied an interview with Rahul for her book, but was not even granted the most basic information about Rahul's studies, his time as a management consultant in London or his business in India, which appears to have gradually died a death. 'The secrecy that surrounds almost every affair of the Gandhi family accompanied Backops as well,' Ramachandran wrote.[12]

Rather than bother himself with the day-to-day politics, or the challenge of running a ministry, Rahul Gandhi instead set out to rebuild the Congress Party, whose dynamism and internal democracy had been laid waste by his grandmother. Like his father Rajiv and his uncle Sanjay before him, Rahul was to make his debut running the youth wing of the party, taking charge in 2007 of the Indian Youth Congress and the National Students Union of India. His idea was to create a meritocracy where talent, rather than loyalty, was rewarded, where the energy and passion of youth were harnessed, and where the leaders of the future would be identified and developed.

Rahul still lists his profession on the parliamentary website as 'strategy consultant', and Ramachandran argues persuasively that he approached the reform of the Congress Party very much as a management consultant would. His approach, she says, was heavily influenced by the Toyota Way, a principle whereby decisions are made 'slowly by consensus, by thoroughly considering all options and then implementing those decisions rapidly'.[13] But a consideration of the drawbacks of that approach in the real world of Indian politics seemed to be lacking: the emphasis on process and systems over people, of strategy over political vision, soon ran into trouble, she argues.

The first step in the effort to create a meritocracy was to reintroduce inner-party elections for posts within both organizations.

Unfortunately, many of the posts on offer were captured by the children or relatives of senior, established politicians. It costs money even to run for office in the party's youth wing – to register new members who will support them or arrange transport for supporters at state-level meetings – and senior party leaders were still able to use their influence to manipulate the process. Nor did successes in some states in recruiting new members translate into electoral success in those states. Rahul's strategy for the youth, it seemed, did not amount to much while the rest of the party continued to behave as it always had done.

Rahul's other big, and not unrelated, project was to revive the Congress Party in India's political heartland of Uttar Pradesh. In this, so far, he has not achieved success. Rahul had campaigned in the state in the run-up to the 2009 national elections, where Congress had performed much better than expected, winning twenty-one seats out of eighty on offer, up from just nine in 2004. But it was the 2012 state elections on which he had staked his reputation, taking control of campaign strategy and becoming the party's main face in the field. He addressed 211 rallies and spent forty-eight days on the campaign trail. The party talked optimistically about winning fifty seats of the 403 on offer, up from twenty-two at the last poll in 2007. In the end, it bagged just twenty-eight seats, and wound up in fourth place.[14]

I watched as Rahul had kicked off the campaign from Nehru's original constituency at Phulpur, just outside the town of Allahabad, on 14 November 2011, the anniversary of his great-grandfather's birth 122 years before. A buzz swept through the crowd as his helicopter came in to land, a swirl of yellow dust rising into the air as necks stretched to catch the first glance of the 'crown prince' of Indian politics. But the early excitement did not last. Rahul proved an unconvincing campaigner, failing to generate much emotional connection with the crowd. There was no humour to get people on his side, and his own anger failed to ignite. His speech was typical of his entire campaign: everything was fine in the good old days when you voted Congress, he told people, but since you threw them out the state has started 'going backwards'. The sleeves of his white kurta were rolled up, and his 'baby face' was covered with a new beard, apparently designed to show he meant business. 'Mafias and criminals are representing you now,' he said. 'Ministers are behind bars but there is still no progress. Now, your generation has to come up and fight against this.'[15]

He reminded people of all the times he had fought for their cause, using his clout in the corridors of power to bring welfare packages for struggling weavers or drought-prone pockets of rural poverty. He reminded them how diligent he had been in learning about the problems they faced, spending nights in their huts and eating their bread. 'I drink the dirty water from their well, and get sick,' he said. 'But unless I drink that water and get sick, how can I know, how can anybody know what lives they are leading?'

Afterwards, I spoke to some of the people who had attended, people who were there either for curiosity's sake, because they supported Congress, or because someone had paid them to attend. Some, it is true, said they were impressed with his 'simplicity' and 'dedication'. But for others, the dissonance was too much to ignore. Here was a senior leader of the Congress Party, the heir apparent of India's first family, railing against the evils of the political class. How could he be a harbinger of change? 'Corruption and inflation are the main things we care about,' said the 24-year-old medical student Tapasya Diwarker, to murmurs of assent from people around her. 'That's why we don't like politicians, and why we weren't cheering.'

Rahul tried to woo Muslims with a promise of a quota system for them in the allocation of government jobs in the state, a system that is widely used in India to offer opportunities to disadvantaged groups. He tried to woo castes and sub-castes by selecting candidates who were supposed to bring a community's votes with them. But it all seemed slightly unconvincing, too little, too late to make a difference in a state where the party lacked a network of organizers at the ground level or strong local leaders. Above all, it seemed to me to lack a vision. I was struck at Phulpur by the lack of any talk of development, of

economic growth or of aspiration: it sounded more like the old politics of handouts and dependency than a new politics of opportunity.
It failed to ignite the imagination, or offer a convincing break from
the past.

Rahul has been tirelessly advanced by his supporters as the face of
the younger generation, someone who is looking forward and can
connect to the modern India's hopes and dreams. Time and again,
he has failed to don that mantle in any convincing way, or indeed to
make that connection. Two missed opportunities stand out in
particular. The first came in August 2011 at the height of the India
Against Corruption movement, as the media and much of the
nation was transfixed by his campaign to establish a strong anti-
corruption ombudsman and millions of Indians expressed their
support. With Sonia Gandhi away in the United States for a surgical
procedure that remains undisclosed to this day, Rahul was one of
four senior Congress figures left in charge of the party. Without her,
they seemed to go into a panic.

After a meeting of the party's bigwigs, including Rahul and
Manmohan Singh, instructions were issued to the police to arrest the
anti-corruption movement's leader Anna Hazare on the morning of
16 August, just as he was setting out to begin a hunger strike in the
heart of the capital. It was an extraordinary blunder, galvanizing
support behind Hazare and making the government look unreasonable and inept. But instead of taking charge, Rahul left for a trip to
the western state of Maharashtra, where three farmers were reported
to have been shot dead during a protest over land grabs. Hazare was
finally released on 19 August, but as the government furiously tried to
negotiate an end to his hunger strike, which was by now receiving
wall-to-wall TV coverage, Rahul remained completely silent.

Finally, on 26 August, he turned up in parliament to make a speech
that he would later describe as a 'game changer'. It was anything but.
Out of nowhere, Rahul argued that the anti-corruption ombudsman,
the Lokpal, be given autonomy under the protection of an amended
constitution. Alongside that initiative, he suggested government

funding of political parties and elections, proper regulation of sectors that fuel corruption like land and mining, transparency in public procurement, a grievance redressal mechanism to improve delivery of public services, and reforms to reduce tax evasion. It was an eminently sensible list of reforms. The problem was that Rahul had built no political consensus around any of them, nor even made much mention of them in the past. Nor were they exactly the sort of suggestions that India's power brokers were going to accept without a fight. Not surprisingly, much of his speech was simply ignored, while the party's later attempt to introduce a constitutional amendment to establish the Lokpal was half-hearted and ended in failure.

The next example was, if anything, even less forgivable. As India reeled with horror and grief at J's gang-rape and murder, Rahul vanished again. There was no attempt to reach out to the protesters, a group that was dominated by the very same young people Rahul was supposed to represent; there was no public appearance, nor statement. When parliament debated and ultimately passed a new set of laws meant to protect India's women on 19 March 2013, Rahul did not even bother to show up. In a country where twenty-four-hour television news channels and the growing importance of social media have changed the nature of the political debate, his insistence that he needs to consult, learn and cogitate before saying anything looks increasingly out of touch – especially for someone who claims to talk with and for the young.

When Rahul set out in politics, the headline writers quickly named him 'the crown prince' of Indian politics. But gradually that epithet began to give way to other, less flattering ones. Soon Rahul became the 'reluctant prince', or, with a weary cynicism, 'the inevitable one'. The columnist Santosh Desai wrote a piece memorably entitled 'An absence called Rahul Gandhi',[16] while the leading historian Ramachandra Guha described him as 'a well-meaning dilettante'.[17] Novelist Shobhaa De virtually called him nice but dim – her exact words to me were 'not terribly bright, but with his heart in the right place', while the best-selling author Chetan Bhagat

widened his aim to target the whole family when he wrote causti-
cally about 'The silence of the Gandhis'.[18]

All the while, Rahul's ratings dropped. *India Today* magazine regularly asks Indians who they believe would make the best prime
minister. In August 2010, Rahul Gandhi was the favourite of 30 per
cent of those polled, comfortably outpacing BJP strongman and
Gujarat Chief Minister Narendra Modi on 9 per cent. Two years later,
Rahul's ratings dropped to a low of just 10 per cent, some 11 percentage points behind Modi. (Although Rahul has since recovered some
ground in the ratings, he still trailed his main rival by similar margins
at the time of writing.) Opinion polls are notoriously unreliable indi-
cators of the voting intentions of India's diverse electorate, but this
trend could scarcely be ignored.[19]

In September 2012 I attended an extraordinary book launch in
New Delhi, for Aarthi Ramachandran's book *Decoding Rahul Gandhi*.
The discussion afterwards was built around the question 'Can Brand
Rahul save the Congress, come 2014?' when national elections were
due. Ramachandran had written a balanced portrait of Rahul, which
she felt was already in danger of being captured and taken out of
context by one side or the other. For an hour, a representative group
of New Delhi's leading thinkers sat and debated 'Brand Rahul' and
what this man stood for. What was extraordinary was this: after two
years of following Rahul, and researching him as exhaustively as his
overprotective inner circle would permit, Ramachandran finally
admitted to being no closer to finding out what Rahul stood for, or if
there really was a 'Brand Rahul'.

For an hour, as we debated Rahul, I realized that no one in that
room, neither panellists nor members of the audience, had stood up to
defend Rahul Gandhi. No one had had a good word to say about him.
In a city where criticism of the Gandhis is often politely avoided, where
Sonia still seems to float above it all, that was a strangely unnerving
experience. Invited to choose between Rahul and Modi as the next
prime minister of India, Ramachandran was forced to admit that the
choice scared her, that they were equally frightening prospects.

Finally, it fell to the veteran British journalist John Elliott to ask Ramachandran the question to end the evening – was there anything positive to say about Rahul, and if so, what? After the laughter subsided, and she paused to reflect for a few seconds, Aarthi Ramachandran offered this verdict: 'He has the right intentions. His heart is in the right place,' she said. 'Unfortunately, he hasn't found a way to route this through politics.'

Rahul's heart-in-the-right-place kind of politics probably wouldn't matter very much if it weren't for what he represented, the dynastic nature of Indian politics and the lack of internal democracy within its main political parties. Not only has this blocked people with talent and political skills from rising to positions of influence, but it has also contributed greatly to the fragmentation of Indian politics, as people like West Bengal's firebrand politician Mamata Banerjee found her path to the top of the Congress Party blocked, and split from the party to form her own grouping, the Trinamool (grassroots) Congress. Rahul is not just an empty space or a missed opportunity, he represents a clogging of the arteries of Indian politics that is preventing fresh blood from emerging to enliven politics and reform the system from within.

In *India: A Portrait*, Patrick French analysed the make-up of India's parliament after the 2009 elections. He found that 156 of the 545 MPs in the 15th Lok Sabha had entered politics as a result of their family background (not counting seven members of old princely royal families). More than a third of Congress MPs had arrived through the family route, and nearly 70 per cent of women in parliament were there because of family connections. But then French began to dig deeper, and that is when it got really interesting. 'This was a shocking result. Every MP in the Lok Sabha under the age of 30 had in effect inherited a seat, and more than two thirds of the 66 MPs aged 40 or above were HMPs (hereditary members of parliament),' French wrote. 'If the trend continued, it was possible that most members of the Indian parliament would be there by heredity alone, and the nation would be back to where it had started before the

freedom struggle, with rule by a hereditary monarch and assorted
Indian princelings.'[20]

Think back for a minute to Prem Shankar Jha's analysis of the
'clientelist' networks that were established at constituency level to
fund election campaigns.[21] When a member of parliament dies, the
easiest way to ensure that this network will not be disturbed is to
elevate the dead leader's wife, son or daughter. The disease of dynasty
is particularly rampant within the Congress Party, where a younger
generation of ministers and aspiring chief ministers, many of them
seen as close to Rahul Gandhi, are all children of former powerful
party stalwarts.

The preponderance of hereditary politics within Congress is also a
product of Indira Gandhi's paranoia about challenges to her power,
and the way she had perfected the ancient art of 'divide and rule'.
Even today Congress does not declare its candidate for the post of
Chief Minister during an state election campaign; instead, someone
is picked, by royal command, after the vote has taken place, as if to
emphasize that the mandate to rule comes from on high rather than
directly from the people. Congress has developed a deeply sycophantic culture since Indira's day, which Rajiv and Sonia did nothing to
dispel. It has become so deeply ingrained that it has become almost
embarrassing. Is there not something a little wrong when a senior
cabinet minister, Salman Khurshid, proudly declares that his primary
duty is to his political party (and for that, read Sonia Gandhi) rather
than to his government or his prime minister? In what country would
the same man, now promoted to the job of Foreign Minister, offer to
lay down his life for his party leader, or call the party leader's untested
son his 'commander'? It smells of stale, suffocating air.

Of course the Gandhis are far from the only dynastic family in
Indian politics, and the Congress Party far from the only sinner. In
Kashmir, for example, the current chief minister, Omar Abdullah,
represents the third generation of a family that has dominated politics
in the Himalayan state since Independence; in Tamil Nadu, five times
Chief Minister Karunanidhi is well on the way to establishing his

own dynasty, and has helped two of his sons and one of his daughters take senior positions in his DMK party; in Odisha, two-time Chief Minister Biju Patnaik passed the mantle on to his son Naveen, who currently occupies the same office.

To India's young city-dwellers, surveyed by the *Times of India* in January 2012, 'dynastic politics' was identified as the biggest threat to the nation's democracy by 44 per cent of those polled, even above 'money and muscle power'.[22]

Even before I met Rahul, my first brush with the Gandhi family came in early 2004, at the height of the election campaign, in their Uttar Pradesh homeland. Through brown fields where wheat had just been harvested, along narrow, potholed roads, I had followed the convoy of white cars that was Sonia Gandhi's roadshow, as she stopped every few miles to rapturous crowds of a few dozen people to several thousand.

At the smaller villages, at roadside stops under small tents or in the blazing sun, she had seemed natural and full of life, bringing a simple message – that the BJP-led government had done nothing for the poor – drawing energy from the crowds as they chanted 'Sonia Gandhi Zindabad' (Long Live Sonia Gandhi) and showered her with rose petals. But at the bigger stops, on a stage reading a prepared text in her accented Hindi, dressed in a red saree with a long scarf or dupatta draped over her hair, she had seemed much more stilted.

Finally, at the end of a long hot day, she agreed to a few minutes on camera with Reuters. She was confident about the upcoming elections, even though exit polls from early rounds of voting had shown the Congress trailing the BJP (her confidence was, it turned out, well placed). But she had also been very clear on one thing: that her struggle was against the 'politics of temple and mosque' that had divided the country since her husband had lost his life. The BJP had ridden a Hindu revivalist wave to power in the 1990s, striking at the secular ideals championed by the Gandhi family and exploiting demands for a Hindu temple in the northern town of Ayodhya to rev up distrust

of the country's Muslim minority. Now, Gandhi said, she felt a duty
to fight back. 'The main reason which made me actively decide to
participate in politics was that, at that point in time, it looked as if
anti-secular forces were becoming stronger,' she told me. 'I felt I could
not just sit by and watch this happening, given that the family to
which I belong fought, lived and died to see that such forces do not
gain strength.'[23] To me now, reading back between the lines, I begin
to see how Sonia views her role in politics, not as the active, activist
reformer who will clean out the Augean Stables of corruption and
nepotism, but as someone whose role is much simpler – to preserve
her family's legacy of secularism until her son is ready to take up the
reins of power, to intervene here and there on behalf of the poor, but
not to challenge the nature of the Congress political beast. During the
interview, Sonia's eyes had sparkled, and she had seemed optimistic,
upbeat and charming. When the camera shut off, I expected that
mood to continue for a few moments at least, but the transformation
was abrupt. The barrier went up, the regal expression reasserted itself,
and the ice queen swept out of the room.

Sonia Gandhi, it is sometimes said, consciously modelled herself
on aspects of her mother-in-law, from the imperious way she exer-
cised power to the regal wave with which she greeted her supporters.[24]
But the real inheritor of Indira Gandhi's charisma is her granddaughter Priyanka. They do not just share a similar hairstyle or a superficial
resemblance, they share an ease with people, a natural spontaneity
and ability to connect that both Sonia and Rahul lack. Much is also
said about how the Gandhi magic is waning with each passing generation, but following Priyanka as she campaigned on her family's
behalf (admittedly on their home turf) was a reminder of what might
have been.

She would stop at a small village where party workers had set up
a microphone for her to reel off a few slogans. But Priyanka would
simply ignore the microphone and spend a while mingling with the
villagers who had turned up, relaxed and smiling all the time. Here
and there she would just descend from the car to chat to women

about their problems. Faced with a bigger crowd, she would be forced to take the stage, but instead of a long, prepared speech, would simply start by asking people what their needs were. Halfway through the day, we spoke on camera. 'I have seen how people live, and I think it is important to do something to better the way they live,' she told me.[25]

While Rahul revelled in his dead father's shadow, called him his 'hero' and promised to complete the work he had started, Priyanka didn't want to be drawn too far into a comparison with her grandmother. 'I have my own personality, I think I am different actually,' she said, 'but I'd be honoured if I did resemble her.' Like her mother, she expressed strong distaste for the BJP's 'politics of manipulation and communalism', and for Modi's failure to prevent the deaths of hundreds of Muslims during riots in Gujarat in 2002. Like the entire family, everything was framed not in terms of leadership but in terms of service to the people, and even her family tragedy was downplayed. 'Look at the suffering you see when you go around the villages,' she said. 'Who can say their lives are less tragic? So this tragedy and suffering are part of life.' As words on the page, they may not look so different from what her brother might have said, but somehow Priyanka manages to pull it all off with less effort and more charm.

Later, we followed Priyanka's convoy again, as she made her way towards an evening rendezvous with her brother Rahul. At a level crossing, we stopped, and Priyanka climbed on top of her car. All around the crowd shouted 'Priyanka Gandhi Zindabad'. With the moon above her, a shower of rose petals was caught in a camera's flash as it fell across her; an image that I can still picture in my mind's eye. Somehow, Priyanka simply projects that indefinable star quality that her studious and earnest brother lacks.

It has always been obvious that it was Priyanka and not Rahul who had the family's gift for politics, and were she not the mother of two young children, things might have been very different. Nevertheless, in an interview with the television journalist Barkha

Dutt in 2009, Priyanka presented her refusal to follow in the family business as a personal choice, a tough decision but something she was very clear about, a process of emerging from the shadow of her grandmother and becoming her own person. 'There was a time when I was about sixteen or seventeen when I was absolutely sure this [politics] is what I wanted to do with my life, but I think I wasn't very clear about my own identity,' she said. Then, in 1999, with the clamour for Priyanka to enter politics at its peak, she 'disappeared' for ten days' meditation, and finally made up her mind. 'I thought I'd better know what my mind is, rather than what other people want of me,' she said. 'I did idolize my grandmother. I grew up in a household where she was the head and she was a very powerful woman. Not only politically powerful, but she was a powerful human being to be around. So being a little girl, and seeing this woman who was very strong and stood for so much, it did have an effect on me, so I think my own identity was confused.'[26]

Perhaps Priyanka is romanticized to some extent because she has removed herself from the political frontline; as we shall see in Chapter 10, her husband Robert Vadra and his controversial business dealings could be a serious handicap if she were to run for major office. Nevertheless, her decision to stay back was one that many people in Congress did not readily accept. Somewhere within the party, despite the anointing of Rahul, one suspects there is a still a group who are Waiting for Priyanka (to change her mind).

In November 2012, Rahul Gandhi was put in charge of the Congress Party's strategy for elections due by May 2014. In January, at a special two-day meeting, they appointed him to a specially created role, the new vice-president of the party, second only to his mother. There were, of course, no challengers, and there was no election. In front of a packed auditorium of party workers, Rahul gave what his fawning fans called the speech of his life, his 'Obama moment', oratory that moved them en masse to laughter and to tears, and finally to a standing ovation.

What he said deserves a closer look. His analysis of what he called 'the tragedy of India' was on one level a passionate call for change, and for a new way of politics. On another level, it was also breathtakingly hypocritical.

The voices of a billion Indians are today telling us that they want a greater say in government, in politics and in administration. They are telling us that the course of their lives cannot be decided by a handful of people behind closed doors who are not fully accountable to them . . .

. . . we don't respect knowledge. We respect position. And it does not matter how much wisdom you have, if you do not have a position, you mean nothing.

Why is our youth angry? Why are they out on the streets? They are angry because they are alienated and excluded from the political class.

Every single day every single one of us are faced with the hypocrisy of this system. We all see it. And then we pretend it is not there. People who are corrupt stand up and talk about eradicating corruption: and then people who disrespect women every day of their lives talk about defending women's rights.

We need the aam admi [common man] to participate in politics. Because even as I speak their future is being decided in closed rooms. There is a young and impatient India and it is demanding a greater voice in the nation's future. Let me tell you that they are not going to watch silently. Our priorities are clear. The time has come to question the centralized, unresponsive and unaccountable systems of decision-making in governance, the administration and politics. The answer is not that people say we need to run the system better. The answer is in not running these systems better. The answer is to completely transform these systems.[27]

This, of course, came out of the mouth of someone who barely deigns to participate in parliament, while boasting on the campaign trail of his ability to influence policy in New Delhi because of his influence behind those very same closed doors. It came from someone who miserably failed to engage with India's youth when they took to the streets over corruption or violence against women, someone who had just assumed one of the most powerful positions in Indian politics without ever having demonstrated any real talent or track record of success, and without any pretence of intra-party democracy. Read his speech once, and you might agree with everything he said; read it again and it might come across as a savage indictment of everything his position stands for.

It was, of course, also a conscious throwback to a famous speech his father had made, when he had complained in 1985 to another major Congress gathering about 'the brokers of power and influence' within his own party, who ride on the back of honest party workers and 'dispense patronage to convert a mass movement into a feudal oligarchy'. Rajiv had inveighed against the 'self-perpetuating cliques who thrive by invoking the slogans of caste and religion and by enmeshing the living body of the Congress in their net of avarice'. Rajiv, of course, had failed in his quest to breathe new life into Congress and rid it of these cliques and their culture of patronage. Now it was his son's turn to achieve what his father had failed to.

Finally, Rahul brought his audience to tears with the most personal account he has ever given of his family's tragedy, a history to rival that of the Kennedys.

This morning I got up at 4 a.m. and went to the balcony. I thought now you have a big responsibility in front of you and people are standing behind you, people are standing on your side. It was dark and it was cold. I decided I was not going to tell you only what you wanted to hear. I decided I was going to tell you a little bit about what I feel. I want to tell you about hope and I want to tell you about power.

When I was a little boy I loved to play badminton. I loved it because it gave me balance in a complicated world. I was taught

how to play, in my grandmother's house, by two of the policemen who protected my grandmother. They were my friends.
Then one day they killed my grandmother and took away the
balance in my life.

I felt pain like I had never felt before. My father was in Bengal
and he came back. The hospital was dark, green and dirty. There
was a huge screaming crowd outside as I entered. It was the first
time in my life that I saw my father crying. He was the bravest
person I knew and yet I saw him cry. I could see that he too was
broken. In those days our country was not what it is today. In the
eyes of the world we had nothing. We were seen as worthless. We
didn't have money; we didn't have cars. Everybody said that we
were a poor country. Nobody thought about us.

That same evening I saw my father address the nation on television. I knew, like me, he was broken inside. I knew, like me, he was
terrified of what lay in front of him. Then as he spoke on that dark
night I felt a small glimmer of hope. It was like a small ray of light
in a dark sky. I can still remember what it felt like. The next day I
realized that many people had seen it too.

Today as I look back – I have a political career of eight years and
I am forty-two years old – I can see that it was that small ray of
hope in the darkness that helped change India into what it is today.
Without hope you cannot achieve anything. You can have plans,
you can have ideas, but unless you have hope, you cannot change
things; you cannot move things the size of India.

Now I want to talk to you about power.

Last night everyone congratulated me. Many of you came and
hugged me and congratulated me. Everybody congratulated me.
But last night my mother came to my room and she sat with me
and she cried. Why did she cry? She cried because she understands
that the power so many seek is actually a poison. She can see it
because of what it does to the people around her and the people
they love. But most importantly she can see it because she is not
attached to it. The only antidote to this poison is for all of us to see

it for what it really is and not become attached to it. We should not chase power for the attributes of power. We should only use it to empower the voiceless.

And for a moment I was actually moved. Until my colleague Rama gently reminded me of the thousands of Sikhs who had died at the hands of angry mobs – mobs that had been led by Congress leaders who remain in politics to this day – and had simply been airbrushed out of Rahul's story. Sonia Gandhi's distaste for power is, on one level, entirely genuine, born out of bitter experience: but it is also easy for a family for whom power is their permanent companion to insist they are not reaching for it, when they exercise their power without true democratic accountability. The dissonance simply won't go away when it comes to the Gandhis.

In the end it was a 'decent speech', wrote the Indian-born British economist and Labour peer Baron Meghnad Desai. But Rahul should not fall for all the sycophantic praise he received from the Congress lackeys. 'They would have hailed him even if he had read out the alphabet.'[28]

The Nehru–Gandhi family continues to exercise a strangely magnetic attraction over many Indians. One friend of mine says she still loves looking at their old family photos – of a young Rajiv and Sonia being served ice cream by a vendor at India Gate in New Delhi, or of pictures of Rahul and Priyanka as children – even though she is no fan of their politics. Like the Kennedys, their private tragedies have been splashed across the front pages. Indians feel like they have lived through the family's trials and tribulations, their strife and decay. The two great Hindu epics, the Ramayana and the Mahabharata, are both family dramas, and there are parallels in the errant son Sanjay, the reluctant prince Rajiv and the matriarch Indira. Whether or not they like them, many Indians respect them for sticking around through thick and thin, and understand Sonia when she says she entered politics through a sense of duty to her dead family members, so that she could hold her head up high in front of their portraits.

They are, perhaps, a reassuring presence to many people, and they have undoubtedly been the glue that has bound the Congress Party together. But many of those same Indians who gaze at and gossip over the Gandhis no longer want them to monopolize political power.

In October 2013, Rahul could have won praise for his role in forcing the government to back down over its ordinance allowing convicted criminals to remain in politics. Instead, he was criticized and mocked for the manner of his intervention, for only joining the bandwagon late in day, for completely ignoring party and government protocol, and for his distinctly unstatesmanlike choice of words (for which he later had to apologize) – for the angry young man act, in other words, from the ultimate son of political privilege.

In the person of Rahul Gandhi, in the sycophantic, unmeritocratic air of the Congress Party, the cure to India's democratic malaise seems elusive. For that, we will have to look elsewhere, and that means looking outside politics, looking into India's villages and at the power of information.

5

Is There Something I Should Know?

The Right to Information Act returns power to India's citizens

'*India has a history of reverence, of touching the feet of elders, but the Right to Information Act is helping us break down the negative aspects of that reverence. The common person is now looking you in the eye, not looking down when speaking to an upper-caste person. That gumption is the greatest success of the Right to Information. People who don't have gumption can't make democracies work.*'
Shekhar Singh, leader of the RTI movement, to the author, 2011

In a small village in the wilds of western India, a crowd of around 200 people had gathered to listen to a group of activists equipped only with a portable PA system and a few pieces of paper. The activists had no food or medicine to distribute to the destitute villagers of Kot Kirana, but what they had with them turned out to be infinitely more valuable. On the paper was information, names and numbers that when mixed with the crowd that had gathered that day proved explosive. It was information that the government and bureaucracy of India had always guarded extremely closely, because here in rural India, information meant power.

The activists were holding handwritten copies of the accounts of local development work carried out in and around Kot Kirana, the names of the people who had carried out that work, and how much they had been paid. As soon as they had everyone's attention, they started reading out the names. The crowd came to life.

'At least half the people on that list were dead,' said Nikhil Dey, one of the activists present at that meeting in December 1994. 'There were people who had never lived in the area. There were chunks of the voters' list just copied out. There were the names of goats and cows.'

The poor were outraged, because the wages for that work should have come their way. Instead, they had evidently been stolen. An army officer with a handlebar moustache was even more outraged when his wife's name was read out. 'I am on the border defending my country, and you put my wife's name down as a labourer?' he said. 'You make my wife a common thief? My wife has never picked up a labourer's implement in her life.'

Then it came to the work itself. The revenue officer's building was supposed to have been rebuilt. A large sum of money had been paid for the roof slabs. 'Everyone started laughing,' said Dey. 'We turned around and looked at the building. There was no roof.' There were bills for limestone to cover the roof, and for fenugreek and jaggri (molasses sugar), used to bind the limestone together. 'It was dramatic, comic, funny and serious,' said Dey. 'That's when we realized the power of information.'

In the first chapter of this book, we saw how India's young people rose up in disgust and anger over the rape and murder of J, and woke up to the desperate state of women's rights in their country. But the roots of that awakening lay not just in the TV studios of Arnab Goswami, nor in the social media campaigns of the urban elite; they lay here, in this fly-blown village in a conservative corner of India, and in the simple realization of the power of information.

What the activists in the western state of Rajasthan had exposed was the kind of scam that has become a way of life for the petty officials of rural India. Bills for development work are vastly inflated; workers' rolls puffed out with the names of people who don't exist or who never received any money; false claims submitted for raw materials, and the difference pocketed by officials running the programme.

Seven years before, three people had moved together to live in a small mud house in a remote village in Rajasthan. One was Dey, then just twenty-four, fresh out of law school, a degree he says he only completed to keep his parents happy. Another was a local grassroots activist, Shankar Singh. The third was the ringleader, a woman of forty who had turned her back on a prestigious career in India's civil service to join the struggle to help the poor. Small in stature but with a penchant for large spectacles, her name was Aruna Roy, and today she is one of India's most famous and most influential social activists.

The ramshackle house they chose had no electricity, no phone line and no running water, The aim was to live amongst the poorest people of India, spend a few years gaining their trust, and then help them stand up for themselves against a state that was predatory, corrupt and rotten to the core. They believed in democracy and not violence, but they were radicals nonetheless.

Over the next two decades, what they were to achieve went way beyond anything they could ever have imagined. The actions they undertook in that small village were to reverberate across India and effect the most fundamental change to this country's democracy since British rule was thrown off in 1947. That house, in the tiny hamlet of Devdungri, was to be the birthplace of India's Right to Information movement.

Today there are more than ninety countries with Right to Information laws on the books. The pioneer was Sweden, which enacted a law of public access to information in the eighteenth century and has a long tradition of open government.[1] US President Lyndon Johnson pushed through a Freedom of Information Act in 1966, and the American government now receives more than 650,000 requests a year. Britain followed suit under Tony Blair in 2000, and is already pulling in more than 45,000 requests annually. In India, former Chief Information Commissioner Shailesh Gandhi estimates that there were between five and eight million applications filed in 2012.[2]

The place the trio chose to establish themselves was one of the poorest and most conservative corners of India, 90 miles by road southeast of the desert town of Jodhpur. Alongside the Aravalli Hills, just off the national highway linking Delhi to Mumbai, the hamlet of

Devdungri has around fifty homes. In this part of the world, women wrap their faces in veils when they talk to strangers; men wear turbans and grow long twirly moustaches. Girls here are often married in their early teenage years, and as wives have very little status in their new families. Many children are malnourished, and huge numbers drop out of school early to work in the fields. Villages are riven by caste discrimination. Landholdings are tiny, and, with little irrigation, support just one maize crop a year at the best of times. Many young men migrate in search of work.

When the trio arrived, a hard life had become even harder, as the district reeled under the effects of a disastrous six-year drought. Many of the poor were getting by on just one meal a day; the middle classes (a relative term here) had sunk all their savings into just keeping their cattle alive. The three activists' idea of settling in gradually soon went out of the window, as they rolled their sleeves up and tried to help.

The first thing they discovered was that people desperately wanted work, rather than handouts, to give them the financial breathing space they needed. But the middle classes had cornered most of the government work that was available, and the remainder was being offered at rates way below the legal minimum wage of 22 rupees (35 US cents) an hour. For the trio of activists, the battle began as a struggle to make the government pay its own legal minimum wage; in it, they were gradually joined by many of the villagers who lived in the area.

Local government officers would claim that a proportion of the wage was being withheld because people had not worked hard enough. It was all recorded, they said, on documents called 'muster rolls', which showed who had worked on each day, and for how long. But when Dey and the others demanded to see those muster rolls for themselves, to verify the facts that they recorded, they were told the rolls were secret government documents that couldn't be shared with the public. Slowly, almost inexorably, the activists' battle shifted into a battle for information.

It was information that local bureaucrats guarded jealously, hiding behind the Official Secrets Act, a 1923 relic of British colonial rule that had sunk deep roots into the mindset of India's bureaucrats. The Indian state, as we shall see elsewhere in this book, had taken on some of the bad habits of British rule, absorbing provisions relating to land seizure or parliamentary functioning that worked to the advantage of the government of the day. Similarly, secrecy was a tool to protect officials, and to set them above their minions; information was a source of power and status. Gradually, Roy, Dey and Singh began to prise the information away from them, but each step was slow and painful. Thanks to their pressure, one sub-district magistrate, the most senior official in the area, was forced by his superiors to conduct an inquiry into whether people had actually been paid what the muster roll showed. But as he interviewed the workers one by one, he clutched the muster rolls close to his chest, tilting them at an acute angle so as to keep them away from the prying eyes of Dey and his friends. His privileged information would be guarded, no matter how comical he looked.

Another, the works foreman or 'mate', simply refused to surrender the rolls even after instructions had come down from on high to cooperate. 'It is a government document and I won't give it,' Dey recalls him saying, as he folded it and tucked it protectively under his arm. Dey and the others chased him around a cactus bush, trying to get the document off him. 'We looked so stupid,' Dey said. 'Finally he ran with the muster rolls up a hill, and we just couldn't follow him any more. We returned home completely crestfallen.'

On 1 May 1990, the trio formed the Mazdoor Kisan Shakti Sangathan (MKSS), the Organization for the Empowerment of Workers and Peasants. Just as the Berlin Wall was coming down and the Soviet Union was collapsing, the group's name made them sound like a throwback to a discredited era. But in the battle for information, they had found a cause that could unite left-wing social activists with free marketeers, just as it had united the lowest-caste workers of Kot Kirana with the moustachioed army officer. What free market, after all, can function without the free flow of information? The battle to get government work for the poor had divided the village, pitting them against the more privileged classes; but the fight for information brought everyone together. Even the middle-class residents of Kot Kirana could see that they were being robbed when development work was billed and not delivered. Much later, the battle for information was to unite rural and urban India too.

But as the 1990s dawned, that national battle was a long way ahead, as Roy, Dey and Singh tried to mount a sustained campaign in one small corner of India. They and their supporters in the village went on two separate hunger strikes in 1990 and 1991 to demand that groups of workers be paid the minimum wage. But the tactic wasn't working – officials would bully or buy off some of the villagers, and then convince the holdouts to abandon their fast by promising to fulfil their demands, only to renege later on. Each day they fasted, every day their health deteriorated, the self-inflicted pressure on the hunger strikers mounted. The officials, by contrast, seemed blasé. 'Their system is to tire you out,' said Dey. 'It's a deliberate method.'

Although progress was slow, their efforts were catching the imagination and admiration of the people in whose villages they lived. The state's obdurate and obfuscatory response brought an equally obstinate response from the villagers, who could see for the first time in their lives exactly how they were being cheated. It was then that one of the elderly villagers, known only as Mohan-ji, composed a song that was to inspire their movement for years to come. Mohan-ji was a Dalit, a man from society's bottom rung whose one-room house was completely bare, but who joined the right to information struggle wholeheartedly until his death in February 2013. Its rhythm works better in Hindi, but even in English it retains some of its power. These are three of its couplets:

> It's a time of bribery and corruption,
> The state is full of thieves . . .

> The thieves of the past used to stay in the jungle,
> The thieves of today stay in bungalows . . .

The thieves of the past used to kill with guns,
The thieves of today kill with the pen.

Buoyed by this support but frustrated at the official response, the activists decided to change tack. Their interactions with the people gave them energy, they realized, but their interactions with officials sapped that energy. Instead of protesting outside government offices, instead of fasting, they took their protests back to the village. With information they had gathered from a few helpful bureaucrats, they began in Kot Kirana with the first 'public audit' of government development work in India's history.

Inadvertently, they had stumbled upon a tradition of democratic, public audit reaching back to ancient Rome, when audit literally meant the 'hearing of accounts', from the Latin *audire*, to hear. They discovered, almost by chance, that this kind of public audit was immensely powerful, and laid bare fraud that a solitary clerk or accountant would have struggled ever to reveal. In Kot Kirana, for example, the government had been billed for the purchase and transport of the stone used in the revenue officer's building; immediately, the villagers pointed out that the stone had simply been recycled from the old revenue officer's building, at no extra cost.

But most important was the way the hearings shifted the power equations. No more were the villagers and their activist supporters cast in the role of supplicants whose complaints were entertained only on the sufferance of the local bigwigs: now, the balance had shifted, and the local government was forced to send its own officials to listen in on the public's proceedings.

From the day of that first hearing on 2 December 1994, the campaign to put these government documents in the public domain only grew. There was massive resistance from the local bureaucracy in Rajasthan – the village administrative officials, or gram sevaks, went on strike all over the state at one point. There were inquiries, and promises by politicians that led nowhere; and finally the growing band of activists staged a year-long campaign all across the state.

Gathering support as they went, they travelled from town to town, staging sit-ins at each central marketplace that galvanized urban support for a campaign everyone could appreciate.

Slogans like 'Hamara paisa, hamara hissab' (Our money, our accounts) synthesized and popularized the message in just four words. Journalists wrote about the public hearings and carried the word around the country. Retired Supreme Court Justice P. B. Sawant, then chairman of the Press Council of India, helped the activists draw up a draft Right to Information Law, and publicize it.

All over the country, political parties began to latch on to a cause that was growing in popularity. Several incorporated the right to information in their election manifestos. States like Tamil Nadu in the south, Goa in the west and then Rajasthan all ended up passing their own versions of the Right to Information law. In 2002, the Bharatiya Janata Party introduced a weak version of the law at a national level, the Freedom of Information Act, although the government lost power before it was ever put into effect.

The breakthrough came when the Congress Party incorporated in its manifesto a promise to improve on the BJP's weak and ineffective law. When it won the election at the head of a coalition, Congress Party leader Sonia Gandhi turned down the job of prime minister in favour of her trusted lieutenant Manmohan Singh. But to give herself a role, and the status of a cabinet minister, she established a new body called the National Advisory Council, with herself at the helm.

The NAC was made up largely of activists, academics and retired bureaucrats; its mandate was to ensure that the coalition government adhered to its agreed Common Minimum Programme, a synthesis of its election promises. It was to give that amorphous and unelected group known as 'civil society' unprecedented power to shape government policy. Among its founding members was Aruna Roy; among its first orders of business was a new, strong, Right to Information Law.

It is very doubtful that the law would ever have been passed in its current form if politicians and bureaucrats had recognized its significance and power. As it progressed through cabinet and parliament, there were various attempts to subvert it by limiting its powers or jurisdiction, but each time Sonia Gandhi, encouraged by the NAC, stood firm. Prime Minister Manmohan Singh was reluctant to even meet the activists, let alone lend his support, arguing that the law was too harsh, would punish bureaucrats for honest mistakes and would put an end to discretion in decision-making. But in the end, Gandhi instructed him to set aside his reservations and move ahead. In December 2004, a few days before the House adjourned for Christmas, the bill was introduced in parliament, but even then there was a last-minute hitch. As activists including Roy, Arvind Kejriwal and others gathered to celebrate over a glass of sparkling wine, one of them broke away to examine the fine print of the legislation, only to discover that it had secretly been emasculated at the last minute to exclude India's twenty-eight state governments from its jurisdiction. Only a last-minute lobbying effort with Sonia Gandhi restored the bill's scope.

Sonia Gandhi receives a lot of very justified flak for wielding huge power in India without any real accountability; she is also rightly criticized for presiding over a deeply corrupt and inept government that has squandered India's economic miracle. But here, at least, she showed her mettle. In 2005, India enacted one of the strongest Right to Information laws anywhere in the world.

What made the act unique, and immensely powerful, was the extent of the grassroots support behind it. The law allows citizens to request information from a public authority and demands a reply within thirty days. But it also requires authorities to publish and disseminate certain information proactively, so that the public does not have to keep filing requests. It set up an Information Commission in New Delhi and in each state with the power to adjudicate when officials decline to release information, to force them to divulge it and to fine them if they fail to do so.

Shekhar Singh, a veteran, white-bearded activist who joined the national leadership of the RTI movement, said that in the past bureaucrats had often allowed politicians to pass progressive laws, knowing that they could control the degree to which that law was implemented, or subvert anything that damaged their interests. 'But this time, within eight or ten months, the bureaucrats realized they had miscalculated,' he said. 'Ninety-nine per cent of laws give powers to bureaucrats to regulate people, and it is in the hands of bureaucrats how they are implemented. RTI is one of those laws that gives power to the people to regulate bureaucrats.'

In a country where the poor are routinely denied access to public services unless they pay bribes, a country where most of the government money earmarked for the poor is stolen, the Right to Information Act has won countless battles in its first nine years. It has helped the poor obtain everything from food ration cards to places at public schools earmarked for low-income families. In Rajasthan in 2001 an RTI-led investigation of public development work exposed fraud by a single official amounting to $140,000, and in New Delhi Arvind Kejriwal used the RTI law to expose a vast network of embezzlement in municipal corporation works. If the Internet is the empowering expression of the information revolution for the middle class, the Right to Information Act is its expression for the poor.

The Right to Information Act played a major role too in uncovering and exposing the huge corruption scandals that erupted in 2010 and formed the backdrop for Manmohan Singh's fall from grace. RTI requests yielded a series of damning documents that shed disturbing light on the waste and corruption involved in the Commonwealth Games; they were later used to ask why the authorities appeared to be dragging their feet in prosecuting those responsible.[3]

RTI requests played an important role in the 2G spectrum scam, for example in exposing an embarrassing note sent by the Ministry of Finance to the Prime Minister's Office that appeared to lay some blame for the debacle on one of the government's seniormost ministers, Palaniappan Chidambaram, for failing to insist on an auction.[4]

The Act has, in other words, been at the heart of India's democratic reawakening, by unleashing the power of information to make the nation's politics more transparent and its politicians much more accountable. Information is power, and the RTI Act has prised a significant share of that power out of the grasp of the political class and given it back to ordinary Indian citizens. It set India off on the road that led to the popular protests against corruption and rape in 2011, 2012 and 2013.

Given the massive and ingrained corruption that was, and still is, taking place in India, it is hardly surprising to discover there have been setbacks. The system is powerful, has deep roots and is skilled in subversion. Pinning down the Indian state must sometimes seem like pinning a huge nation-sized jelly to the wall, or perhaps fighting a giant, immensely crafty octopus. All over India, people filing RTI requests have received death threats, and more than two dozen have been killed.[5] Meanwhile the backlog of unfulfilled RTI requests keeps getting longer;[6] responses, when they arrive, are often late or unhelpful; requests are routinely denied on the flimsiest of grounds;[7] and awareness in many parts of India is still too low. The job of Information Commissioner is far too often given to a retired senior bureaucrat, and many have proved extremely reluctant to rock the system or the colleagues they left behind. It is easy to think that the octopus is winning.

Shailesh Gandhi, a former RTI activist, served as Information Commissioner from 2008 to 2012 and was one of the best. But he says that 90 per cent of the appointments to the role are now based on patronage rather than suitability – a posting given as a reward for a compliant bureaucrat rather than to the best-qualified candidate.[8] So twisted has the appointment process become that we recently had the bizarre spectacle of a former head of India's Intelligence Bureau, Rajiv Mathur – a man whose job it had been to guard the nation's secrets – being appointed an Information Commissioner, through a hiring process which in itself lacked any transparency.

Meanwhile, pressure is almost continuous to limit the scope of the law. Bureaucrats and politicians constantly argue that the burden of RTI requests is somehow a distraction from their normal work, or is overloading the system. One of the leading critics, ironically, is that supposed champion of clean government Prime Minister Manmohan Singh, who has expressed concerns that the Act 'could end up discouraging honest, well-meaning public servants from giving full expression to their views', or complains that 'frivolous, vexatious' applications are a drain on public resources.[9] In the process, the once-lauded prime minister demonstrated his cautious, bureaucratic side, his lack of ease with the norms of democratic accountability in a modern state.

Shailesh Gandhi believes that Singh's comments represented a worrying hardening of attitudes within government against the Act, a backlash of sorts and an attempt to limit its advance. 'The bureaucracy and the government is clearly very unhappy, and given the chance they will try and push it back,' he told me in early 2013.

The history of India is littered with good laws that have in the end been subverted and sometimes virtually forgotten. Gandhi could see that the corrupt heart of Indian politics would not dissolve away without a fight. 'It is going to be a tussle,' he told me at the time. 'I see a threat, and I feel we need to fight that threat.' His words proved prophetic. As we saw in Chapter 3, the showdown between RTI supporters and the political class broke into the open at last in the summer of 2013. The Central Information Commission's ruling that political parties were subject to the provisions of the RTI, and therefore had to open up their books for public inspection, provoked a serious backlash, with the government threatening to pass an emergency ordinance to amend the RTI Act and subvert the ruling.

There was, however, an extraordinary public outcry, which forced the government to backtrack, at least partially, by referring the matter to a parliamentary standing committee.

'Citizens will have to continue their effort of engaging with the political class,' wrote Shailesh Gandhi in an emotional email in

September 2013. 'But for today let us celebrate the success of democracy. This is the way to go. Citizens and politicians engaging in
discussions and the politicians showing they are sensitive to our
voices. Can there be a better proof that democracy works? A victory
for RTI and democracy.'

How that battle plays out remains to be seen. But despite all of
these threats and setbacks, the RTI has already wrought profound
changes in a system that thrived on secrecy and where accountability
was only to one's immediate superior rather than to the public at
large. No bureaucrat in India today picks up a pen to write a note on
a file, or makes a written submission about an issue, without having
the RTI in the back of his or her mind. The idea that they could one
day be called to account for what they are doing enters their brains,
even if it does not necessarily change their course of action.

The RTI is sometimes criticized for the paralysis that has gripped
India's governmental machinery in the past few years. Bureaucrats
are often scared of making decisions because they don't want to be
held accountable – so they simply pass the buck. A decision deferred
is a lot safer than a decision taken, especially when the eyes of the
world are looking over your shoulder. And if decisions have to be
taken, they have to be taken by the most unimaginative and uncooperative reading of the rulebook possible. Accountability to the
public is such a novel concept in Indian bureaucracy that it simply
fuses the system.

To frame this as a complaint, however, completely misses the point.
Yes, the system is struggling to cope in a new era of greater transparency and accountability, but it will have to learn to cope. Decisions
do have to be taken and files have to be moved. Sooner or later
bureaucrats will have to learn how to do so more honestly and openly.

Indeed, the solution to the malaise of inaction, inertia and inability
to make a decision is not to turn one's back on transparency and
accountability. Rather, it lies in giving performance incentives to
bureaucrats who perform their duties in a timely manner, and penalties to those who simply sit on files or shirk decisions. In December

2011, partly in response to the India Against Corruption movement, the government tabled a bill called 'The right of citizens for time bound delivery of goods and services and redressal of their grievances'. More commonly known as the Grievance Redressal Bill or the Citizens' Charter, it is supposed to ensure the timely delivery of government services, from passports to death certificates and pensions. It allows for officials responsible for the delay to be fined 250 rupees ($5) a day, up to a maximum of 50,000 rupees.

Ironically, the Prime Minister's complaint about the frivolous nature of RTI requests was rumbled – by another RTI request that forced his office to admit that there was no data to back up the claim. On the contrary, a study of some 18,000 RTI applications across India later discovered that nine out of ten were simply applications for information the government should have supplied anyway: a woman selected for a government job in 1998 who then heard nothing for seven years about what the exact job would be or when to start work; a man who complained the police had seized his land, who then successfully forced the government to carry out a survey of the land in question, but was never shown the survey's findings.[10] 'They were for things that any self-respecting government would have told people,' said Shekhar Singh. 'What are we talking about, it being a distraction? What are we talking about, it coming in the way of good governance?' Indeed, the number of RTI requests is still relatively small compared with the number of government employees in India, some 20 million.

That research puts India's millions of RTI requests into context. Most are for public services that an individual in a Western country would either expect or, if they were not delivered, would simply pick up the phone and find out what had happened. In India, there is no point in phoning a government department in a quest for information, any more than in trying to fight for one's rights through the overburdened judicial system. The Right to Information is, in many cases, the only recourse.

A study by researchers from Yale University[11] looked at people who tried various ways of accessing basic government services like food rations or state pensions. Those who simply requested the service were largely ignored, while those who used contacts in the NGO world did not get much better service either. The two groups who were most successful at accessing those services (and were roughly at the same level) were those who paid a bribe and those who had filed an RTI application. For the middle classes it may still be easier to pay a bribe, but for the poor, for whom 500 or 1,000 rupees is a lot of money, the RTI has become an extremely useful, and empowering, alternative.

But it is in places like rural Bihar, one of India's most impoverished and crime-ridden regions, that the power of information to upset the old order is most dramatically exposed. The story of Sanjay Sahini and Ram Kumar Thakur shows the tremendous potential that the Act has unleashed, and the battle that has been joined as a result, between ordinary people and a powerful nexus of corruption and crime. It also demonstrates the risks some people are prepared to take to stand up for their rights.

The tale begins in August 2011 with Sahini, a 26-year-old electrician from the village of Ratnauli who had migrated, like so many Biharis, to the capital New Delhi to set up a small roadside kiosk in a suburb there. On his occasional trips home, Sahini says friends started complaining about irregularities in a flagship government programme, the National Rural Employment Guarantee Act, known as NREGA. The scheme, another brainchild of the National Advisory Council supported by Sonia Gandhi, was supposed to provide 100 days of guaranteed employment a year in public works programmes for millions of the rural poor, but Sahini's friends were complaining that the public works projects in and around their village seemed to have been cornered by the village headman and a few local contractors. Villagers were not really getting a look in.

In Rajasthan today, thanks to the work of MKSS, more than 100,000 walls across the state have been painted with meticulous lists of each person in each village who has worked under NREGA, and how many days' work they have done. As a result, the opportunity for fraud has been significantly curtailed. But in Bihar, nothing of the sort had taken place.

Sahini's kiosk in Delhi, a tin shack with a sign saying Sanjay Electricals in Hindi, was situated next to a cyber café. One evening, after finishing work, he wandered in to take a look at the banks of people busy on the computers. He watched them for a while as they brought up the Google home page, typed in some information, and were instantly transported somewhere else. He was intrigued. When a booth came free, he sat down and tried to have a go. He had never used a computer before. 'I am more or less illiterate in English,' he said, 'and I didn't know how to even write Ratnauli in English, so I just typed in "NREGA Bihar".' He soon found himself confronted with a list of districts, and then a list of villagers, and finally, after just a few clicks, made his way to a huge long list of all the people who had worked in his village under NREGA. 'The café owner stood behind me, scolding me, saying I would break the computer, but I just carried on,' he said. Pretty quickly, he noticed the name of a man, Lal Kumar Singh, who had not been seen in the village for five years, as well as names of people from a certain caste who do not inhabit his village at all. They were obviously fictitious names.

Intrigued, Sahini returned the following day and printed out a massive list that he says ran to 3,000 pages and cost him 9,000 rupees ($160), some of which amount he still owes the café owner. Then, with the list in his hand, he set off for home. Once there, he travelled from house to house, trying to verify the information. That is when the intimidation began. 'The village head turned up at my house, and started threatening me, saying he would file all sorts of criminal cases against me,' Sahini said. 'I was getting a little bit scared, so I went back to Delhi.' There, he tracked down Nikhil Dey.

With a population of 83 million people, Bihar is India's poorest state on a per capita basis, and has long been a byword for crime, destitution and caste division, as well as for the mass migration of many of its young people to other states in search of agricultural or construction work. In recent years, its determined chief minister, Nitish Kumar, had improved law and order, and had the economy growing fast; NREGA had helped provide jobs at home and slow the outward migration. But still Bihar was deeply corrupt, often violent and desperately poor. Ratnauli was a typical large village of around 12,000 people that enjoyed between two and four hours of electricity a day, and suffered from very low literacy levels. In the surrounding fields, people grew wheat, rice, corn and pulses, but schools here stopped at the eighth grade.

Luckily, Dey was friends with a senior official in the bureaucracy in the state capital Patna, who straightaway promised to help. Sahini visited the bureaucrat and they agreed to convene a social audit. In January 2012, officials arrived from Patna as well as the district capital Muzaffarpur. Sahini gathered hundreds of villagers. Among them was Ram Kumar Thakur, a 36-year-old local lawyer and RTI activist from Ratnauli, who had latched on to Sahini's work and was keen to help. But the headman was there too, along with his goons. Sahini described him as a thuggish man, with a moustache and a completely bald head – a bit like the Indian actor Amrish Puri at his most villainous.

The inquiry began in a tense atmosphere. A man's name was read out. Thakur piped up, saying that the man had left the village years ago to live with his in-laws. Immediately, the headman's thugs surrounded him and starting slapping, punching and kicking him. Sahini was struck too, and before long the entire event had dissolved in chaos. A police complaint was lodged against the assailants, although it was never followed up.

By now, though, Sahini and Thakur were starting to build up a fairly good idea of the scale of the swindle that was taking place, with the headman pocketing most of the NREGA funds, working in league with a few local contractors who carried out some token public works projects. Thakur filed a formal complaint about corruption to the district office in Muzaffarpur, and an RTI request. In response, the village headman concocted two cases against him, for supposedly hitting a pregnant woman in the stomach, and abusing a Dalit he was supposed to have employed. Only a public demonstration of support at the local police station kept Thakur out of jail, but he was beaten up more than once, as was his brother Janardhan.

As the threats to his life continued, Thakur fought in the only way he knew: writing to the state police chief; turning up at a public forum held by Chief Minister Nitish Kumar and appealing for his help; even writing to the Prime Minister of India for protection. Still no action was taken.

On 23 March 2013, as Thakur returned from court on a bicycle, six men on two motorbikes surrounded him, including the village headman and his son. His nephew was not far behind him, and watched in horror as Thakur was shot in the stomach at point-blank range, on the instructions of the headman's son.

Thakur was still breathing, so the nephew tied a piece of cloth around his stomach to stem the bleeding, called an auto-rickshaw and rushed for the nearest hospital. But before they had gone far, police stopped them and offered to give him a lift. The police said they would take the injured man to the local hospital and promised to meet the nephew there. Inexplicably, his family and friends say, they then headed for a much more distant hospital, got stuck in traffic and delayed his arrival by two hours. 'They took as long as they could, and by the time Ram reached hospital, he was no more,' said Sahini.

'Why were the cops lying in wait for him?' Thakur's brother Janard-han asked. 'My brother was a very brave man determined to do what he must. So many times he asked for protection but it was overlooked. But what good is it? He is survived by three brilliant children, two daughters and one son.'

Sahini has carried on undaunted. His work has attracted the attention of thousands of people living nearby, and he now helps people in thirty-five villages to get the work to which they are enti-tled under NREGA, and the wages they are entitled to receive. The headman, his son and his goons from Ratnauli have all disappeared, but there is no sign of a police manhunt. Sahini, though, is still getting threats, and his colleagues still getting beaten up, as they enter new villages, expose new scams and embarrass a whole new set of village headmen. But he has no doubt that the powers of the old village elite are on the wane. 'Villagers now get together and jointly decide what work needs to be done,' he said. 'Power has passed from the village heads to the villages. It's like a storm, this change that has come, it's going to last a long time.'

Sahini had been transformed from a humble electrician to a local leader in his own right, but one with the conviction of an activist and none of the arrogance of a politician. He shrugs off the risks to his life, and says more and more people are joining the movement every day, making it harder and harder for the crooks to oppose them. He speaks fast, with a strong Bihari accent, a bag of papers always at his side, a full, dark beard covering his small face. But Thakur's family, he sadly adds, is struggling to make ends meet.

There is little justice for the many whistleblowers who are attacked and killed in India today, their murders rarely investigated properly and the corruption they were trying to expose rarely dealt with. In the final days of 2011, the lower house of India's parliament passed the Whistleblowers Protection Act in an attempt to correct that situation. The legislation is meant to allow whistleblowers to conceal their identity when they feel at risk, and makes it an offence both to reveal their identity and to victimize them in response to a complaint. The bill wasn't perfect – it lacks, for example, an essential provision that would force authorities to urgently investigate whistleblowers' original complaints if they come under serious attack.[12] But it would have been a step forward. Sadly, the political will to pass the bill in the upper house of parliament was lacking, and it is now languishing, like many important pieces of legislation, on parliament's to-do list.

Yet nothing in India is ever as bleak as it sometimes appears at first sight. My own favourite application of the RTI Act has come not in the holding of India's army of bureaucrats to account, but in the way it has been used to shine the spotlight on the country's elected representatives.

It started with Anjali Bhardwaj, a bright and lively woman with master's degrees in economics from Delhi and in environmental management from Oxford, who left her job at the World Bank to join the Right to Information movement in its early days. She worked for a while with Arvind Kejriwal in a group called Parivartan (the Hindi word for change), which helped expose massive fraud in municipal works contracts in Delhi. Then she split with Kejriwal to form her own organization, the Satark Nagrik Sangathan or Collective of Vigilant Citizens, working in the slums of Delhi, at first to help the poor access food rations and other entitlements.

Five out of ten people in India's capital live in slums, but many of the places where they live are unregistered and unrecognized by the city authorities. Every now and then, the city embarks on a clean-up drive, and some slum or other is demolished to make way for more modern homes or development projects, or big marquee events like the Commonwealth Games sports tournament. Millions of people live with the constant background fear of having their homes demolished, although they are supposed to be told before that happens.

As Bhardwaj worked, she started to notice a pattern. In the weeks leading up to a local election, the women who normally attended her public hearings would suddenly stop coming. A few weeks after the election, they would start coming back. The same thing happened the following year, around the time of elections for a different level of local government. She looked for the reason.

In the run-up to elections, it turned out, politicians would spread a rumour that the slum was about to be demolished (forcing anxious householders to stay at home and miss the meetings, in case the bulldozers arrived suddenly while they were away). Then, the same politicians would reassure voters that they alone could prevent the demolition from taking place, that a vote for such and such a person would protect the slum-dwellers from the demolition drive.

A deftly filed RTI request soon exposed the lie. There had never been any plan to demolish the slums in question in the first place; it was all a ruse. Once again, the power of information became apparent. That's when the slum-dwellers started asking Bhardwaj for something more than their food rations: they wanted to hold their political leaders to account. These politicians – these 'netas' who turned up once every five years with folded hands promising to serve the people, and then disappeared back to their luxury homes and plush offices never to be seen again – what were they actually doing?

Even though they sit at the bottom of the pile, and even though they are denied access to the most basic public services, the poor in India still turn out to vote in large numbers. Voting is the only leverage they have on a system that otherwise excludes them; whether they sell their vote for money, whether they use it to support someone from their caste or religious community, to voice a protest, or in the hope of effecting change, there is no doubt that it has value to them. In a middle-class district of Delhi, turnout in a local election might be 10 or 15 per cent; in a slum it might be 90 or 95 per cent. As a result, slum-dwellers are an important vote bank for India's politicians. The problem is that only voting every now and then was not getting Delhi's poor very far – sure, some of the corrupt, good-for-nothing politicians could be turfed out, but they would only be replaced by a different corrupt, good-for-nothing politician. The key to making democracy work in India lies in somehow making those politicians perform their duties outside election season.

The first step in Bhardwaj's journey was to find out what politicians were supposed to be doing: what the roles and responsibilities of an elected representative were. She filed countless RTI requests to every branch of government, but in the end the establishment was forced to admit: we don't have an answer. There was nothing written down.

'Somehow, elected representatives in India exist in a space which is totally unaccountable, where there is very, very little information on what their roles are and even less on what their performance is,' she told me. 'It is almost insulting someone if you ask, "What are you doing?" – they are treated with such kid gloves. But when we are facing the kind of breakdown of governance that we are in India now, people find it extremely useful to know how effective their elected representatives are.'

Bhardwaj, her colleagues and some friendly lawyers searched India's constitution and the country's laws themselves. They came up with three principal roles for a member of the national parliament or a state legislature:

- Attending the national parliament or the state legislative assembly, asking questions and passing laws;
- Managing local area development funds – money that was granted to them to spend at their discretion in their constituency;
- Taking part in various committees meant to supervise the functioning of the executive branch of government – committees supposed to monitor the distribution of food rations or address grievances against the police for example.

The next step was to file RTI requests for every elected member of Delhi's legislative assembly, and find out what they had been doing. According to the RTI law, the results were supposed to be delivered in thirty days, but in fact they took a year. When they came they were almost unintelligible – masses of acronyms that no one without experience of the bureaucracy could hope to unravel. Who but a bureaucrat would know, for example, that P/L of CCR stood for the Providing and Laying of Cement Concrete Roads? The acronym-heavy response was a classic act of subversion, an example of how bureaucrats try to wriggle out of the demands that freedom of information places upon them. Nevertheless, with the help of an honest, retired official, Anjali and her team did eventually unravel the data, and what they discovered was startling.

Residents of one slum, for example, would wake in the middle of the night to line up in front of a water tap that was turned on at 2 a.m., for just one hour. For seven years, the people of Malviya Nagar had visited their local elected representative and pleaded for a tube well, only to be told that he had no money. No one ever mentioned that a development fund even existed.

The information gleaned from RTI requests showed not only that their representative had received $650,000 annually to spend on development, but also that he had spent a quarter of it in the past year building or refurbishing fountains – which would probably never be turned on – in a neighbourhood renowned for water shortages. Suitably shamed, the official turned up just before election day to inaugurate a tube well.

In her office, Bhardwaj and her colleague Amrita Johri sat with me and leafed through folders packed with similar examples. In one year, one lawmaker had spent 500,000 rupees ($10,000) on 'designer decorative poles and lights' for public parks; another in one of the capital's poorest constituencies had spent half his funds in public parks on things like ornamental gates, a water feature, a shelter and a tree plantation. All very noble, except that the work was so shoddy it was in ruins in a few months, while the slums went without water and electricity.

With no oversight at all, most of the money was simply disappearing into the pockets of the politicians and their pet contractors. If a politician ever deigned to actually help people by building a well, he would usually pretend the money came out of his own pocket.

Nailing the lies, though, was still nerve-racking work. Since the point of the whole exercise was to empower the poor, the RTI requests would all be filed by the residents of the slums themselves. If the government failed to respond, an appeal would be convened and the complainant subjected to cross-examination. Surrounded by officials and public works engineers, one woman was asked about her husband and her children, and then told to go home and look after them. 'It is not the job of a woman to question so much,' she was told. 'These NGOs are just instigating you, but you can easily be picked out. These are very powerful people you are asking about, be grateful you are allowed to live in Delhi.' On another occasion, another slum-dweller was casually accused of being a 'habitual blackmailer'.

Many people backed out under this pressure, but some, with the pride and dignity that seems so common to the poor in India, dug their heels in.

The next step for Bhardwaj was to make the information more readily available, demanding that the government provide it proactively, 'without people having to stick their necks out and ask for the information and get threatened'. This was a key provision of the RTI Act, and among its most powerful, but also perhaps its most widely ignored. The government agreed first to post the information online in English, a token gesture that would have made it inaccessible to Hindi-speaking slum-dwellers who lack Internet access. Bhardwaj appealed to the Information Commission, requesting the information be posted on wooden bulletin boards across the city.

In February 2011, the Central Information Commission ruled in her favour, and gradually a few boards started coming up. At first, many were left blank; some didn't go further than the iron scaffolding, but gradually, after another appeal, the government was forced to accept the inevitable. Today, painted wooden boards exist in each of Delhi's seventy legislative assembly constituencies, all in Hindi, detailing exactly how the politicians have spent their funds. Perhaps even more encouraging than that, though, is what the boards show – a gradual shift from 'decorative lights' and 'ornamental gates' to projects that actually matter, like school buildings and drains. 'It is very heartening to see the boards,' said Bhardwaj. 'It just makes people's engagement with their elected representatives so powerful and so meaningful.'

More detailed 'report cards' on Delhi's politicians and what they were doing have been prominently published in local papers, and the initiative is catching on around the country. Similar work was carried out for members of legislative assemblies in two of India's poorest states, Bihar and Jharkhand, and report cards were published for 250 members of India's national parliament before the 2009 elections.

The efforts have exposed scores of lawmakers who had spent an entire year without raising a single question in parliament, as well as tens of millions of dollars in development funds that were left unspent, and committees that were formed to supervise the distribution of food rations to the poor – through 'fair price shops' – but never convened.

A group of academics from Harvard, MIT and Yale carried out a detailed statistical study of Delhi's 2008 state elections and found that slum-dwellers exposed to those newspaper report cards on politicians' performances 'responded by increasing turnout and rewarding incumbents who spent more in slums and attended fair price shop oversight committee meetings'.[13] In other words, people voted for politicians who performed their duties, and against those who didn't, once those voters had the right information.

'The idea that voters in an otherwise well-functioning democracy might be severely constrained by information about the candidates' qualifications and past record is both striking and important,' Abhijit V. Banerjee, Selvan Kumar, Rohini Pande and Felix Su concluded. 'We see that voters when given the information move quite substantially and if this information had reached the entire constituency, outcomes may have been quite different. We also see evidence that voters are somewhat sophisticated in how they use the information, allaying fears that information would simply confuse them.'

Despite the threats from the political class, I believe the RTI Act is bringing about a fundamental change in the way Indians think about their government and their democracy. There is no doubt that the hydra of Indian corruption and patronage is not going to be slain by one Act alone, and the monster will look for new ways to subvert every new law, just as hackers find ways past every new security wall that is presented to them.

As we will see elsewhere in this book, India's democracy is far from fully functioning. It is not enough to pay your taxes, vote and go away and let the government and one's basic rights do the rest. The individual in India has very few rights, especially if he or she is poor, and those rights that are mandated by law are routinely denied by the bureaucracy. The RTI is one of the few pieces of legislation that actually empower the citizen outside of election day, and that is its extraordinary impact.

'What we have in India is a defective elective democracy,' said Shailesh Gandhi. 'Voting by itself does not make a democracy. The soul of democracy is the concept of individual sovereignty . . . and this has been missing here since Independence. The fact that the RTI Act empowers individual citizens – this changes the paradigm of democracy in India, and in that sense it is extraordinarily valuable.'

In the end, perhaps the most profound change the Act has brought could be cultural, in a country where traditional hierarchies of status, caste and age have often left those in authority unchallenged.

In the old days, Delhi's politicians would visit their constituencies surrounded by drummers and armies of sycophants, touch the feet of a few community leaders and be garlanded in return. These days they are stopped, and asked uncomfortable questions – Why has the public toilet in our slum not been fixed for seven years? Why don't we have any water? In the old days, the poor would beg and scrape before authority. Now, emboldened by the RTI Act and the presence of people like Shailesh Gandhi and Anjali Bhardwaj, they are standing up for themselves, passionately and with real determination.

'India has a history of reverence, of touching the feet of elders, but the Right to Information Act is helping us break down the negative aspects of that reverence,' said Shekhar Singh. 'The common person is now looking you in the eye, not looking down when speaking to an upper-caste person. That gumption is the greatest success of the Right to Information. People who don't have gumption can't make democracies work. People are beginning to say, "I have the right to ask, and if you are not going to tell me, I am not going to vote for you."'

Yet the Right to Information movement cannot take all of the credit for breaking down that reverence, or for empowering people to ask questions and demand answers. For at the same time as activists were toiling away alongside the nation's poor and downtrodden, another man in a suit and tie was fighting a very different battle in a television studio in Mumbai – a battle for ratings, and to hold the nation's politicians to account, a battle that was to have equally revolutionary results in reshaping Indian democracy. That man was Arnab Goswami, and his channel, launched in January 2006 just three months after the RTI Act became law, was Times Now.

6

Headline Hustler

The twenty-four-hour news television helps awaken a nation

'The competition is already looking for places to hide. . . . 'What you are doing today is revolutionary. What you are doing today will be written about ten years, twenty years from now. It will be remembered.'[1]
Arnab Goswami, in a speech to his staff at Times Now
television in January 2009, two months after the channel cemented
its place at the top of the ratings with its live coverage of the Mumbai
attacks in which Pakistani militants killed 166 people

'It's open season on the media. At one level, we're the whipping boys because perhaps we have more power.'
Rajdeep Sardesai, editor-in-chief of CNN-IBN, quoted
in *Outlook* magazine, 5 December 2011

The President's son repeated his mantra over and over again. Abhijit Mukherjee, speaking in the heavy Bengali accent he shares with his father, said he had 'withdrawn' and 'apologized for' his remarks referring to the Delhi rape protesters as 'dented-painted' women who had emerged from discos to join the candlelit vigil. His apology, he said, should be the end of the matter.

'The matter will not end there.' Arnab Goswami, the nation's leading television anchor, was not so easily brushed aside. 'What are dented and painted women?' he barked. 'Who are dented and painted women? The question is in the public domain. You will have to explain what you meant by dented and painted women. My English is not very good, Mr Mukherjee, but yours must be better. I want to know what dented and painted means. I want to understand your mindset that made you use these words.

'Mr Mukherjee,' Goswami went on, his exasperated tone more evident each time he used the politician's name, 'you are avoiding the question but I will not let you . . . Mr Mukherjee, it's not going to be so easy to get away unfortunately . . . I want you to admit tonight that your comments were chauvinistic, and anti-women.'

'Hello, hello, your voice is breaking,' Mukherjee bleated, pretending that he could not hear the question, while blinking myopically behind his glasses.

'I am told,' Goswami replied, without missing a beat, 'the audio line is very clear.' The attack was unrelenting. 'There may be two reasons why you have withdrawn your comments. One, because you don't want to embarrass yourself, and you don't want to embarrass your father. The other is because you believe what you said was wrong, misogynistic, anti-women and uncultured, and is not something that should be said in the modern age.'

It was vintage Goswami, the take-no-prisoners, brook-no-bullshit style of television-presenting that he had made his own. His nightly *Newshour* debate has been described as a kangaroo court with Goswami acting as judge, jury and executioner, but it is nothing if not engrossing television. It is often described as India's version of Fox News. At his best, he skewers the corrupt, incompetent and hypocritical with conviction and courage; at worst, he whips up nationalistic fervour with scant regard for the facts.

Half a dozen guests are typically arrayed in boxes either side of the dominant figure of Goswami, while a series of straplines below ask the heavily loaded question of the night, or deliver the verdict that has already been ordained. 'Death to all rapists?' 'Govt to brazen it out.' 'Pak butchers, shirks responsibility.' 'Will India stand up to China?' To his credit, Goswami invites everyone to take part, as long as they speak good English and hold widely opposing views; from retired Pakistani generals to supporters of Kashmiri separatism on one side to rabid right-wing nationalists on the other; but then, he never fails to nail his own colours to the mast. 'Oh my God,' he sighs theatrically, before cutting his Pakistani guest off. 'Oh no.'

India has, of course, long had a flourishing newspaper tradition, and the investigate magazine *Tehelka*, whose name means 'Sensation' in Hindi, has set the standard for investigative journalism since its founding, initially as a website, in 2000. The magazine, whose motto is Free-Fair-Fearless, has carried out important work in exposing rampant corruption in the defence industry, documenting the role of politicians in fanning communal riots and protesting against injustice from India's heartland to its fringes. But for five decades after Independence, Indian broadcasting was dominated by the stately and staid All India Radio and its sister television network Doordarshan. Like a national sedative, it sanitized the news and enshrined the idea that information would flow in one direction only, from the top down, with no answering back. Politicians were there to deliver pronouncements, and the public were not expected to question them. In the past decade that model has been shredded by an explosion in twenty-four-hour news channels, and a new dynamic: for sanitized, read sensational; for state-run monopoly, read ruthless private-sector competition; for pronouncements by politicians, read interrogation of them.

In just a few years, television has become the king of the media in India. In the 1990s, my colleague Rama recalled, she used to tour India with notebook and pen in hand, and villagers would ask, 'Are you BBC?' Today, in less than a decade, that question has vanished, to be replaced by another set of questions. 'Which TV station do you belong to? Where is your camera?' Rama is asked. 'Once I say I am not a TV reporter, they lose interest, very visibly,' she said.

In the process, over the past decade, television anchors have joined the ranks of Bollywood stars, cricketers and politicians as India's icons, the new elite, one day revered and parroted, the next torn down and despised. Perhaps the three foremost in the English-language sphere are Arnab Goswami, the vehement anchor of the Times Now channel, Barkha Dutt, the fearless reporter-turned-editor for rivals NDTV, and the combative Rajdeep Sardesai, who was the boss of the other two at NDTV before leaving to form his own channel.

Each have played important roles in developing a new culture of transparency and political accountability. But this is the story of Goswami, the most controversial of the trio, a larger-than-life figure whose catchphrase 'the nation wants to know' has been ridiculed for its self-indulgent pomposity even as he sets the daily news agenda. He is bossy, bombastic and relentlessly opiniated. He is nasty and nationalistic at times, but never irrelevant. He poses as the nation's conscience-keeper, as prosecuting lawyer, judge and jury. But if Goswami is not to everybody's taste, he is undoubtedly also very good at what he does. He has an eye for a story that will capture the public gaze, and he pursues that instinct relentlessly. And, in a world where journalists all too often get sucked into cosy relationships with the elite, Goswami plays the role of outsider to perfection.

It was Goswami's channel that relentlessly exposed the corruption in India's staging of the Commonwealth Games in 2008, Goswami who kept up a steady stream of outrage at every scam and scandal that followed. It was Goswami whose incessant championing of the India Against Corruption movement brought the campaign to life and gave it the platform to challenge the government. Times Now's decision to do the same for the Delhi rape protests undoubtedly played a role in fuelling the fire.

When Prime Minister Manmohan Singh invited senior television editors to a rare televised news conference in 2011, Goswami's pointed questions about corruption brought a rebuke from the PM's media adviser. 'This is not,' said Harish Khare, 'an interrogation of the Prime Minister.' With India drowning in a sea of corruption, many viewers could have been forgiven for thinking it should have been.

* * *

Goswami was born to an eminent family in Assam, a state in India's often marginalized northeast. His grandfathers practised law and politics; his father was an army officer, his uncle a minister in the short-lived anti-Congress government of V. P. Singh that ruled India from 1989 to 1990. He is smart, with a master's in Social Anthropology from Oxford and a spell as a visiting fellow at Cambridge, but he burns with resentment, that the kid from the boondocks of Assam never quite belonged in New Delhi society.

After a short spell at a newspaper in Kolkata, his first big break had come with NDTV 24x7, the first independent English-language news channel to take advantage of India's new media freedoms in the 1990s. A friend remembered the ambitious and up-and-coming young television reporter as 'diligent and disciplined' but also resentful – in this case, that his boss, Rajdeep Sardesai, was not him giving the breaks or airtime he deserved. On one occasion, Goswami had called the studio with breaking news, desperate to be plugged straight on air. Sardesai imperiously declined, recalls a friend who was with Goswami at the time. 'If it was Barkha calling,' Goswami complained to his friend, referring to NDTV's star female reporter, 'he would have spent his own money to send an OB [outside broadcast] van.'

Despite making it to the post of national editor and co-hosting his own NDTV show in his early thirties, Goswami could not shed the feeling of being stifled and undervalued – until the nation's largest media company, the Times Group, decided to back him as head and main anchor for their new channel.

It was the beginning of 2006, not long after parliament had passed the landmark Right to Information Act to herald a new awakening of Indian democracy. The media had shaken off the shackles of the past, and television was coming into its own as a strong force to hold politicians to account. They were heady days in the Times Now newsroom, a channel staffed with young, hungry and often painfully inexperienced television reporters. Goswami was only thirty-two when the channel launched in January 2006, burning with a fierce mix of ambition and, again, of resentment, of NDTV and of Sardesai, who went on to found another of his competitors, CNN-IBN. There was never any doubt in Goswami's newsroom that NDTV, in particular, was the dragon to be slain, the complacent product of the elite who had never quite accepted him. 'His aim was to kill NDTV come what may,' recalled one former colleague, 'and make Rajdeep into an afterthought.'

'He had a sense of mission,' said another, 'and that was: let's see if we can provoke and shake things up. NDTV was seen as a training ground for the sons and daughters of Delhi politicians. It was leftist, and elitist, modelled on the BBC, just politics and poverty but nothing of relevance to the kind of people Arnab was aiming for.' But mixed up with Arnab's desire to shake apart the elite was his determination to prove himself, to satisfy his ego, 'to prove he is a player, an influencer, someone who matters'.

Times Now had begun with a mix of business and general news programming, but had struggled in the ratings war with the already established NDTV and the other new kid on the block, CNN-IBN, which boasted a powerful American partner. Reuters, which had taken a minority stake in the channel, had also enforced a code of ethics that talked about holding accuracy sacrosanct and not taking sides, but the rules gradually began to feel more like a straitjacket than a spine. Goswami was under pressure to perform and bring home the ratings: his boss at the Times Group, Samir Jain, had famously compared the media business to selling toothpaste, and this was no vanity project. Goswami was expected to make television to make money. With his back to the wall, he soon turned the pressure to his advantage, convincing his backers to abandon business news and quietly push the Reuters principles to one side. 'He understood that if we let Reuters run it, it would look like NDTV,' a colleague recalled.

As Goswami was finding his feet, Indian television was also finding its own – as an active shaper of public opinion and champion of a 'cause'. In July 2006, live coverage of a five-year-old boy trapped in a sixty-foot borewell transfixed the nation and dominated the ratings

– in shades of the 1951 Kirk Douglas movie *Ace in the Hole*. Children often fall into uncovered borewells in India; ordinarily, the boy might have been left to die, but when cameras were lowered into the well, the fate of the boy, known only as Prince, became a national concern. The Hindi-language channels were first on the scene, but the English channels quickly caught on. Unlike in the Hollywood film noir, there was a happy ending: after an ordeal lasting fifty hours, soldiers dug a parallel shaft and rescued him.

That same year, an outcry – driven initially by a campaign on NDTV – forced a retrial in the case of a model and celebrity barmaid, Jessica Lall, who had been shot in cold blood, in front of several witnesses, seven years earlier because she refused to serve a drink at 2 a.m. to the son of an influential politician. The culprit had been acquitted in February 2006. Ten months later, after rallies, email and text-messaging campaigns, and several candlelit vigils, he was sentenced to life imprisonment.

I had met Goswami even before Times Now was launched, when he visited the Reuters office in New Delhi. Straightaway, I sensed him lose interest when I talked about the prospects for peace with Pakistan – had I been banging the drumbeat of war, I felt instinctively, I might have received a more engaged response. It was my first hint of the nationalism that was a powerful driving force behind Goswami's particular brand of journalism.

But my first clear sense of what Goswami was all about came in November 2006, ten months after the channel had launched. That was when a note surfaced at the airport in the southern city of Tiru-chirappalli, found and handed to airport staff by a cleaner. Written in the Tamil language of southern India, and signed 'Allah Osama', it claimed that 'al Qaeda terrorists' had infiltrated five airports in south-ern India and planned to carry out attacks. It did not have a ring of authenticity. The police dismissed it as an obvious hoax, and a local NDTV reporter had already chosen to ignore it.

But Goswami was not going to let breaking news – or officialdom – get away that easily. It is possible the Times Now reporter on the ground was not aware that the police had branded the note a hoax, but it is equally likely that Goswami simply did not care. With ratings to secure, terrorists to denounce and national security to defend, he now warned his viewers of a full-blown al Qaeda attack in the offing. Such was his conviction that a nervous police chief was forced to admit that he could not take any risks, and that extra security would be immediately dispatched. So loud was Goswami's drumbeat that every other major channel, including NDTV, was forced to give the bomb scare coverage. Reporters turned up en masse at the airport, to find that there was no extra security to speak of. The police came under more pressure, and, finally, the promised security arrived.

Remarkably, it worked. Not for the air travellers, of course, whose planes were delayed and bags repeatedly searched. It worked for Arnab Goswami, because of the power of his conviction in what made news. For the first time since its launch, Times Now climbed to the top of the ratings for English-language news, albeit (as I remember) for males in the prime target age group, and in the afternoon. But it was enough of a success for Reuters to issue a note to staff in Asia promoting the new channel's arrival.

'It's an old saying – never let the facts come in the way of a good story,' one former colleague observed, before delivering the usual grudging praise that Goswami often receives. 'Nobody can stand up to him and tell him he is wrong,' he said. 'Arnab is not an idealist. He doesn't have a political agenda. He just wants to be the number one player in the media. But grant this to him, he has pulled it off. He sets the agenda on a daily basis.'

Goswani is a force of nature, even if he is perhaps less charming to his staff than he has always been to me. Many of his reporters scarcely dare look him in the eye, and no one can interrupt him in full flow. He famously once swore so vehemently at a member of staff in front of the entire newsroom that he dislocated his shoulder: the same person who had been the target of his anger ended up helping to put his shoulder back in its socket. He is opinionated, sometimes unethical, but always watchable. And there's no doubt that Goswami has played a major role in holding India's leaders to account over the past six years, relentlessly exposing their corruption and lies. Goswami has many faults, but the way he brings politicians down to the level of ordinary people is perhaps his greatest contribution to a democracy, especially in a hierarchical society where those in power guard information closely. He is the antithesis of Doordarshan, and that is why India's gerontocratic politicians often loathe him, and why viewers flock to him.

'The impact of the fight against corruption only became prominent when television took it up as a campaign,' Goswami told me in an interview in early 2012, remarking on what he called an 'inflexion point' in India journalism as big scams broke one after the other in 2010–11.[2] Then he aimed a small swipe at his rivals. 'However, I feel that the greatest problem is that a very large part of the media choose to please the establishment too much. They don't maintain distance with people in power. But change is happening, you see.'

The independent member of India's upper house Rajeev Chandrasekhar says the pendulum of power in India was completely on the side of the politician three decades ago, but has now swung towards the citizen, the common man and the activist. 'The institution of government, that was impervious, unknown and invisible to people, has now been breached,' he told me. 'The information coming out was a trickle, but now it's a torrent.' The Right to Information Act had played a role, but much of the credit, he said, goes to a 'ballsy media'. And when you talk about a ballsy media, the name Arnab Goswami springs immediately to mind. 'Journalism is about guts,' said Chandrasekhar, 'and on that you can't fault him. He has taken the fight to the system fairly single-handedly.'

Goswami's great rival for the title of India's best-known journalist is Barkha Dutt, another tough-talking and fearless dispenser of wisdom, but one who stayed with NDTV and rose to become the channel's head of English news. Although she hosts talk shows and debates, she is equally at home in the field and has won countless awards for her reporting over the years, starting with her battlefront dispatches during the conflict between India and Pakistan over the mountains of Kargil in Kashmir in 1999. The daughter of a well-known newspaper journalist, she is immensely respected within the industry for her fearlessness and integrity. My *Washington Post* colleague Rama once gave a talk to some journalism students in New Delhi; in conversation afterwards, many spoke glowingly about wanting to follow in the footsteps of Barkha Dutt. She has been called the Oprah Winfrey of India, or perhaps more accurately, by the *New York Times*, a blend of 'the hard-charging bravado of the young Christiane Amanpour with the feel-your-pain empathy of Anderson Cooper'.[3]

Dutt is more balanced than Goswami, more committed to hearing both sides of the story. They are at once alike, and polar opposites. Both are at their strongest when holding those in power to account, but both have come under criticism for their breathless, hysterical style. While Goswami often infuriates Indian liberals, Dutt often elicits equally strong distaste from the right. While Goswami poses as the indignant 'outsider', Dutt is the consummate 'insider', with well-cultivated sources in the corridors of power – something that is both her strength and her weakness. In 2010, her Achilles heel was exposed when tape recordings surfaced of telephone conversations, in which she appeared to be acting as a go-between between the ruling Congress Party and a potential coalition ally, and which caught her conspiring with a corporate public relations executive to pass information between the two sides.[4]

Dutt maintained she was merely gathering newsworthy information from a source, and playing along with the pretence of passing messages to string the source along. Nevertheless, the fact that the pair discussed the potential cabinet portfolios that were at stake, including the possible reappointment of the tainted Telecoms Minister A. Raja to the cabinet, and that the corporate lobbyist, Nira

Raadia, also represented business leaders who had their own interests in the outcome of the negotiations, made the tapes uneasy listening.

In an internal note to staff, Goswami called the revelations against Dutt and the prominent editor Vir Sanghvi a low point in the news business and 'downright shameful'. He took the opportunity to remind staff that his channel would not be cosying up to the rich and powerful, under any circumstances. 'We believe in fierce editorial independence and complete personal honesty,' he wrote. Goswami is sometimes portrayed as completely unprincipled in his quest for ratings and to satisfy his ego, but I believe this memo sums up a fundamental view about how the profession of journalism should be conducted. (Notice how he neatly wraps a warning about loose talk and disrespect to the organization into his warning to staff.) 'No gifts, no favours, no lobbying, no free dining and wining, no cash, no kind, no pass, no trip, no holiday, no promise, no passes, no special treatment, no tall or short claims, no disrespect to the organization that you represent and the group that we are all a part of, no loose talk, no flexibility on values, will be accepted,' he wrote. 'If I hear of any, we will come down hard, and no exceptions will be made.'[5]

Asked in February 2012 about Goswami, and whether he had changed the rules of the game, Dutt's reply was carefully worded. 'I may not personally relate to a certain style adopted by him, but style, as I said before, is a very personal thing,' she said. 'Some viewers like a much more aggressive, combative, in-your-face, judgemental approach to news. Others prefer a more "take a step back". It's a deeply personal thing . . . There's space for all kinds of styles, all kinds of journalism, and I don't necessarily agree with you . . . that he has changed the rules, or Times Now has changed the rules of journalism.'[6]

The Mumbai attacks of 26 November 2008, when Pakistani terrorists stormed India's financial capital and killed 166 people during a three-day siege, was the moment that seemed to swing the nation's

middle-class viewers behind Goswami. While Dutt manned the barricades outside the Mumbai hotel where the terrorists were holed up,
Goswami stuck to the studio and unleashed his unholy rage on the
'professional killers' who carried out the attack, on their Pakistani
backers and the Indian politicians whose various failures allowed the
attack to take place. His rage caught the mood of the nation.

At other times, though, Goswami can strike the wrong chord.
His obsessive championing of India's security forces makes him
dreadfully one-sided when it comes to Kashmir, dismissive of the
anger of Kashmiri youth or of the victims of army and police brutality. His anger at Pakistani terrorism is often justified, but sometimes
feels more like posturing than journalism. His outrage over perceived
Chinese snubs and threats may occasionally shake a complacent
Indian bureaucracy out of its stupor, but often feels alarmist. His
rants are sometimes so over-the-top that a friend's wife, on arriving
in India and tuning in unprepared, thought she was watching the
Indian equivalent of American political satirist Stephen Colbert, a
caricature rather than the real deal. (Indeed, Arnab looks a little like
a heftier Colbert, with his small rectangular glasses, his taste in dark
suits and his slick, oiled black hair.) Arnab and his viewers are so
addicted to outrage, it has become the default position; it has made
The Newshour the show that dominates the English-news market on
a daily basis, but it does not always make attractive viewing to an
outsider.

In January 2013, Goswami was not alone when he went into over-
drive over the news that two Indian soldiers had been killed by their
Pakistani counterparts who had crossed the Line of Control that
marks their disputed border in Kashmir. One of the soldiers had
apparently been beheaded, and his head carried back to Pakistan by
the intruders.

Over menacing music, with a grainy video of soldiers patrolling in
the snow relentlessly replayed over and over again, Times Now fanned
the flames throughout the day. By the evening, the straplines on *The
Newshour* denounced 'Pak's open aggression' and asked: 'Can India

continue the dialogue process with Pakistan despite an unprovoked ceasefire violation?' Goswami opened his show by denouncing 'the mutilation of Indian martyrs' on Indian soil. A retired Indian general with a luxuriant moustache and a green army cap lined up alongside Goswami to take potshots at his Pakistani guests, and the tone of the kangaroo court was swiftly set. The Geneva conventions and all norms of military professionalism had been breached by the barbaric foes that India was facing.

All over Indian television, retired officers urged that the army be unleashed to teach Pakistan a lesson. Newspapers denounced Pakistan's 'butchery',[7] and opposition politicians demanded the resignation of India's defence minister. On NDTV, Barkha Dutt said the beheading had changed the 'moral compass' in her eyes. The quest for ratings and eyeballs in India's congested media market yielded a kind of competitive nationalism that impacted directly on government policy. Under pressure to share a nation's anger, the Indian government spoke of the 'barbaric and inhuman mutilation' of the corpses and denounced the 'ghastly' and 'dastardly' act.

The whole thing was, as one respected Indian journalist argued, 'close to poppycock'.[8] That journalist was Praveen Swami, then a senior reporter and editor for *The Hindu* newspaper, who actually bothered to fill in the context and background behind the tale. Crucially, citing senior military and government officials, he reported that both armies had beheaded enemy corpses in tit-for-tat exchanges the previous year.[9] (Indeed, he later reported on long-standing Pakistani complaints about the torture and decapitation of half a dozen of its soldiers in the previous fifteen years, as well as about the massacre of twenty-two villagers in Pakistani-held territory by Indian-backed militia forces in 1998.)[10] The latest incursion by Pakistani troops appeared to have come in retaliation for an attack by Indian troops a few days earlier, Swami reported, in which one Pakistani soldier was killed. Moral high ground, it seemed, was all relative in the Himalayas.

Dutt, whose moral compass had apparently been reset by the

incident, had previously confessed to having seen the severed head of a Pakistani soldier proudly and excitedly displayed by Indian soldiers during the Kargil conflict in 1999.[11] She also confessed to not having reported that story while the war was still on; she seemed to have totally suppressed that memory in her outrage at the Pakistanis a decade and a half later. In her defence, Dutt is subject to constant sniping and often vitriolic attack from the right for being unpatriotic in her reporting, and can be forgiven for occasionally swimming with the tide on a national security issue like this, especially when the mood of the nation was so firmly moving in one direction. But the episode showed how strongly that tide was flowing in 2013, thanks to some blatantly jingoistic reporting.

The rest of the media had resolutely ignored Swami's reports into the context of the attack. India's army chief held a press conference, where General Bikram Singh called the beheading gruesome and unpardonable, and said he had told his commanders to retaliate aggressively if provoked further. Incredibly, no one asked him to respond to the allegations that the Indian army had carried out similar acts in the past.

Manmohan Singh, his policy of engagement with Pakistan by now utterly in tatters, ruled out 'business as usual' with Pakistan after an act he called 'barbaric'. India summoned the Pakistani ambassador to lodge a 'strong protest'. Progress in promoting trade and tourism ties was instantly stalled. Pakistani hockey players playing in India's league were asked to go home, a programme of visas on arrival for elderly Pakistani visitors was placed on hold, and shows by two Pakistani theatre groups were cancelled.[12]

While the imperative of peace with India was becoming increasingly obvious to many opinion leaders in Pakistan, India's hawks had once again forced their nation to turn its back on its neighbour, lamented the veteran Congress politician Mani Shankar Aiyar.[13] The blame, he said, lay in the ratings war being waged by hysterical and 'utterly irresponsible television anchors screaming, "The Nation wants to know," as if they were the nation': in other words, the blame lay with Arnab Goswami.

Given the sea change in Pakistani attitudes I experienced under Musharraf's rule, and the way India failed to grasp the opportunities on offer, it is hard to escape the feeling that the media deserves some of the blame. But Aiyar is overstating the case in shifting the blame entirely, or even mainly, onto television. It was the government and the intransigent bureaucracy, after all, which had turned its back on Musharraf's peace overtures in 2004/05, before Times Now was even on air. The power of the media in modern India to set the agenda is partly a reflection of the weakness of the government, especially under Manmohan Singh and his bumbling administration. (Nor is it surprising or unusual to see a nation's media take a jingoistic or nationalistic line towards a foe that has so often proved treacherous in the past.) Without a coherent foreign policy – apart from being nice to everyone – with a senior leadership scared of talking to the media, and the next rung down prone to shooting their mouths off, the government often comes across as unsure, uncoordinated and reactive. The space for someone as brimming with self-confidence as Arnab Goswami to set the agenda instead is obviously magnified. Singh had lost the initiative in terms of policy towards Pakistan some years earlier, after the ill-timed declaration at Sharm-el-Sheikh. No wonder others had claimed it.

In the same way, the powers of the judiciary, the Comptroller and Auditor General (CAG) and of activists have expanded in the past decade, into the vacuum created by Singh and his cabinet. When government and parliament have been slow to react to the public mood, other actors have taken over. Sometimes, those new powers claimed by non-governmental actors have been overused, abused or misdirected, and the actors themselves have often seemed unaccountable in the ways they have wielded them. The CAG, for example, has been accused of straying into areas of policy formation; the anti-corruption movement, as we will see later in this book, has been accused of usurping parliament's rights to draw up laws, the media of acting as judge and jury. In the short run, that has produced a lot of angst among the Indian elite, but in fact these may be positive developments in the deepening of the nation's democracy. If and when a stronger central government emerges, it will surely reclaim some of those powers for itself, but not all of them. What will emerge in years to come will be a stronger CAG's office, a more confident civil society movement, a media that cannot be cowed and a judiciary that is not scared to challenge the legislature and executive. Future governments in India will be more respectful, less dismissive of the powers of the other pillars of Indian democracy. In essence, I believe, we are seeing a strengthening of the checks and balances that can guide India's democracy in decades to come.

But it will be a slow and painful process, with almost as many steps back as forwards. At NDTV, executive director Vikram Chandra says that an over-dependence on advertising revenue coupled with unrepresentative and often manipulated ratings data is skewing Indian television coverage dangerously towards the hysterical end of the spectrum.

Most Indian programming is delivered by cable operators who charge viewers a pittance, but charge channels a fee for carrying them – with hundreds of channels competing for limited capacity on cable networks, those carriage rights can cost a fortune, and channels like NDTV haemorrhage money to ensure they reach enough homes. Meanwhile, Chandra complains, the Television Ratings Point (TRP) data is based on very narrow samples of viewers, who have specially designed boxes in their homes recording what they watch. The people who take part in the surveys tend to be lower-middle-class, more prone to the type of Goswami-induced hysteria than the more sober tones of Chandra and Dutt, he complains. In a tiny sample of just 9,000 people across India, not many more than 100 might watch English-language news, NDTV says, making the ratings data prone to wild swings from week to week depending on individual viewers' preferences. More worry-ingly, NDTV argued in a $1 billion-plus lawsuit against ratings provider Nielsen, the data is often rigged.[14] The channel says it obtained supposedly confidential lists of homes where the boxes were installed, as well as evidence that viewing data was being delib-erately doctored in return for bribes. Some homes, for example, had an extra television installed, attached to a viewing meter and tuned to certain channels, while the family watched a separate television themselves, the lawsuit alleged.

What is required, Chandra told me over lunch, is a change in the business model, one that he hopes is coming as analogue services are phased out and television services become fully digital. That should reduce carriage fees significantly and actually raise subscription rev-enues: at the same time, NDTV is waging war on the ratings data, in an attempt to show advertisers who is really watching what. But for now, it is hysteria that sells; for now, nightly adversarial debates draw in the ratings more effectively (and more cheaply) than documentary-style coverage of issues. Although NDTV has some high-profile and successful weekly shows like *The Big Fight*, from day to day Goswami is the master of this genre.

So adept in fact, that he sometimes seems to value ratings danger-ously far above any other measure of journalistic value. In his book *Pax Indica*, the former Minister of State for External Affairs Shashi Tharoor complains about an unnamed anchor (widely assumed to be Goswami) whipping up 'mass hysteria' over allegations of racist attacks on Indians in Australia. In a break during a recorded interview on the subject, Tharoor says he challenged the anchor, asking if he was really serious about the allegations he was making. 'How does it matter?' the anchor supposedly replied. 'I'm playing the story this way, and I'm getting 45 per cent in the TRPs. My two principal rivals are trying to be calm and moderate, and they are at 13 per cent and 11 per cent respectively.'[15]

But even Times Now eventually grew tired of the wild weekly swings in the ratings data, and the way that it appeared to be significantly under-recording their viewership. In June 2013, it joined NDTV and several other leading channels in temporarily withdrawing or threatening to withdraw from the ratings system in protest. Negotiations over a fairer system are continuing.

Goswami once told me we were all just 'doing a job'. Reservations about the reliability of the data aside, it is clear that as far as he is concerned success in that job is based on achieving higher ratings than the competition. But it would be wrong to suggest that his motivation is always wholly cynical. 'There is a sense of social justice, but it is tough to distinguish between his belief that India should be better, and his own ego,' said one former colleague. 'It is a combination of where he wants to be, and where he thinks the country should be.'

In an interview with Indiantelevision.com in 2010, Goswami talked passionately about the 'opportunity to make a real change in society', but also about the youth and energy of his newsroom, his relentless focus on hard news, his disdain for sensationalism and his pride in the channel's success.[16] 'Hard news is what I believe in; it is the only thing that we do, and the only reason why Times Now is No. 1.' But hard news, he went on to say, does not mean impartiality. 'To not take a position is not a virtue, to prevaricate is not a virtue, and to be unsure of news is not a virtue. You look at all the stories recently, and you ask yourself which channel do I remember? Answer is Times Now,' he said. 'If there is an obvious case of right and wrong, I can't pretend not to know what is right and what is not. And if in that situation, I prevaricate or choose to be silent, then that is wrong.'

Whether or not one agrees with Goswami's relentless editorializing, he has a point when he complains that the media is often unfairly blamed for what has become known as 'negativity'. 'You expose a scam, and you are being negative. You bring out documents through legitimate RTI applications, and ask warranted questions on why irregularities happened in procurements worth thousands of crores, and you're being negative,' he wrote in a 2011 column.[17] 'You ask the only direct question in a news conference aimed at clarifying the air on scams, and you are being negative. "It's journalists who are bringing the country down" is their new argument. "The country will not forgive you for focusing on one scam after another," they say. "Think of the country, think of our image internationally, think of the long-term consequences of what you're doing," they say, in a tone that wavers between fear and anger. "History will remember you only for being negative," they accuse bitterly. In the last one year, their accusations have become more and more intense. And predictable.'

Goswami is right: much of the criticism of the media is a smoke-screen, designed to protect the powerful from scrutiny. That is not to say, though, that there is not plenty to worry about when it comes to the Indian media, or that the critics lack some basis in truth. Mixed in the hysteria and lack of context is a frequent disregard among large swathes of the journalistic profession of the basic principle of accuracy. While conducting training courses for journalists from across India, I have been I was shocked by the inability of many of those reporters to record a quote with even the most basic level of accuracy. Some years before, I had been interviewed by a reporter for the *Brunch* weekend magazine of the *Hindustan Times* for a light article about foreign correspondents reporting from New Delhi. I had been a little surprised to notice that she wasn't taking notes as we spoke – part of me wondered whether what I was saying was not really all that interesting. I later realized that I shouldn't have worried: the reporter obviously went back to her office and wrote the piece up from memory, or else made it up. I don't think a single quote was verbatim, and some were plainly things I would never have said. No harm was done in this case, but it goes without saying that a disregard for the basic standards of reporting will inevitably court problems on more important stories.

The fact that politicians in India often appear to be above the law encourages the media to step into the breach. When the court system is so backlogged it seems sometimes to have completely broken down, when the government plainly interferes in the work of the foremost police investigating agency in the country, the Central Bureau of Investigation, it is perhaps not surprising that journalists sometimes imagine they should play the role of judge and jury. But there is no due process on Indian television, no presumption of innocence until proven guilty, no right of the defendant to lay out his case clearly in his own terms. There is enormous power in the television journalist's position, power that is not always wielded with appropriate responsibility.

There are, of course, other problems in the way the media is set up in India that pre-date the advent of cable TV news. A bigger problem perhaps is the under-representation of Dalits, 'tribals' and other underprivileged members of Indian society in the country's newsrooms.[18] The tribulations and achievements of a quarter of India's population are largely ignored in the media (while the coverage of the wider majority of the nation who live in the countryside is barely any better). The urban middle class may be disenchanted with the power of their vote, but they use the media extremely effectively to articulate their concerns. The poor vote in larger numbers, but have much less power to influence the national debate through the media. The absence of their voice on the national stage often allows resentment to bubble up, sometimes destructively, as evidenced by the Maoist uprisings in the forests of eastern and central India.[19]

To make matters worse, the Indian media is extremely Delhi-centric. One of the first things I realized about India was that the problems, issues and experiences of India's states were all very different, but that they were often relatively poorly understood by media people stuck in Delhi newsrooms and TV studios. From the conflict over the planned car factory in Singur to the trials and tribulations of India's northeast, there was far too much written and said from afar, and too little good-quality reporting from the ground.

At the same time, the media in individual states is often less energetic, less professional and less free. Local journalists are much more often threatened, intimidated or even killed than national reporters, while local newspapers often come under significant pressure from state governments who will withdraw lucrative advertising from papers they deem excessively critical. That is one reason why India always scores surprisingly poorly on global rankings of press freedom.[20]

Ramachandra Guha laments the fact that India's TV channels intensify the hostility and animosity between the country's two main political parties, and are often better at highlighting issues than at promoting a deeper understanding of the roots of the problems and their potential solutions.[21] The media also fosters a messianic syndrome, he says, presenting people like Anna Hazare, Arvind Kejriwal or Narendra Modi as the answer to all the nation's problems.

Finally, as elsewhere in the world, there is growing concern about the rising influence of corporate money on the media in India. India's leading industrialists, including India's richest man, Mukesh Ambani, have made significant investments in media companies. Some are clearly doing so to buy protection or expand their influence – an industrialist who owns a television channel or newspaper will be ushered into a chief minister's office almost immediately, whereas he might otherwise have been forced to wait indefinitely. There is no doubt that the Indian media is far more adept, and far more courageous, when it comes to exposing corrupt politicians than it is at exposing private-sector corruption.

On top of that, Indian newspapers and television channels also increasingly indulge in the illegal practice of 'paid news', where politicians or business sponsors can actually buy so many inches of favourable editorial copy. In many cases, warned a parliamentary report in June 2013, media houses take equity stakes in other companies in return for advertisements and 'favourable coverage'. In the political sphere, the 'paid news' phenomenon had become enmeshed in the corruption and money power that is already undermining Indian democracy. The report quoted from a Press Council of India study that outlined how the clandestine operation worked and cited hundreds of cases during the 2012 Gujarat state elections:

> So-called 'rate cards' or 'packages' are distributed that often include 'rates' for publication of 'news' items that not merely praise particular candidates but also criticize their political opponents. Candidates who do not go along with such 'extortionist' practices on the part of media organizations are denied coverage. Sections of the media in India have willy-nilly become participants and players in such practices that contribute to the growing use of money power in politics which undermines democratic processes and norms – while hypocritically pretending to occupy a high moral ground.

The report was largely ignored by the Indian media.

But it is not just at election time that 'paid news' rears its head in the Indian media. The report cited the example of Munir Khan, a quack who allegedly paid significant sums of money to secure frequent television interviews about a potion he was promoting, coverage that was significantly more effective than advertisements in promoting his product. (Sale of the potion, called Body Revival, was later banned in Khan's home state of Rajasthan after complaints that it was ineffective.) New cars often receive favourable coverage in newspapers and appear on television news segments on or before their launch, the report alleged; and just before a major new Bollywood film was launched, its two main actors suddenly popped up on Indian television reading the news.[22]

There are accusations of extortion too, the most notable coming in October 2012, when the leading industrialist Naveen Jindal accused senior employees of Zee News of trying to extort a huge sum of money from him, in return for not running a story alleging he was involved in the Coalgate scam. The matter has since gone to court.

*   *   *

In Gorakhpur in northeast India in 2011, I had travelled with the reporter for a local television channel. As we passed a house, he excitedly told me that this was the scene for his greatest 'exclusive'. An alien had come to earth, and then disappeared in a flash of blinding light and intense heat, he told me. So intense was it that the screws flew out of the door hinges, and the windows melted – all that was left was a single, large footprint. 'It was his exclusive,' his friend in the front seat underlined. 'No one else had that story.' Harmless enough perhaps, until a leading Hindi news channel devotes hours of breathless coverage to warn viewers that an asteroid is about to strike the Earth. There sometimes seems to be more astrology and quackery masquerading as religion on some channels than actual, properly reported news.

It is hardly surprising that the Indian media comes in for unrelenting assault, both from the government and from the elite. Even the Chairman of the Press Council, an eccentric retired Supreme Court Judge called Markandey Katju, joined in the open season that has been unofficially declared on the media in 2012. In a country where, according to the venerable Katju, 75 to 80 per cent of people were living in horrible poverty, it was wrong for the media to be devoting 90 per cent of its coverage to 'the lives of film stars, fashion parades, cricket, disco dancing, reality shows, astrology etc'.[23] The problem, the opiniated Katju admitted, was that 90 per cent of Indians are 'very backward, of poor intellectual level, full of caste-ism, communalism and superstition'. The solution, he said, was for the media to play a role in transforming society for the better, as the European media did during the Age of Enlightenment in the seventeenth and eighteenth centuries. Voltaire, Rousseau, Tom Paine, Diderot or Helvetius, these should be the role-models, Katju said – certainly not Goswami or the television reporter from Gorakhpur.

But is this really fair, to expect Indian media to do much more than reflect the society in which it survives? Indian news has gone from a state-run monopoly to the chaos of the digital age in the blink of an eye, even as the country is catapulted into another age.

Is it fair to expect this feisty infant to be invested with all the wisdom of the venerable BBC? Come to that, and looking around the world, does Arnab Goswami really compare unfavourably with American cable news networks, or some of the anchors at Fox News? Is the Indian media really any more prone to jingoism than the American or British? Does it indulge in phone-tapping, or make stories up any more blatantly than Britain's *News of the World* or America's *National Inquirer*?

Does Arnab fuel a gladiatorial form of politics, or does he reflect the polarization of Indian society today? The answer is probably both. From questions about the economy or the environment, about the welfare state or the free market, about peace with Pakistan or proud nationalism, the debate in India is often polarized and conducted at a high decibel level. Perhaps in this crowded nation of 1.2 billion people, after sixty years of waiting for the state to act, amid unimagined wealth and unimaginable poverty, shouting is the only way to make oneself heard. Impatience has become the norm.

Compared with the other three pillars of Indian democracy – the legislature, the executive, and the judiciary – it would be hard to argue that the media is the weakest link. Far from it. In holding the powerful to account, it fulfils its basic function imperfectly, but still with gusto, courage and no little style. India is a land of politics, and the media brings politics into every living room. Are journalists less professional in carrying out their duties than policemen, bureaucrats or judges? Investigative journalists may not be flourishing, but there are still some formidable practitioners of the art around; magazines provide a platform for some great writing and some more in-depth reporting; newspapers supply a daily choice of news and opinion that has educated and enlightened me about this country as much as it has infuriated and frustrated me. As we will see in the next chapter, television also helped to energize and unify a land rights movement in the past decade that prevented the rich and powerful from turfing the poor off their land with minimal compensation. And finally, television – the most powerful medium of all – has led the charge against the corrupt and the incompetent in modern-day India, a charge that has left the crooked on the defensive and imbued the young with new hope and drive.[24] The media has helped wrench information out of the tight grip of the powerful elite, and helped deepen India's disorderly democracy. Love him or loathe him, Arnab Goswami has to be given some credit for that.

7

This Land is Your Land

Farmers stand up for their rights, and politicians look for answers

'The British had to leave our land – they understood our sentiments. Now we have a government which wants to become rich by selling our land – but we won't let that happen.'
72-year-old Sheikh Moslem, in Nandigram in the east Indian state of West Bengal, speaking to the author in February 2007

'The days are gone when you can impose yourself, surround yourself with goons and policemen, and browbeat every Tom, Dick and Harry. It's not going to work, it's not a long-term solution at all.'
Sanjeev Zutshi, head of Vedanta Resources alumina refinery at Lanjigarh in Odisha, speaking to the author in March 2007

They were supposed to be flagship projects of the new India: one, a factory to build the world's cheapest car, would show how India was leading the world in 'frugal innovation'; the other, a special economic zone, was meant to attract billions of dollars of foreign investment. Both were to be built in a state run by a communist government, proof that even left-wing politicians in India were alive to the needs of industry and the importance of building a globally competitive manufacturing base.

But the projects, at Singur and Nandigram respectively, were to blow up in the face of the government, and help to end more than three decades of communist rule in the state of West Bengal. Foreign investors found the door slammed in their faces, and one of the country's most respected companies, Tata Motors, was forced to relocate its factory, at considerable expense, to the other side of the country.

It all came down to land, as so much does in this crowded nation of 1.2 billion people.

Land lies at the heart of some of worst corruption and misgovernance in today's India, as politicians and property developers work hand in hand to reap vast profits in ways that hark back to the era of the robber barons in the nineteenth-century United States. But at the same time, land is the scene of a growing struggle between rural and industrializing India, as farmers fiercely resist government efforts to throw them off their land to make way for factories, houses, infrastructure or mines. For some it is a classic example of how India's dysfunctional democracy is standing in the way of progress, holding the nation back in ways that authoritarian China can simply bypass. For me, though, land offers hope – that democracy can force India to change for the better.

India dreams of rivalling China's rapid surge to industrial prosperity, a process that requires the rapid conversion of farmhand to factory worker, and inevitably of farmland to factory. China's dash to 'modernity' is happening on a scale and at a pace that are unprecedented in global history. Britain's Industrial Revolution was a much more leisurely affair by comparison, yet still caused immense social dislocation at the time. But while China literally bulldozes its way to industrial prosperity, in India the people whose land is being acquired also happen to be voters.

Here, the decades-old way of doing business – abusing the law to grab land and bullying opponents into submission – just isn't working any more. Projects worth around $100 billion have been halted as farmers have found their voice and said no.

At the beginning of 2007, I travelled to both Singur and Nandigram to find out what was happening.

The village of Singur lies less than an hour's drive north of the state capital Kolkata, beside the best highway in West Bengal. It has an abundant supply of fresh water, with ponds and channels irrigating fields of rice, mustard and potato. It was, in short, a decent place for a farmer, but an even better place for a car factory.

The communists of West Bengal had enjoyed three unbroken decades in power thanks partly to an aggressive policy of land redistribution and reform that had given tenant farmers or sharecroppers greater rights over the plots they cultivated, boosted agricultural production and reduced rural poverty. But they had also infiltrated every aspect of public life during their long rule, from education to the police, and their militant trade unions virtually controlled the factories. But, with agricultural growth rates slipping, they had decided that economic reform was vital to their survival. Just like their Chinese brethren, they had recently discovered the joys of capitalism, and were keen to show the world that their state was open for business. 'Communists are not fools, we are realists,' the state's then chief minister, the moderate and respected Buddhadeb Bhattacharya, told me in a library inside the party headquarters, surrounded by books on Marx and Lenin. 'Earlier we fought for land, now we are fighting for industry.'[1]

What better way to demonstrate this new-found belief than to attract Ratan Tata, the venerable head of the Tata Group, the grand old man of Indian business with as close a reputation to ethical business here as one was likely to find? Tata had dreams of his own: to build the world's cheapest car, to be called the Tata Nano, and sell it for what is known here as 'one lakh', 100,000 rupees – a little less than $2,000. After looking around the country, he had chosen West Bengal, and had promised to employ 10,000 people. It was to be a 'special project, one of a kind', Bhattacharya's savvy Industries Secretary Sabyasachi Sen told me. 'West Bengal suffered for a long time with a perception problem, and the stamp of approval of the Tatas is very important.'

The problem was that in its eagerness to attract Ratan Tata, the government took precarious shortcuts, mainly in failing to get the agreement of the very farmers who formed the backbone of their support. Instead of a public consultation, communist cadres went around manufacturing consent. Instead of consensus, the government invoked an 1894 colonial-era land law that allowed it to forcibly acquire land deemed to be in the 'public purpose'. It put a fence around nearly 1,000 acres of land and invited the Tatas in.

Ironically, the British had seldom invoked the land-acquisition law during their time in charge in India, simply because their need for land was relatively modest, apart from the needs of government and the creation of India's vast railway network. In comparison, modern India's thirst for land appears insatiable.

For decades, India's politicians had been abusing the provisions of that colonial-era law. Public purpose was loosely defined as anything that might benefit the economy as a whole; land was seized and farmers paid a small premium on a government-determined 'market rate'; and if they objected, the police would soon shut down their protests, with a heavy hand if needed. But, in modern India, the old ways were to backfire.

In Singur, I met 78-year-old Gopal Chandra, standing beside land he shared with his five brothers, land that had belonged to his father and his grandfather before them. 'The day they started putting up the fence, we knew our land was gone,' he said, his white stubble and sunken cheeks not masking a quiet dignity. 'I felt like trying to stop it right away, but all I could do was stare.' A few yards away, on the other side of the fence, an Indian policeman, clad in full riot gear, stared back.[2]

The protests, by this stage, had already turned violent, and had attracted the support of the opposition leader Mamata Banerjee, who was determined to use the issue to stoke up her lifelong campaign to oust the communists. Banerjee, a schoolteacher's daughter, fifty-one years old, had been frequently beaten by the police while protesting against communist rule, and even hospitalized – many years later she showed me the scars on her wrists and arms.[3] In Singur, dozens of people had already been hurt.

The government claimed that the flat land of Singur was not so very fertile, mostly supporting just one crop a year. The white-haired and bespectacled Bhattacharya told me the compensation package on offer was 'the most exemplary in the country' and said 95 per cent of the 14,000 affected families had already accepted it.

But even a day spent reporting in Singur cast serious doubt on those claims. 'This is the third crop this season, and we will get two more,' 62-year-old Haradhan Adak told me, a red and white checked scarf or gamcha wrapped across his shoulders and chest. 'How can they say this isn't fertile land?'

Some people said they had accepted cash for their land. Others had sold because the party had promised them factory jobs, or because they saw no point in holding out. But in village after village, farmers told me they had not signed consent forms. 'People have been intimidated by party workers,' 62-year-old Anil Shantra told me. 'They brought out a list of people who agreed to sell, but someone had signed on my behalf.'

The presence of hundreds of tenant farmers on the Singur land further complicated matters. Some would get a limited compensation payment, but others, unregistered with the government, would not qualify for any money at all.

Although the government was paying several times the market rate for the land, economics professor Abhirup Sarkar calculated that, allowing for prevailing levels of interest rates and inflation, investing the money would probably not produce the same returns as farming. More importantly, farmers knew that the capital would not last for ever. 'You have marriages, illnesses, the money will just drain away,' said Shantra. 'What do we do then?' Inside the fence, a thin line of protesters, perhaps 300 in all, snaked through a small village called Gopalnagar. 'Sticks and bullets will not make us budge,' they chanted. 'The fight is going on. Everybody join us.'

At the time, I hadn't given the protesters much chance of resisting the tide. Tata had just started work on building the factory, was already giving scores of men job-training and organizing women to supply food to construction workers. It seemed only a matter of time before enough people were bought off for the protests to fizzle out. In the media, instead of ground-level reporting on the economics and the farmers' grievances, the issue had been reduced to a political face-off: the calm and rational-sounding Bhattacharya versus the mercurial and populist Mamata Banerjee. It was industry and progress against agriculture and the village. 'Mad Mamata', as she was dismissively nicknamed by some in the intellectual elite, did not seem to have the press on her side.

Nandigram changed all of those calculations.

I travelled there shortly after leaving Singur, and it made that dispute seem restrained in comparison. By the time I entered this coastal district to the southwest of Kolkata, six people had already been killed and more than fifty injured in weeks of protests, since a leaked government document had revealed plans to seize 19,000 acres of fertile land on the banks of the Haldi and Hooghly rivers, home to thirty-eight villages and 100,000 people. It was supposed to be just one among hundreds of Special Economic Zones the Indian government wanted to establish across the country in a bid to lure foreign investment and close the gap with China. Deals had already been struck with the state-owned Indian Oil Corporation and Indonesia's Salim Group to build a refinery and chemicals complex there.

I rode in on the back of a motorbike. Deep trenches had been dug in every road leading into Nandigram. Every few metres, a barricade of rocks or logs blocked the way. Piles of broken red bricks were strewn across the road, while knots of angry men kept a wary eye on intruders. Police and government officials dared not enter.

As soon as we paused, crowds began to gather. Hasina Bibi, choked back the tears as she remembered her eighteen-year-old son Salim, who had been killed in a violent confrontation with Communist Party workers trying to protect their family's modest plot of land. But, sitting in the midst of an angry crowd of villagers, she was unbowed. 'I lost my son, I can't do anything about that, but I can save my land – even if I have to sacrifice two more of my sons,' she said, a pink patterned veil half pulled over her face, a gold stud in her nose. 'The land gives us a morsel of rice every day. What will happen to us if we give up our lands, how will we get our rice?'⁴

In the decades after Independence, several popular films and books focused on the Indian farmer's deep connection to his land, and warned that severing that connection would lead inexorably to suffering, humiliation and loss of dignity. The 1953 film *Do Bigha Zameen* (Two Acres of Land) is a classic, where a small farmer is cheated out of his land by a rich landlord, and his family ruined in the process. In the final scene, farmer, wife and young son gaze through a wire fence at a factory being built on land that was once theirs. 'Mother, look, right there from where the smoke billows, was our house,' the boy says. 'And right there was my kitchen,' his mother replies. As they leave, the farmer reaches through a hole in the fence to pick up a handful of earth from land he once owned, but is angrily sent packing by a security guard; silhouetted against the sky, the three of them trudge up a hill, to the sound of mournful strings and a future of probable destitution.

Nandigram was not just fertile land; it was home to a vibrant Muslim community, with many mosques. We wandered past houses where women were weaving cotton cloth; we saw fish-farming in the pools that dot the countryside. Canals took abundant river water to irrigate fields of paddy, mustard and potato. Farmers pressed forward, one offering a fistful of lentils as if to prove the point, another holding a bucket of lobsters. But there was an emotional attachment too to the land. 'My father and grandfather are buried here,' said forty-year-old Rahajuddin Shah, his voice laden with emotion. 'They are sleeping peacefully. I don't want anybody to disturb them.'

Singur and Nandigram illustrated another of the problems of India's land-acquisition process: that much of the best land for industry and infrastructure is often close to cities, with good road or rail links and abundant supplies of water. It is often equally popular with farmers, and densely populated.

In Nandigram, a local Communist Party office stood as testament to the violence that had already erupted there, rocks and broken glass littering the floor, the window frames smashed and burnt. Just over the road, 28-year-old farmer Sheikh Hafrul Islam paused from his work in the paddy field to say he had voted communist all his life, but never would again. 'The left always told us "We are for the farmer, we will protect your land," but now they are snatching our land and our food,' he said. 'But we won't let them do it.'⁵ By the time I left Nandigram, I was certain that the West Bengal government would never be able to claim this land.

Back in Kolkata, Bhattacharya told me he had taken 'a wrong step' by not consulting the farmers of Nandigram before agreeing to sell their land, but insisted his party had learnt from its mistakes. Given time, the farmers would still be convinced to move, he added – assurances that turned out absolutely hollow.

A few days after we spoke, a policeman who dared to venture into Nandigram was killed by an angry mob, according to local media reports. The blockade of Nandigram began to seem like an intolerable challenge to the authority of the police and the Communist Party. On 14 March 2007 thousands of police and armed communist cadres tried to force their way into Nandigram, only to be met by a wall of residents: men, women and children. In the subsequent police firing, fourteen people were killed. Public opinion and the media flipped. Suddenly, the heavy-handed communists were the bad guys. 'The Killing Fields of Nandigram', the media proclaimed. Some of Kolkata's leading intellectuals and artists joined hands to protest, while the state's largely ceremonial Governor, Gopalkrishna Gandhi (the grandson of Mahatma Gandhi), spoke of his 'cold horror' on learning about the violence.

At the time, there was talk that Maoist insurgents, whose long-running rebellion still flared in the forests of eastern and central India, had stoked the violence in Singur and Nandigram, and there is no doubt that they tried to take advantage. Hundreds of sympathizers blocked a busy road junction in Kolkata in the aftermath of the Nandigram deaths chanting 'Maobad Zindabad' (Long live the Maoist movement), and Jiten Marandi, a senior leader of the

Maoist-backed political group the Revolutionary Democratic Front, told me that Maoists were 'seizing the opportunity to recruit more members'.[6] They may have played a role, but when I was in Singur and Nandigram there was no sign of radical politics or violent troublemakers, just farmers, genuinely worried and extremely angry about the potential loss of their livelihoods.

In the wake of the violence, Bhattacharya was forced to tear up the agreements to build an oil refinery and chemicals plant on the farmland of Nandigram. The protests at Singur were re-energized, and the government's hands more firmly tied. In 2011, Mamata Banerjee ended thirty-four years of communist rule by winning West Bengal's state elections, with the land-acquisition issue one of her main campaign planks.[7] Bhattacharya lost by a landslide in his own constituency. One of Mamata's first acts as Chief Minister was to declare that much of the Singur land would be returned to the farmers, although the courts ironically stayed the decision, arguing that there was no provision in the law for the return of land once acquired. But even before the election, the Tatas had given up, relocating their Nano factory to a new home in the western state of Gujarat.

But the significance of the events at Nandigram reverberated way beyond West Bengal. A group of farmers had successfully resisted the march of industry and thrown back clumsy attempts to rob them of their land. Their protests had received wall-to-wall coverage on India's energetic new twenty-four-hour cable news channels, and penetrated every corner of the country.

For decades, all over India, powerless small farmers had seen their lands seized to make way for factories and mines. Isolated and alone, they had been easy prey for policemen and politicians in the pay of big business. But now, Nandigram became their rallying cry; their protests too began to attract television cameras and journalists. Gradually, each group of protesters began to feel part of a broader struggle, each victory over the bulldozers emboldening the next group.

For me, this was a Eureka moment, the point when I realized that twenty-four-hour news television was changing the game in India and helping to deepen democracy. In the short term, of course, the media attention on the great Indian land grab and the parallel movement for farmers' rights has paralysed development. For the past five years, industry has struggled to acquire the land it desperately needs, with the result that several major infrastructure and investment projects have ground to a halt. But in truth Indian industry had only itself to blame, after decades of seizing land with impunity and caring little for its owners and occupants.

In the five years that followed the Nandigram violence, five separate bills were drawn up to regulate land in India, and in particular the acquisition of farmland for other purposes, as a consensus emerged that the 1894 land law had to be changed. Politicians were seeking a way to ensure that business gets the land it needs and farmers receive the compensation they deserve. Indian democracy might have complicated matters, but it was also groping towards a fairer, more sustainable solution to the problem.

In the neighbouring state of Odisha, events at Nandigram had emboldened farmers in their struggle against India's largest-ever foreign investment project, a $12 billion steel plant planned by South Korea's POSCO. 'This has had a very good effect on the people struggling against the POSCO project,' protest leader Abhay Sahu told me in the small village of Dhinkia in March 2007. 'Now is the time to move forward.'[8]

Odisha's government had staged its own 'Nandigram' the year before, when twelve villagers and one policeman died during a protest over a steel plant outside the small town of Kalinganagar. Without such compelling television footage, the death of a dozen 'tribal' people had not resonated in quite the same way nationally, but had become a major embarrassment within the state. Odisha's government was treading carefully, and Sahu was already taking full advantage. Supporters and opponents of the POSCO project had recently clashed, leaving scores of people injured, and a bamboo barrier had been erected across the road leading into Dhinkia to keep outsiders away.

Sahu had greying hair and a grey moustache, and dark glasses. He was dressed, like every Indian politician, in a long white-cotton shirt or kurta. He had struck me as a self-important man, grandstanding to his assembled supporters as we faced each other on plastic chairs in the shade of a roadside palm tree. He had been a member of the state politburo of another of India's communist parties, which held a marginal position in opposition in the state, and he had descended on the villages of Dhinkia, Nuagaon and Gadakujang in 2005 with the express purpose of fomenting opposition to the POSCO project. He complained that the multinational's plans would destroy traditional lifestyles and the environment, but also groused about the lack of trade unionization allowed at POSCO's headquarters in South Korea. The people of these villages, it seemed to me, were pawns in Sahu's game.

Sahu seemed like the classic example of the opportunist that many industrialists and miner owners complain about, who inserts himself into these kinds of situations for ideological reasons or in the hope of reaping political or financial benefits. Was he that different from the 'goondas' or thugs often hired by politicians and industrialists to bully villagers into submission? I wasn't sure, but a day spent talking to the people of Dhinkia made me realize that it was the arrogant way that ordinary people had been brushed aside in India's rush to development that gave people like Sahu the opportunity to sow distrust. In the past, the state-run Indian Oil Corporation had taken land in the area to build a refinery, villagers told me, but the promises of jobs for the locals had never materialized. How then should they trust POSCO, they asked.

Land in India is often divided into such tiny plots that an industrialist would seldom be able to buy enough contiguous land to build a factory without some help from the state. There has never been a comprehensive survey of land ownership in India since Independence, and land records are also a complete mess, a mass of conflicting claims written on slips of paper and held in government offices and private homes. My colleague Rama Lakshmi had visited a patwari, or land records officer, in the state of Haryana in 2009, and seen piles of handwritten land records, yellowed with age and under attack from rain, mice and termites. His main reference was a sixty-year-old tea-stained map of the village, drawn on a folded piece of cloth and carried around with him in his tote bag.[9]

So contentious was the problem that 80 per cent of the cases before India's lower courts relate to land, experts told me, while crime statistics record that property disputes were the cause of nearly 10 per cent of the murders in the country.[10]

There was no way, industrialists argued, that they could disentangle the mess and adjudicate between someone who claims ownership of land based on a decades-old piece of paper and someone else who has been occupying or farming the land for almost as long. Unless the government intervened to arbitrate between disputes, the process of land acquisition would collapse in discord.

Finally, in 2013, the government and the opposition BJP agreed to introduce a new bill meant to regulate more fairly the acquisition of land. Eventually passed by both houses of parliament by overwhelming majorities in September 2013, The Right to Fair Compensation and Transparency in Land Acquisition, Rehabilitation and Resettlement Act marks a step forward in the quest for a more equitable way of acquiring farmland, although far from an ideal solution.[11] The government will stay play a role in land acquisition but the agreement of farmers and land users will be more explicitly sought. When private companies wish to acquire land, the consent of 80 per cent of project-affected people will need to be secured; when public–private partnerships (a method the government hopes to use to significantly boost infrastructure investment) wish to do so, 70 per cent of those affected would need to consent. This condition is waived for public-sector bodies, but even they will need to subject all projects to social-impact assessment. Tenants as well as landowners would be entitled to compensation, while compulsory relief and resettlement packages would also be offered to the displaced.

Industry complained that the bill had swung the pendulum too far back the other way. The Associated Chambers of Commerce and Industry of India (Assocham) said the hurdle of 80 per cent consent would make land acquisition 'difficult if not impossible', while the Federation of Indian Chambers of Commerce and Industry (FICCI) said the bureaucratic process of acquiring consent and carrying out social impact studies could delay the land acquisition process by four to five years.[12]

More fundamentally, the way a fair price for that land was to be fixed also showed how imperfect the market for land remained.

Buyers and sellers of land, it was implicitly recognized, routinely declare to the authorities a much smaller price for their transaction than the amount that really changes hands, in an attempt to avoid stamp duty and registration fees. Typically, around half the transaction might take the form of an undeclared cash payment, often being paid in the office of the property registrar itself – so that everyone involved can see they are getting a fair cut of the (illicit) proceeds. So prevalent is this system that real estate agents in India will simply not deal with a buyer unless he or she is prepared to make a significant part of the payment in cash, explained Barun Mitra, an expert on land issues and founder of the Liberty Institute think tank in New Delhi. I last met Mitra over a coffee in the India Habitat Centre in 2013; a small, enthusiastic man with a flourishing grey beard, he was fired up about the land issue. 'In twenty-two years living in New Delhi, I only know of one property transaction that was done legitimately,' he said. 'That was only because the seller was moving to Mumbai, and buying something worth ten times as much there, so he wanted to prove to his bank he had enough legitimate money.'

Recognizing that the recorded market price is usually (if not always) much lower than the real market price, the government arbitrarily decided that, when a private sector operator buys land, he or she should pay a significant premium over the recorded price in the market (twice the recorded market value in urban areas, four times in rural areas). The mark-up was supposed to also take into account the fact that the recorded market price might not reflect the value of land for those who do not wish to sell, as well as providing farmers with a greater share of the profits of development. Predictably, industry complained this formula would push up the price of land to levels at which economic development would become unprofitable. But the fundamental problem was that the mark-up was completely arbitrary. In effect, the state was acknowledging corruption and market failure, but simply throwing (other people's) money at the problem, instead of trying to solve it.

Despite all of these reservations, The Right to Fair Compensation and Transparency in Land Acquisition, Rehabilitation and Resettlement Bill, 2013, represents a sincere attempt to tackle a problem that has bedevilled India's economic advancement and where vested interests have long blocked reform. Thanks to a sustained effort by activists and considerable media coverage, the issue of land rights has been properly recognized in India, and is high on the national agenda. Individual states have the power to modify the law and its provisions – perhaps some may find ways to keep industry happy in order to attract investment while still protecting farmers' rights. It may take several more years before an equitable compromise is found between the needs of landowners and land developers, but the process of negotiation has at least begun in earnest.

In the long term, though, Mitra argues, the only answer lies in creating a properly functioning market for the buying and selling of land, and removing the distortions that prevent market forces doing their work (distortions that politicians and power brokers exploit for their own profit). For example, the government in West Bengal imposes restrictions on how much land an individual farmer may own, preventing the consolidation of land holdings into more economically viable plots, and ensuring that the fragmentation of holdings that so hampers land acquisition is perpetuated. Tenant farmers are given the right to remain permanently on land they have long cultivated, but these rights cannot be bought or sold: in this way, the value of the land to the owner is depressed, while a tenant is effectively trapped on the land with no way to realize the value of his or her right to farm it.

The way that land is zoned in India also causes a huge distortion in the market, and is one of the single largest sources of corruption in the country today – the reason that property came top of that KPMG survey[13] of the most corrupt business sectors. Most of India's land is classified (zoned) as exclusively for agricultural use; in order to build a factory or a block of flats, the land needs to be re-zoned for that purpose. The problem is that there is a huge demand for such re-zoned land (for land classified as suitable for industrial or residential use), and an acute shortage of supply, raising its price.

What this means in practice is that a property developer can reap huge rewards by buying agricultural land and then convincing officials to have it re-zoned for housing or other development, a decision that raises the value of the land by a large multiple in an instant. In other words, re-zoning land can generate huge profits overnight at the stroke of a bureaucrat's pen. The system, as we shall see in Chapters 10 and 11, has been exploited to enrich politicians and politically connected business people. Indeed, it has become a major source of illicit campaign finance in India today.

Since the state clearly cannot not be trusted to allocate land fairly, or to arbitrate honestly in disputes, Mitra argues that the only solution is to let market forces do their work and remove all of the government-imposed restrictions. Abolish stamp duty, registration fees and taxes on land transfers, and the incentive to lie to the authorities about the true market price of land is removed. Abolish zoning restrictions, and the yawning imbalance between supply and demand, and the absurd, immense power of a bureaucrat's pen, will be dramatically reduced. No more second-guessing of farmers' desires or intentions: let the market set the price of land, and let landowners decide whether they want to sell at the price industry or government is offering, or not.

Land is the primary asset of hundreds of millions of poor people, but – because of market failure – not an asset they can easily monetize. A government survey in 2006 found that roughly 40 per cent of Indian farmers would like to sell their land and move to more profitable occupations, but can't find buyers.[14] Archaic land laws are preventing them capitalizing their only asset, just as they are preventing huge capital investments in development projects. Rewriting them to create a true market for land could be the most empowering reform any Indian politician could dream of undertaking.

Mitra has other radical suggestions, too, like decentralizing the power to set land regulations to local governments. Individual communities, he argues, would then have a more direct say in whether they wanted to attract industrial or residential development, or mining projects, to their areas, rather than policy being set in distant state and national capitals. 'Experimentation by local government would be a good learning experience for all stakeholders. The better-performing local governments would attract investment, and the worse-performing ones will experience flight of capital. Both will have an incentive to learn.' It might seem like a pipe-dream at the moment, but the idea would allow local people to hold their elected representatives to account more directly, and cut corruption too. Mitra calculates that the amount of 'black money' generated each year from land and property transactions accounts for between 1 and 2 per cent of gross domestic product, and could amount to 25 per cent of local domestic product in cities like New Delhi and Mumbai where property prices are astronomical. 'No wonder,' he rues, 'there are no takers within any of the major political parties for such fundamental change.'

Of course, to create a free market for land requires confronting the issue of contested titles that affects hundreds of millions of plots. Mitra has an ingenious solution, which is essentially to build a new computerized set of land records from the grassroots up. His Liberty Institute, together with a rural development organization in the western state of Gujarat, Action Research in Community Health, has set out to help villagers map their plots and submit those claims to the authorities. They have lent out hand-held GPS sets, and shown

villagers how to use them. Local village bodies would approve or
reject the claims that are documented in this way; rival claimants
would have a fixed time period to appeal against the rulings.[15]

He was taking advantage of a bill that was passed by the government in 2006 that gave tribal groups and long-established
forest-dwellers title rights to the land they were cultivating, much to
the dismay of environmentalists. This was an opportunity to lay
down a new database of land titles, in areas where none had existed
until now.

So far, the project is only being rolled out in a few villages on forest
land in the western state of Gujarat. But it could spread, he hopes,
and provide some ground-up momentum for the proper recording of
individual plots, as well as popular pressure for people's rights to buy
and sell those plots. It could, Mitra hoped, be the first step towards a
free market for land.

Singur, of course, was not the first flagship project in India to run into
opposition over land.

Dams were the 'temples of modern India', a central plank in
Prime Minister Jawaharlal Nehru's vision of a state-directed semi-
socialist industrial transformation of the new nation. There would,
of course, be victims – ordinary people pushed out of the way – but
they were relatively unimportant in the very grand scheme of things,
when the future was being built. But then a young woman called
Medha Patkar, the daughter of social workers, who was studying at
the Tata Institute of Social Sciences in Mumbai, went on a study
tour of the Narmada Valley in the early 1980s. What she saw there,
in terms of the suffering of people displaced by a new dam, changed
her life, and India's path.[16]

The multi-billion-dollar Sardar Sarovar Dam was the centrepiece
of efforts to tap the waters of the Narmada, one of thirty dams planned
or being built on India's fifth-largest river. It promised electricity and
drinking water to tens of millions of homes and irrigation to nearly 2
million hectares of farmland through 50,000 miles of canals, longer

than the country's railway network. But it also threatened to displace hundreds of thousands of people.

For two and half decades, Patkar has led a campaign to rescue the poor of the Narmada Valley from losing their homes and their fields in the rising waters of the Sardar Sarovar. The Narmada Bachao Andolan, known as the NBA or Save the Narmada movement, has been a titanic struggle, one of the world's most celebrated social and environmental campaigns. The now grey-haired and steel-willed Patkar has staged several hunger strikes, fought protracted legal battles and organized countless mass demonstrations. There were riots, and even a suicide by self-immolation. The author and activist Arundhati Roy has written heartbreakingly about towns and villages submerged in the rising floodwaters, and argued passionately against the idea of big dams.[17]

In 2006, as China put the finishing touches to the Three Gorges Dam just nine years after first breaking ground, I travelled through the Narmada Valley beside Patkar on one of her many tours. Wherever she went, hundreds turned out to listen and cheer her on. Among her entourage she inspired devotion and not a little fear, her sheer force of will seeming at times all that was holding the waters back. The dam's benefits had been radically overstated, she told me: if all the promised canals were built, there would be scarcely any water left to power the turbines. 'They promise dreams and heavens,' she told me in an interview in the lee of a house beside the river. 'The benefits of the dam have always been overstated but the reality is different.'[18]

At that point, the Sardar Sarovar had already taken nearly three times as long as the Three Gorges Dam and was still far from complete. Nearly a decade had been lost to a dispute between rival states over the sharing of power and water from the dam before Patkar even emerged on the scene. Earlier, in front of the huge concrete wall of the dam, I had spoken to the affable project manager Pankaj Patel. 'The delay has been due to democracy,' he told me. 'We want to take a decision consensually, and for that we have to pay.'

This is India's lament, 'the cost of democracy' in time and money and missed opportunities. Some rue delays caused by the tiresome business of getting popular consent for major infrastructure investment projects, others rail against the country's corrupt and inept politicians or blame the poor's reluctance to embrace economic reforms that businesses might welcome. Some people cheerfully accept the cost of democracy, others complain bitterly, looking enviously at their giant northeastern neighbour. But as I contemplated the economic benefits but huge social and environmental costs of the Three Gorges Dam, I wondered if the cost of democracy was actually that high.

In the end, Patkar has slowed but not prevented the government of Gujarat from gradually raising the height of the dam; but she won her battle to force the state to significantly raise the resettlement and rehabilitation packages it offered the displaced. She helped force the World Bank to pull out of the project and to re-examine its policy towards big dams; even today she is still fighting to force the state to honour its promises to the displaced.

It is hard to make a considered independent judgement of the Sardar Sarovar Dam until the project is complete – unless and until, for example, its promised irrigation canals are built and filled. But it is worth noting that the Supreme Court of India judged in 2000 that the dam's promised benefits far outweighed the costs to the displaced. Nevertheless, without Medha Patkar, the debate would not even have taken place: the people in the dam-affected area would simply have been pushed aside.

China may one day come to regret the environmental and social consequences of its ruthless rush for riches, and the Three Gorges Dam will not necessarily be remembered as a triumph of Communist rule. While India still dreams of damming more rivers to feed its ever-growing need for energy, it is much less likely to treat the displaced as though they don't exist.

This is the strength of Indian democracy, its ability to empower those who would ordinarily not have a voice, its ability to broker a compromise between powerful vested interests at the top of the tree and everyone else down below. Without democracy, those vested interests would surely corner the benefits of economic advancement even more thoroughly than they already do, and the poor would be further marginalized. The compromises reached are often messy, they often take an age to negotiate, and are seldom optimal. Like many compromises, they seldom make everyone happy, but they may be better than the alternative.

In March 2007, I travelled to the site of a planned bauxite mine in the forested Niyamgiri Hills, in a remote corner of the eastern state of Odisha, where the 8,000-strong Dongria Kondh tribe were resisting the plans of Britain's Vedanta Resources to strip the top off their ancient hilltop home and dig a huge opencast mine. So sure were Vedanta of the official go-ahead for their project that they had already constructed a $900 million alumina refinery beside the hills.

As dusk drew in and the lights of the refinery dominated the night sky, I visited the village of Bandhaguda, right up against the wall of the plant. There, villagers told me that Vedanta had already walled off part of their land to build the refinery, cutting them off from their pond, cremation ground and some of their fields. When they staged a peaceful protest, thirty-two of them had been jailed for seven days and held with scarcely any food and water.

The refinery manager, Sanjeev Zutshi, contested that version of events, but in the process he revealed much about the way India had operated, and the way it was gradually changing. 'The days are gone when you can impose yourself, surround yourself with goons and policemen, and browbeat every Tom, Dick and Harry,' he told me. 'It's not going to work, it's not a long-term solution at all.'[19]

That a company like Vedanta, which is no stranger to controversy, was beginning to think like that – or at least pay lip service to the idea – was a true leap foward. (Much later, the Supreme Court was to rule that mining could not be undertaken in the Niyamgiri area without the consent of the local community.)

It should be obvious from these accounts that the state cannot be trusted to arbitrate between the rival claims of big business and small farmers to land in India, and indeed that collusion between the government and the private sector has been a disaster; that dishonest property deals are a major source of the corruption in India today; and that huge vested interests are opposed to reform.

Democracy and the media have exposed these facts as never before, and helped farmers stand up for their rights. But in the years that followed, it was not just farmers who were fighting against the predations of the corrupt elite. The battle to rid India of the cancer of graft, to end the abuse of power that had become embedded in its political system, shifted from India's villages to its urban centres. At its forefront were not rural folk, but young, middle-class residents of the nation's fast-growing towns and cities. By 2011, huge swathes of urban India had risen against corruption.

8

Get Up, Stand Up

India Against Corruption galvanizes the middle class

'You have lit a torch against corruption. Do not extinguish it until India is free from corruption.'
The India Against Corruption leader, Anna Hazare,
speaking to thousands of cheering supporters
as he was released from jail in August 2011

It was the summer of 2011, a year of global protests, of the Arab Spring and Occupy Wall Street, and India had risen up too. People had taken to the streets in their millions. They were not trying to overthrow a dictatorship, but to effect a change that was, in a sense, no less fundamental. They wanted to overthrow a system of corruption, nepotism and vested interests, to expose a cosy conspiracy between the nation's political and business elite, and to excise the rotten heart of its bureaucracy.

Thousands of people had gathered on a scruffy expanse of grass and dirt in the heart of New Delhi to support a 74-year-old man who had threatened to starve himself to death unless the government established a strong, independent authority to investigate and prosecute the corrupt. Everyone in that crowd had a story to tell, such as Amit Bharadwaj, a 28-year-old call centre worker, a thin, bearded, bespectacled man with a chain of small beads around his neck, who was still troubled by the bribe he had been forced to pay three months before to get a birth certificate for his newborn son.

On his first visit to the registrar's office, he had been turned away, supposedly because there wasn't a stamp. When he returned a second time, he was told that no doctor was available to sign the form. Finally, the official gestured to him, to make it clear that he wanted money. Reluctantly, Bharadwaj handed over 1,000 rupees ($20).[1]

'I hated it,' he said, miming how the official had greedily counted the notes in full public view. 'I had hatred for myself and for him. This was the first thing I did for my newborn son.'

It was hot, humid and intermittently drizzling, and there were puddles of water on the ground. Outside, turbaned old men in long white kurtas, with dhotis wrapped around their waists, stood hunched over their walking sticks in the queue to get in, next to groups of women in colourful floral printed sarees, and university students carrying Indian flags. Inside, on a small stage, the white-haired Anna Hazare sat cross-legged on his fast, dressed in homespun white cotton and a white Gandhi cap, under a huge black and white image of the Mahatma. Close by, musicians played devotional and patriotic songs, and activists and ordinary people came up to the microphone one by one to give short messages of support. Thousands of people sheltered under a massive tent, chanting, singing, reading newspapers and handbills, or crowded around at a desk to buy placards, flags and caps with the words 'I am Anna' written down each side in Hindi. The mood was full of promise and optimism, a sense that the wrongs they had suffered could at last be redressed.

There were retired bureaucrats who had been passed over for promotion throughout their careers because they had refused to sanction corrupt deals, young people who had joined the movement through Facebook and Twitter and were now showing up in person, schoolgirls who had seen the headlines and wanted to catch a glimpse of Anna Hazare. There were retired bank employees like Balbir Singh, who had been transferred far from home because he refused to sign documents allowing his bosses to falsify accounts, and said it was 'difficult to breathe if you want to be honest in this country'. There were public-sector workers like Triloki Nath Sharma, who had been denied his pension for over a year because he refused to bribe the pension officers.

'People just kept accepting all the injustices and corruption silently for too long,' he said. 'I told them: "This is my money that I earned with my blood and sweat, this is my right." But they kept delaying. They would say, we can't find your file. Or the officer is on leave. Or you need to bring some more papers and sign on more files. I finally got fed up and paid them. I was very angry but finally I had to surrender.'

Soft-spoken 24-year-old Jaipreet Singh, a turbaned Sikh, had just joined his father's business making filters for ships. 'In our business, we have to apply for government tenders,' he explained. 'And it is impossible to get a tender without giving a bribe to the officials. My father built this business, but he used to pay bribes to get ahead, win tenders. But I told him I would not pay bribes. Why should we? We lost a tender recently because I refused to pay. There are a number of arguments between my father and me at home over this.'

The India Against Corruption movement had galvanized the country, and the government was bewildered and on the run. From Facebook to fasting, it had married India old and new in a blitzkrieg campaign; it had cobbled together a crowd-pulling line-up of leaders, including two yoga gurus with huge followings and vast business empires, a smattering of activists and lawyers, all grouped under the supposedly Gandhian figure of Hazare. They were a motley crew, but for a while the chemistry worked and the spark ignited.

The flames were fed by India's brash new twenty-four-hour television news culture, which was engaged in a cut-throat battle for ratings and had recently discovered the power of anger and outrage to draw in middle-class viewers. This was an issue made for TV. But the flames were also surely fed by a feeling of deeply hurt pride in the way the huge corruption scandals that erupted in 2010 had dragged down India's national image and sense of self. Exasperation with a government that seemed weak, incompetent and irredeemably corrupt was part of the story, fuelling a feeling that corruption was now eating away at the nation's soul. An interventionist Comptroller and Auditor General can also take some of the credit. But the flames were also fed by the oxygen of social media, which was for the first time consciously employed in India to mobilize people behind a cause. Just as social media had been critical elsewhere is the world in giving people a voice and building support behind a cause before people even took to the streets, so in India Facebook proved critical in mobilizing a young urban middle class behind the anti-corruption movement. India Against Corruption represented an important moment in the deepening of Indian democracy by engaging an entirely new set of people in a mass movement, and fusing the anger of the middle class with the impatience of youth, to offer a quick answer to an age-old problem.

The man who sensed and exploited this moment – but who admits to being staggered by how quickly the movement took off – was a former tax inspector-turned-RTI activist named Arvind Kejriwal, a small, slightly built man, with spectacles and a moustache, his clothes worn loose and his shirt often untucked. Indeed, so staggered was he by this phenomenon that Kejriwal told me he had been forced to reconsider his previously held atheism, to consider the possibility that his movement was being directed by a higher power.

Kejriwal's life as an activist had begun while he was still with the income tax department, founding an organization called Parivartan that started out helping citizens with income-tax issues and obtaining food rations. He joined the campaign for the Right to Information Act, and then used the law to expose massive corruption in public works in New Delhi. In one hard-hitting study, they found that seven out of ten projects run by the Municipal Corporation of Delhi were 'ghost projects' where no work had been carried out at all. A former colleague remembers him as 'dynamic, full of energy and idealism, with a spirit that is very infectious, also . . . a decent man when all is said and done'. He was the sort of man who would wake up at 2 a.m. and start working if something occurred to him. But with Kejriwal's tremendous drive also came extreme 'impatience' – a word I was to hear over and over again when talking to people who worked with him – and a lack of tolerance for other points of view. 'I didn't find his way of functioning very democratic,' the former colleague said. 'He didn't have very much time for other people's ideas, and there was certainly not much space for dissent.'

By 2010, Kejriwal had become a major figure in the National Campaign for the People's Right to Information (NCPRI), alongside Aruna Roy, Shekhar Singh and Nikhil Dey, the umbrella body that was shepherding the entire movement. This was the time of the massive scams that had undermined Manmohan Singh's government, with the media baying over corruption in the Commonwealth Games and in the allocation of 2G telecom spectrum. For all the noise, heads had not yet rolled, and the government was doing its best to bury its head in the sand. Something, Kejriwal decided, needed to be done.

Kejriwal began working with his colleagues at the NCPRI on a series of initiatives meant to build on the success of the RTI Act, looking at a series of measures to establish an anti-corruption ombudsman, protect whistleblowers, clean up the judiciary and improve the delivery of public services. The solution he came up with was typical Kejriwal, bundling everything up into the office of a powerful new Citizen's Anti-Corruption Ombudsman, the Jan Lokpal, with the authority to prosecute corruption at every level of government, from the Prime Minister right down to the lowliest bureaucracy and across to the judiciary. The idea of the agency, or Lokpal, had been around since the early 1960s, and there had been many unsuccessful attempts to get legislation through parliament in the decades that followed. But Kejriwal's idea was to give the Lokpal almost unlimited scope and power, and so to create a magic wand that could wish away corruption in a flourish. Many of his fellow travellers in the RTI movement were uncomfortable with that idea, fearing it would create a parallel bureaucracy and police force without the necessary checks and balances, but Kejriwal brushed off their objections and went straight to the people for support.

The RTI campaign had been built on years of patient grassroots activism, almost one 'muster roll' at a time. Kejriwal had no time for this kind of approach. The time was ripe for a nationwide anti-corruption movement, and the crowds just needed to be summoned, he believed. His recruits were designed to do exactly that, even if the seeds of the movement's eventual demise can arguably be traced back to the allies he chose in such a hurry to assemble the crowds.

Baba Ramdev was India's most popular yoga guru, with an empire of his own, a massive following among the lower middle classes and in the small towns of India, and at least 30 million viewers for his daily two-hour television show.[2] To add a touch of polish, there was Sri Sri Ravi Shankar, another popular New Age spiritual leader with a reputation for catering to the rich and famous through his Art of Living Foundation. Then there was the figurehead, the man who could represent simplicity and honesty and draw in both the middle classes and rural folk, the movement's Mahatma Gandhi, as the media soon began to call him: Anna Hazare was a former army truck-driver who had championed the Right to Information movement in the western state of Maharashtra, and ousted several ministers. But he was also a rural ascetic with a simple, earthy charm, who was reputed to have turned his home village of Ralegan Siddhi into a model of development and alcohol-free clean living.

There were others too, who provided a bit more intellectual depth and a stronger track record of activism. Kiran Bedi had first come to public attention – and earned the nickname Crane Bedi[3] – when in 1982, as a young member of the Delhi Traffic Police, she had dared to tow Indira Gandhi's car for a parking violation while the then prime minister was visiting the United States. She went on to have a distinguished career in the police force, known for her outspoken views and for reforming Delhi's notorious Tihar jail before resigning in 2007 to involve herself in social work. There was the distinguished father–son team of lawyers, Shanti and Prashant Bhushan,[4] who had been involved in a long campaign against corruption in the judiciary, and had also played a key role in legal efforts to expose the 2G spectrum allocation scam, as well as public interest cases against Enron, Pepsi and Coca-Cola. Justice Santosh Hegde, a former Supreme Court judge, had served with distinction as the anti-corruption ombudsman in the southern state of Karnataka and exposed a massive illegal mining scam.

Together, the media soon christened them Team Anna.

They made a relatively muted entry on the scene in October 2010, demanding the government level charges against those responsible for swindling the nation in the run-up to the Commonwealth Games, and calling the government's inquiry committee an 'eyewash'. But, thanks largely to tireless work behind the scenes from former journalist Shivendra Singh Chauhan, the campaign started to gather momentum on Facebook. On 30 January 2011, on the anniversary of Gandhi's murder, around 5,000 people gathered in New Delhi to demand the Jan Lokpal be established. Organizers said that demonstrations were staged in sixty towns and cities across India, as well as among Indians in New York, Washington, Chicago and Los Angeles.

In April, Hazare staged a dramatic hunger strike at the Jantar Mantar protest site in New Delhi, threatening to fast until death unless the government agreed to establish the Jan Lokpal. But it was only when the media led by the aggressive and populist Times Now channel swung behind Hazare that momentum really snowballed. The channel's editor and anchor Arnab Goswami had already been using the stick of corruption to beat the government, and – once he had overcome his distaste for social activists – this seemed like perfect territory. On Tuesday, when the fast began, Times Now added its weight to the campaign. 'India's crusade against corruption,' it proclaimed as it kicked off breathless live coverage of the event, 'India in one voice.' 'India for Anna.' If you were a real patriot, a true citizen of India, Goswami told his viewers, you'd be at Jantar Mantar. By Wednesday, a profile of Goswami in India's *Caravan* magazine later reported,[5] the two other main English-language channels had dispatched reporters and satellite trucks to the venue. By Thursday, there were forty-two outside-broadcast vans at the venue, and tens of thousands of Indians. They were of all ages, but mostly English-speaking. In just a few days, a powerful symbiosis had developed between India's new issue-driven and sensation-hungry visual media, and the activists' need for a force multiplier. It would very likely have happened without Goswami, but he had certainly staked his claim as the leader of the pack. The government panicked, inviting 'Team Anna' to take part in a joint committee, with five members from each side, to draft a new Lokpal Bill. On Saturday, Anna called off his fast. 'Like Tahrir Square in Egypt . . . history will show that Jantar Mantar was the moment that triggered change in our country,' wrote Rajeev Chandrasekhar.[6] It was a widely held view.

Sadly, things were not to be quite that easy. When the drafting committee convened, neither side appeared in much of a mood to compromise, or frankly even to negotiate seriously. The two sides were miles apart on the question of the scope of the new anti-corruption agency. Should it target just politicians and senior bureaucrats, or everyone in public office, including judges and the Prime Minister? Would there be separate bodies in each of India's states to combat corruption there? How would the new body's chief be chosen? The government wanted to pack the selection committee with ministers, Hazare and Kejriwal wanted a committee dominated by independent figures. The government came across as insincere, while 'Team Anna' was intransigent.

In retrospect, the government may have miscalculated in the composition of the committee who were constituted to draw up the Lokpal law. Excluding opposition parties left Congress looking isolated, while a failure to insist on the inclusion of people like Aruna Roy, who could have represented a broader spread of 'civil society' opinion, as well as people from other walks of life, only served to bolster Team Anna's self-regarding claims to be speaking for the entire nation.

As negotiations broke down, the atmosphere turned nasty. The government's draft bill was a 'cruel joke', said Anna, as he promised to go on another fast on 16 August, the day after India celebrated its Independence from British rule. The Hazare team were 'armchair fascists, overground Maoists and closet anarchists', said Congress party spokesman Manish Tewari,[7] while Anna himself was 'corrupt' because a trust he ran had supposedly spent money illegally for his birthday celebration. The nation's twenty-four-hour news channels, such allies in getting the movement off the ground, now began to have a more pernicious effect on proceedings, endlessly repeating the barbs that were thrown until the other side was goaded into an equally intemperate response. A negotiation conducted in the full glare of a news media that thrived on conflict and drama soon proved to be an impossible act to sustain. But such was the anti-corruption movement's fascination with their new-found television stardom that they seemed unable to retreat behind closed doors.[8]

At the same time, the first cracks began to appear in the once united front against corruption. Kejriwal's no-compromise style had alienated many of his fellow leaders from the RTI movement: Team Anna's declaration that the bill should be passed without a comma being changed seemed to negate the very principle of public consultation that they so passionately believed in. The implication that anyone who opposed Team Anna's vision was a government toady only alienated the activists further, and gradually they started giving voice to their objections. The RTI had been successful because it had empowered individual people, argued Aruna Roy, while Kejriwal's Jan Lokpal would concentrate power in the hands of a vast and bloated new anti-corruption bureaucracy and police force. 'It could become a Frankenstein's Monster,' she warned in an interview released in August, warning of the dangers of evil things created by good men.[9]

At the time, Hazare and Kejriwal and their team were widely accused of undermining the great institution of Indian democracy. Critics blamed them for holding parliament to ransom by staging hunger strikes and demanding their version of legislation be passed. They were accused of an attack on the sovereignty of parliament, of an unconstitutional form of blackmail. But that analysis ignored the fact that parliament's credibility had been undermined not by Kejriwal and Hazare, but by parliamentarians themselves, through their criminality and contempt for proper debate.

It was also self-evident that a Lokpal could not be established by any other method than by an act of parliament, and lawmakers would only vote if they felt it was in their interests – in other words, if popular pressure made it so. Indeed, what better way for parliament to restore some of the credibility it had frittered away than by taking effective measures to curb corruption? Kejriwal and company were uncompromising in their rhetoric, but that was, after all, *rhetoric*, the lifeblood of any democracy.

Indeed, in some senses, Kejriwal had given Indian democracy a shot in the arm. Traditionally, Indian politicians looked to the rich for money and to the poor for votes – the middle class were neither big enough as a constituency nor involved enough in politics to matter. Indeed, India may be unique in the world in having a higher turnout among the poor than among the middle classes, at least in big cities like Delhi, Mumbai and Bengaluru. Kejriwal, by harnessing social media and with the support of twenty-four-hour television news, had brought the middle classes onto the streets and into the centre of the debate. And since when had a single piece of legislation been so endlessly debated, both on the television screens and between ordinary Indians? Agree or disagree with Kejriwal's proposals, but outrage seemed far healthier for the nation than complacency.

By August, 12 million people had registered their support for the anti-corruption movement by ringing a campaign hotline and logging a missed call, while more than 60,000 had sent emails to government officials. Their engagement was not entirely transitory. Less than eighteen months later, long after the anti-corruption movement peaked, the middle class was out on the streets again, to protest against the rape and murder of J and to call for stiffer laws to protect women. Many of the people I met at those protests in New Delhi had also attended Hazare's second fast at Ramlila Maidan; they had glimpsed the possibility of change, and of making a positive contribution to that change, and they wanted more of the same. When Justice Verma called for suggestions from the public about what laws needed to be changed to protect women better, he received an unprecedented 80,000 submissions from all over the country, and says all were carefully considered: how was that for popular participation in democracy?

My own dealings with Kejriwal did not start happily in the summer of 2011. We met for a brief interview, but there was a succession of interruptions as aides rushed in or calls needed answering, so I never felt I had his full attention. Some time later, I asked if he could help us meet Hazare, only to be told that the movement's figurehead was not currently doing interviews. Pretty soon we established that this was not actually true, when my colleague Rama Lakshmi tracked Hazare down through an aide and spoke to him at some length over the telephone. It was my first inkling of the control that Kejriwal was trying to exert over the message, and the hidden rivalries that would later emerge between the two men. Indeed, I quickly began to suspect that India Against Corruption was already descending into a battle of egos, after another member of the team complained on more than one occasion that I had interviewed him but not used his name in a story, quoting Kejriwal and Hazare instead. That the story was sympathetic to the cause seemed, to this person who I will still not name, to be of secondary importance.

More and more Indians started to feel a little uncomfortable with the movement and its leaders. The drawbacks of Kejriwal's impatience started growing more obvious. Team Anna had been assembled with one overriding objective in mind – its ability to pull in the crowds, and pull them in quickly. But in the process Kejriwal had taken on board a distinctly loose cannon in Baba Ramdev.

Ramdev was associated with the Hindu nationalist right wing, and in particular with its paramilitary volunteer wing, the Rashtriya Swayamsevak Sangh (RSS), an organization that has used charitable work to spread its ideology but with which many Indians are uncomfortable. All over the country, members of the RSS and its sister political party, the BJP, took up prominent roles in the India Against Corruption movement, fostering a sense of partisanship that began to make some people uncomfortable.

Ramdev[10] cut a striking figure, with his bushy black beard and ponytail, with saffron-coloured robes slung across his shoulders. He had a genius for self-promotion, and always seemed to know where the cameras were – the image I most associate with Ramdev is seeing him greeting some filmstar or politician, but at the same time twisting his body so that his broad smile faced the lens and his hairy chest filled half of the shot.

Born to illiterate parents in a poor farming family, Ramdev had built up a multi-million-dollar global business empire based on yoga, deep breathing and herbal medicine. His ashram in northern India boasts a yoga school, a hospital, and a factory making herbal medicine based on ancient Hindu texts. His reach spans the planet, with more than forty satellite centres across the world and a remote Scottish island – renamed Peace Island – where he planned to establish another ashram.

Controlled breathing techniques, yoga and a daily intake of 'holy' basil leaves can cure cancer, he taught his followers. Sex education in schools should be replaced by yoga classes to stop the spread of HIV and AIDS, he argued, while homosexuality is a mental disease that only yoga can 'cure'. He was also determined to purge India of polluting foreign influences, denouncing the World Health Organization as an agent of Western pharmaceutical companies, recommending multinational companies be thrown out of India and foreign goods boycotted, and deriding Pepsi and Coke as 'toilet cleaners'. The corrupt should be put to death, he said, along with rapists, murderers and terrorists. It is one of the many contradictions of Ramdev that he himself has been accused – notably by investigative journalists at the magazine *Tehelka*[11] – of having built his own empire on a network of corrupt deals and tax evasion. The government eventually served him with a demand for more than 5 crore rupees – 50 million rupees – for unpaid taxes on his yoga camps stretching back years.[12]

It was always going to be hard to keep Ramdev chained to someone else's movement, and so it proved. In June he launched his own hunger strike in New Delhi, with a call for 'black money', the proceeds of corruption that have been stashed in foreign bank accounts to evade the law and the tax man, to be seized for the nation and repatriated. The government panicked. Four ministers rushed to receive Ramdev at the airport where he arrived in his private jet, but they failed to convince him to call off his fast. Four days later, at midnight on 5 June, they took an altogether different approach, the police wading in with tear gas to break up the protests. Ramdev's protest had been something of a family affair, with children and grandmothers from around the country camped out on Ramlila Maidan to see and support their guru. The police were indiscriminate, allegedly beating anyone who crossed their paths with lathis, the steel-tipped canes that serve as a primitive form of crowd control here. One man died. Under the cover of darkness, Ramdev snuck away, dressed in women's clothes, presumably under a big veil to cover his dense black beard.

Looking back, Kiran Bedi told me Ramdev's solo protest was the first crack in the anti-corruption movement's unity, and the first chapter in its eventual downfall. But the government's brutal response papered over that crack, and kept public sentiment squarely behind the movement. Failing to reach agreement with Team Anna, the government introduced its version of the Lokpal Bill into parliament. Anna Hazare announced that his second fast would begin on 16 August, and threatened to continue 'unto death'. With the nation standing together, he said, the government 'will fall short of batons and bullets'.

On the morning of 16 August, as Hazare and his colleagues were preparing to set out from their homes and headquarters in New Delhi, the police swooped again. Hazare, Kejriwal, Bedi and Shanti Bhushan were all arrested, on the grounds that they lacked official permission to stage the protest at their chosen venue. Refusing to call off their protest, they were sentenced to seven days judicial custody and dispatched to Tihar jail, where, ironically, they joined the disgraced Telecom Minister A. Raja and Commonwealth Games organizer Suresh Kalmadi, the very people whose transgressions had inspired their movement. Police said 1,400 protesters had been detained in Delhi, while activists claimed 20,000 people had been detained across the country. It was a monumentally stupid move by the government, surrendering every inch of the moral high ground to Hazare. Protests erupted all over India, and 'I am Anna' caps were suddenly the nation's most fashionable headgear. Within twenty-four hours, 120,000 Indians had signed an online petition demanding his release, while hundreds of thousands more signalled their approval on Facebook and Twitter. 'Corrupt, repressive and stupid' was the verdict of the respected newspaper *The Hindu*.[13]

By the evening, the government was desperately trying to back down, but Hazare, sensing the power of his position, refused to emerge from jail unless the police relaxed their restrictions on the venue and the length of protest that would be allowed. Hazare once more donned the mantle of Mahatma Gandhi, declaring in a video message that the 'second freedom struggle' had begun. 'The protests should not stop,' he said. 'The time has come for no jail in the country to have a free space.' Thousands of supporters gathered outside Tihar, carrying placards saying 'The corrupt are selling the nation' and chanting 'We are with you Anna'.[14] They were farmers, tradesmen, retired army officers, government employees, teachers and even schoolchildren in uniform. 'We have had a fire in us for a long time, but we have never found this kind of an opportunity and a leader we can trust like Anna,' said 63-year-old retired insurance company executive Om Prakash Bakshi. 'We have woken up now. Nobody can stop us. We will root out this corruption from the nation's blood.' My colleague Rama asked police officer Kuldip Singh if he supported the protests. 'Must you ask?' he replied, and laughed. Many other policemen said they also backed Hazare's demands. These were heady days, full of optimism, with India's desire for a fresh, clean start drawing attention all over the world.

On 17 August, Manmohan Singh accused Hazare of trying to circumvent democracy. 'The question before the nation is who drafts the law and who makes the law,' he said in parliament, speaking from a prepared text in an almost unintelligible monotone to jeers from the

opposition. 'We will not allow anyone to question the sole prerogative of parliament to make the law.' Hazare, he said, might be 'inspired
by high ideals' but his attempt to impose his will on parliament 'is
totally misconceived and fraught with grave consequences for our
parliamentary democracy'.[15]

But the nation was not listening, at least not to Singh. As he spoke,
a friend wondered on Facebook what the 'droning sound' was in the
background. 'Was it a mosquito perhaps?' But the problem was not
just Singh's wooden delivery, nor the wording of a proposed piece of
legislation: it was about the right to protest and the government's
ham-fisted attempts to deal with the crisis. 'Has the government lost
all sense of statecraft, or how a political agitation should be dealt
with?' asked the senior BJP leader Arun Jaitley at his scornful best,
accusing the government of smugness, arrogance, and of trying to
silence its critics. 'The truth is that India today is exasperated with
corruption. India today is exasperated with the political leadership of
this government.'

The very next day, Hazare won Round One, receiving permission
to stage his protest at Ramlila Maidan, a bald patch of land in front
of Delhi's historic Red Fort, for at least two weeks. The Ramlila
ground hosts religious festival celebrations and political rallies, but is
perhaps best remembered for a huge protest against Indira Gandhi in
the hours before she imposed emergency rule in June 1975. Hazare's
choice of venue sent a very deliberate message to Indira's successors at
the helm of the Congress party. A sea of people greeted his emergence
from jail on 19 August, and surrounded his vehicle as it made a slow
procession from the jail to the protest venue. Lawyers, trade associa-
tions, and even business leaders spoke out in support, or turned up in
protest.[16] Finally, parliament bowed to the popular mood, passing a
'sense of the House' resolution accepting Hazare's three main demands
– for a citizen's charter to punish officials who failed to deliver public
services on time, for the Lokpal to cover the lower bureaucracy as well
as its top ranks, and for parallel anti-corruption bodies to be established in each of India's states. The Prime Minister wrote to Hazare

assuring him on the same three points. On 28 August, in front of
what the media called 'a sea of humanity', after twelve days without
food, Anna Hazare 'suspended' his fast, and the country celebrated.

Ironically, that was the movement's peak. Over the next few
months, Hazare and Kejriwal repeatedly misfired as they attempted
to maintain the pressure on the government to pass a strong Lokpal
Bill. Hazare's insistence that he was the voice of India's 1.2 billion
people did not strike quite the right note of humility. Nor did he stick
to the Gandhian script of non-violence, proclaiming first that corrupt
politicians should be hanged, and then that alcoholics should be
flogged. When an anti-corruption demonstrator struck an Indian
politician in the face, Hazare hastily tweeted 'Just one slap?' before
quickly retracting his words. An October vow of silence, another
Gandhian practice rooted in Hindu tradition, was more farcical than
forceful, as Hazare kept up a steady stream of tweets and statements
throughout his nineteen days of supposed restraint and reflection.

At the same time, Hazare's credibility suffered as he moved into the
dangerous world of electoral politics, and cemented the impression
that the movement was cosying up to the Hindu nationalist opposition. First, he told his supporters to vote against a candidate from the
ruling party in a parliamentary by-election in October, then he
branded the Congress party 'traitors' for again watering down the
Lokpal Bill. Invited to condemn the BJP in similar terms for failing
to endorse some of his key proposals, he simply walked out of a news
conference.[17]

In the second half of 2011, the government also began a concerted
campaign to investigate and smear Team Anna, striking a damaging
blow when they accused Bedi of falsifying her travel expenses. It was
the usual tactic, ignore the message and attack the messenger, but this
time it appeared to be partially successful. By December, the government had backed away from its promises and had watered down the
Lokpal Bill, but Hazare and Kejriwal seemed to have lost the nation
and the media's attention. The very rigidity, dogmatism and single-
mindedness that had been an asset in their early days had begun to

sound tiresome, and the debate over the finer points of the legislation had failed to hold the popular imagination. (Indeed many people may have supported the movement without being entirely convinced by every comma in the proposed Jan Lokpal Bill.) In December, Hazare staged another fast in Mumbai, but only a few thousand supporters showed up – the empty spaces cruelly highlighted by the same media who had once championed their cause – and the protest was abandoned after only a day, ostensibly because of Hazare's health. He would later claim that he had been forced into the hunger strike against his better judgement, and was ill for months afterwards.[18]

In parliament, a series of bills were drawn up to increase the accountability of the judiciary and the bureaucracy and to protect whistleblowers. As we will discuss in more detail in the next chapter, the watered-down Lokpal Bill itself was passed by the lower house of parliament, but failed to win the backing of the upper house as a mass of amendments divided the government and the opposition. With a special session of parliament descending into chaos, the speaker suspended proceedings at midnight on 29 December 2011, and the momentum was lost.

Bedi says she now realizes that the movement should have declared victory in the summer, and then let parliamentary debate run its course. A weaker Lokpal might have been passed, but could have been improved upon at a later date. Instead, the maximalist position adopted by Team Anna turned off the movement's supporters, weakened its credibility, and let the government off the hook. 'We had the trophy right there, and we could have grabbed it,' she told me in an interview in her New Delhi office. Bedi has stayed close to Hazare, and laid the blame on Kejriwal's 'impatience' and the unsuccessful December fast. 'We didn't come to the finishing line. We were so close and yet so far. His impatience brought us to the running track, but his impatience also stopped us from getting over the finish line.'

Kejriwal had played the media and the numbers game beautifully at first, but both proved fickle friends. Media fatigue and popular fatigue fed off each other, and when numbers were disappointing, the cameras were trained not on the crowds but on the empty spaces.

The following year, the movement split in two. Again, Kejriwal was cast as the instigator, after he and Prashant Bhushan resolved to form a political party to push for change from within the system itself (a story we take up in Chapter 10). Hazare and many others were uncomfortable with the idea, and wanted to remain outside.

In the summer of 2012, the split was formalized after a bizarre protest in the Indian capital, and a staged show of public consultation. Another hunger strike was launched, with the diabetic Kejriwal now centre stage and only joined at a later date by a reluctant Hazare: its demand was patently unrealistic – an inquiry into the movement's allegations that the Prime Minister and fourteen of his cabinet members were corrupt – and there was even talk of martyrdom. But there was also a request for the public to advise them on how to carry the movement forward. In early August, they called off the fast. Kejriwal announced that the people had advised him to enter politics; a few days later Hazare and Bedi vowed to launch a fresh movement for a Jan Lokpal. Team Anna was formally disbanded.

This was classic Kejriwal, critical former colleagues asserted. 'Arvind doesn't like to listen,' said one activist who worked with him closely in the anti-corruption movement. 'Or rather, he generally consults only when he has already taken a decision.' A former friend from the Right to Information campaign agreed, saying Kejriwal's changes in direction and strategy tend to disorientate his fellow activists: 'He gives the impression of listening, but only accepts minor suggestions that fit in with the stream in which he is moving. And because the stream shifts so rapidly, others are not quite aware of where it is going. By and large, he ends up being surrounded by people who are really quite enamoured of him, and are willing to move and shift along with him.'

For Kejriwal, the split in Team Anna was a temporary setback, in a career that still had plenty of headline-grabbing gas. For the battle against corruption, it was perhaps a bigger blow, leaving many thousands of activists unsure of where their loyalties lay now and a lot less starry-eyed about the movement's leaders. For Bedi, it was a cruel defeat that has left her once again returning to her social work and her speaking engagements. The prize of the Lokpal is still within sight, she says, 'but it is gathering dust'.

'The first time [Hazare went on a fast], the system was shivering and we were really hurting their vote bank. Now people have lost interest, we've split, and people don't trust us any more. When we lost the trust, the gainer was the vested interest. They've bounced back.'

There is little doubt that Kejriwal overplayed what was a strong hand. And yet, despite all the dashed hopes, despite Bedi's bleak assessment that the vested interests had won, all was not lost. The anti-corruption movement did have lasting value in awakening this country to the evils that lurked within the state. In the end, a bill will probably be passed by parliament to establish a Lokpal in India, and although it will not be as strong as Kejriwal and Hazare had wanted, that might be a good thing. Legislation to protect whistleblowers and allow citizens to demand better service from the government is also surely not too far away, and although many people outside the anti-corruption movement can also take credit for this, those bills would represent significant progress.

While the country's two main political parties are arguably as corrupt as ever, the perils of public exposure are growing. The Congress-led coalition has been forced to sack five ministers for corruption since taking office in 2004, and the BJP was forced to turn its back on its only chief minister in the south of the country, Karnataka's B. S. Yeddyurappa, over corruption charges. Corruption may not be the sole factor determining electoral outcomes in India, but there is no doubt that it is a growing concern among voters. The young and aspirational middle class has woken up to the need to clean up the country, and is becoming a force for change. This is down, in part, to Kejriwal and people like him.

The issue that now faces India is whether this desire for change can translate into votes and political will. Will the people who took to the streets in 2011 shrug their shoulders, go back to their lives and decide that campaigning for change is futile? Or do they represent a deep disillusionment with the current political class that demands a reaction?

The question is whether enough political leaders can emerge in India who realize that honesty and good governance are not electoral liabilities, but are qualities that today's voters can relate to. And whether they can rise to the top of the parties to which they belong, and whether parliament, the beating heart of the nation's democracy, can truly reflect the Indian people's desire for a new way of governance. That is to say, can people's power trump entrenched vested interests?

9

How Can You Mend a Broken Heart?

The heart of India's democracy, parliament, is barely beating

'Whatever the Constitution may or may not provide, the welfare of the country will depend upon the way in which the country is administered. That will depend upon the men who administer it . . . There is a fissiparous tendency arising out of various elements in our life. We have communal differences, caste differences, language differences, provincial differences and so forth . . . Would to God that we shall have the wisdom and the strength to rise above them, and to serve the country which we have succeeded in liberating.'
Rajendra Prasad, President of India's Constituent Assembly, in his closing remarks to the Assembly, 26 November 1949. Prasad went on to serve as India's first President, from 1950 to 1962.

'People are asking, and I can hardly answer, that what is the purpose of retaining the Parliament of India? . . . It has become the place of political confrontation, not for the service of the country. Politics has become based on conflict between each other, only as a methodology to come to power, not for service to the people.'
Somnath Chatterjeee, Lok Sabha Speaker 2004–09, on NDTV's *The Big Fight*, 4 May 2013

It was 29 December 2011, and expectations could hardly have been higher. After months of nationwide street protests, after fasts and Facebook campaigns, after acrimonious negotiations between the

government and the anti-corruption movement, this was finally
parliament's moment. Before the lawmakers was a bill meant to
establish an anti-corruption ombudsman, a weaker body than Anna
Hazare and Arvind Kejriwal had demanded, but a potential mile-
stone nonetheless in the battle against corruption, a historic piece of
legislation being considered in the building that represented the
heart of Indian democracy.

The lower house of parliament, the Lok Sabha, had already given
its approval, and proceedings had moved to the upper house, the
Rajya Sabha. But time was running out fast. The government had
dragged its feet, and it had only scheduled one day to debate and pass
the bill before the year's end; the opposition and reluctant members
of the ruling coalition had introduced an incredible 187 amendments,
and discussions had been going around in circles. Failure to put the
bill to a vote before parliament was adjourned would force the whole
process back to square one, and momentum would be lost. At the
same time, however, it was becoming apparent that the government
faced defeat on several of these amendments as its coalition's fragile
unity crumbled. As the clock ticked, the televised debate transfixed
the nation, the ratings for live parliamentary proceedings surpassing
even those for the popular TV reality show *Big Boss*.

Then, with just over an hour to midnight, there was high drama
that might have seemed more appropriate to the reality show than to
the 'august House'. Government minister V. Narayanasamy was
replying to the debate, when the white-bearded lawmaker Rajniti
Prasad left his seat and approached him. As Chairman (Speaker) of
the House, Vice-President Hamid Ansari waved his hands rather inef-
fectually. 'Please go back to your seat,' he said. 'Please stop it. This is
wrong.' But Prasad was undeterred. He snatched a copy of the Lokpal
Bill from Narayanasamy's desk, tore it into two pieces and theatrically
threw the two halves up into the air, from whence they fluttered down
onto the floor. 'The Lokpal would not work,' he shouted, as parliament erupted.

For the next hour, there was chaos. Narayanasamy ploughed on with his speech, but the interruptions grew more frequent. Many of the troublemakers, like Prasad himself, came from parties that were supposed to be part of the ruling coalition government. Tempers rose so high that the Chairman, Ansari, was forced to order a fifteen-minute adjournment. The government blamed the opposition for introducing a 'web of confusion' with their amendments; the opposition appealed in vain for a vote, and accused the government, with some justification, of consciously choreographing the entire debate in such a way that voting would be impossible, in order to avoid an embarrassing defeat. They appealed to the Chairman to extend the session past midnight, and if necessary into the New Year.

The official parliamentary transcript[2] makes troubling reading. Picture India's bespectacled Vice-President Hamid Ansari in the chair, with receding hairline and white goatee, his bushy eyebrows rising and falling, his voice forlornly pleading for some respect.

MR. CHAIRMAN: Please . . . (Interruptions) . . . Please. This is not right . . . (Interruptions) . . . You can't do this. This is disgraceful . . . (Interruptions) . . . Hon. Members, an unprecedented situation has arisen. There appears to be a desire to outshout each other . . . (Interruptions) . . . Please . . . (Interruptions) . . . Let me finish. . . . (Interruptions) . . . Let me finish.

SHRI ARUN JAITLEY (BJP): Sir, there is a desire to avoid the vote . . . (Interruptions) . . .

MR. CHAIRMAN: There is total impasse . . . (Interruptions) . . .

SHRI S. S. AHLUWALIA (BJP): They are not . . . (Interruptions) . . .

MR. CHAIRMAN: Just a minute . . . (Interruptions) . . . The House cannot be conducted in this noise . . . (Interruptions) . . .

DR. V. MAITREYAN (AIADMK): No, Sir . . . (Interruptions) . . .

SHRI TAPAN KUMAR SEN (BJP (M)): Sir, let them . . . (Interruptions) . . . Let the Bill be taken up for consideration . . . (Interruptions) . . .

MR. CHAIRMAN: I know, but that requires . . . (Interruptions) . . . that requires orderly proceedings . . . (Interruptions) . . . I am afraid . . . (Interruptions) . . . I am afraid, the Chair has no option . . . (Interruptions) . . . most reluctantly . . . (Interruptions) . . . Please. . . . (Interruptions) . . . Just a minute . . . (Interruptions) . . .

SHRI S. S. AHLUWALIA: You can call for voting . . . (Interruptions) . . .

MR. CHAIRMAN: I am afraid . . . (Interruptions) . . . You can shout and nobody is heard . . . (Interruptions) . . .

SHRI TAPAN KUMAR SEN (BJP (M)): Sir, I asked for your ruling . . . (Interruptions) . . .

MR. CHAIRMAN: What ruling can I give in this noise? . . . (Interruptions) . . .

SHRI SITARAM YECHURY: Can we sit after 12 o'clock? . . . (Interruptions) . . .

MR. CHAIRMAN: I am afraid . . . (Interruptions) . . . I am afraid I can't do anything. If this is how the Rajya Sabha is going to behave, then we all better go home . . . (Interruptions) . . . National Song . . . (Interruptions) . . .

(The National Song, 'Vande Mataram', was then played.)

MR. CHAIRMAN: Now, I adjourn the House sine die.

'The House then adjourned sine die at 00.02 hours of the clock,' the transcript concludes.

Members of Anna Hazare's team called it 'the murder of democracy', arguing that parliament had clearly defied the will of the people. BJP's leader in the upper house, Arun Jaitley, called it 'the single greatest fraud' any government had ever played on the nation's parliament. The media called it 'Parliament's most shameful hour'.[3] While most commentators put most of the blame on the government, the impression was hard to shake that neither side really wanted to push through anti-corruption legislation that could have threatened their entire way of working and raising money. With the momentum behind the anti-corruption movement waning by the end of 2012, India's political class had wriggled off the hook. Although the government promised to reintroduce the legislation the following year, a new Lokpal Bill is still nowhere to be seen.

How had it come to this? How could parliament in the world's largest democracy so blithely ignore the apparent will of the people? How could deliberations over one of the most important pieces of legislation facing the nation descend into such demeaning chaos? Had the heart of Indian democracy really stopped beating?

In 1952, India embarked on that great experiment, granting the franchise in one go to the largest mass of people in history. Before the vote, there was widespread scepticism, from foreign diplomats and elite Indians alike: how could a mass of largely illiterate people really be trusted to elect their own lawmakers? Would demagoguery and dishonesty not triumph over reason? Even Nehru himself, the champion of Indian democracy, worried about the quality of the men who might be selected by the great Indian public. Yet in the end, the world was moved to banish those doubts: Indians of all castes and creeds lined up largely peacefully, and with great enthusiasm, to cast their votes in a national election for the first time in history, and elected a parliament that, by and large, took its legislative responsibility seriously.[4]

The parliamentarians they elected belonged mostly to the Congress Party, which won 364 out of 489 seats in the national assembly thanks to the first-past-the-post system, despite having won just 45 per cent of the popular vote. But there was a sizeable and determined opposition, and there were many impassioned debates in the years that followed. It was a young lower house by comparison with today's parliament, but a poorly educated one: just over a quarter of its members were under the age of forty but just under a quarter lacked secondary education. (In 2009, just 14 per cent of those who won seats in the Lok Sabha were under forty, and just 3 per cent lacked secondary education.)[5] But it was imbued with a sense of responsibility.

The tone was set by Nehru himself, who made a point of dutifully attending parliament's daily question hour promptly and regularly, and many of the debates too: indeed, he would often decline engagements when parliament was in session to ensure he could attend – a habit not followed by his successors. In a famous speech to the Lok Sabha in March 1957, before India's second general election, Nehru spoke eloquently about the merits, and the risks, of parliamentary democracy. That speech is worth remembering today for the lofty ideals it aspired to. 'Surely,' he said, 'there can be no higher responsibility or greater privilege than to be a member of this sovereign body, which is responsible for the fate of the vast number of human beings who live in this country.' Whether or not parliamentarians were worthy of that responsibility was, he admitted, 'another matter', but overall his verdict was an optimistic one.

'Parliamentary democracy demands many virtues. It demands, of course, ability. It demands a certain devotion to work. But it demands also a large measure of cooperation, of self-discipline, of restraint,' India's first prime minister said. 'Parliamentary democracy is not something which can be created in a country by some magic wand.

We know very well that there are not many countries in the world where it functions successfully. I think it may be said without any partiality that it has functioned with a very large measure of success in this country. Why? Not so much because we, the Members of this House, are exemplars of wisdom, but, I think, because of the background in our country and because our people have the spirit of democracy in them.'⁶

Today, India's parliament is still a thrilling place to visit, especially during an important debate. The sense of history and tradition, the momentous responsibilities contained inside its walls, still convey a sense of awe. Designed by Edward Lutyens and Herbert Baker, it was built in the 1920s; its domed Central Hall played host to the transfer of colonial power in 1947 and the framing of India's constitution in the years that followed.

But in the nine years that I have lived in India, parliament has more often than not failed to live up to its illustrious past and Nehru's fine words. In July 2008, lawmakers from the Bharatiya Janata Party brandished wads of cash on the floor of the House, claiming they had been given the money by members of the ruling coalition government to support it in a crucial no-confidence vote. Time and again, over the years, I have seen MPs competing to shout each other down, waving papers and even rushing into the supposedly neutral space in front of the Speaker's chair known as the well of the House; it was painful watching successive Speakers Somnath Chatterjee and Meira Kumar vainly trying to calm proceedings. Again and again, proceedings were adjourned as the opposition protested over one corruption scandal after another, demanding investigations, resignations of ministers, or even of the Prime Minister himself. When he did make a rare speech, the same prime minister was often unable to make himself heard over the din. In the spring of 2013, with a whole series of important bills pending – including the Land Acquisition Bill, the Grievance Redressal Bill and the Whistleblowers' Bill – the country's fifteenth parliament set course to become the least productive in the nation's history. The famous dignity of the House was in tatters.

Some might cynically observe that all this isn't surprising when the House is staffed with so many crooks and charlatans. As the chief architect of India's constitution B. R. Ambedkar observed: 'however good a Constitution may be, it is sure to turn out bad because those who are called to work it, happen to be a bad lot.' When a Congress MP was caught on CCTV in October 2012, brandishing his rifle at a toll plaza because a lowly booth attendant dared to ask him for the 80 rupees ($1.50) toll, it only seemed to confirm that cynical reading. When, in the same month, the ruling coalition allowed A. Raja and Suresh Kalmadi to take up posts on parliamentary committees – at a time when both were on bail for corruption relating to the 2G auction and Commonwealth Games respectively – it seemed to show that the realm of cynicism stretched right to the top.[7] Yet there are far more complex forces at work than this simplistic reading might suggest.

The first problem is the utter breakdown of trust between the country's two main political parties, the Congress and the BJP, fuelled by the nation's sensationalist twenty-four-hour TV news culture. It is, perhaps, one of India's least attractive imports from the United States, where a culture of confrontation, of sound bite and fury, has replaced honest debate, and where points-scoring replaces any attempt at bipartisanship. At times it makes the rows between the Democrats and the Republicans in Washington look like a tea party.

For many US and Indian cable news channels, ratings seem to follow rows. A good television news show just doesn't seem complete without at least two people shouting at each other, and preferably a full panel of eight screaming heads. India's politicians are the all-too-willing victims, often getting sucked into this game without a moment's thought or reflection. In September 2012, India's then Information Minister Ambika Soni was asked by a senior editor at a private function why she had joined in the attack on the *Washington Post* over my article criticizing the Prime Minister. She apparently replied that someone had put a camera in front of her face, and she had to say something.

With the cameras watching, and scandals erupting every few days or weeks, India's opposition parties have tried to drive home their disgust by disrupting the House. It has had a corrosive effect on parliament's effectiveness.

In the 1950s, India's newly established Lok Sabha sat for an average of 127 days a year. Since the year 2000, it has managed an average of just seventy-two days a year. The actual hours of sitting have fallen to around 70 per cent of the hours available. And with less time at its disposal, parliament has achieved less. Between 1952 and 1989, it typically passed nearly sixty-five bills a year. That number has fallen steadily, to below forty in recent years, according to data from the private non-profit body PRS Legislative Research.[8]

This breakdown in governance, which is evident in both the United States and India, comes at a time when both countries are wrestling with a particularly challenging set of economic and governance problems, whether over runaway deficits or runaway corruption. They are issues that require responsibility, bipartisan cooperation, negotiated consensual solutions, not filibuster and fury.

Yet not every failing can be laid at the government's door. The BJP's vision of opposition over the past nine years has seemed to consist of blindly opposing almost every single measure the government has proposed. The Hindu nationalist party championed a closer strategic cooperation with the United States during its time in government, but vehemently opposed it while in opposition. It enacted reforms to liberalize the economy while in office, but opposes them now. It has left me, and millions of Indians, scratching our heads and wondering what on earth the party actually stands for, if many of its principles can be so easily tossed aside. Some people argue the strategy is supposed to keep the government under pressure, to prevent it from scoring easy parliamentary wins, to force it to carry its entire, unwieldy coalition with it on every vote. But at what price does that pressure come? The price, perhaps, of making the opposition look equally incoherent.

The breakdown in parliament's effectiveness is causing the nation enormous economic damage and actually costing lives – every day's delay in passing an effective land bill, for example, meant another day when the nation's industrial and infrastructural progress is being undermined. But with the weakness of one of the institutional pillars of democracy, another pillar has grown stronger and partially filled the gap. Parliament's inability or unwillingness to legislate effectively has allowed the judiciary to step into the breach, with the Supreme Court passing a series of judgements in the past two decades that might ordinarily have been seen as the prerogative of the elected body.[9] In retrospect, many of those rulings might seem progressive and of lasting benefit, especially rulings that have enshrined people's rights to education or food, but this is not the way democracy is supposed to function.

Around the world, the increasingly adversarial nature of politics, and the erosion of any sense of parliamentary common purpose, gives room for movements that hold parliament, government or politicians in contempt, from the Tea Party in the United States to the India Against Corruption movement. It contributes to a general disgust with politicians and an unhealthy disillusionment with democracy, summed up for me in one shocking poll carried out by the CNN-IBN news channel and *Hindustan Times* newspaper in November 2011. It was far from representative, covering just 821 people in eight cities between the ages of twenty-five and fifty, but it was interesting nonetheless as an indication of middle-class apathy or downright hostility towards democracy.[10]

Only 19 per cent, less than one person in five, said elected leaders should govern the country in a democracy. A further 10 per cent wanted the political class to use professionals to govern key sectors, but the remainder seemed happy to do away with democracy entirely. Some 22 per cent wanted a technocratic government, run by experts and professionals who were not answerable to political leaders; 15 per cent said the army should run the country, while more than 33 per cent, one in three people, said India should be governed by a 'a strong leader who does not have to bother about contesting elections'.

Should politicians in India care? Some seem to hold the middle class in mutual contempt, knowing that it is the poor, not the comfortably off, who are not only more numerous but also much more inclined to vote. To me, that is short-sighted and dangerous. Not only is the middle class growing rapidly in numbers, its enthusiastic participation in the India Against Corruption movement suggests it may also be becoming more politically engaged. But the poor are getting smarter too, less willing to be fooled again and again by the same old appeals to caste and community, and more demanding that their political leaders actually deliver.

Part of the problem lies in a fragmentation of Indian politics that has seen the vote shares of both Congress and the BJP declining over time, so that both parties are dependent on small, regionally based allies if they are to form a government. As we have seen, that fragmentation has partly arisen as a result of the lack of internal democracy within Congress, which has forced popular regional leaders to break away from the mother ship and form their own parties. Its effect has been to make governance significantly more challenging in modern India. It is the root of Manmohan Singh's eternal complaint about coalition *dharma*, or duty, although it has to be said that previous Prime Minister Atal Bihari Vajpayee seemed better able to manage a coalition than this successor has been.

While some of those regional parties are governing relatively well in their respective states, they tend to lack national vision or any strong ideology, apart from a vague commitment to stick up for the perceived interests of the poor in general and the communities that elected them in particular. In the first half of Manmohan Singh's second term in office, for example, Mamata Banerjee's Trinamool Congress held the balance of power in parliament as a small but crucial partner in the ruling coalition. Elected on a populist pro-poor platform in West Bengal, with the protection of farmers' land rights over the demands of industry a central campaign platform, the Trinamool Congress blocked Singh's attempts to liberalize the Indian economy, for fear that reforms would hurt the poor. Other regional parties only seem interested in being part of the ruling coalition so that they can use national ministerial posts as opportunities for extortion, to raise party funds or bolster their personal wealth. This, allegedly, was why DMK from the state of Tamil Nadu was so keen that A. Raja should hold the telecoms portfolio in Singh's cabinet, with ultimately disastrous consequences for the government's credibility in the form of the 2G spectrum scandal.

Coalitions are often kept together not with ideological glue but with a very primitive carrot and stick – the carrot is money, the stick the threat that the government will unleash the nation's Central Bureau of Investigation to pursue corruption charges against any leader who dares to leave the coalition. (That is one reason, incidentally, that the government will always resist any effort to make the CBI constitutionally independent, and why the agency is sometimes nicknamed the Coalition Building Initiative.)

In the past, Indian legislators were often bribed to switch sides during important debates or no-confidence motions. To prevent that happening, an anti-defection law was passed by parliament in 1985. It allows for legislators to be disqualified if they defy the party's leadership or whip on a vote. But corruption and coercion usually find ways to work around the rules, with efforts these days concentrated more on getting the support of entire parties through their leaders than trying to influence individual members. The law has also had one important unintended consequence, dramatically reducing legislators' freedom of choice and making parliament less of a forum for debate and more of a rubber stamp. Combine that with the almost total lack of democracy within political parties in India, and you have a situation whereby the party leadership has almost total control over who is selected to represent the party within parliament, and how those people vote once installed in the House. It is a fundamental flaw in India's democracy that seriously constrains voters' choices and undermines the proper functioning of parliament, argues Professor Jagdeep Chokkar, one of the founders of the Association for Democratic Reforms who we met in Chapter 3.

To underline parliament's dysfunctional nature, data from PRS

Legislative Research shows that the length of time debating important bills has fallen sharply since the 1980s: the budget, for example, used to command more than a hundred hours of parliament's time; but in recent years has been passed in less than forty. At least twenty-nine bills have been passed in the latest parliament without any debate at all.

The situation in India's twenty-eight states is even worse.[11] The state assemblies in Arunachal Pradesh sat for an average of just eight days a year in the first decade of this millennium, while Haryana managed just fourteen days a year on average. More than 90 per cent of the bills in Bihar, West Bengal and Haryana were introduced and passed on the same day, and very few bills in all states are scrutinized by committees (just five out of the 476 bills passed by Tamil Nadu's legislative assembly between 2000 and 2010 went through committees for example).

The dysfunctional and disorderly nature of India's parliament has led to periodical calls for India to adopt a presidential system, a call notably made by Congress Party MP Shashi Tharoor in a piece for the investigative magazine *Tehelka* in December 2011.[12] 'Pluralist democracy is India's greatest strength,' he wrote, 'but its current manner of operation is the source of our major weaknesses. India's many challenges require political arrangements that permit decisive action, whereas ours increasingly promote drift and indecision. We must have a system of governance whose leaders can focus on governance rather than on staying in power.'

Tharoor and others have argued for a two-round direct presidential vote that would elect an eventual winner supported by a majority of Indian voters. But a presidential system is hardly a panacea for the ills of a polarized and constipated legislature, as the United States can bear witness. Nor does neighbouring Sri Lanka offer an attractive model of presidential rule, unless you like your presidents distinctly dictatorial, your minorities marginalized and your freedom of speech curtailed. But the simplest argument against Tharoor is this: it is not going to happen. Parliament will surely never agree to anything that would limit its powers in this way.

More realistically, there is plenty that could be done to make parliament function more effectively, as one of India's most articulate and thoughtful MPs, Baijayant 'Jay' Panda, has persuasively argued. Panda is a graduate of Michigan Technological University and had a background in engineering and management in the corporate sector before joining politics for the Biju Janata Dal in his home state of Odisha: he spends fifteen days a month touring his constituency on a motorbike and listening to his constituents, but also takes part in parliamentary committee work, television debates and writes op-eds. In his own words, he represents the 'new face' of Indian politics, and I have met him several times to discuss democracy and some of the ideas in this book.

Panda points out that many of the rules of Indian parliamentary functioning were established in 1919, during British colonial rule, when the appearance of some political power was granted to the 'natives' but control was firmly kept in the hands of the Viceroy. As a result, the government retains a veto on what can be debated, and which debates can be voted on, except when it comes to a no-confidence motion. One of the chief roles of parliament is to hold the government to account, but the rules of parliament make this much more difficult. The opposition, blocked from holding debates or setting up parliamentary inquiries on controversial subjects, often feels it has to disrupt proceedings just to get itself heard. In Britain, the combined opposition is granted twenty days in parliament's annual calendar when it sets the subject of debate, while private members' business is discussed on Fridays. There is much less incentive to disrupt proceedings in Britain, while parliament also sits for much longer – around 150 days a year, more than twice what Indian lawmakers currently manage.

Panda would like to see the rules changed so that a certain number of MPs could club together to demand a debate on a subject of their choosing; a greater number, perhaps a third of parliament's strength, would be required to force a vote. Removing the requirement that the President's approval is required for private members' bills, and changing the convention so that they are voted on rather than just debated, would also encourage more active participation from ordinary legislators. Amending the anti-defection law, so that party whips are limited to no-confidence motions and important money bills, would give lawmakers much greater autonomy.

Rajeev Chandrasekhar, IT-billionaire turned independent member of the Rajya Sabha, was so frustrated by the lack of debate that he wrote to the Prime Minister in 2011 appealing for three special sessions of parliament a year, each of five days, for nationally televised debates on the main issues facing the country.

'If parliament can be convened especially to hear President Barack Obama of America, surely we can convene a special session to discuss priority issues like poverty that affect more than 400 million fellow Indians,' he wrote. Chandrasekhar says his petition has received considerable support from fellow lawmakers and ordinary Indians. So far, though, there has been no response from the Prime Minister's Office.

The sad reality is that, despite the best efforts of people like Panda and Chandrasekhar, neither major party is seriously interested in reform. Both resent parliamentary scrutiny when they are in power; both seem to see short-term gains in disrupting parliament when in opposition, even if the long-term effect is to degrade the legitimacy of the House itself. In 1997 and again in 2012, the Rajya Sabha commemorated important anniversaries by adopting resolutions solemnly promising to 'uphold and maintain the dignity of parliament', to refrain from 'transgressing into official areas of the House, and from any shouting of slogans', to 'maintain the inviolability of question hour' and even to enact electoral reforms. Neither resolution had any noticeable effect.

Panda argued in 2012 that a campaign by civil society could conceivably push lawmakers to agree to some of these reforms, to secure those 'low-hanging fruits' that were both feasible and far-reaching.[13] Panda believes, and I think he is right, that parliament cannot keep behaving in such a dysfunctional way, that inevitably the pressure of popular expectations has to force change. But when we last met in May 2013, he said he believed it would take a Gorbachev-like figure to come to power from within the system itself, and unleash the next round of desperately needed reform.

'The irony is that it is all a gigantic missed opportunity for political parties and their leaders,' Panda wrote in one op-ed in November 2012.[14] 'They could either defend themselves against charges or distinguish themselves from the rest as the viable, untainted alternative. The proliferation of satellite and cable television in even the remotest areas has ensured that literacy is no longer a prerequisite to get voters to engage with such issues. Many politicians, however, are still rooted in an earlier paradigm, where parliamentary debate did not afford such an opportunity to make their case to the masses.'

Despite all the disruptions, Panda is very far from the only lawmaker who takes his or her job seriously and who sees parliament as an important part of doing that job effectively. Every year, a communications specialist from Chennai, K. Srinivasan, holds an awards ceremony to recognize the members of parliament who have contributed the most to proceedings over the past year.[15] The awards, known as the Sansad Ratna, which translates as 'parliament's jewels', often end up recognizing the same people: Shiv Sena MP Ananda Rao Adsul has raised an incredible 971 questions over 282 sittings of the current parliament between 2009 and 2012; BJP MP Hansraj Ahir has raised the highest number of private members' bills, twenty-seven, in that time; BJP MP Arjun Meghwal has participated in 345 different debates, and Congress MP S. S. Ramasubbu was also celebrated for a good all-round performance, contributing to 132 debates, raising two bills, asking 821 questions and being present 97 per cent of the time. The comparable figures for Rahul Gandhi and his mother Sonia were just one speech each, no questions, no bills and less than 50 per cent attendance; Prime Minister Manmohan Singh, as historian Ramachandra Guha points out,[16] betrays his own lack of respect for parliament by not even standing for election to the Lok Sabha; former Telecoms Minister A. Raja has still not spoken a word during this parliament, although he did spend fifteen months of it in jail.

Ramasubbu is the son of a Congress politician, and prides himself on his connections to the concerns at the 'grassroots' in his constituency. He frequently uses parliamentary questions to raise their concerns, on issues ranging from education to loans and the welfare of fishermen. When an outbreak of dengue fever led to around fifty deaths in his constituency, many of them children, partly because of a lack of blood platelets, he used parliament to draw attention to the crisis, forcing the government to send a health team to his area. Free medicines were distributed, stagnant pools of water where mosquitos breed were cleaned up and many lives were saved.

He is as frustrated as anyone with the constant disruptions to parliament, which he blames on the opposition, but says his good work is not really recognized outside his constituency, even by his own party. 'The Congress Party must recognize and select more people like us from the grassroots,' he said. 'I am from the village level with no connections with top-level Congress politicians at the centre. It would be better for the party and its image if more politicians who work at the village level are given national centre stage.'

The media, too, is giving parliament more attention these days, but not always the right kind, he says. 'It is the corrupt and the sensational they always want to talk about and highlight. There are so many more parliamentarians like me who are working so hard who never get any space in the mainstream media.

'There are all kinds of people in the parliament. Some politicians come here for power since they already have money. Some come for only money and some for both power and money. There are a few like me who are here to work, for what they are supposed to do, work for the people without any greed for either power or money. So for parliament to work, people must recognize genuine politicians.'

With the possible exception of Ahir, who was the whistleblower in the Coalgate scam, none of the people recognized by Srinivasan are household names in India. While the media zooms in every time parliament is disrupted, it shows little interest in the actual business of the House when it does take place. Political parties reward politicians for their ability to raise money, or to suck up to the party's top leaders, or for their supposed ability to deliver the votes of key communities, but not, generally speaking, for doing a good job in parliament. 'We have some very good parliamentarians, but they are not recognized by the media, they are not recognized by political parties, or by society,' Srinivasan said, echoing Ramasubbu's complaint. 'In a humble way, I am trying to gather people together to give them respect and honour; and to say that we must elect good people.'

Srinivasan gets his data from PRS Legislative Research, a private body that is doing a truly amazing job of trying to help India's parliament function more effectively. It was set up in 2005 by two friends, one a graduate of the Madras Indian Institute of Technology, C. V. Madhukar, whose initial idea it was, and M. R. Madhavan, who left a lucrative job as a currency strategist at Bank of America in Singapore to join the team. The House of Commons in London boasts eighty people doing pure research, while every MP has a staff of four or five people all funded by the taxpayer. The US Congressional Research Service has a budget of more than $100 million. Members of India's parliament get an allowance of 30,000 rupees ($550) a month to hire their entire staff, including a driver, and appointments secretary. PRS aims to help fill the gap.

Parliament cranks out an incredible mass of paperwork; a lawmaker might receive 4,000 documents a year, each perhaps ten or fifteen pages long. Helping make sense of it all, PRS produces crisply written and non-partisan analyses of all the major bills before parliament, after extensive interviews with the officials who drafted the law and the stakeholders who might be affected. The major points of each bill is highlighted, context supplied and attention gently drawn to potential points of conflict or controversy, without taking sides. Twice a week it conducts briefing sessions to which all MPs are invited. The main event, when an external expert is usually invited to speak, takes place each Wednesday morning at 9 a.m. sharp, and regularly draws a couple of dozen attendees from across the parties; one of them regularly arrives in his golf clothes, complaining that he has missed the final nine holes just to come along. Away from the TV cameras, 'they behave in a parliamentary way,' Madhavan told me, adding that parliamentary committees also tend to work reasonably well off camera.

Indeed, Madhavan says many MPs are actually extremely hardworking. By 7 a.m. a summary of the previous day's proceedings is delivered to each of their residences, and many are already beginning work. Many continue until late into the evening; Madhavan says he has often been called for long meetings beginning at 8 p.m. on a Sunday night. Excluding government ministers, there are around 700 lawmakers in both Houses; Madhavan says around 400 interact with PRS when parliament is in session, and between eighty and 100 are in contact with his organization on average once a week. Srinivasan is looking at similar numbers: he says 100 out of the 545 members of the lower house account for between 50 and 60 per cent of the questions, debates and private members' bills.

Those, then, are the encouraging signs within the great gloom that envelops parliament in modern India. But they are not yet enough to lift that gloom.

In May 2013, just as I was about to sit down to write this chapter, NDTV's Managing Editor Vikram Chandra invited me on his weekly prime-time debate show, *The Big Fight*, to discuss the cost of parliament's constant disruption.[17] Chakshu Roy, who works with Madhavan at PRS, was one of my fellow guests, and we were looking forward to a productive debate. But Chandra had also, for perfectly good reasons, invited onto his show representatives of the country's two main parties, Mani Shankar Aiyar for Congress and BJP spokeswoman Meenakshi Lekhi. Both are smart, and quick with their jibes, but the debate swiftly lapsed into a shouting match.

'They are so uncoordinated, they are so incompetent, I have never seen such a useless opposition as we have now,' said Aiyar, as tempers started to flare. 'They are not only useless they also are totally disruptive.'

Chandra looked on with his pen held to his mouth, a bemused smile playing on his lips.

'The country is facing the crisis and the disaster because we have yet to come across a more corrupt government than the one we have presently,' Lekhi countered, as Aiyar reached across to clap sarcastically.

'Why don't you bring a no-confidence motion?' bellowed Aiyar twice, as Lekhi tried in vain to continue speaking. 'Why don't you bring it? You don't have the guts. It is the most cowardly opposition I've seen. They know they'll lose so they don't allow it to take place.'

'Mr Aiyar is a loudmouth, which we can all see,' she said.

Eventually the two of them just stood there shouting above each other, reeling off the names of corruption scandals the other party had been involved in, from Bofors to Bellary.

'That's really entertaining,' Chandra said, when he finally got a word in, 'but we really wish you were doing this in parliament . . . May I now be allowed to speak without interruption?'

Within a quarter of an hour, the 'debate' disintegrated again.

'I am beginning to know what the Speaker feels like,' a beleaguered Chandra was finally forced to admit. 'I know I don't want the job.'

Chandra's sentiments would be shared by many Indians today, for parliament often looks like a pale shadow of its former self. Adversarial, often more interested in protecting vested interests than representing the will of the people, demagogic rather than deliberative, the heart of Indian democracy has not stopped beating, but the pulse is weaker than it should be.

As they ponder this sick patient, many Indians wonder whether a new leader might emerge in India, from within the system (as Panda predicts), or from outside it, who could clean out the clogged arteries of Indian parliamentary democracy and rekindle the vigour of its youth.

In the autumn of 2012, one man presented himself as the answer: the outsider who could enter politics and clean up the system from within. Still buoyed by the national outpouring of anger against corruption, and undeterred by the breakdown of the movement he had begun, that man was Arvind Kejriwal.

10

Fight the Power

Arvind Kejriwal launches his political career in uncompromising fashion

'*Our aim is not to come to power. Our aim is to prepare the people for a complete systemic overhaul. We are in politics to change the politics of this country.*'
Arvind Kejriwal, to the author, November 2012

'*The reasonable man adapts himself to the world; the unreasonable one persists in trying to adapt the world to himself. Therefore all progress depends on the unreasonable man.*'
George Bernard Shaw, in 'Maxims for Revolutionarists', from *Man and Superman*

The chatter rose to fever pitch in the run-up to his latest news conference. Who would Delhi's anti-corruption crusader expose this week? This business leader? That politician? Some other conspiracy? There were any number of potential targets, after all.

Arvind Kejriwal strode onto the lawn at the Indian Press Club, looking steadily ahead, an expression of grim determination etched onto his face.[1] More than forty television cameras faced him as he took his seat, every major news channel preparing to beam his press conference live. After the inglorious end to the dreams of Team Anna, Kejriwal had not been down for long. By November 2012, this slight but manically determined man had bounced back with a vengeance, and the media was once again transfixed. With a nation's eyes upon him, Kejriwal took aim at India's richest man, Mukesh Ambani, widening his target from corrupt politicians to the business leaders he says are in league with them. In retrospect, though, this stunning event might come to be seen as his high-water mark.

His new political career had been launched just a month before: not with a manifesto, or even, yet, with a name for his party, but in typically uncompromising fashion with an assault on corruption at the very peak of Indian society. He trod, with the zeal that had become his trademark, where the Indian media normally dared not go. His first target, in October, was Robert Vadra, the husband of Rahul Gandhi's sister Priyanka, the son-in-law of Sonia Gandhi herself, a taboo-busting assault on an unpopular figure who had until then largely escaped the scrutiny of the press. The Gandhis are the closest thing to a royal family that India has, and have somehow remained largely above the mud-slinging fray of Indian politics. Sonia is criticized, of course, but it is rare to see an all-out no-holds-barred attack on her in the Indian media.

It was an open secret that Vadra had amassed vast wealth since his marriage to Priyanka, but not one that was often written about. Kejriwal disdained such niceties, alleging that Vadra had engaged in a series of land deals with a state government and a leading property developer that had seen him rise from being a small-time exporter of brassware on his marriage to become a major property baron.

According to Kejriwal, the idea was a simple one: Vadra would buy agricultural land cheaply off farmers, then use his political clout to convince the Haryana state government to 're-zone' the land for commercial use: in the stroke of a pen, the value of the land soared. Vadra would then be able to sell the land for a vast profit to a property developer. In the process, Kejriwal said Vadra's assets had risen from $100,000 in 2007 to $100 million in 2011.[2] He demanded an immediate investigation, brandishing documents that supposedly proved his sensational allegations.

The charges were resolutely rejected by Vadra, who called them 'utterly false, entirely baseless and defamatory', and concocted in order to gain 'cheap publicity'. True or not, they certainly succeeded in putting Kejriwal back on the front pages. By bringing them, the activist-turned-politician had not only punctured the protective halo surrounding the Gandhis, but shrewdly chosen an unpopular in-law, rather than 'Madam' herself (as Sonia is fawningly referred to in Congress circles), as his target. Indeed, the mystery of what the charming Priyanka saw in her short, moustachioed and brawny husband Vadra was one of impolite society's eternal talking points. Vadra, it was said, talked mainly about the gym and his workout programme, and had a penchant for being photographed in tight T-shirts and sunglasses, sitting astride motorbikes. There was already resentment about the fact that Vadra was the only person listed by name, rather than by rank or title, as being exempted from searches at airport security checks. Kejriwal had crystallized that resentment, and given people reason not to like him. Taking Kejriwal's lead, the media soon forgot its reserve, and turned on the man *Outlook* magazine christened 'His Royal Son-in-Lawlessness'.[3]

In the process, Kejriwal had also blown a huge hole in another unwritten convention in Indian politics: to stay away from a political leader's relatives. 'There are ethics in politics. Never attack family,' Congress Party spokesman Digvijaya Singh pompously tried to lecture Kejriwal. The Congress spokesman went on to say that his party possessed ample 'evidence' against family members of the opposition BJP's two elder statesmen – former Prime Minister Atal Bihari Vajpayee and his deputy Lal Krishna Advani – but had never cared to use it.[4] But was he really saying that he had evidence of criminal behaviour but had not made it public because it is wrong to attack your opponents' relatives? Were politicians really arguing that it was acceptable to turn a blind eye to corruption, that politicians' relatives were above the law?

The social commentator Santosh Desai told my colleague Rama Lakshmi that Kejriwal had made politicians uneasy by breaking the 'off-camera set of rules' that protected the elite. 'It's like the peace that exists between gangs,' he said. 'That code of silence has now been broken by Arvind Kejriwal.'[5]

Nor was Kejriwal finished. He swiftly followed the Vadra exposé by attacking the wife of Law and Justice Minister Salman Khurshid for allegedly misappropriating money meant for the disabled through a charity she runs. It was a scandal first exposed in the Indian media, which alleged that stamps and signatures had been forged by Trust members, and the funds pocketed. Kejriwal jumped on board, demanding arrests. Then he rounded on BJP president Nitin Gadkari, accusing him of misusing his political clout to influence land deals in his native state of Maharashtra. The subject of each news conference was a closely guarded secret ahead of time, stoking the fires of rumour to colossal effect.

Once again, there were critics. Kejriwal was not providing proof of his charges that would stand up in a court of law, many pundits said, and was flitting from target to target too quickly, in a bid to remain on top of the news agenda. Yet again, however, the government's attempts to fight back were a public relations disaster, a sign that senior figures within Congress continued to misread the public mood, and underplayed the extent of popular anger against corruption.

Since his split from Hazare, Kejriwal had replaced the words 'I am Anna' on his white cap with the words 'I am the common man', a jibe at the Congress Party's 'aam admi' or 'common man' campaign slogan. But 'aam' in Hindi can also mean mango. Vadra thought he was being funny when he facetiously dismissed Kejriwal and his gang as 'Mango people in banana republic' on his Facebook page. It came across as an insult to the entire nation, and Vadra soon deleted his entire Face-book profile.

Congress leaders fell over themselves trying to defend their beloved first family. One cabinet minister accused Kejriwal of lying like Hitler's propaganda chief Joseph Goebbels, while another erupted in self-righteous anger on television to call the attack 'shameless and shameful'. The Information Minister, Ambika Soni, accused Kejriwal of making the accusations to boost his own image, and accused the media of helping him by airing them, neither of which seem like such grave offences. Law Minister Salman Khurshid vowed to lay down his life for the Gandhi family. It was a defence, wrote *Indian Express* Editor-in-Chief Shekhar Gupta, not built on facts, but around 'counter-abuse and outrage' that showed the party losing 'its political judgement, instinct, discretion, everything'.[6]

Kejriwal had also, perhaps, tapped into something deeper, a resentment of the English-speaking elite who flit in and out of the country from their houses and penthouses in Manhattan and London, and have disdain for Indian law and for the vast majority of its people.[7] Their morals are Western and decadent, in the eyes of conservative, small-town India, and their privilege propped up by the politics of appeasement and the vote bank, of 'pseudosecularism', of pandering to Muslims and the lower castes through policies of reverse discrimination that only narrow the space for the aspiring lower middle classes. Vadra's disdainful Facebook comment only confirmed those prejudices, and showed that Kejriwal had tapped a rich political seam.

Khurshid did no better at responding to the charges. True, he and his wife brandished photographs and papers of their own that purported to show the money had been properly spent. But he too started to lose his foothold on the moral high ground when he described Kejriwal as a 'guttersnipe . . . worse than an insect, a snake that moves in gutters'. He shouted at a TV reporter and told him to 'shut up'. Later, he was caught on camera apparently daring his accuser to visit his constituency in the northern town of Farrukhabad and return home safely. As Law Minister, he said, he told his supporters that he had worked with the pen, but he could also 'work with blood'.[8]

For good measure, Digvijaya Singh weighed in as well, calling Kejriwal a 'self-serving ambitious megalomaniac' with a 'streak of Hitler' in him.[9] Fellow cabinet member Beni Prasad Verma leapt to Khurshid's defence by saying the sum allegedly stolen, some 7.1 million rupees, was 'a very small amount' for a cabinet minister (presumably, too small for him to bother stealing). But the Comptroller and Auditor General had confirmed, in a preliminary report, that funds had been misappropriated, and Khurshid seemed to be floundering.

In a move that seemed brazen to many, it was at that point that Manmohan Singh decided (or was told) to promote Salman Khurshid to the post of the country's new foreign minister. Loyalty to the Gandhi family clearly has it rewards.

In November 2012, I accompanied Kejriwal as he took the fight to Congress and Khurshid, staging a large political rally in Farrukhabad itself and promising to field a disabled candidate against the minister when elections rolled around.[10] He was in bullish mood, comparing the India Against Corruption movement to two great historical movements against misgovernance and corruption in the nation's past, the 'Total Revolution' of Jayaprakash Narayan against Indira Gandhi's government in 1975, and V. P. Singh's later defeat of Rajiv Gandhi in 1984 in the wake of the Bofors scandal.

Narayan – JP as he was known – had been a hero of the freedom struggle who refused Jawaharlal Nehru's entreaties to join the post-Independence cabinet and enjoyed huge moral authority in the country. In 1974, JP joined a movement against a particularly corrupt and incompetent government in the impoverished state of Bihar, and turned it into a national campaign against Congress party misrule. Like Hazare, JP had implicitly compared himself to Gandhi, and there was talk of a 'second freedom struggle' against the corrupt rule of the Congress party, which was likened to the British colonial government. In March 1975 he brought an estimated 750,000 people onto the streets of Delhi – a crowd far bigger than Hazare ever managed to draw in – for a march on parliament, calling for the dissolution of the government in Bihar and the establishment of tribunals to investigate Congress leaders accused of corruption. 'Vacate the throne, the people are coming,' said one of the placards held aloft, clearly aimed at Indira, according to Ramachandra Guha's history of post-Independence India. While JP was accused of undermining democracy by asking for the dismissal of an elected government, the more serious blow to Indian democracy came three months later, when Indira Gandhi declared a State of Emergency and locked up thousands of her opponents, including JP himself and leaders of other political parties.[11]

Indira, of course, revoked the Emergency two years later and called elections, only to be soundly defeated. But the coalition that took power, independent India's first non-Congress government under Morarji Desai, had been united only in its opposition to her rule, and soon fell apart. By 1980, Indira was back in power.

In 1989, it was the turn of Indira's son Rajiv to suffer electoral defeat, at the hands of a former member of his own cabinet, V. P. Singh. As Finance Minister, Singh had attacked the nexus of politics and business by conducting raids on some of India's leading companies on the grounds that they were evading tax; but his supposedly reformist prime minister failed to stand by him. Singh was first moved to the defence ministry, and then removed from the cabinet completely. He was to leave Congress and return to parliament as an opposition lawmaker. Later, as the Bofors arms-procurement scandal engulfed Rajiv Gandhi's government, Singh's reputation as the only honest Indian politician rose still higher. Leaving Congress, he contested and won a parliamentary seat for the opposition in 1988. The following year, he was sworn in as independent India's second non-Congress prime minister. He lasted slightly less than a year.[12]

That Kejriwal had modelled the anti-corruption campaign on Narayan's movement was no surprise. In 2011, India Against Corruption's choice of the Ramlila Maidan to organise their protest had seemed like deliberate throwback to a famous rally by Narayan against Indira Gandhi's rule at the same venue in June 1975. Then, when Kejriwal announced his foray into politics in August 2012, he had echoed his predecessor's call for 'total revolution'. Now, he admitted he had similarly grand ambitions for his new party. 'The kind of wave that existed during Jayaprakash Narayan's time and V. P. Singh's time, a similar kind of wave exists in the country today also,' Kejriwal told me, as we travelled in his car on the way to Farrukhabad. 'That means we have the necessary conditions existing in the country to change the government in the centre, and it is possible that this movement is able to actually get a majority.'

JP Narayan and V. P. Singh, he explained, had lacked a vision beyond ousting a corrupt Congress government from power. His movement, Kejriwal explained, was working hard to put a blueprint in place before it came to power. The Jan Lokpal Bill was one important element, as well as a plan to radically decentralize power to village and town councils, and hold regular referenda at district or state level. Yet aside from those two points, Kejriwal can often sound a little vague, saying that the process of policy consultation is only just beginning – indeed the party's website lists just one item under the banner 'Agenda', and that is the Jan Lokpal Bill.

Nevertheless, in the course of various conversations with Kejriwal and party workers, some key elements of his 'blueprint' begin to emerge. Candidates for office would have to take a pledge not to live in the fantastically expensive bungalows where today's MPs luxuriate, and to refuse the perks of office that can so frustrate the 'common man' – the flashing red lights on top of their cars, and the supposedly status-enhancing armed security details assigned to political VIPs. Natural resources, land, water and forests, would not be acquired without the consent of their owners or, in the case of common land, the consent of the village council. Voters would have the right to recall or reject politicians and bureaucrats they deemed to be corrupt, through locally organized popular no-confidence votes.

Kejriwal wants to establish India's first major party that is transparently funded and internally democratic. Unlike every other major party, the Aam Admi Party would not choose candidates with criminal backgrounds, he said, nor would it sell tickets to stand for office to raise money for the party. Instead, candidates would be chosen after a rigorous process of popular consultation, with people canvassed to suggest candidates and raise objections to those who were shortlisted. Campaign funding would be transparent, with every single donation to the party listed on its website, something he said had cost him backing from some business leaders who had requested anonymity.

But where was the economic message, I asked him in the car, how did his party connect with the aspirations of middle-class Indians not just to end corruption but also to enjoy the fruits of a growing economy?

'I want to allay the fears that we are anti-business,' Kejriwal told me, reminding me that Mahatma Gandhi had himself enjoyed the backing of members of the business community. 'We are in favour of ethical business, but we are opposed to corrupt business. So therefore we are against the corrupt system that exists today where a business can thrive only through corruption. We want to create conditions in our country where a businessman can actually lead an honest life and they can do honest business.' And how about the reforms of the past two decades, I asked, did he support them? The answer was long but came down to this: Kejriwal supported reforms that promoted honest competition, but not those that led to a cosy collusion between business and politics, to corner the proceeds of corruption. About the last two decades, he had nothing good to say. 'I don't think the delivery of services has improved, it is just that the corruption, the bribe money, which was shared by a large number of people earlier, is now going into the pockets of a few industrialists. That's it. That's all that has changed. If this is reform, then I am against these reforms.'

For many aspiring Indians, Kejriwal's message on governance and the economy seemed to lack a little substance. The impression that he was better at exposing the corrupt than he would be if he were left in charge of anything himself always seemed to lurk in the background. That's not to say, of course, that his party won't or shouldn't get votes: many Indians will surely feel that a protest vote against corruption might be a vote worth casting, or that Kejriwal, however imperfect, might be distinctly better than anything else that is on offer. Just having him inside parliament could make Indian politics significantly more interesting, if only because of what he could expose from within the system.

If he can just maintain that connection to India's middle classes, he could yet be a powerful force for change, because the urban middle class are a growing force. Using some admittedly pretty optimistic economic projections, India's National Council for Applied Economic Research estimated that the numbers of middle-class Indians could swell to nearly 500 million people, or 40 per cent of the population, by 2025, from 160 million in 2011. Perhaps it won't be Kejriwal who ends up getting their votes, but he has certainly reminded a few people of the votes that are out there.

As we talked, the convoy of cars swept on its way to Farrukhabad, horns blaring and flags flying from the cars. At small towns along the way, knots of people had turned out to lend their support, and as the cars slowed, Kejriwal would greet them through an opened window.

Manmohan Singh, Kejriwal went on to say, had allowed corruption to take place within his cabinet, signing off on the deals central to the 2G telecom spectrum scam, just so that he could remain in office. He might not have received any money from the deal, but that did not, under India's Prevention of Corruption Act, make him any less guilty, Kejriwal said. 'You don't need to take bribes. If you abuse your position and do something illegal you can be put behind bars for a maximum of seven years. So to that extent, Prime Minister Manmohan Singh is guilty of corruption. If there was an honest investigation, I am very sure he would be adjudged guilty.' Indeed, a few weeks later, Kejriwal told the press that 'corrupt ministers' would be sent to jail within six months of his party coming to power.[13]

But is India ready for this kind of uncompromising talk, for Kejriwal's vision of 'total revolution' and a 'complete systemic overhaul'? Is it ready for this former tax inspector to launch (the tax office's trademark) pre-dawn raids on the entire establishment? And was he really strong enough to take on the entire system? 'It is only the most powerful and the rich people who have a vested interest in keeping this system alive,' he said. 'A vast majority of the population wants to change the system, they want to lead an honest life.'

Kejriwal still takes an early morning walk near his modest home in a New Delhi suburb, without police protection. 'I sincerely believe that my life is in the hands of God,' he told me. 'No one can take away my life as long as God wants me to be here. Every human being comes on earth with some mission . . . and until such time as that mission is incomplete, that person has to stay. So I very strongly believe in that, and I am not very worried about my security.'

Thousands of people had assembled in Farrukhabad to hear what he had to say; locals mixed with party supporters in white caps from around the country. As he sat on the stage waiting his turn to speak, a white cap perched forward on his head, his bare feet crossed under his body, the slightly built man would have been easy to miss. His oiled hair and baggy, untucked shirt give him a slightly schoolboyish look at times. But when he took the stage, his ambitions seemed to bolster his stature. 'We haven't let the powerful enjoy a good night's sleep since we announced the formation of a political party,' he told the crowd. 'We will teach them a lesson in politics.'

One by one, disabled men were lifted onto the stage, one in a plastic chair, others in people's arms. Many had the stick-thin limbs typical of polio victims. Pieces of paper were brandished that, Kejriwal said, proved that the men had been listed as receiving tricycle wheelchairs from Louise Khurshid's charity. One by one, the men said they had received nothing. One was listed as having been given a hearing aid, but limped on stage to say he had received nothing. 'I have a problem with my legs, now Salman Khurshid has finished off my ears as well,' he said, to laughter.

Kejriwal does have an ear for politics, connecting corruption with the rapidly rising prices of recent years in ways that ordinary people could understand. He speaks in sound bites, a very different style from the long and laborious lectures of his former associate Hazare. His impatience, his certainty, his unshakeable belief that he has the answers to India's problems, all speak powerfully to the nation's youth. He speaks to the same impatient India that Pepsi targets with its frenetic advertising campaign 'Oh Yes Abhi!' (Oh Yes Right Now!), where the Bollywood actor Ranbit Kapor jumps out of his taxi in a traffic jam because he can't wait to eat Pani Puri[14] and drink Pepsi at a roadside vendor's, where Priyanka Chopra is an impatient bag of nerves as she can't wait to get onstage to sing for her adoring fans, and a young woman has 'Now or Never' tattooed on her shoulder.

Rahul Gandhi says the young people of India are impatient and are demanding change, but in the next breath demands that they be patient, for change cannot come overnight, nor can it be achieved by one person's efforts alone. India, Gandhi says, believes in 'the man who comes in on a horse, the sun in the background, a billion people waiting, and he is going to fix everything. No, that's not going to happen.' Change, he says, will only come by giving a billion people the chance to solve their own problems.[15]

Kejriwal, by contrast, has no qualms about presenting himself as the Messiah, about flaunting his own impatience. That is a large part of his appeal. It is a quality he shares with Gujarat's chief minister and the BJP's prime ministerial candidate for the 2014 elections, Narendra Modi, and in the media world with Arnab Goswami: that messianic drive to present himself to an impatient public as the man on the horse, riding to India's rescue.

But it is not only young people who are attracted by the message and who turn up at his rallies. Sixty-seven-year-old retired naval commander Sudhir Kumar was typical of the decent, honest and frustrated people one typically meets at India Against Corruption events. He said he had travelled for a day and a half to attend the rally, sleeping overnight in a railway waiting room. 'There is going to be a huge change,' he said. 'People who feel patriotism, they are all being connected.'

A few days later, on 9 November 2013, I was at the Indian Press Club, to watch Kejriwal – at his peak – unveil his latest exposé. In it, Kejriwal accused business leaders of stashing huge sums of money in Swiss bank accounts to evade tax, and perhaps for use as slush funds for bribes. A major international bank was colluding, he said, and when evidence of wrongdoing had first emerged in 2011, the government's reaction had been to sweep the whole affair under the carpet.

The reporters were all given sixty-one-page booklets with

photocopied police statements. Page numbers were cited, important sentences underlined and read out. In the old days as a social activist, Kejriwal used to smile a lot. This time, his smile was absent. When a colleague spoke, he surveyed and sized up the mass ranks of the press with a imperial gaze. At other times, his lower lip protruded in an expression that bordered on a sulk. He had mastered the idiom of television news perfectly, and pointedly only spoke in Hindi – even though his English is perfect – to reinforce his links with 'the common man'. 'When I read these papers, I feel repulsed by this government. It is fallen and inferior,' he said in his typical style. 'The government is encouraging criminals, the government is protecting criminals.'

But this, perhaps, was a taboo-busting performance too far, because the person in Kejriwal's crosshairs that day was none other than India's richest man, Mukesh Ambani. Ambani, the head of the country's largest business empire, Reliance Industries, was wielding undue influence over government policymaking, Kejriwal alleged, and was also evading taxes. The problem was that Ambani was not just wealthy but also litigious too, and a media baron in his own right. India's media often treads softly around men like this, and this was obviously uncomfortable territory for the powers-that-be back in the news-room. Suddenly, Kejriwal's regular press conferences started to disappear from the airwaves. A formal launch of his political party – under the name of the Aam Admi Party – was largely ignored. There was coverage from time to time, but that bank of television cameras had shrunk considerably. Had the media had enough of this maverick muckracker, or had Kejriwal simply overreached himself?

In another interview, this time in his modest new party offices on the outskirts of Delhi, with skyscrapers looming through the smoggy haze, Kejriwal offered his version of events. Ambani, he told me, had tried to 'intimidate' the media into silence by threatening to sue them directly if they broadcast any more of what the mogul's lawyers called 'false and grossly defamatory material' being circulated by Kejriwal.

As evidence, he produced one of the letters from Ambani's lawyers, A. D. Dayal & Associates, that reminded media companies of their client's numerous awards and the recognition he had received for his business leadership over the years. The letter castigated the television channel for broadcasting Kejriwal's accusations without attempting to verify them. We contacted several media houses about the letter, but none wanted to comment. Nor did Reliance Industries. But a reporter at one major TV network confirmed to me that instructions had gone out internally: Kejriwal's accusations should no longer be broadcast unless the channel had carried out its own investigation.

In the streets, targeting Ambani was probably a shrewd move. The industrialist had recently built what *Forbes* magazine called the world's most expensive private residence, a 27-storey building in Mumbai worth an estimated $1 billion, that included helipads, a spa and parking for 168 cars. *Forbes* estimated Ambani's net worth at $21 billion in 2012. But did Kejriwal's tactics cost him the support of the press? 'Each of the media houses have to decide on what side they stand – with the politicians, Ambani and all these corrupt groups on one side, or with the people on the other side,' Kejriwal told me at the time. 'The battle lines are clearly drawn.'

The problem for Kejriwal, though, is that he expected the media to join him in a battle against the entire establishment, an elite that many senior editors were part of socially, and perhaps also financially. Once again, Kejriwal had ridden the media tiger beautifully for a while, but was in the end at risk of being thrown off and devoured. Big business had invested in Indian media companies partly to buy insurance from such charges, and Kejriwal could not break those kind of bonds single-handedly.

By the spring of 2013, Kejriwal's ambitions had considerably shrunk. He was still using social media intelligently to get his message across, with YouTube and Twitter to fall back on when the mainstream media ignored him. Meanwhile there are at least twenty-five Facebook pages and groups advocating him as India's new premier, the most popular of which, 'We want Arvind Kejriwal as Indian PM', had 24,661 likes in mid-April 2013. But the man himself had turned his sights on the

Delhi legislative elections, and his ire on the head of the city government, Chief Minister Sheila Dikshit. From Arvind for PM, it was
starting to become Arvind for CM (chief minister).

In early April, Kejriwal was fasting again, this time not against an
entire system or an idea like corruption, but against 'inflated power
and water bills' in New Delhi. Advocating a campaign of civil disobe-
dience by non-payment of bills, he argued that Sheila Dikshit was
colluding with private companies to cheat the poor. It was a nakedly
populist stand, which took the barest interest in the actual economics
of utilities supply, and was painted on a much smaller canvas than his
previous campaigns. It made no economic sense at all as far as I could
see, threatening to reverse the local government's hard work in putting
the electricity sector on a more sustainable financial footing. (Indeed,
the knee-jerk distrust of private profit, and the faith in the state to
provide a solution, if only more money is spent and more safeguards
are put in place, is typical of civil society groups in India, and arguably one of their greatest weaknesses.) Nor was advocating the
non-payment of bills a message likely to resonate among the more
well-off and influential sections of the middle classes. Kejriwal later
told me that a million people had signed his petition promising not
to pay their utilities bills, and promised to cut electricity prices in
half. Quite how he would afford to do that was anybody's guess.

The event was staged in the narrow streets of the low-income
colony of Sunder Nagri, ostensibly because he did not want a 'grand
show' but probably also because he knew he could no longer easily
stage one.

On 6 April, after fifteen days, without achieving any breakthrough
but believing that he had made his point, Kejriwal called off his fast.
Perhaps as many as 3,000 people crowded in the narrow alleyways of
Sunder Nagri, most of them men, waving Indian flags and wearing 'I
am a common man' caps. Older supporters craned for a look from the
balconies of neighbouring buildings, and a few television OB vans fed
a few minutes of the event onto a few channels. It was a far cry from
the vast crowds and wall-to-wall coverage of Ramlila Maidan nearly

two years before. Old Bollywood songs blared out and there were chants of 'Vande Mataram' (I bow to thee, my motherland) as Kejriwal broke his fast, and dry colours from the recent festival of Holi flew through the air. 'The next battle will be on water and electricity in the next Delhi elections,' Kejriwal said from the small podium, to applause. 'If AAP comes to power, it will reduce the tariff for both.'

I met Kejriwal for a fourth time in his very small and modest apartment on the outskirts of Delhi. With its dowdy curtains, simple sofa and bare bathroom, this was clearly not the flat of a man who was corrupt. Over a cup of tea, he denied that he was dictatorial, arguing that he could not have sustained such a huge anti-corruption movement without being inclusive. Today, his Aam Admi Party contains 'fiercely independent' people like Yogendra Yadav and Prashant Bhushan, he pointed out. But he agreed wholeheartedly that he was impatient.

'The time has come when everyone in this country has to become impatient. Because the time left is so little. If we do not wake up and do something urgently I think India will cease to exist, the way it is being looted by these parties.'

Kejriwal, though, has had to temper that impatience with the realization that a political party cannot be built overnight. Morarji Desai and V. P. Singh had both served in government before defecting from Congress, and had brought other parties together under an anti-Congress banner. Kejriwal is effectively starting from scratch, and he now seems to realize what lies ahead.

'The mood of the people is still the same, but they look at us as anti-corruption activists,' he said. 'In order to create a political space for yourself, to be perceived by people as a political alternative, you have to make a beginning somewhere, and Delhi, I think, is going to be the beginning. As far as becoming a political force is concerned, I completely concede that it is a long haul. People are very agitated and very angry against the existing political parties, that is one part. But for them to see you as a credible political alternative, as a ruling party, that is a long way.'

If the Delhi fast had seemed something of an anti-climax, Kejriw-al's political career has been anything but. In December 2013 his Aam Admi Party surprised almost everyone with an extremely impressive debut showing in the Delhi legislative assembly elections, bagging 28 of the 70 seats on offer and coming second only to the BJP. Equally astoundingly, Kejriwal thrashed three-times Congress Chief Minister Sheila Dikshit in her own constituency by nearly 26,000 votes, more than doubling her tally. 'This is not my victory, this is the victory of the people of Delhi,' a beaming Kejriwal told hundreds of his white-cap wearing supporters outside the party office, many of them swirling the brooms that are the new party's election symbol. 'In many ways, the result is historic. Our democracy has been subservient to political parties governed by caste, religion, money-power, muscle-power and corruption for too long. People were exhausted with this kind of poli-tics and decided to contest elections themselves.'

This was no hyperbole. Indian friends called Kejriwal's victory a triumph for democracy, a sign that democracy was alive and well: one told me she was jumping for joy when the results were announced. Suddenly, there was fresh hope that the nation's cynical politics could really be cleansed, that voting could really make a difference. Turnout in Delhi was over 65 per cent, a new record, as Kejriwal drew new support from across class and caste lines. Rahul Gandhi admitted that the Aam Admi Party had 'involved a lot of people who traditional parties did not involve,' and made a fairly empty vow that Congress would do the same in ways 'you cannot even imagine right now'. Pratap Bhanu Mehta of the Centre for Policy Research called the results 'absolutely spectacular' and a sign of the potential for progres-sive, creative politics to seize the day. 'In a paradoxical turn, the party that was accused of being anti-politics has rejuvenated politics to a degree no one could have imagined,' he wrote.[16]

Kejriwal had also stayed true to his word and made every contri-bution to his new party public, publishing each one online.[17] When the party felt it had enough money, he said, it even stopped taking contributions, a step that may be unprecedented in political history, and withdrew one candidate when reports surfaced about his possible corruption.

Kejriwal went on to form a government in New Delhi with the backing of Congress, and on 28 December 2013 was sworn in as the capital's seventh Chief Minister. His political career is only just beginning, and he will have to work hard to maintain this momentum. Yet it is increasingly clear that he is no shooting star: it seems fairly certain that he will be irritating the corrupt and the complacent for many years to come. One magazine called Kejriwal 'The Demolition Man'; George Bernard Shaw might simply have called him an 'unreasonable man', just the kind that revolutions need, and perhaps just the kind of man India sometimes needs to challenge the cosy circle of complicity at the highest levels of power. There is no doubt that Arvind Kejriwal is a flawed hero of modern India, a man whose energy and impatience helped to bring corruption to the centre of the national debate and helped to engage the middle class in ways that other activists have signally failed to do. His ego and his extreme self-righteousness are his greatest assets, and they may also be his greatest weaknesses; but for all his faults, Kejriwal has inspired many people to make a stand against the corruption they see around them, and now he has also inspired people to vote for him too.

Another man to take a stand was Ashok Khemka, who went to the same college as Kejriwal before making his way into India's bureaucracy. As Kejriwal set out his grand plans for political change in the autumn of 2012, Khemka emerged into the limelight as another hero of the struggle against corruption, an ordinary citizen who was not scared to sacrifice his own career in the interests of clean government.

11

Hard Times for an Honest Man

Whistleblowers under attack in India's bureaucracy

*'People like me who fall foul of the system, who see through their game,
they try to badger you, to bully you. All these kinds of threats, they make
life horrible for you.'*
Ashok Khemka to the author, October 2012

Ashok Khemka is a troublemaker. He says he has a 'sixth sense' for corruption, and in every job he has been given in India's bureaucracy, the 47-year-old Khemka has done his best to sniff out and stamp out the stealing that surrounds him. To say that this does not always go down well with his bosses is something of an understatement. In twenty-one years of service in the northern state of Haryana, Khemka's determination to follow the proper rules and procedures has seen him transferred out of his job more than forty times,[1] and moved to another department on average every six months. In 2012, Khemka became a national celebrity and a hero in the battle against corruption, when he took on the might of the Nehru–Gandhi family.

It happens that Khemka had been at the same college as anti-corruption activist Arvind Kejriwal, both of them attending the prestigious Indian Institute of Technology in the West Bengal town of Kharagpur. But while Khemka studied computer science, Kejriwal was a mechanical engineering student. The pair lived in different hostels and never knew each other. But twenty-three years after they graduated, their paths were to cross in a more meaningful way.

It was the beginning of October 2012, and Khemka had recently been appointed director of land registration in Haryana. Quite why the state government had let a known stickler for honesty anywhere near the most corrupt sector of the Indian economy I have never been able to establish, but there he was – at the exact moment that Kejriwal burst back onto the national scene with his sensational accusations that Rahul Gandhi's brother-in-law, Robert Vadra, had amassed a fortune through corrupt land deals in Haryana. This was Khemka's patch, and it was not the sort of thing that a man of his nature could ignore: on 8 October he summoned his staff to a meeting, and ordered an immediate investigation. At the same time, he asked for all the relevant land records to be sent to his office. 'In case the allegations are false, the fair name of our registering officers will be cleared in public,' he wrote in his spidery handwriting in an internal memo. 'In case the allegations are correct, it is appropriate that Shri Robert Vadra compensates the state the underpaid stamp duty and penalties, After all, Robert Vadra is a citizen and is amenable to the rule of law like any other ordinary citizen.'[2]

Unfortunately, Khemka was wrong, because Robert Vadra was not just any other citizen. Within a few days, bureaucrats in two districts told him they could not comply with his request to send over the relevant land records because of instructions 'from the top'. It was like a red rag to a bull, not the sort of answer Khemka could possibly accept. 'I said: "Look, Robert Vadra is not above the law. If you don't do it, I will address you a letter, and it will become a media storm."' It was typical of the way Khemka was willing to raise the stakes, but its effect was not what he intended – for the storm broke over his career. At ten o'clock that night, a note arrived at Khemka's modest apartment in the state capital Chandigarh telling him he had once again been transferred, demoted to a more junior role running an arm of the government developing and producing seeds for the state's farmers.

Shortly afterwards, I met him there, in his large but bare office in the Haryana Seeds Development Corporation, and sat on a dowdy orange-checked couch as he set out the whole story. Khemka, with a thin moustache and spectacles, looks every inch

the bureaucrat. He passed one of the most competitive examina-
tions in the world to join the Indian Administrative Service, has a
PhD in computer science and a mind full of rules and regulations.
His conversation is laced with references to sections of the administrative rulebook, to land laws and to the constitution. As he
talked, he paced about his office as though he were lecturing and I
was his audience.

The Vadra affair, he explained, had its roots in India's rigorous
zoning laws, which have created an artificial scarcity of industrial
and residential land. As we have seen, a simple bureaucratic decision
to re-zone land can raise its value by a large multiple, the benefit of
which is 'cornered by politicians, bureaucrats and business'. Vadra's
business model was brilliant: he had married a Gandhi, and in the
process became semi-royal. He was now, it is alleged, using his name
and political influence to play the system and corner some of those
benefits for himself.[3]

In March 2008, Vadra's company Skylight Hospitality had allegedly bought 3.5 acres of farmland close to the fast-expanding city of
Gurgaon, a forest of skyscrapers on the outskirts of the capital, for 7.5
crore rupees ($1.4 million). Gurgaon had grown in the past two
decades from almost nothing to become one of the world's premier
outsourcing and offshoring centres; land prices were soaring. Within
twenty-four hours of the purchase going through, Skylight had been
given a licence to exploit the land for commercial use, a re-zoning
process that would normally take months to process, Khemka said.
The licence fee cost an additional 8 crores ($1.5 million), but the
decision sent the land value soaring. Within sixty-five days, Skylight
was alleged to have agreed to sell the land to the property developer
DLF for 58 crores ($10.6 million).

So far, so clever. Few people would argue that Vadra's name had not
been a huge asset in getting the land re-zoned so quickly, and enabling
him to cream off vast profits for himself. It certainly seemed improper
for a member of such an important political family to use his influence in this way. But was it actually illegal? It appeared so, argued first

Kejriwal and now Khemka. The first question was whether the land had been correctly valued when Skylight bought it, and therefore whether the correct amount of stamp duty had been paid. The second was whether the transfer of the land to DLF had been carried out legally.

Although most of the money was paid to Skylight in 2008 and 2009, the land title and its accompanying (and immensely valuable) licence remained in the name of Vadra's company for several years, Khemka said. 'Either he didn't inform the [land] department [of the sale], or he informed the department and they took no action,' he said. 'In both cases the situation talks of a serious governance deficit. If you had sold the land, the licence would have to be cancelled, since the licence is to a person.'

The licence stipulated that the owner of the land should develop it within two years of its purchase, but nothing was done. In 2011, an extension to Skylight's licence was granted, even though it was not clear at that stage who actually owned the land. Finally, and in direct contravention of the rules, the land – and the licence – was transferred to DLF's name in 2012, when the remainder of the money was paid to Skylight. Such a transfer would normally require fresh government permission, fresh registration of the land, and a fresh payment of stamp duty to the government. None of those steps appeared to have been taken, Khemka said.

Khemka did not know for sure whether the Vadra affair had led to his transfer, because it was not the only controversy he had embroiled himself in. Shortly after entering the land records office, he had ordered a separate investigation into the transfer of farmlands to realtor companies, some of which, mysteriously, had only been created a few days earlier. Khemka claimed to have evidence that land had been deliberately undervalued, and that forest land had also been illegally taken to create 'prime plots near highways to build farmhouses or resorts'.

Whatever the reason for his transfer, Khemka was dismayed. He wrote to the state's Chief Minister, Bhupinder Hooda, a Congress party bigwig known to be close to the party's elite in New Delhi. The civil service rules stipulate a secure tenure of at least two years, he argued, something that is supposed to protect public servants from just this kind of pressure. 'I am threatened that I would be subject to transfer every month so as to humiliate and demoralize me and create road blocks for regular and timely release of salary,' he wrote in the letter. 'My family feels threatened due to certain vested elements whose interests were adversely affected by the exposure of scams in this department. I plead for security and fixed tenure in a cadre post befitting my seniority.'[4]

The Chief Minister ignored his appeal. With nowhere else to turn, the transferred Khemka turned to the media, making multiple appearances on India's scam-hungry twenty-four-hour television channels. But he was at pains to insist to me that he was not criticizing government policy, which would in itself be a breach of his own rules of employment. 'Crony capitalism and corruption is not government policy,' he said. 'I am just lending my voice against my superior decision-makers in the hierarchy, who are blatantly disobeying government policy and engaging in this kind of racketeering.'

Not surprisingly perhaps, his television appearances simply stoked the fire. Hooda denied that his transfer was a punishment, and promised the allegations against Vadra would be investigated, but, more menacingly, threatened that if they were found to be false 'appropriate action' could be taken against the bureaucrat who had levelled them.

Congress leaders used loyal journalists to launch a whisper campaign in New Delhi about Khemka's character, and an old letter from a bureaucrat questioning his 'mental stability' was dredged up – even though the bureaucrat's claims had subsequently been investigated and dismissed. Government loyalists asked whether he was simply someone who could not hold down a job. 'Is he the only Mr Right and all others evil ogres, or is there a fundamental problem that is being overlooked?' asked the Congress spokesman Manish Tewari.

The problem, of course, was not in Khemka but in the corruption he encountered at every turn and in his stubborn refusal to be co-opted. In 1993, as a local magistrate, he was asked by the then chief minister of Haryana to procure government trucks to transport people to a Congress party rally. He refused, and was transferred. Later, he successfully fought against the use of asbestos in warehouse walls and water pipes, overcoming a powerful asbestos lobby in league with local politicians. He blew apart a cartel supplying poor-quality bricks to the government, and exposed the illegal transfer of prime land just outside New Delhi to a builder at a cheap rate. His efforts won him a national anti-corruption award in 2011,[5] the prize money for which he says he donated to research to fund cancer and tuberculosis treatment.

By the time we met, the stress was clearly affecting Khemka, who said he had scarcely slept all week. 'People like me who fall foul of the system, who see through their game, they try to badger you, to bully you. All these kinds of threats, they make life horrible for you,' he said. I asked for details. 'I received threats that Vadra is a very big man, that the Indian army is behind him, that he will finish me off.'

Ashok Khemka is compulsive in his determination to root out corruption wherever it exists, because, as he explains it, wherever there is corruption, there is always a victim. But he is not immune to the pressure that his compulsion brings with it. 'In the last one or two months, most of my friends, or some of them, have deserted me, for the reason of fear, or part jealousy,' he said. 'I will not walk into an office very comfortably. Sometimes I feel a sense of uneasiness, that I am not one of them.'

Yet Khemka is not completely alone. His junior colleagues are often proud to be associated with him, he told me, and he had received messages of support that week from retired senior bureaucrats – including a former boss – as well as from Indians all over the world. That support had helped him through this 'nightmarish experience' – that, and his conviction that you have to remain inside the system if you want to reform it. 'This cronyism must stop,' he said. 'The sense of rule of law only comes when those at the top are made to pay the penalty of their crimes.'

Khemka had told me his only fear was losing his job and not being able to provide for his family. After his workday was over, we went to the family home, where I met his long-suffering wife Jyoti, an artist and art historian and the mother of their two boys. She supported him, had faith in him and didn't question his decisions, she told me, just as he did not challenge the way she ran the household. But I imagined Khemka as a tough man to please at home as well as at work: his younger, teenage son Ganesh wandered in, and said he wanted to be a lawyer rather than a bureaucrat, because he wanted to contribute to society, but didn't want to end up reporting to his dad. Mother and son agreed they were proud of Khemka, even if he hadn't always been the perfect father. As a boy, I remembered reading, Khemka had once cried when he scored only 99 per cent in a maths exam and was consigned to second place. I imagined him to be an exacting father.

Later, I checked out Khemka's background. Journalists and lawyers in Chandigarh dismissed the government's smear campaign: Khemka had an unrivalled reputation for honesty and for making the corrupt uncomfortable wherever he was posted. 'In my experience, there are two kinds of government officers – officers who work only to please their political masters, and other officers who work to uphold the law, who work for justice and the poor,' advocate Kuldip Tiwari told me, in a comment that was typical of the responses I received. 'I put Mr Khemka in category two. So far as his honesty and integrity is concerned, no one can doubt it.'[6]

In his job at the land registration department, Khemka was trying to clean out the most corrupt sector of India's economy. And he was doing it in a state where there is little or no social stigma about being corrupt, where, in his own words, there was something 'macho' about being wealthy through gaming the system. The nexus between politicians, bureaucrats and builders in Haryana was a powerful source of ill-gotten wealth, especially as land prices soared close to Delhi. An investigation by *The Hindu* newspaper, published in February 2013, claimed that 1,350 acres of land had been acquired from poor farmers at cheap rates since Hooda had taken over as Chief Minister in 2004, and later licensed to builders for vast profits.[7] The 1894 land law had been abused, the report alleged, to force farmers to part with their land 'for public purpose', only for the eventual benefits to flow to the builders and politicians instead of the farmers or the public. 'In many instances, valid objections of senior officials are overruled to benefit the builder,' the newspaper alleged.

But even outside Haryana, Khemka and his ilk are swimming against the tide. In January 2012, a Hong Kong-based consultancy firm, Political and Risk Consultancy, rated India's bureaucracy the worst in Asia, giving it a rating of 9.21, compared with 2.25 for Singapore, where 10 is the worst possible score.[8] Officials were willing to accept under-the-table payments and business executives were tempted to pay in order to overcome bureaucratic inertia and gain government favours, the Press Trust of India reported. Bureaucrats were rarely held accountable for wrong decisions, something which the report said gave them 'terrific powers' and could be one of the main reasons they are perceived so negatively.

Yet that is not the whole story. In the way that he relentlessly pursues corruption, Khemka is extraordinary. But I believe there are many bureaucrats who are honest in their personal dealings, but silent about the corruption they see around them. I have met many such people, often now retired, at Anna Hazare's and Arvind Kejriwal's rallies. They may not blow the whistle, but their careers have often suffered because of their honesty.

Bureaucrats in India are typecast as lazy, conservative, arrogant and corrupt, says the best-selling author Chetan Bhagat, but not all of them deserve that description. Many are committed, hard-working and trying to make a difference, often for a fraction of the salary they could earn in the private sector.[9] But virtually none, he argues, have any guts, and most are too petrified of bosses to fight for change, too accepting of a hierarchy that does not reward initiative.[10]

Manmohan Singh, a man who spent much of his life working within India's bureaucracy, certainly seemed to see the need for reform in the way it functioned. In 2005 he set up an Administrative Reforms

Commission to provide 'a detailed blueprint' to revamp public administration.[11] The six-member commission toiled away for four years and produced fifteen reports. Among its many recommendations were the reduction in the number of ministries at central and state level, the 'democratic decentralization' of power to local governments that were closer to citizens, the strengthening of the power and autonomy of industry regulatory bodies, and the passing of the long-mooted law to set up a Lokpal, or anti-corruption ombudsman. It was an eminently sensible set of recommendations that, if implemented, might have protected India from the scandals that blighted Singh's second term in office. Sadly, most of the recommendations are still gathering dust; faced with opposition from within the establishment, and with many other battles to fight, Singh seems to have lacked the political will or political clout to push them through.

Politicians often blame bureaucrats for failing to take decisions, but the problem, lamented lifelong civil servant Shailaja Chandra in an op-ed for the *Indian Express* in 2012, is that the signals coming down from on high are all wrong.[12] Risk-taking is not celebrated in India's bureaucracy and dishonesty seldom punished. 'Not even a fraction of those who deserve punishment ever get penalized and instead a number of honest officers get stigmatized by remaining under investigations for years together,' she wrote. 'In the ultimate analysis, all civil servants agree that connections and sycophancy overshadow hard work and probity.' Incentives need to change to reward risk-taking, investigations need to be concluded quickly and transparently, and an impartial board appointed to hear officers' grievances, she wrote. 'Investment in levelling the playing field could give birth to some rare daredevils.'

Sanjiv Chaturvedi is like Khemka, another man who couldn't resist blowing the whistle. And when he saw how rotten the system was, how shamelessly it punished him for his honesty, he blew it again and again. Also like Khemka, he was a very bright young man. After completing a degree in electrical engineering, he too joined the bureaucracy, coming second in a national examination to join the Indian Forest Service in 2005, eleven years after Khemka. His is a story of persecution and harassment for daring to cross Haryana's Chief Minister Bhupinder Hooda, a strife so unrelenting that his marriage fell apart. But unlike Khemka's tale, it has some good guys in it, people who stood up for Chaturvedi when he most needed it; and it has a happy ending.

I met Chaturvedi in New Delhi, in his office at the All India Institute of Medical Sciences (AIIMS), where he was posted in 2012. He sat beneath a huge poster setting out the lessons of time and karma, which concluded with the words: 'Time is more powerful than you, so be good and do good.' His father was an electricity board engineer in Uttar Pradesh, his maternal grandfather a freedom fighter 'who was imprisoned by the Britishers'. His elder brother also works for the Forest Service. He framed his conversation by telling how tough the Jat people of Haryana were, how corruption was not seen as a social stigma there, how people were prone to what he called 'vulgar displays of wealth'. He wore a red thread around his right wrist to ward off evil, and a ring with a green stone on the little finger of the same hand. While Khemka had quoted from the Hindu holy book, the Gita, in the course of one of our conversations, Chaturvedi frequently mentioned how he had been saved at various points in his battle because of 'divine intervention'.

His first posting was in Kurukshetra, a destination that appealed to him because of its importance in Hindu scriptures, where he was put in charge of the Saraswati Wildlife Sanctuary, one of Haryana's last remaining forest areas and home to the endangered hog deer. Almost at once he discovered that a 400 crore ($73 million) irrigation canal was being built right through the sanctuary, without environmental clearances or any respect for the reserve. Heavy machinery was ripping up the earth, and trees were being felled on a massive scale. Appalled, Chaturvedi put his foot down, even going so far as to have trenches dug around the reserve to stop the diggers coming in.

It was, of course, a deeply provocative move to the Haryana elite.

Not only were irrigation projects seen as good politics in a state with a permanent shortage of water and a falling water table; they were also a good way for politicians to make money in collusion with contractors, even if they produced few lasting results in terms of irrigation. Chaturvedi says Hooda was furious with him, and the sycophantic senior bureaucrats who surrounded the Chief Minister decided that this young upstart should be taught a lesson. He was transferred to Fatehabad, but he was soon in trouble again, after he objected to a plan to use government money to construct a 'herbal park' on private land owned by an influential politician. Within a month, he had stopped the work; within two he was suspended, and given a formal charge of insubordination that threatened him with dismissal from the service.

Chaturvedi told me he felt shattered and utterly humiliated, as the government now forced him to sit at home with nothing to do, and with friends and relatives continuously asking him what he had done wrong. Whereas Khemka appears to have accepted his repeated transfers, Chaturvedi's back was now against the wall. Buoyed by 'very, very strong emotional bonding' within his immediate family, and by his faith in God, he decided to fight on. Knowing that the people who had written India's constitution and the rules of its administrative service had built in certain safeguards to protect bureaucrats from politically motivated persecution, he appealed to the central government for help, and even filed an RTI application to force Haryana to divulge the reason for his suspension.

What followed was extraordinary. States in India guard their constitutionally mandated autonomy very jealously, and don't take kindly to being told what to do by the central government in New Delhi. But, in Chaturvedi's case, the Congress-led government in New Delhi took the extraordinary step in January 2008 of revoking his suspension order, sending the Haryana government a letter from the office of the President himself.[13] It was even more extraordinary because of Hooda's close ties to the Congress elite, but it failed to calm the waters. Hooda took the snub badly, trying to push Chaturvedi into one undesirable junior-ranking post after another. Still, the young forestry officer resisted, successfully appealing against the transfers to the bureaucracy's Central Administrative Tribunal, with his friends and supporters in the bureaucracy clubbing together to cover his legal costs.

Finally, Chaturvedi was sent to a place called Jhajjar, the constituency of Hooda's son, Deepender. If it was an attempt to place the young bureaucrat somewhere he could be supervised and controlled, it did not work. This time, Chaturvedi uncovered the brazen theft of government money meant to pay for forest plantations that simply didn't exist. Working against the clock before he was transferred again, he managed to force an independent investigation that saw more than forty people suspended for corruption. By this stage, the threats were mounting; there were even demonstrations against him staged outside his office. He was transferred again, and charged again.

By August 2010, Chaturvedi approached the President's office once more, complaining of having suffered twelve transfers over five years and having been kept without a posting at all for more than two years. In January 2011, the President's office again wrote to Haryana, ordering the charges against the forestry officer to be dropped, in what can only be described as an extremely rare intervention by New Delhi in the business of a state government.[14]

That's when things really turned nasty. Chaturvedi says the investigations into his private life were pretty intense by this stage, but there was apparently little to uncover – he told me that as a Brahmin, Hinduism's priestly caste, he did not drink, smoke or 'have extra-marital affairs'. Eventually, though, the police found something they could – at a stretch – try to pin on him.

One of the officials who had been suspended for corruption in Jhajjar was found dead some months later. Although Chaturvedi was long gone from the district at the time, and there was nothing to link him to the case, nor even to suggest the man had taken his own life, the young government officer was charged with abetment to suicide.

At this point, one gets the feeling that even the politicians and bureaucrats in New Delhi must have thought enough was really enough. Chaturvedi paid tribute to Environment Minister Jairam Ramesh[15] and his successor Jayanthi Natarajan for rising above party considerations and supporting him. The central government asked for Chaturvedi to be transferred back to Delhi. Hooda refused to sign the order releasing him for several months, only to be eventually, and unusually, overruled again.

The young man was exhausted. The stress had affected his marriage, and the constant upheaval had meant he and his wife had not really been able to set up home together, living apart for long periods. The 'normal issues' in a marriage were magnified, and eventually they had divorced. At work, papers accusing him of one crime or act of insubordination after another were piling up in his in-tray. But his ordeal was not quite over. It appeared that Hooda had used his considerable influence in Delhi to blacken the young man's name, and one ministry and institution after another – from Kapil Sibal's Human Resource Development Ministry to S. Y. Quraishi's Election Commission – refused to take him on. Finally, the top bureaucrat in the health ministry came to his aid, getting his minister to approve Chaturvedi's hire by the simple ruse of not briefing his boss about the young man's past.

He landed up at AIIMS, India's premier medical institute, where I met him some months later, happy and settled and working as the Chief Vigilance Officer, whose job it was to prevent corruption.

Of course, knowing Chaturvedi, there had to be one final twist in the tale: soon after he had arrived at AIIMS, he had uncovered systemic corruption in the procurement of medical supplies there, and won the enmity of the most senior bureaucrat at the hospital, the deputy director in charge of administration. Pretty soon, the Health Minister, Ghulam Nabi Azad, found out who Chaturvedi was, and duly ordered him transferred to another institute, in charge of ayurvedic medicine, yoga and homeopathy. Fortunately, AIIMS is so high-profile that parliamentarians take notice of what happens there. Azad's plans were thwarted by a parliamentary committee,

Chaturvedi kept his job and the deputy director's contract was not extended.[16] His replacement, Chaturvedi assured me, was an extremely honest man.

Today, Chaturvedi is frequently asked to deliver lectures to trainee bureaucrats, as well as police officers, on his ultimately successful battle against the dark forces of corruption in India. Many of the junior officers he meets in these events come up and tell him they too want to work honestly. The tragedy, of course, is that many will get those ideals bullied out of them in the course of their careers.[17]

One could argue that Chaturvedi is living proof that the checks and balances built into the system do have some power to protect the honest bureaucrat (even if he does attribute the biggest role to God's grace). Without the independent backing of the Central Administrative Tribunal and the support of the central government, Chaturvedi's career would have been buried long ago. All along, he had support from his subordinates, he says, and, of course, from some influential people in New Delhi. The media, one of the biggest checks and balances in any properly functioning democracy, consistently backed him – from a campaign by the *Times of India* newspaper to frequent spots on twenty-four-hour TV channels like NDTV and CNN-IBN. And he wouldn't have survived without the Right to Information Act, he says: he reckons he has filed around 100 RTI requests just to get to the bottom of what he was being accused of at one stage or another.

Yet a more cynical reading would suggest that Chaturvedi was just lucky, because he had the position, the education and the self-confidence to win; to exploit the system and use the media to protect himself. The story of the whistleblower Ram Kumar Thakur in Bihar from Chapter 5 shows that many people are not that lucky, and do not have as many levers to pull.

The essence of any functioning democracy is this system of checks and balances, which prevent the abuse of democratically granted power by any arm of authority, whether executive, legislature or judiciary. Each pillar of democracy is supposed to supervise the others.

But the establishment cannot be expected to always police itself effectively: a properly functioning democracy also requires active supervision by ordinary citizens. It needs whistleblowers like Khemka, Chaturvedi and Thakur to be protected.

There is now an Act before parliament supposed to do just that, and protect whistleblowers in India: one suggested provision is that any information a murdered RTI activist is seeking should be immediately released and disseminated widely – a measure supposed to ensure that death will not silence a whistleblower's complaint. But the southern state of Andhra Pradesh has found a different way to expose corruption and simultaneously protect those who speak – by institutionalizing 'social audits', where work done under the National Rural Employment Guarantee Scheme (NREGA) was read out in public gatherings, just as it had been in Kot Kirana.

The audits have been a resounding success. Already nearly 5,000 government officers or contractors have been sacked, more than 1,000 suspended and more than 13,000 punished in some other way for scams uncovered in the audits of NREGA alone. More than 684 million rupees ($12 million dollars) in 'misappropriated' government funds have been identified, and nearly one third of these recovered from the swindlers. The audits reach 30,000 villagers and employ 1,200 young men across the state, drawn from poor rural backgrounds, as facilitators.

But the numbers tell only part of the story. There are audits under way every day all across the state, each one attended by hundreds of villagers, as well as local politicians and bureaucrats, with the meeting sometimes lasting from 11 a.m. until the early hours of the next morning. They have quickly become embedded in rural culture in Andhra Pradesh, and are so successful that they have already been extended to other rural welfare schemes, including pensions, scholarships and a midday meals scheme meant to encourage children to attend school.

What is extraordinary about this scheme is that it has uncovered a huge nexus between local bureaucrats, politicians and contractors at the village without generating reprisals, and with the backing of the state government – something that has astonished Sowmya Kidambi, who has been running the social audits in Andhra Pradesh for nearly three years. 'We haven't had one person shot or killed,' she said. 'And to the credit of the state government, in the past six or seven years there has been not one call from the Chief Minister's office, or from anyone's office, saying don't do a public hearing or don't release this report.'

One of the secrets was a chief minister named Y. S. Rajasekhara Reddy, popularly known as YSR, who wanted to differentiate himself from his predecessor by courting the rural poor. Former Chief Minister Chandrababu Naidu had been the darling of the urban middle classes and the media for his efforts to turn Hyderabad into an IT capital. He was visited by Bill Clinton and Tony Blair, voted South Asian of the year by *Time* magazine in 1999, and nicknamed the 'Laptop Minister'.

But he neglected the state's vast rural hinterland, and let corruption run wild in the villages. He was trounced in elections in 2004. Reddy cast himself as a hero for the rural poor – if there was to be corruption in his state, he decided (and there was, of course, still massive corruption), it should not come at the expense of rural development programmes. He issued strict instructions that anyone caught stealing from these programmes shouldn't come running to him for sympathy.[18]

Kidambi said that when the social audits began in 2006, they found that 90 to 95 per cent of the money allocated for a food-for-work programme was being 'siphoned off' by local officials and contractors. Since then, the deterrence value of the social audits has brought that number tumbling down.

Naidu had followed a traditional political model in rural India, treating the village heads, or sarpanches, as vote banks – letting them steal all they want, on the condition that they deliver their village's vote. Reddy, seeing this model was no longer working, went straight to the people themselves. Rajesekhara Reddy was corrupt, said Kidambi, but he remained a hero to the people because he delivered services like housing, education, work, schools and pensions. 'In that sense he was a political genius.' By the time of his death in a helicopter crash in 2009, the social audits were so successful in the state that there was no turning back.

There are good and honest people throughout India's bureaucracy, but the ruling ethos has become accountability to one's boss rather than to the people. Partly perhaps as a result of bad habits inherited from British colonial rule, and partly because of India's hierarchical, caste-divided society, the bureaucrat in India often seems to behave less as a public servant and more as a lord of his or her domain. What is most astounding about the social audits is how effectively they have challenged that mindset.

'The attitude of the system is that they are accountable only to somebody who is their superior,' said Kidambi. 'The constant refrain in the first few years was "This person is only a fourth-class pass, and I am supposed to answer to him? What is his status in life, to come and ask me a question?"' Bureaucrats complained the audits humiliated them and made them feel like criminals, she said. 'How someone who was not their boss could ask them a question was beyond them.'

Now, India's central government wants to extend the experiment across the whole country. The tragedy, says Kidambi, is that most of the other states which have carried out pilot schemes have carried them out in so 'dismal' a way that they have been rendered ineffective. There are still too few politicians, it seems, daring enough to realize that honesty and efficiency in public service delivery can actually win more votes than corruption and nepotism.

Kidambi had started out as an activist with MKSS, the organization run by Aruna Roy and Nikhil Dey in Rajasthan, in 1998, before joining the social audit programme in Andhra Pradesh in 2005. She admits to being very cynical at first about government, but says she discovered that there were people she could work with, and ways to get around. The real credit for the introduction of the social audits, she explained to me as we delved deeper into the subject, was not really due to Chief Minister Reddy but to an extremely committed and honest bureaucrat, K. Raju, who was then acting as rural development secretary to the government. It was Raju who had convinced Reddy that there were votes in delivering services to the rural poor more efficiently; winning him over by talking to him in a language he could understand. Reform in Andhra was only possible because an influential section of the bureaucracy was willing to embrace it, she said: without bureaucratic will, reforms are impossible, no matter how often people take to the streets and call for change.

Her comments reminded me of Khemka's determination to reform the system from within, yet she seemed to offer more hope of sustainable change. Honest bureaucrats could make a difference, she said, if they strategize well: when an opposition politician asks for a report that might damn the government, Kidambi will tell him or her to file an RTI request, so that she cannot be accused of leaking information to the government's opponents.

An hour or so after I put the phone down on Kidambi, I was speaking to Khemka again. This was the beginning of April 2013, and he had been transferred again, out of his job at the head of the Haryana Seeds Development Corporation. The organization's role was to buy seeds from suppliers and sell them to farmers at subsidized rates. Not surprisingly, Khemka believed he had found evidence of collusion between bureaucrats and the suppliers to overcharge the government and share out the proceeds. He had also, he believed, found evidence that vast quantities of fungicide were being imported by the state, at considerable expense, to protect Haryana's wheat seeds from a variety of diseases, under false pretences. The fungicide did not even protect the seeds from a common disease known as karnal bunt that afflicted a significant proportion of Haryana's wheat crop, he concluded; someone, somewhere, appeared to be making money illegally.

The government, predictably, was not interested in Khemka's complaint. But the scandal leaked to the media in Chandigarh, and local seed-growers took the government to court. On 4 April 2013 an officer several ranks junior to him turned up in Khemka's office, the same place we had met four months before. 'He told me: "I am now the MD [of the seeds corporation], you have to relinquish your charge,"' Khemka said. 'Then he just continued to sit before me, so I could not even finish up my work.'

Khemka was told to go home and await his transfer orders, which were duly posted on the Internet at 7.30 p.m. that night. He had been posted to head up the Archives Department, where he is now supposed to be in charge of dusty files that date back to the British colonial era, and even before that to Mughal rule – somewhere the government obviously believed he could do no harm.

'In this post, I am truly archived,' Ashok Khemka told me.

Although the national spotlight has moved away from Ashok Khemka these days, he remains an important figure in the struggle to counter corruption and afford better protection to those who blow the whistle, an inspiration to India's honest bureaucrats.[19] But democracy in this country has other heroes too. There is one whose sacrifices are even greater than Khemka's, whose lonely struggle for justice on India's remote northeastern fringe is all too often forgotten by the mainstream media. Her name is Irom Sharmila.

12

Isolation

One woman's lonely struggle to rein in the powers
of the army in India's remote northeast

'My protest needs some time, to awaken our people, our leaders . . .
I never feel lonely, but I just feel I am missing something, someone who
will be my life partner, my soul mate.'
Irom Sharmila, speaking to the author outside a courtroom in
Manipur after her fortnightly appearance before a judge,
February 2013

'The brutality of the armed forces in border areas leads to deep disen-
chantment . . . Serious allegations of persistent sexual assault on the
women in such areas and conflict areas are causing more alienation.'
Retired Justice J. S. Verma, head of the committee asked to look at
ways to protect women in the wake of the Delhi gang-rape,
January 2013

It was 11 July 2004, and the small hill state of Manipur on India's far
northeastern border with Burma was deeply embroiled in a bloody
separatist insurgency that had left thousands of people dead. On the
outskirts of the state capital, Imphal, 32-year-old Thangjam Manorama Devi was at home asleep, with her mother and two of her
brothers in adjoining rooms. Not long after midnight, soldiers
surrounded the house and burst in, dragging the family out of bed at
gunpoint, separating Manorama from the others. The house was
searched, although nothing was found. Manorama was interrogated,

accused of being a member of an insurgent group, of making bombs, of killing soldiers; judging by her screams, she was tortured, in her own home, within earshot of her own family. At 3.30 a.m. she was taken away.[1]

Shortly after dawn, villagers found the bullet-ridden body of Manorama Devi by the side of a paddy field a couple of miles from her home. The gunshot wounds to her genitals prevented doctors being certain she had been raped, but the semen stains on her sarong were strong evidence to suggest she might have been. Her body was scratched, bruised, and bore a large gash to her thigh, relatives and witnesses said.

The army was later to claim that Manorama had led them on a merry dance that night, promising to lead them to the hideout of another insurgent, but constantly changing her mind about its whereabouts. Eventually, they said, she had wanted to relieve herself by the roadside, and was shot while attempting to escape. Yet there has never been any attempt to explain why a group of young, fit soldiers had been unable to outpace and peacefully apprehend a woman wearing a tightly bound sarong and whose hands had been tied. The lack of bullet casings or blood at the scene made human rights groups believe she had been killed elsewhere and her body dumped. The police surgeon and forensics specialist later testified that the bullet wounds suggested she had been shot while lying down, while the injuries to her body seemed to confirm the torture that her family had overheard.

The Indian army was not popular in Manipur: the suspicion and contempt with which it treated the state's citizens had created a tinderbox of resentment. Manorama's death lit the fire. For months, thousands of people took to the streets, defying a curfew. Government offices were torched, hundreds of protesters were beaten, hundreds more arrested. One man died after setting himself alight, and three others suffered severe burns. But one protest, above all, caught the nation's consciousness. A dozen middle-aged and elderly women took off their clothes in front of the main army barracks in

the Manipuri capital Imphal, and paraded behind a sign that said
'Indian Army Rape Us'. It made front-page news in Delhi, and briefly
alerted a nation to the suffering of its remote citizens.

For Manipur, this was the equivalent of the rape and murder of J
more than eight years later in the national capital, an outpouring of
anguish and rage that demanded a response. Yet for eight years the
Indian government has systematically blocked the release of a judicial
investigation into Manorama's death, let alone the prosecution of
those responsible, fighting a long legal battle that has now reached the
Supreme Court. While the Delhi protests caused India to re-examine
the way it treated and protected women, the death of Manorama changed nothing. The disappearances and murders of innocent
civilians went on, and the struggle for justice in Manorama's case
continues to be blocked to this day. Attitudes were too entrenched,
the army too powerful, politicians too scared of their own shadows to
impose any accountability on the nation's own armed forces.

Manipur, 1,500 miles from New Delhi, was too far from the
nation's consciousness to tug many heartstrings. Manipur encapsu-
lates the limits of Indian democracy, both to rein in the army where
'security' is supposedly at stake, and also just to rule the extremities of
this vast nation fairly and with respect.

One of them almost forgotten in India's remote northeast, the
other constantly in the news on its northwestern border, the states of
Manipur and Kashmir are two lonely outposts of the nation where
democracy seems to be singularly failing to function. Both chafe
under virtual military rule. In both, the armed forces operate above
the law and have been accused of atrocities against civilians. Visiting
both places first in 2004 and 2005, I saw how the absence of democratic civilian rule created widespread alienation from the rest of the
nation, and fomented violence. It is often said that without democracy India would never have survived as a nation after the British left.
In Manipur and Kashmir, perhaps, where democracy was failing, here
was the proof. My visits to both these places made me properly appreciate the democracy the rest of the country enjoyed – for all its obvious

faults, it offered an important pressure valve and, more than that, helped to foster a sense of nationhood.

Yet, even here, there is hope that things could get better. In 2013, most Kashmiris and Manipuris are sick of violence, and yearn for peace, development and respect from the rest of the country. While some continue to wage war on an Indian state they see as deeply oppressive, most are simply getting on with their lives. Nevertheless, both populations nurture a deep sense of hurt, and they need to heal; it is important that those who are struggling peacefully and democratically for justice are not ignored or made light of. This chapter, in a sense, is their story, the struggle of hundreds of women who have lost their husbands and their sons in the past three decades, abducted, 'disappeared', and in many cases executed by the army and police. Justice must be delivered to them if India is to draw a line under the violence, and embrace both Manipur and Kashmir properly into its national, democratic fold.

The Verma Committee, set up in the wake of J's rape and death to look at laws to better protect India's women, realized this, and lent its own weight to the struggle in January of 2013. Its chairman, retired Supreme Court Justice J. S. Verma, demanded that soldiers accused of raping civilians be tried in civilian courts, rather than hiding behind a draconian law that gives them virtual immunity from prosecution in conflict zones.[2]

Then, a few weeks later, thanks to the tireless work of human rights activists and lawyers, I sat in a New Delhi conference room, beside a woman whose husband had been kidnapped and killed by security forces more than four years earlier, and listened as army officers were finally forced to give their accounts of what happened during some of those disappearances. It was a tiny, incremental sign of progress, but it represented a glimmer of hope that India's democratic institutions could be goaded, slowly and painfully, into some kind of action.

To tell the story of Manipur, we have to return to the year 2000 – four years before Manorama was killed and the mothers of Manipur bared their bodies in protest – and talk about another young woman, who put her own body on the line to fight the injustice she saw around her.

Irom Sharmila Chanu was always a loner, a quiet woman who didn't even mix much with her eight brothers and sisters. She had two or three friends, her closest brother Singhjit recalls, but often she just liked to sit by herself inside the temple or under a nearby banyan tree and read books. She used to study the Gita, the 700-verse Hindu scriptural work that Mahatma Gandhi described as 'The Gospel of Selfless Action', but she also read the Bible, the Koran and Buddhist scriptures. Sometimes she wrote poetry.

Her mother remembers her as someone who cared little for the way she looked. She never wore make-up, and only dressed up on one occasion, for a relative's wedding. Sharmila was largely vegetarian and 'a little finicky about her food', her mother said. She preferred natural cures. She was also interested in women's rights, and wrote an occasional column for a local newspaper on social issues and nature. Then, at the age of twenty-eight, Sharmila got involved with a campaign that was to change her life, and thrust this shy, spiritually inclined woman into a spotlight in which she has never been entirely comfortable. Today, she is celebrated as the world's longest hunger-striker, and has won several international and domestic awards.

In 1958, faced with a separatist insurgency in the adjoining state of Nagaland, the government had introduced a draconian piece of legislation called the Armed Forces (Special Powers) Act, commonly known as AFSPA, which gave the army sweeping powers to search, arrest and shoot to kill suspected militants, even if the soldiers were not facing an imminent threat. It also gave the troops virtual immunity from prosecution. Under its provisions, no one can start legal action against members of the armed forces without permission from the central government: permission that is, in practice, almost never given.

The law was modelled on a similar piece of legislation introduced by the British in 1942 at the fag end of colonial rule to give the army free rein to counter India's growing freedom movement. But India's new rulers had failed to learn from the mistakes of their British predecessors: instead of dousing the fires of independence and insurgency, the imposition of virtual martial law in the hills of its remote northeast only made those fires burn more brightly, and helped ensure that the spirit of Nagaland's rebellion had spread to neighbouring Manipur.

When AFSPA was first introduced in the northeast there was just one insurgent group in the region, representing the Naga people; now there are more like fifty, local human rights activist Babloo Loitongbam told me. There were perhaps 100 militants, now there are at least 20,000. 'Instead of fighting insurgency, it has spawned insurgency,' he said, during one of our many conversations on the subject.[3]

The insurgency in Manipur began in earnest in the late 1970s, and since then a dizzying array of armed groups had sprung up in the state, demanding independence from India, or autonomous territory for their particular tribal grouping. The Indian army had responded by sending in tens of thousands of soldiers, who swarmed through the streets of the capital Imphal and set up armed roadblocks throughout the territory. Turn a corner, and an army truck would disgorge a large group of uniformed men; turn another, and a jeep would whizz by packed with soldiers, automatic rifles at the ready.

Manipur is an alien land for the Indian army. The people here are Tibeto-Burman in origin: although most of them are Hindus, they look much more Burmese than they do Indian. They have a completely different language, a different script and a different cuisine. Imphal lies in a broad river valley; its bright green paddy fields stand in striking contrast to the darker green of the forested hills that surround it on all four sides. It is known as the Land of Jewels, and was described by former Viceroy Lord Irwin as the Switzerland of India. Arriving there is like stepping out of India and into South East Asia. It is spectacular, but for Indian soldiers distinctly unwelcoming.

Send young men into a violent and culturally unfamiliar land far from home – where civilians and insurgents are hard to distinguish – give them guns and bullets and grant them immunity from prosecution, and you are asking for trouble. Throw in a rewards system that doles out cash and promotions for killing militants, and trouble is pretty much guaranteed. Not surprisingly, as the years went by, the accusations against the soldiers – of disappearances, extrajudicial executions, torture and even rape – began to pile up.

AFSPA has also been applied in India's restive northwestern state of Jammu and Kashmir, where flagrantly rigged elections, appalling misgovernance and Pakistani interference have combined to keep an Islamist insurgency alive for the past two and half decades. Here too, allegations of dreadful human rights abuses by the army have multiplied. The mistrust the mainly Hindu and Sikh troops feel towards the mainly Muslim people of Kashmir is all too apparent. It is summed up for me by a large sign that greets the soldiers just before they leave the main air force base outside the capital Srinagar, reminding them never to let down their guard. It reads simply: 'Respect All, Suspect All'.

From the start, Manipuris had chafed under AFSPA. Some took up arms, others took to the law, but a legal challenge to the constitutionality of the Act had foundered in the Supreme Court a few years before.

Undeterred, Babloo's organization, Human Rights Alert, set out to prove that the court's judgement had overlooked the human cost of the law on the people of his state. Babloo is a passionate 43-year-old who has become a friend over the eight years I have known him. His mixture of good humour, calmness and gentle determination make him an inspiring person to be around. He has been my guide on two trips to Manipur, and we have met several times in New Delhi.

With a group of volunteers, Babloo started trying to catalogue what was really happening in Manipur under the cover of this law, combing old newspaper reports and interviewing victims and their relatives. Sharmila, he recalled, came to every meeting, often sitting anonymously at the back, the sort of person who might approach you afterwards for a quiet word but would never raise her hand. No one really paid her much attention. But Babloo remembers she had been upset after she interviewed a young woman in the hills who had been raped by soldiers in front of her father, a village headman.

Then, on 2 November 2000, the army committed an act that set it violently at odds with the people of this state. An improvised bomb exploded as an army convoy was travelling down a main road just past the airport to the south of Imphal. Stopping, the soldiers came under fire from insurgents and two were injured. In the confusion that followed, the soldiers appeared to open fire indiscriminately, killing eight civilians waiting under a tree at a bus stop at a place called Malom. Two more people were shot in a culvert in a nearby village. The victims included a 62-year-old woman and an eighteen-year-old boy, who had won a National Bravery Award twelve years before, as well as his brother and his aunt.

In an attempt to catch the culprits, a curfew was imposed in Imphal for two days, while soldiers carried out what was described by one human rights group as a 'brutal combing operation' in the surrounding countryside, injuring dozens of other people in what seemed to villagers like simple retribution. The army insisted that two of the dead were what is known here as UGs (underground insurgents) while the other victims were shot as they fled the scene in a different direction. But the armed forces' excuses were met with widespread disbelief, especially because the law virtually precluded an independent inquiry. The incident became known as the Malom Massacre. Today, a small memorial park has been constructed at the site, behind the bus stop and beside the tree, beside the open paddy fields, and inscribed with the names of the dead.

It was a Thursday, the weekday Sharmila had set aside to fast since her childhood, following a Hindu practice meant to appease the gods and promote physical and mental well-being. The following day, with the dead bodies of the victims prominently displayed in local newspapers, Sharmila approached her mother and asked for her blessing for a 'programme' she was about to undertake. Ongbi said she really had no idea what her daughter was up to, but she gave her blessing anyway. The young woman ate some pastries and sweets with her mother, set off to Malom, and announced she was starting an indefinite hunger strike until AFSPA was repealed.

Three other women went along at first, but soon gave up – they had husbands and children to look after, and were really only trying to make a point. But Sharmila was serious, more serious than anyone imagined at the time. She took no food or water at all. When the police came to arrest her and take her to hospital, her health was already deteriorating. When she still refused to eat or drink, the doctors had little choice but to insert a plastic feeding tube into her nose.

Today, more than twelve years after that tube was first inserted, AFSPA remains in place, and Sharmila has refused to abandon her fast. So determined is she not to let any water pass her lips that she even cleans her teeth with a piece of damp cotton cloth. She does not even wash her hair. The clear tube, attached to her nose by a small piece of white medical tape, is still her only lifeline – five times a day, nurses pump a liquefied mixture of proteins, carbohydrates, vitamins and laxatives down it. Sharmila has won herself the nickname the 'Iron Lady of Manipur'.

At first, Babloo recalls, Sharmila's fast was barely taken seriously. There was even a little bit of resentment among the activist community of this unknown woman who seemed to be thrusting herself into the forefront of the Manipuri struggle. Slowly, though, as people began to see how serious she was, she started to earn their respect.

Manipur is one of eight states in India's northeast, pinched between Bhutan, China, Burma and Bangladesh, and attached to what the region's people call the Indian 'mainland' by a thin chicken's neck of land just 14 miles wide at its narrowest point. The biggest state, Assam, sits astride the broad valley of the Brahmaputra River, the others nestle in the hills and mountains on either side. That this region is even part of India is largely an accident of colonial administration; that it is so cut off from the rest of the country is an accident of the Partition of the subcontinent that accompanied

Independence in 1947, and the creation of what was then East Pakistan and is now Bangladesh.

In Manipur, the Meitei people who dominate the sweeping Imphal valley trace their history back through seventy-four kings to AD 33. One of the kings converted his subjects to Hinduism at the beginning of the eighteenth century, and a British political agent was stationed in Imphal in the nineteenth century, but it wasn't until 1891 that the British formally and forcibly absorbed Manipur into their Indian Empire after a brief war. It was the last territory to be incorporated into the Raj. When Independence came in 1947, the princely state of Manipur had visions of going it alone, but two years later the Maharaja was pressured into signing its full accession into the nation of India.

Still, many Manipuris were not unhappy at the time to be associated with their Hindu brethren in the project of building a new India. Sadly, their optimism soon turned to profound disillusionment.

Over the decades that followed, India's rulers in far-off Delhi treated the Manipuris as little better than colonial subjects. In Kashmir, the government can perhaps try to excuse its record by pointing a finger at Pakistan and the suspicion and paranoia that Islamabad's interference generated, but here there were no such excuses. Manipuri hearts were India's alone to lose, and that they lost them cannot be blamed on anyone else.

India's economic development of the past six decades has largely passed Manipur by. There are no industries to speak of here, and few jobs outside government service to employ school-leavers and graduates. To get those jobs, you have to bribe. New Delhi does send money – 90 per cent of the state government's budget is funded by the central government – but it seems to care little if that money is spent wisely or is stolen by local bureaucrats or politicians. It has created what one Manipuri professor called a 'culture of dependency manufactured by the government of India'. It was, Professor Nubakumar Singh told me, 'the life of a beggar'.[4]

But it is the attitude of many of their fellow Indians to the people of the northeast that cuts most deeply, an attitude that can often seem openly racist. Babloo once told me that he had been brought up as an Indian, and said his father had wept when the country's first prime minister, Jawaharlal Nehru, died. But he described his first stay in New Delhi, at university there, as a traumatic one. 'Nobody recognizes you as an Indian,' he said. People say "you Chinky" because we look Chinese. They treat you as a secessionist, and as morally lax.'

There is a long tradition of women leading protests in Manipur. At the beginning of the twentieth century, they led a successful agitation against forced labour, until the British political agent withdrew the practice in 1904. In 1939, they led what has become known as the Nupi Lan, or Women's War, a protest against the export of rice outside the territory at a time of huge shortages that expanded into a broader call for political reform. The dramatic naked protest against Manorama's death in 2004 was carried out by members of the Meira Paibi, or 'Torch Bearers', a group of Manipuri mothers who had started out trying to tackle social issues like alcoholism and drug use, only to join the campaign against human rights abuses and AFPSA.

Much later, I met one of those tough Manipuri women, the 62-year-old grandmother Lourembam Ngangbi, who has been jailed five times over the years for taking part in a variety of protests. Friendly and welcoming, she laughed off the risks to which she had subjected herself. We sat on a mat on the floor in her one-room house in the village of Bishnupur, set on a small rise with a view over the valley. Over tea and biscuits, served by her daughter Lianalimparani, she remembered how the mothers of Manipur had felt when they heard of Manorama's death, and why they felt they had to stage such a dramatic protest. 'We were frightened,' she said. 'We could not sit still because our hearts were jumping, like I cannot describe.'

The national spotlight that the protests shone on Manipur also reached Sharmila, as her hunger strike, by now approaching its fourth anniversary, finally started to catch people's imagination.

As the pressure of the protests mounted, the state government in Manipur ordered an inquiry in July 2004, chaired by a retired district judge, C. Upendra Singh. The Assam Rifles, whose soldiers had been involved, repeatedly refused to cooperate with the inquiry, or to respond to a series of summonses. Eventually, Singh was forced to put the names of the soldiers in a local newspaper. Only then did some of the troops agree to interviews, on the proviso that the meetings took place within the army barracks.

Singh's report was swiftly concluded, but its findings have never been made public, thanks to a concerted legal campaign by the Indian government to block its release. Predictably, depressingly, its argument is that, under the rules of AFSPA, the local state government did not have the right to investigate the actions of the army, a central government force.

As Manipur burned, Indian Prime Minister Manmohan Singh finally visited the state in November, and promised an inquiry. Skirting the issue of who was responsible for the Manorama incident, he promised a broader 'review' of armed forces law. In doing so, he employed a tried and tested tactic around the world, and one that is particularly popular in India – form a committee of inquiry and park its eventual conclusions in the long grass. For a while, however, it succeeded in calming things down.

A five-member panel was established under former Supreme Court judge B. P. Jeevan Reddy, and the following June it submitted its report to the government. But even this report, which pointed no finger of blame at anyone, was shelved, hidden from parliament and the public. Despite the outpouring of anger and alienation on its northeastern fringe, the government of India seemed determined to ensure that the death of Manorama Devi would change nothing.

I visited Manipur for the first time in the summer of 2005. It had taken some doing – foreign journalists required something called an Inner Line Permit to visit the state, and I had had to jump through quite a few hoops at the foreign and home ministries to get one. One official, whom I had to visit on more than one occasion, exuded a studied indifference to my entreaties for a while, until a broad hint was dropped. A previous foreign journalist seeking his signature on a similar permit had supplied him with a year's subscription to his magazine, the official casually remarked.

Without bribing the official, but by dint of a little more legwork and a few more cups of tea, my permit was granted, for Manipur, and for the neighbouring state of Nagaland too. There was, however, one proviso – while in Manipur, I was not to leave the Imphal valley. Oh, and there was one more thing they didn't warn me about. As soon as I landed at the airport, I was to be assigned a 'minder', one of those low-level intelligence agents supposedly there 'for your own protection, sir' but obviously meant to keep a close watch on who you meet and where you go.

Luckily for me, my minder seemed almost as indifferent to the whole process as I was frustrated by it, usually staying in the car as Babloo and I trailed around town meeting academics, activists and ordinary people. I met Sharmila's gentle brother Singhjit and her elderly mother Ongbi at their family home for the first time, then we crossed town and met Manorama's mother.

A wizened lady in her sixties, Shakhi Devi sat on a tiny plastic stool on the swept ground outside the family home, her shawl wrapped around her shoulders, as she recounted how soldiers kicked her senseless on that night in July 2004. When she awoke, she said, her daughter was gone. 'My daughter was snatched from me, she was harassed, tortured and spoiled,' she told me. 'She is gone, but I want to make sure she rests in peace.' Now, Devi can only wait for a justice that might never come. Until then, she said she had still not completed the Hindu rituals of mourning. 'The justice delivery system is very slow,' she said, 'but because my daughter is innocent, I am still expecting justice.'

That night, I told my minder we'd be starting late the following day. I had some writing to do, I said, 'so let's meet around noon at the hotel'. In fact, I had other plans. Sneaking away before breakfast with a translator, I drove south on the road to Burma, past an unmanned roadblock on the outskirts of Imphal and a short way up into the forested hills. No one asked to see my permit. My destination was the village of Angtha, and the parents of Yulembam Sanamacha, a fifteen-year-old boy whose arrest by the military and subsequent disappearance seven years before had caused something of an international outcry.

There I met Sanamacha's parents, his mother Arubi, and his 76-year-old father Jugol, and heard about how drunken soldiers had come and dragged away their son in the middle of the night. I saw cardboard boxes, sacks and piles of cards from well-wishers from all four corners of Britain, after Amnesty International had organized a letter-writing campaign on his behalf.[5] But I found no sign of any effort by the Indian authorities to investigate his disappearance or prosecute those responsible.

A few hours later, I sneaked into my hotel by the back door and up the back stairs. Casually walking back down a few minutes later, a few smudges of Angtha mud still on my trousers, I wished my minder good morning, and off we went for another day's reporting together in Imphal.

I met the Indian army's spokesman in Manipur too, Lieutenant-Colonel Santanu Dev Goswami. The army and defence ministry is normally pretty reluctant to set out its case for the continuance of the sweeping powers it enjoys under AFSPA, and I have had several requests for a briefing in New Delhi to set out the army's case ignored.

But Goswami, at least, came to my hotel and sat down over a cup of tea for the best part of an hour to set out their point of view. The army, he said, was facing a 'challenging job out here', called in by the government to fight insurgents and maintain security, which, he explained, was not the job it was trained to do. 'Every day, every night, we put our lives in danger, fighting our own brothers and sisters to bring them to the mainstream,' Goswami told me. 'Every time you kill a militant, you can't go to court.' The army cannot be expected, he continued, to put itself at the mercy of 'vested interests with sinister designs of their own, who are trying to tarnish the image of the armed forces'.

But what about Manorama's death, and the way the inquiry was blocked? I asked. 'An unfortunate incident,' Goswami said. 'Manorama has taught us a good lesson. We have to carry out people-friendly operations.' In practice, what that means is bringing along local police on raids, and female officers when women are to be arrested – provisions blatantly ignored in Manorama's case. Of course there were some problems, Goswami admitted, but they were 'aberrations', and the army dealt with them through its own internal boards of inquiry.

Underlying all these arguments is the sense of grievance the armed forces feel. We didn't ask to be here, it isn't really our job, we are surrounded by people who are trying to kill us and are generally out to get us, the argument runs, so don't you dare put us at the mercy of these people and their silly lawsuits. Sometimes, the argument is accompanied by a threat – don't expect us to serve in these conflict zones if you remove the protection that AFSPA allows us.

The problem with all of this, say critics, is that no institution, and no individual, in a democracy should be above the rule of law. The army would be expected to abide by the Geneva Conventions if it were fighting abroad, so why can't it abide by the normal laws of India when it is at home? Nor, they argue, should it be the army's decision in a civilian democracy to decide where and how it should be deployed.

On one afternoon, we called in at Imphal University, where a group of students had gathered to meet me in a large sun-filled and wooden-floored room on the first floor. It didn't take long for the conversation to catch fire. Some of the young men and women indignantly insisted the rebels were 'freedom fighters' rather than terrorists, as the government would have us believe. Others, though, were not so sure. 'They are in insurgent groups because they are lazy,' complained one female student. 'They want easy money.' Not everyone in that room saw their future outside India, but everyone wanted more respect from the Indian government, and more opportunity to join in India's boom.

Around 2,000 students graduate in Manipur every year, another university professor later told me, and gave me the same lament that I have heard almost everywhere in India: expectations, fuelled by television and easier travel, have risen faster than opportunity. At the time, that mismatch was fuelling the insurgency, the professor said; these days it tends to simply fuel a mass exodus of many of the best and brighter Manipuris to other parts of India. Since my visit to the university campus in 2005, sympathy for the insurgents has probably waned still further in Manipur. To fund their struggle, the rebels extort money from almost every citizen of the state, government servants included. To function in Manipur these days requires the protection of one insurgent group or another, and many people are just tired of constant war. But the Indian government would surely be mistaken if it interprets that weariness as a sign of progress, or of any lessening of the sense of alienation that many Manipuris feel.

In October 2006, Babloo pulled off a stunt that raised Sharmila's profile immeasurably in New Delhi. From the outset, she had been charged with attempted suicide, a crime carrying a maximum jail term of one year, and kept under armed guard in a government-run hospital, in a damp and shabby room with peeling walls measuring 12 feet by 20. Every two weeks she was produced in court and asked if she was determined to continue her fast; when she said yes, she was taken back to hospital in the company of two female police officers. Once a year she was released, and, within a day or two, rearrested.[6]

This year, though, Babloo had other plans. On her release from hospital, he whisked her off to his home, throwing the media off the scent with promises of a press conference the following morning. At dawn, with everyone's hearts in their mouths, they guided Sharmila, in a wheelchair because she was so weak, through Imphal's high-security airport, where a flight to Delhi had been booked in the name of I. Chanu. Yet their elaborate plan was so nearly rumbled: just as they were waiting to board, a local intelligence officer stationed at the airport spotted them, and was about to come over. Fortunately, at that exact moment, Manipur's chief minister arrived from New Delhi, surrounded by officials, flunkeys and armed guards. The intelligence officer was swept up in the minister's entourage, and Babloo and Sharmila boarded the flight without obstruction.

In New Delhi, I was waiting for them at Raj Ghat, the memorial to India's Independence hero Mahatma Gandhi, who made fasting such a potent political weapon against British colonial rule. There, in the middle of a manicured lawn, on top of a black marble platform, an eternal flame burns for Gandhi in a glass case, marking the spot where he was cremated in 1948, after his assassination at the hands of an extreme Hindu nationalist.

Sharmila walked falteringly to the memorial supported by her brother Singhjit, throwing marigolds on the marble platform and joining her palms in respect. Shortly afterwards, she joined me on the lawn, sitting cross-legged with a white shawl over her matted, curly black hair. She looked pale after her long incarceration. Her breath was slightly stale from dehydration. I sprawled on the grass beside her. Her visit was a personal pilgrimage to the cremation site of a man who she had always admired. 'If I have to die without my demand being fulfilled, before I am lying on my death bed, I would like to get his blessings,' she told me.

We talked about her incarceration. She spent her time reading books and newspapers, as well as letters from well-wishers. She practised yoga to keep fit, she told me, but the government does not allow her outside to get some sun. There were none of the privileges of a political prisoner here; Sharmila felt she was treated like a criminal. Her English is halting, and her shyness is an additional handicap. She does not have a natural presence that commands attention, but she spoke with force about the conditions that had forced her into this drastic fast. The Indian government, she said, had betrayed Gandhi's memory in its reaction to her peaceful protest, and in the way it treated the people of Manipur. 'I would like to follow his tradition, his ideology,' she told me. 'Maybe you call it a sacrifice but to me it is simply a bounden duty.'[7]

After her visit to Raj Ghat, Sharmila made her way to Jantar Mantar, the home of protest in New Delhi. There, the media swarmed around her. She demanded that the government release the Jeevan Reddy report into AFSPA, which was said to have recommended the law's repeal. Again taking no food or water, without her nasal tube, her health soon began to deteriorate. The Indian government started to feel the pressure of all the television coverage, and the Home Minister sent emissaries.

The minister, Shivraj Patil, seventy-one years old at the time, is perhaps best described as a dandy, his hair always immaculately combed back on the top of his head. Dapper isn't a word I use much, but it always springs to mind when I think of Patil, because dapper is precisely how the minister seemed to see himself. Indeed, in September 2008, Patil was to be severely embarrassed by the media when he was seen in three different sets of clothes on the same day that five bombs had exploded in New Delhi, killing thirty people. Patil, the media bayed, cared more about how he looked than he did about the victims.

In New Delhi, Sharmila offered to accept medical attention if the government released the Reddy report. Patil called Babloo and the rest of Sharmila's team to his office to negotiate. Throughout the meeting, Babloo told me, the minister refused to even look at the Manipuris, addressing all his comments to the Indian television journalist who had accompanied them. His offer was not much less insulting than his manner – that Sharmila should call off her fast entirely, and he would send someone to read out to her the main findings of the Reddy Commission report – actual copies would be denied them. Not surprisingly, the offer was refused, and that night hundreds of armed police descended on Jantar Mantar. There were only five or ten activists left there with her, Babloo recalls. Singing 'We Shall Overcome', they were led off, and Sharmila was taken to the All India Institute of Medical Sciences hospital in Delhi.

Sharmila's team did, however, record a partial victory. One of India's leading journalists, Siddharth Varadarajan procured a leaked copy of the Reddy report. In a dramatic news conference, Babloo and the others shared its findings. It recommended unambiguously that AFSPA be repealed. The army should stay in Manipur, it said, but had to be accountable and could not be above the law.[8]

By late 2011, the debate on AFSPA had shifted back to Kashmir. The insurgency there had waned considerably over the past few years, and the youngish Chief Minister, Omar Abdullah, had made what seemed like a modest request. The Act should no longer apply to two districts in the state where the Indian army no longer even conducted operations, he suggested. Casualty rates from the insurgency had halved in the preceding year, and were less than 5 per cent of what they had been a decade ago. The Kashmiris, he argued, deserved to see a 'peace dividend'. The gesture would be largely symbolic, the 41-year-old Abdullah told me on a visit to the state, but still an important test of the Indian government's political will to solve the Kashmir question.

Tens of thousands of people have died in the state since the insurgency began in 1989, after elections two years before were widely seen as rigged to deny separatists a democratic foothold. The dispute between India and Pakistan over their rival claims to the Himalayan territory lies at the heart of their long enmity and caused two of their three wars. 'At some point in time, we have to have the courage to take what appear to be risky decisions, with the belief that this is an important component of the peace process,' Abdullah told me. If New Delhi can't even go this far, 'how are you going to resolve the overall Kashmir issue, that is going to require much tougher decisions?'[9]

Three of the previous four summers had seen repeated violent protests reminiscent of the Palestinian intifada, with demonstrators throwing stones at police and officers responding with live fire. Yet many Kashmiris would, I believed, still respond in an overwhelmingly positive way if they could only be convinced that New Delhi trusted and respected them – especially when the prospect of joining a collapsing Pakistan held less attraction than it used to. It was time, said Noor Ahmed Baba, the head of the political science department at Kashmir University, for the Indian leadership to show 'vision, guts and courage'.

The government of Manmohan Singh either disagreed, or lacked the courage. Despite repeated entreaties from Abdullah, his request was turned down flat. AFSPA was to remain in place throughout Kashmir, and hundreds of thousands of troops would stay too. But there was to be no serious attempt to heal the wounds, or lessen the alienation of the Kashmiri people. The abuse of democracy in Kashmir by the Indian government would continue.

In April 2013, Abdullah was reduced to making an impassioned appeal, as one newspaper put it, that Kashmiris were normal people too. 'All Kashmiris are not terrorists,' he was quoted as saying.[10] 'Don't view every Kashmiri with suspicion. Every Kashmiri is not out to destroy this nation. Every Kashmiri does not carry a rifle under his phiran [shawl].' Kashmiris, he complained, were facing harassment and discrimination when they went for work outside the state, with landlords refusing to rent them flats. The tendency to 'suspect all', rather than 'respect all', obviously ran deep.

Yet just when one despairs of India's sclerotic democracy, it springs a surprise. Justice Verma had been serving Chief Justice when the Supreme Court had ruled that AFSPA was not unconstitutional. But his panel came to a rather different conclusion when it considered whether AFSPA was just, and what its implications were for the nation's women.

People from northeast India had appeared before the committee. Verma was shocked. Such was their alienation, he later recalled, that they talked about 'India' as though it were a separate place. This had upset the panel. 'We have to do something about that,' he told the press.

The report's conclusions were unequivocal. 'The brutality of the armed forces in border areas leads to deep disenchantment,' Verma said. 'Serious allegations of persistent sexual assault on the women in such areas and conflict areas are causing more alienation.' Fellow committee member Gopal Subramaniam took up the argument at their joint news conference. 'At the outset we noticed that impunity for systematic and isolated sexual violence in the process of internal security duties is being legitimized by the Armed Forces (Special Powers) Act which is enforced in large parts of our country,' he said. 'Sexual violence against women by members of the armed forces or uniformed personnel must be brought under the purview of ordinary criminal law.' There was an 'urgent need', he continued, to review whether AFSPA had any place in India at all.

Yet again, the government's response was predictable – to hide behind the army. Palaniappan Chidambaram was one of the government's most powerful and competent ministers, and had taken over from the hapless Shivraj Patil as Home Minister in November 2008, shortly after his wardrobe controversy. During Chidambaram's tenure as Home Minister, he had proposed three amendments to soften AFSPA, but had failed to push them through. Now, back at the finance ministry and attempting to breathe life back into India's ailing economy, he nevertheless took charge of the government's response to the Verma report. While many of its recommendations were accepted, there was to be no budging on AFSPA. 'We can't move forward because there is no consensus,' he said in a speech on national security issued shortly after its release. 'The present and former army chiefs have taken a strong position that the act cannot be amended.'[11]

Since the government would not act, activists turned to the judiciary. Perhaps the courts would provide an escape route from the tensions that had built up in Manipur. Babloo and his colleagues had documented an incredible 1,528 extrajudicial executions that they alleged had been carried out by the army and police over the past three decades.[12] He had helped the widows of Manipur set up a self-help group, the Extra-Judicial Executions Victims' Families Association of Manipur, whose acronym, EEVFAM, means bloodstain in Manipuri. In December 2012, in response to a petition filed by the widows, India's Supreme Court appointed a respected three-person commission to look into the allegations. It was just another committee of inquiry perhaps, but there seemed to be some real hope it could add to pressure on the government of India to roll back the blanket of impunity that was suffocating Manipur.

I returned to Manipur in February 2013. The insurgency had waned since I was last there, and the requirement to apply for a special permit had been waived. I still had to register at the airport on arrival, but no one was assigned to shadow me. It was winter, so the paddy fields were brown, not bright green. There were fewer troops and checkpoints on the streets of Imphal, but the city hadn't changed much otherwise.

Once settled, I arranged with Babloo to meet the widows of EEVFAM at their modest headquarters, a newly built and bare wooden common room up a flight of stairs above his office. As I walked up, I heard laughter: half a dozen widows had already assembled to meet me and were sitting cross-legged on bamboo mats on the floor. Reluctantly, I explained who I was and what I was doing. After chatting for some time, I was forced to change the mood and make them share with me the experiences that had brought them there.

Neena Ningombam is EEVFAM's secretary, a well-educated and striking 37-year-old, with straight black hair and full cheeks. Wearing a black and white patterned top with a black scarf draped around her neck, she had intensity in her gaze and a captivating smile. She lost her first husband to diabetes and TB when she was eight months pregnant with her first child. Her second husband, Michael, who had also been her childhood sweetheart, was taken away by the police on 4 November 2008.[13]

There is a huge problem of drug abuse and AIDS in India's northeast, linked to the lack of economic opportunities here and the cross-border smuggling trade from Burma. Most of the drugs are painkillers and opiates, obtained from chemists or manufactured locally, and often injected for a bigger high. Michael was a small-time drugs user and was also HIV-positive. He had even spent some time in prison for buying drugs, but he also loved Neena and the family deeply, and was trying to make a fresh start.

After his arrest, Michael made one brief mobile phone call to Neena at 3.32 p.m. to let her know he had been arrested, and then rang off. Neena called back, but the first few times no one answered. Finally, someone picked up the phone and said Michael was in the bathroom. Then the phone was switched off. Sitting at home, Neena was worried, but it was only when she watched the nine o'clock news that her life collapsed. Her husband's dead body flashed up on the screen, with a Chinese hand grenade planted next to it. Insurgents had attacked the police, the report explained, and one of them had been slain. To Neena, it was a transparent fabrication, an obvious cover story for her husband's execution.

Neena now has two young sons to care for on her own. They are being penalized, she says, because their father has been falsely labelled a terrorist, and will be shut out from scholarships and government jobs in the future.

In one small sense, though, Neena is lucky. Witnesses saw her husband being arrested by police, and for once they have not been intimidated into silence. A local judge investigated the case and found that Michael had never been involved in a militant group, and that he was killed in what is known here as a 'fake encounter'. Neena is fighting the case in court and is determined to clear his name.

Occasionally, women like Neena actually win their cases and receive some compensation payment from the government. But mostly witnesses are intimidated into silence. And even when relatives of the disappeared win their cases, there is never any attempt to properly investigate how their husbands are killed, or to punish those responsible. The widows of EEVFAM are putting their lives back together, running micro-finance schemes and supporting each other, but they are still frozen out by the Indian state.

Neena's story also reflects another sad truth about Manipur today: that the local police have become worse offenders in recent years than the army. The cloak of impunity that AFSPA affords has been stretched to cover up their sins too; their ill-disciplined behaviour goes as unpunished as the army's.

The following day, I left the Imphal Valley and drove through the winding mountain roads to the Burmese border, a trip I had long wanted to make. What I found there underlined for me the gap between the Indian government's rhetoric and reality, between its stated ambitions for the northeast and its actual delivery.

For the past two decades, there has been a lot of talk in India about a policy called 'Look East', that is supposed to herald far greater engagement with the bustling economies of South East Asia.[14] It is a vision supported by the US State Department, which hopes that closer ties between Asia's free-market democracies can help balance China's rise. The recent opening up of Burma has given a fresh impetus to that dream. The road to Moreh and beyond, through Mandalay in Burma to the Thai town of Tae Sot, is already being upgraded. Fresh green signs on its shoulders proclaim its new name, Asian Highway Number One, a road that in theory runs all the way to Japan. A bus service from Imphal to Mandalay is being talked about, and a car rally was staged at the end of 2012 from India to Indonesia, through Imphal and Moreh, to symbolize the new 'connectivity'.

It does not take long to bring those dreams down to earth. Moreh is a friendly enough place, but it is a backwater, a dead end, instead of a potential metropolis. Its narrow dirt streets are patrolled by soldiers and stray dogs, while legal trade flowing across the frontier is both meagre and local, from betel nuts to bicycle spare parts. But, locals told me, there was a much larger flow of smuggled drugs and timber, militants and weapons across the porous, forested and mountainous border.[15] Indeed, two weeks after I left, the sad reality of Moreh and the Manipuri economy was dramatically underlined, and the nexus between the army and politicians in promoting that illegal trade was exposed. The defence ministry spokesman, a Colonel Ajay Chowdhry, was arrested in Manipur, along with an army sepoy, an airline staff member and three locals, with a huge consignment of pseudo-ephedrine hydrochloride-based drugs worth over $3.5 million that was destined for Moreh. The following day, the son of an important Congress Party MP was arrested at his house and another large consignment of drugs seized.

The truth is that Manipur should be India's bridge to South East Asia and China, a commercial and strategic link to the buoyant economies to the nation's east. If it were, there probably wouldn't be any question of an insurgency here. But there is neither the political will nor the courage to turn that dream into reality. Instead, Manipur is a state riddled with corruption and locked in a deep state of dependency – on government money and on drugs. It is a backwater where democracy barely functions, and where its people feel like second-class citizens.

That trip also saw me come face to face with Sharmila for the second time. It was her regular fortnightly appearance in a small courtroom in Imphal – I watched as she quietly told the judge she was set on continuing her hunger strike, and was committed back to custody in hospital. Afterwards, having submitted a written application to the judge, I was granted seven minutes to talk to the defendant before she was taken back into captivity. It was a rushed, unsatisfactory conversation, by the side of the ambulance that had brought her to the court, with a crowd of local reporters crowding around, but it was a rare chance and one that couldn't be missed.

Her white shawl was draped around her shoulders, her plastic tube still attached to her nose. Her toenails needed cutting, her hair was as unkempt as ever, her voice still barely more than a mutter even as her replies were defiant. She leant back against the ambulance, a policewoman in an olive-green uniform and a fawn beret at her side. Was she at all buoyed by the Verma Committee's report, I began by asking. The answer, sadly, seemed to be no. Once bitten, twice shy: Sharmila had lived through the disappointment of the Jeevan Reddy Committee, seen promises broken and a perfectly reasonable set of recommendations blithely ignored by the government. It was an act, she said, by a government intent on deceiving people. So was she losing patience? 'My protest needs some time,' she said, 'to awaken our people, our leaders, so I remain contented. I just want to set myself free.'[16]

For several years now, Sharmila has had a boyfriend, a British national originally from the Indian seaside state of Goa. Desmond Coutinho is a writer and activist who has been writing to Sharmila for a while, has sent her several gifts, and even travelled to meet her in 2011.[17] Even so, I was slightly disarmed by her honest response when I asked what she was missing most about the outside world. 'I never feel lonely,' she said, 'but I just feel I am missing something, someone who will be my life partner, my soul mate.'

It is easy to forget that Sharmila is a real person, with real desires. It is something she often reminds Babloo, that she too gets hungry when she smells food, that captivity and self-denial does not come easily to her, any more than to any human being. She is shy and withdrawn, certainly, but someone who longs for human interaction as we all do.

Before leaving Imphal, I returned to the family home. Her brother Singhjit has a ready smile and a huge amount of affection for his sister; he has supported her throughout the long years of her struggle, while her other brothers and sisters have kept away, preferring to get on with their lives without the constant hassle of being a hunger striker's sibling. But I was interested too in Sharmila's relationship with Ongbi, which seemed at first a little distant. Her elder brothers and sisters had largely brought the young girl up, her mother said, as she talked in a slightly detached way about a daughter who was 'different from the rest'.

Mother and daughter have met only twice since Sharmila began her fast; both times when Ongbi was admitted to the same hospital, once after a bad asthma attack, and once for a cataract operation. Otherwise, Ongbi says she has kept away, worried that it would upset her too much to see her daughter in such a state. As she chatted, I realized this was not an act, nor an excuse, but the only way this mother could cope with the loss of her daughter. A large teardrop formed on her right eye, and she fought hard to restrain more from coming. Her voice broke.

The irony, of course, is that when Anna Hazare went on a fast against corruption in New Delhi in 2011, and when the same city erupted in protest over J's rape in 2012, the Indian government was forced to respond. In Manipur, no amount of popular rage or individual self-sacrifice seems to budge the needle an inch. The Manipuris, Sharmila said, are seen as a different people. 'They treat us like stepchildren,' she said, her final words to me before her guards whisked her away once more, into the back of her ambulance and back to her lonely hospital room.

Manipur is an example of what happens in India when democracy breaks down, a place that the Indian elite treats with the same arrogance and condescension that the British had employed in this country. It is a reminder of the freedoms that the people of 'mainland India' enjoy and sometimes take for granted. Yet for the sake of women like Manorama's mother Shakhi Devi, like Lourembam Ngangbi and the women of the Meira Paibi, like Irom Sharmila and Neena Ningombam, it would be wrong to give up hope entirely. There is a legal process under way, and there is a small, outside, chance that the wheels of justice could yet turn in their favour. But it is a slim hope, and a long battle.

In March 2013, I watched some of the proceedings of the Supreme Court Appointed Commission as its lawyers cross-examined army officers about the disappearances of seven Manipuris, test cases to see if Babloo and EEVFAM's allegations warranted deeper investigation. It was a scrupulously professional and transparent investigation, open to the press and conducted by a team made up of some of India's most respected figures, former Supreme Court Justice N. Santosh Hegde and former Chief Election Commissioner James Michael Lyngdoh, as well as a retired police officer, Ajai Kumar Singh.

Neena sat at the back and quietly watched the proceedings unfold with me. There had been a delay of several hours on the first day, as the army claimed its officers did not have security clearance to appear before the commission, but eventually they showed up. 'When they appeared, we felt a little satisfied,' Neena said later. 'People who felt nothing could touch them; they have to answer some questions now.'

Shortly afterwards, the committee reported back to the Supreme Court. Its findings were explosive. In all six cases it examined, it concluded the dead had not been killed in an encounter nor had the security forces acted in self-defence. 'It would appear that the security forces believed a priori that the suspects involved in the encounters had to be eliminated and the forces acted accordingly,' it reported. It also concluded that allegations against all six – that they had criminal backgrounds or were involved in militant activities – were either unproven or downright false. It called the cases 'egregious examples of the AFSPA's gross abuse'.[18]

'Though the Act gives sweeping powers to the security forces, even to the extent of killing a suspect with protection from prosecution etc., the Act does not provide any protection for the citizens against possible misuse of these extreme powers,' it said, adding there was no evidence of any monitoring system to prevent those powers being abused. Indeed a list of 'Dos and Don'ts' laid down by the Supreme Court to regulate the use of AFSPA has remained largely on paper and they are 'mostly followed in violation', it said. 'Normally, the greater the power, the greater the restraint and stricter the mechanism to prevent its misuse or abuse. But here in the case of AFSPA in Manipur this principle appears to have been reversed. We should not forget that power corrupts and absolute power corrupts absolutely.'

The Jeevan Reddy Committee, after its own hearings, found in 2005 that AFSPA had become 'a symbol of oppression, an object of hate and an instrument of discrimination and high-handedness', the report recalled. 'The Commission has carefully gone through the said Report and is in respectful agreement with the same.'

Momentum continued to build. In May 2013, the United Nations Special Rapporteur on extrajudicial, summary or arbitrary executions, Christof Heyns, submitted his report on India to the UN

Human Rights Council in Geneva, after examining the evidence submitted by EEVFAM and visiting Manipur. In it, he called on the India government to make a public commitment to eliminating the phenomenon of unlawful killings, he recommended a Commission of Inquiry be established to look into extrajudicial executions alleged to have taken place, and he called for the repeal, or at least the radical amendment, of AFSPA.[19] Testifying before the Human Rights Council on behalf of the widows of Manipur and Kashmir was Neena Ningombam. In October, Babloo emailed me with good news: there had been just two extrajudicial killings in Manipur all year, he said, compared with 500 in 2009.

It is still not clear how the Supreme Court will react to its own commission's report, or how the central government will respond when it does. But in one lonely editorial shortly after its release, the *Indian Express* newspaper urged New Delhi not to miss this valuable chance for redress. 'The Centre must build on it,' it argued, 'if it wants to draw Manipur closer to the national mainstream.'[20] The same, of course, could be said for Kashmir. The central government must build on this chance, I believe, to stand up to the army and repeal AFSPA, before India can claim to be a democracy for all of its 1.2 billion people.

13

I Want to Break Free

India's youthful aspirations threatened by a lack of skills and jobs

'It has to be a truly national effort to convert the potential of a demographic disaster into a demographic dividend . . . It will be a dividend if we empower our young, it will be a disaster if we fail to put in place a policy and framework where they can be empowered.'
India's Human Resources and Development Minister Kapil Sibal,
speaking to the author, October 2011

Pedestrians weave their way through a sea of cars, rickshaws and motorbikes, the vehicles' desperate scramble for space just making the gridlock worse. Lumbering buses belching diesel fumes try to bulldoze their way past bullock carts, cyclists and trailer-dragging tractors. The narrow roads are choked and the pavement swallowed up by small stalls and piles of rubbish. The smell of sewage poisons the air from an open drain, while overhead a web of electric cables criss-crosses the sky.

But just above eye-level, a succession of billboards offer the hope of escape from this chaos – Wizard Tutoring, Achievers Academy, the Epitome Institute for Advanced Learning – these are a few of the many private colleges that have sprouted in the northern city of Gorakhpur in recent years, offering a dizzying array of courses and qualifications to help people stand out from the crowd, from MCA to PGDCA, IAS to PCS, UPSEE to AIEE, and SSC to CAT and MAT.

In October 2011, as the world prepared to welcome its

seven-billionth person, I had travelled to Gorakhpur, a growing city in India's most populous state, to start to get a handle on the implications of India's rapid population growth, to ask whether a bulge in young people entering the nation's workforce would represent a 'demographic dividend' or a 'demographic disaster'.

To put it another way, I was looking for answers to the two big questions facing the youth of India today: the first is whether there will be enough jobs for them when they complete their education; the second is whether they will have the right skills to do the jobs that are available.

What I found was a young nation desperately trying to get ahead, its eyes opened and its ambitions stirred by economic growth and freely flowing information, aspiring through education to break free from the circumscribed lives of their parents, to escape from the crowded tangle of small-town India or the limited horizons of its villages, and join the age of opportunity. But I also found myself asking if their ambitions would be realized or whether they would be frustrated, if the calamitous state of India's education system and sluggish rates of job creation would crush their dreams; and I found myself asking what would happen in that event.

India is home to some 1.2 billion people and its population is expected to keep rising until 2060. Before that, by 2025, it will overtake China as the world's most populous country.[1] It will also be one of the youngest countries in the world, with an average age of just twenty-nine. Around 300 million young Indians will enter the workforce between 2010 and 2025. Trained, educated and employed, they should become India's trump card, powering a new economic boom of the kind that East Asia's tiger economies enjoyed in the 1970s. Newly enfranchised by India's democratic awakening, they should be a powerful force for societal change (even if the serious environmental risks of India's ever-expanding population and ever-growing economy cannot be ignored). But ill-trained, jobless and excluded, they risk becoming an entirely different force. For just as the Arab Spring was fuelled by the frustrations of young Egyptians and Tunisians, so too could India risk serious unrest and rampant crime if she fails her young.

I began my reporting journey in the villages just a short drive outside Gorakhpur. This was the heart of eastern Uttar Pradesh, a state of 200 million people, which had increased its population by 33 million in the last decade alone. Here, on the fertile, crowded plains of the Ganges, many of the questions facing India are bound to be answered. Here, though, I found India's family planning policy was still struggling to take hold, despite decades of public information campaigns and a disastrous attempt at forced sterilization under Sanjay Gandhi in the 1970s. Here, I found high rates of infant mortality, low educational levels and the low social status of women contributing to high rates of childbirth. Under the trees in the village of Tarkulahi, the village health worker assembled a crowd, mainly of women in colourful sarees, with veils over their hair and rings through their noses. A couple of plastic chairs were procured to make me and my researcher Suhasini Raj comfortable. We talked to older women, like Chanwati, who had raised eleven children at a time when there was no means of contraception available, of whom two had died as babies; and younger women like 35-old year Sunderi Gupta, who was married to a landless farmhand. 'I only wanted two children, but my husband forced me to have more,' she said, three of her kids at her side. 'None of them have been educated because we don't have any money.'

The local primary school was useless, the villagers complained: the principal only turned up at lunchtime if at all. Saraswati Devi sent her children to a nearby private school, where the education was apparently slightly better, but the prospects of advancement were still bleak. Her oldest son had dropped out of school after ninth grade because the family was so poor, and went away to find work in the faraway southern state of Kerala. 'Now he works as a stone-breaker,' she told me.

Since it threw off British rule in 1947, India has undoubtedly made progress in raising the educational levels of its people. Adult literacy, for example, now stands at 74 per cent, from around 18 per cent at

Independence (although the current figure may overstate people's ability to read much more than their names). Significant investments have been made in building classrooms and employing teachers, so that more than 95 per cent of six- to fourteen-year-olds are now enrolled in schools (even if attendance on any given day is significantly lower, and more than half drop out before completing secondary school). In 2010 the Indian government put into force the Right to Education Act that made schooling both free and compulsory for that age group. But those superficial signs of progress mask some deep and disturbing problems, for it is not just the access to education that matters, but the quality of education that is on offer.

The education specialists Pratham carry out an extensive survey of educational attainment across India every year, partnering with scores of other organizations and reaching even the remotest villages. The organization, founded in 1994 to provide education for slum kids in Mumbai, has expanded into the largest non-governmental body offering education to the underprivileged in India, and their study of attainment has become a national benchmark. In it, they use simple cards that measure children's ability to read simple words and do simple maths, comparing their ability with what the government expects of them at particular grade levels. What they have found is that education attainment is not only way below where it should be, but it is falling further.

Less than half of the children in fifth grade were able to read a simple text in their native language that a second grade child should have been comfortable with. Almost half were unable to carry out a two-digit subtraction like 51 minus 35, again something the curriculum says is a second grade problem. Those proportions have fallen by 7 and 17 percentage points respectively in just two years, from 2010 to 2012. Less than one in four could read a simple sentence in English like 'What is the time?' or 'I have a brother', and a third of those who passed the reading test didn't understand what the sentences meant. There is, of course, enormous variety across India; among the large states, Kerala consistently records some of the highest scores, Uttar Pradesh some of the lowest.[2]

As they move up the grades, the situation doesn't improve. Rukmini Banerji at Pratham told me that the preliminary results from another study in 100 Uttar Pradesh villages found that a majority of the children moving up from eighth to ninth grades were at fourth grade level or below. Yet they proceeded through the system regardless, promoted automatically every year, their own expectations and those of their parents rising with every year in school but their abilities lagging far behind.

Back in New Delhi, a few days before my trip, the Minister of Human Resources Development, the white-haired lawyer Kapil Sibal, had told me that India needed to impart job skills to 500 million young Indians over the next decade, and admitted that the scale of the problem sometimes kept him awake at night. 'It will be a dividend if we empower our young, it will be a disaster if we fail to put in place a policy and framework where they can be empowered,' he said. 'It has to be a truly national effort to convert the potential of a demographic disaster into a demographic dividend.'[3]

But it is clear from Pratham's figures that the government's input-driven approach – getting children into schools and assuming that will be enough to educate them – simply isn't working. The teaching methods and the quality of instruction are not good enough to make that a realistic assumption. Indian schools are often characterized by rote learning and a failure to test understanding, in an environment where children do not feel free to raise their hands to ask questions. The curriculum, designed by academicians in ivory towers, is not realistic for much of rural India, and is pushing children too fast at too young an age, Banerji said, raising the risks that many will be left behind. At the same time, rural parents themselves often lack the educational levels to realize that their children are falling behind, or to help them catch up – often blaming the children if they fail, rather than the system. Although children may complete many years of schooling expecting to be employable, many simply are not, at least not in the jobs they imagine for themselves. It is not hard to see how disappointed aspirations can lead to frustration, and even violence.

Today, just 13 per cent of Indians in the college age group actually attend higher education institutes, a figure that has barely increased from 10 per cent in 2000. In China, the comparable proportion stands at 23 per cent, up from 6 per cent in 2000. Sibal wants to raise India's figure to 30 per cent, and says India needs 700 new universities and 35,000 new colleges to achieve that goal. Again, though, it is as much about quality as it is about numbers. Even the country's celebrated Indian Institutes of Technology (IITs) failed to feature in the top 200 universities in the *Times Higher Education* World University Rankings 2012–2013. Hong Kong and the rest of China have six in the top 200.[4] 'The progress China has made, and the lack of progress in India, is astonishing,' Columbia University professor Arvind Panagariya told me, adding that Sibal's statement of intent rang hollow. 'The government is asleep at the wheel.'

Outside Gorakhpur, in the village of Thakurpur, we stopped at a roadside tea stall and started talking to eighteen-year-old Akhilesh Kumar and a couple of his friends. A farmer's son, Kumar was taking a degree in English and Sociology at a small private college, and said he dreamt of a government job, or of opening a computer institute in his own village. 'There is a big change here,' he said, in Hindi, describing the determination he and his contemporaries have to break free from the constraints of their rural upbringings. 'Many children are studying while also doing part-time jobs to earn money for their families,' he said, as the stallholder brought out tiny glasses of sweet chai. 'Children burn kerosene lamps to study during power cuts. We are more qualified than our parents, so we can do much better.' But Kumar's ambition was undermined by an inability to string together more than a sentence or two in English, the language in which India conducts much of its national and pretty much all of its global business.

Culture and infrastructure are also holding people back. None of Kumar's three sisters went to school at all, nor did their mother. His friend Biswajit Yadav says the lack of electricity and Internet access is also a major handicap in the villages. 'We want education most of all,' he said. 'I am very keen to learn about computers, but there is no scope here. Nothing is available.'

In Gorakhpur itself, computer courses are available for the better off, but their value is questionable. I stopped in at one of the better private colleges, and saw groups of students copying down information in a small windowless room as their instructor, barely any older than them, read out coursework directly from a computer. I interviewed a handful of the students. They all wanted to leave Gorakhpur and most wanted to work as software engineers in Bengaluru or Delhi; they all talked about the dream of earning a lot of money, but I wondered how employable they would be.

On those two fundamental questions – of skills and jobs – there is every reason to be concerned. Not only has the rate of economic growth slowed alarmingly in recent years, but the economy is also not producing enough jobs to keep all those 300 million young people who will enter the workforce by 2025 gainfully employed. In this context, India's failure to foster a vibrant manufacturing sector – which could provide hundreds of millions of jobs – is particularly worrisome. As wages rise in China, India has a historic opportunity to seize the mantle of a top global manufacturer. It is an opportunity the country looks destined to miss.

The World Bank identifies a number of factors that are holding India back[5] – including unreliable power supplies, rampant corruption, barriers to acquiring land for industry, education, and the malnutrition[6] that is impairing children from reaching their potential. While China's cities are engines of growth, India's are clogged by poor infrastructure and lack basic services. Last but not least, the rigidity of India's labour laws acts as a big disincentive to hiring, by making it much harder to then fire someone during a downturn in business. Some firms get around this by hiring temporary workers on contract, but are then less inclined to invest in their training. Nevertheless, it is no coincidence that many of India's most successful manufacturers, including the auto sector, tend to be in capital-intensive industries. It is almost undeniable that relaxed labour laws would boost overall employment levels in India, and that – done sensibly – such a measure would benefit workers in general. But Indian unions seem to hold a veto over the issue, and have so far blocked any real attempt at reform.

At the Indian edition of the World Economic Forum, held in the IT city of Gurgaon in 2012, I sat in on a workshop attended by industry leaders. One frankly admitted to me he saw his permanent staff as a liability rather than an asset, simply because both sides knew they could never be fired. At one point, we split into groups to talk about the barriers to growth, and find solutions. Afterwards, the spokesman for each group stood up; each, in turn, demanded the government drastically relax the labour laws – probably any session held in the past twenty years would have produced similar results. But what struck me was how shallow those demands seemed. I seemed to be the only person in the room – apart from the impressive Arun Maira from the Planning Commission – wanting to examine ways that trust and consensus could be built, or how the unions might be gradually brought on board with a slightly more relaxed regime. There was a lot of bleating but not much constructive thinking.

The other question is whether these employers, even if they are free to hire, will find the sort of skilled workers they need. In 2008, the Indian government set up a National Skill Development Corporation in an attempt to bridge the skills divide, but its boss Dilip Chenoy is already concerned that India will fall short. By 2022, he says, India needs another 103 million skilled workers in the infrastructure sector, 35 million in the auto sector and 33 million in construction.[7] The IT sector, where many of the Gorakhpur students had set their sights, needs just 5 million more people. Already, the Royal Institution of Chartered Surveyors says India needs more than 4 million architects, engineers and planners, but has less than 570,000 of them, a shortfall that is significantly delaying construction work in India's expanding cities.

Students in India, as my colleague Rama Lakshmi reported in March 2013, tend to flock to white-collar professions that are considered more 'respectable': medicine, teaching, business management and software and electronics engineering.[8] Families want to skip the incremental farm-to-factory journey, she reported from the large village of Rajhedi in Haryana, and are hoping to see their children secure office jobs that bring respect and social status. 'Indian families tend to put a lot of emphasis on college degrees as a tool of aspiration and growth,' Chenoy told her. 'So what we have is a whole lot of people with degrees in hand but no relevant skills.'

Already in India there is a growing shortage of skilled blue-collar manpower in textile factories, as well as construction project foremen and machine operators. There is also a huge and growing gap in India's workforce that is stopping the nation from realizing its potential, and that is the under-representation of women. Less than 40 per cent of Indian women aged between twenty-five and fifty-four are economically active, compared with 82 per cent in China and 72 per cent in Brazil. In the cities, that proportion falls to just 24 per cent, and the overall numbers have fallen by nearly ten percentage points in a decade. The reasons, say scholars at the McKinsey Global Institute think tank, are low levels of female participation in formal education and a lack of opportunities, in particular of low- and medium-skilled jobs that offer a path out of subsistence work.[9] There are already concerns that the increased – and increasingly publicized – violence against women in India will make it harder for young women to get permission from their parents to go to work. This would be a tragedy were it to happen. 'As more women join the workforce, the voices against gender-based inequality will grow louder,' observed Jayan Jose Thomas of the Indian Institute of Technology Delhi. 'Equally important, there will be more hands and brains to take the Indian economy forward.'[10] It is common knowledge that educating women pays enormous dividends in improving health outcomes and building a better society. This should surely be one of the nation's highest priorities.

The risks inherent in all this unfulfilled potential, all these unsatisfied aspirations, are fairly obvious. Many millions of children may grow up with a damaged sense of self-worth because years of schooling have failed to impart the most basic of educational skills, blaming themselves or being blamed by their parents for a failure that is not of their doing. Perhaps that is one reason Saraswati Devi's eldest son left school and home after ninth grade to become a stone-breaker in a far-off state. Others, perhaps like eighteen-year-old Akhilesh Kumar or some of the students at the Gorakhpur college, may have inflated ideas of their own employability after completing their education at a private college, and end up deeply disappointed and frustrated with what is on offer.

In Haryana, as we saw in Chapter 1, social workers blamed youth underemployment for the rash of gang-rapes that had broken out in recent years. Gangs of young men without jobs, with a damaged sense of self-worth and time on their hands, are a risk to society, and it only takes a tiny minority to turn to violence and crime to create a significant problem. A lack of educational and job opportunities in India's villages fuels the trafficking of huge numbers of young boys and girls to the cities. Many are abused sexually; the juvenile involved in the gang-rape of J seems to have turned abuser.

In the western state of Punjab, neighbouring Haryana, an epidemic of drug addiction has swept through the ranks of young men, thanks in part to a ready supply of Afghan heroin smuggled over the border from neighbouring Pakistan. Again, I was told, high levels of unemployment, slow economic growth and frustrated aspirations are all pushing people to drugs.

In early 2013, I travelled to Maqboolpura, a village on the outskirts of the city of Amritsar, not far from the Pakistani border. So many men here have died of drug use that this village is nicknamed 'the place of widows'. On the scrubby patch of land surrounding the village, boys as young as twelve offered me opium, hashish and heroin in broad daylight, hoods over their heads, while younger children flew kites from the neighbouring rooftops.[11]

A hundred yards away, I met 23-year-old Deepak Kaur, looking after her three young children in a small brick house, with paint peeling off the walls. Her husband, she told me, was a farm labourer who died of a heart attack in 2010 after taking drugs and alcohol. Her brother-in-law also died of an overdose, leaving two more young children, and a father-in-law who is over seventy as the family's main breadwinner. 'I have no plans for life after my father-in-law is dead,' she said, her children clinging to her side and staring warily at this foreigner in their midst. 'Only God knows how we are going to live.'

In Amritsar, the sociologist Ranvinder Singh Sandhu published some of the only research on the drug epidemic but complained that the authorities had ignored his findings.[12] 'It is a very big problem and our youth is being engulfed in it,' he told me as we drank tea in his front garden. 'Punjabis are very aspirational people, and when their aspirations are not fulfilled, then they are depressed.'

Meanwhile, in the forests of eastern India, a Maoist uprising has found ready recruits among the young and poor, placing large swathes of land outside the control of the state. Here, teenage boys have often picked up guns, not pens, fighting either for the Maoists or for the government-sponsored militia that was set up to oppose them in the state of Chhattisgarh. Similarly in the big cities like Mumbai, the young form impressionable gangs of thugs eager to enforce the will of divisive political leaders, who fuel fear of the city's Muslim minority, or trade on resentment of immigrants from other parts of the country.

According to economic theory, a demographic dividend occurs when fertility rates fall, as they are now doing in India. At present, India is a young country, but as the bulge in young people moves to working age, there will be fewer children following on behind them. That, in turn, means that a higher proportion of the population will be in work, and a lower proportion will be classed as dependents. In other words, there will be a rise in the relative number of breadwinners in the population, boosting the savings rate (because workers tend to save more), and even (as the number of children falls) potentially boosting the number of women entering the workforce. All of this helps the economy. It worked in Japan in the 1950s, China in the

1980s, and it also worked in Ireland after the legalization of contraception in 1979 caused fertility rates to drop. But will it work in India? Only if the education system is given a drastic overhaul and the economy starts producing more and better jobs.

Kaushik Basu, the affable economics professor who worked for a while as the finance ministry's chief economic adviser, warns that the window will not stay open for long.[13] The population bulge in the working age category is followed 'almost like an echo' by a bulge in the old-age population, he said, working its way through the system 'like a kill in a python's stomach'. By 2040, India's chance to take advantage may have passed. 'This is all the more reason for us to sit up and make use of the dividend while it lasts,' Basu told me.

In April 2012, the polling organization Gallup released a survey showing that Indians have become much more unhappy about their lives in the past four years, despite one of the world's fastest rates of economic growth.[14] The deterioration appears to have been driven partly by the expectation, created by politicians and the media, that India's boom would dramatically improve its citizens' standard of living. When many Indians realized that the boom was not significantly benefiting them, their sense of well-being and optimism about the future seemed to collapse. 'It is very dangerous to create expectations and not meet them,' Rajesh Srinivasan, Gallup's regional research director for Asia and the Middle East, told a news conference in New Delhi.[15] Gallup's surveys showed that the number of Indians who rated their lives poorly enough to be considered 'suffering' rose in 2012 to 31 per cent, equivalent to 240 million people, a dramatic rise from just 7 per cent in 2008. India's number is also significantly higher than the global average of 13 per cent. Gallup classifies respondents as 'thriving', 'struggling' or 'suffering' according to how they rate their current and future lives. While 74 per cent of Danes said they were 'thriving', just 13 per cent of Indians said the same thing. The global average is 24 per cent.

The percentage of those saying they had smiled or laughed the previous day fell to 52 per cent in 2012 from 62 per cent in 2006.

Even more worrying was that levels of well-being and optimism were no higher among the young than among the general population. 'In most countries, fifteen- to 24-year-olds are the most optimistic,' Srinivasan said. 'It is very, very depressing to see those numbers are so low [in India].'

Jim Clifton, Gallup's chairman and chief executive, warned that the findings raised the possibility of the sort of social unrest that struck Los Angeles twenty years ago after police officers were filmed beating Rodney King, or the sort of upheavals that roiled Tunisia and Egypt in 2011. 'All you need is a matchstick event,' (to light the fire) he said.

Clifton could be right, but it is a common perspective when a foreigner looks at India, to examine the numbers, to see the poverty and the inequality, and to foretell disaster, perhaps overlooking how democracy, freedom of expression, and a national resilience to suffering have often acted like oil on troubled water. Srinivasan agreed with his boss that India's failure to meet the aspirations of its young people through better education and good jobs could mean more youths 'looking for trouble', and he said that similar levels of perceived suffering had led to 'transformation revolutions' in other countries. 'But I wouldn't forecast something like that for India,' he concluded.

As the eminent Canadian Professor John Kenneth Galbraith once famously said: 'When you think of what is true in India, the opposite is also true.' It is easy to make a case for revolution in India, to argue that the country is inevitably going to rise up in violent frustration at the horrific levels of inequality and routine denial of opportunity that form the fabric of everyday life here. It would be easy to look at the state of the nation's education system and feel not just disheartened but also slightly scared of what the future holds. One very smart Indian friend of mine looks on the youth bulge with fear, forecasting a South African-style descent into violent crime that could engulf its cities. Yet the history of the last century is littered with the predictions of those who thought it could never survive as a democracy or even as a nation. Many of them were foreigners.[16]

If there is one thing that will save India, it is the Indian people. It's hard to argue the case for India when one looks at some of the challenges ahead, but when you find a small, clean primary school outside Gorakhpur and meet young teachers keen to help their students, and equally keen to get ahead themselves, it is hard to be too pessimistic. 'There is a generation gap – nowadays people get a chance for education,' twenty-year-old Ravinda Pratab told me, as he explained how he was teaching at the school to finance his own studies, and dreamt of working in a bank. 'If you are hard-working, definitely nobody can stop you.'

Given the horrific poverty and terrible inequality in India, and given the religious divides that are often inflamed by irresponsible politicians, some outsiders wonder why the country is not more violent already. The answer to that question is not obvious. Perhaps there is something in the genes, perhaps the caste system has prevented the poor from questioning their fate too violently, perhaps Indians, packed cheek-by-jowl into this densely populated land, instinctively realize that no one is safe when violence erupts, that there is nowhere to hide in a nation of 1.2 billion people, that violence will not bring the better future they all yearn for.

But if caste helps prevent violent uprisings, it has prevented and still prevents countless numbers of people from realizing their potential. A rigid stratification of society based on Hindu scriptures, India's caste system mandates four broad classifications of society, or *varnas*, from the priestly Brahmins to the Shudras, the labourers and service providers. Within those broad classifications are 3,000 or more jatis, hereditary and traditionally endogamous groups that further divide people according to occupation and status.

The Dalits (once known as 'untouchables') constitute a fifth group, sitting below and outside the caste system completely. Confined to occupations considered ritually impure, from leatherwork to cleaning latrines, they are the lowest of the low in Indian society, traditionally banned from temples and schools and forced to live outside the village. Yet they make up more than 15 per cent of the population.

Even today, the list of activities from which many Dalits are barred in rural India is mind-boggling and bizarre. Widespread prohibitions recorded in a 2001–02 survey include inter-caste dining (even extending to children in school) and entry into non-Dalit houses or places of worship; also common were bans on Dalits holding marriage processions on public roads or using barbers; more rarely, Dalits in some villages were prohibited from using umbrellas, wearing chappals (slippers) on their feet on public roads, or wearing bright clothes and sunglasses.[17]

Nevertheless, in terms of caste, there are grounds for hope. Economic growth, education and democracy have all combined to break down some of the barriers that were holding India's lowest castes back. A policy of positive discrimination, through quotas in educational institutions and government jobs, has undoubtedly had a major effect, although some argue that it has not always benefited the truly needy and has only calcified caste divisions. But to see a Dalit woman from humble beginnings, Mayawati, being elected Chief Minister of India's most populous state, Uttar Pradesh, was rightly heralded as a 'miracle of democracy' by former Prime Minister P. V. Narasimha Rao – however badly she might have governed the state during her four terms in office.

It is well known and fairly obvious that the modernization and urbanization of India is helping to break down caste barriers in India's cities, but it is much less well known that the economic reforms of the past two decades are also breaking down those barriers in the villages. A radical study of 19,000 Dalit households in Uttar Pradesh released in 2010 found massive changes in everything from grooming habits – most Dalits use toothpaste now, whereas almost none did two decades ago, for example – to eating habits and the rules governing social occasions in the village. The survey reported comments describing the changes as 'night and day' and 'the world turned upside down'.[18]

In the past, almost everything in the village had a 'social marker' of status attached – from what people wore to the type of food they ate.

Green leafy vegetables and radishes, for example, were seen as low-status foods, as were the head, leg or intestine of a goat – they were foodstuffs that were taboo to the higher castes. There were rules as to how dhotis should be worn, what cooking utensils could be used, and even stipulations that the front doorframe of a Dalit house should be below head height, so that they had to stoop on their way in, as one of the report's authors Chandra Bhan Prasad, a Dalit rights activist and columnist, explained to me over drinks at his home.

These days, though, Dalits have turned their backs on many low-status foods, and have adopted diets much more like those of their higher-caste near-neighbours. Everyone uses modern metal cooking pots, and young people of every caste wear jeans. The new goods that have flooded into the villages, from televisions to mobile phones, do not have the older social markers attached, and are available to anyone who has the money. 'Material goods have replaced social markers as the reason for existence,' said Prasad. 'India is moving from a caste-based society to a class-based society. The market is the most secular institution there is. Profit knows no caste, no gender, no nationality.'

These days, Dalits in UP are expected to transport a groom's marriage party to a bride's village in a car or jeep, rather than walking, as they would have been expected to do in the recent past – another sign that they are engaging in social practices that would normally have been the province of the upper castes. They are, indeed, breaking free of the norms that had bound them for countless generations. Economic relationships are changing too, with what the report calls a significant shift of Dalits into occupations like mason, tailor, driver or shopkeeper. Migration to the cities has also been a significant driver of Dalit emancipation, by giving them alternative sources of income and employment, while a ban on bonded labour has also helped.

The gradual empowerment of women in India has provoked a horrifically violent backlash, and may be one of the chief reasons behind the epidemic of rape that is gripping the country. Similarly, the empowerment of Dalits has provoked its own violence. In Tamil Nadu in November 2012, for example, a crowd of more than 1,000 people rampaged through three Dalit settlements, looting and burning as they went, razing more than 260 houses to the ground, stealing goods worth millions of rupees and destroying anything from motorbikes to television sets. The immediate cause was a marriage between a Dalit man and a woman of a higher (but still relatively low) caste – but the underlying tension ran much deeper. It was only one example of a rash of attacks against Dalits in India in recent years.[19]

'India is an extremely hierarchical civilization,' the historian Ramachandra Guha told me in one of our most recent conversations. 'Hierarchy was encoded in scripture and social practice here even more systematically than anywhere else. That applies to Dalits of course, but also to women.' The violence against both Dalits and women, he went on to say, is perhaps best understood as the 'old order striking back', an extremely painful process but part of social change.

'Women, for the first time in Indian history, have conceived of themselves as individuals, which is a good thing, not as somebody's wife, or mother, or daughter, or sister or mistress. Dalits have gained massive dignity and social mobility, but there is a rash of attacks against Dalits in some parts of India . . . If you only focus on the violence,' he said, 'you would think that India is lapsing back into the Middle Ages. But it is the old order striking back – against what is a massive surge in women and Dalits wanting to be recognized as individuals.'

N. K. Chandan stands as an example of what is possible in today's India, albeit a rare one. Brought up in a typical village in Uttar Pradesh, in a poor Dalit family with seven siblings, he passed out with a diploma in electrical engineering from a government polytechnic at the age of twenty-three in 1990 – thanks to his parents' encouragement and his own drive to get ahead. He joined a photocopier company in 1992 as a service and repair technician on 800 ($13) rupees a month. In 2013, after a spell running his own company, he bought the company that first employed him for 20 million rupees ($3.3 million), and renamed it Chandan and Chandan Private Industries.

He is one of a new breed of Dalit entrepreneurs rising up in India who have formed their own chamber of commerce and hope to serve as role models. Many compare their story to the Black Power movement in the United States and look to African-American entrepreneurs for inspiration. But they are also writing their own stories, and their determination to succeed in the face of adversity carries its own power. 'I do business mostly with non-Dalits,' says Chandan. 'Unless he is sure that by dealing with me he is making a profit, unless he starts believing that, why should he come to a Dalit? I never leave any default behind me. I have to win the trust of my business colleagues. I have to go the extra mile.'

India also has to go the extra mile if it is to satisfy the dreams and aspirations of the young people living in and around Gorakhpur, and indeed in every Indian city, town and village. The drive of its people is a constant reason for optimism, but the abject failure of the state has the power to bring this nation's dreams crashing down. Perhaps India's best hope lies in the power of information to force a dysfunctional system to change.

14

The Age of Information

Technology empowers India's people to fight corruption, elect better leaders

'We have to recognize the new and changing India, an India increasingly peopled by a younger, more aspirational, more impatient, more demanding and a better-educated generation . . . our youth is getting more assertive, it wants its voice to be heard.'
Sonia Gandhi, speaking to Congress Party leaders in Jaipur,
18 January 2013

'Things are beginning to change in Bihar. I think the caste factor will be relegated to the back seat for the first time in the coming assembly elections in the state. The polls will witness the majority of people rising above narrow caste considerations to vote for development-centric politics.'
Bihar's Chief Minister Nitish Kumar, in a blog in August 2010, shortly before winning an overwhelming victory in the state's elections, for a second term in office

It was May 2007, four years before the India Against Corruption movement channelled a nation's frustration with its corrupt governing elite. Husband and wife Ramesh and Swati Ramanathan were sharing a drink with a friend and local businessman, Sridar Iyengar, in San Francisco's Bay Area, after a conference on Indian democracy at the University of California, Berkeley. They were all complaining about corruption, but realized they were talking in the dark: no one had really measured the scale of the problem. While 'wholesale corruption' – the siphoning off of large sums of money from government contracts – had already received a lot of media attention over the years, what they called 'retail corruption', the daily, grinding asking and giving of bribes that permeated all aspects of Indian life, had never been effectively studied.

There was no market mechanism to discover the right 'price' for a particular service, with the result that some people paid far more than others. The trio realized they could not control corruption, but they could at least make it more predictable. Their solution, appropriately enough for a conversation held in California, was to crowd-source the answer. The Ramanathans already ran an organization based in Bengaluru dedicated to improving Indian democracy by encouraging citizens' participation in urban governance. Soon after their return to the country, they launched the ipaidabribe.com website.

'How is it that we as a middle class seem to have lost the boundary wall between what is OK to do, and what is not OK to do?' Swati Ramanathan asked me in her office in Bengaluru in early 2013, surrounded by the ipaidabribe team. That signal, that sense of right and wrong, was no longer being sent by the state.

'If we have subverted the system we all boast about it. This reflects our feeling that the state is unfair intrinsically. When the law is intrinsically unfair, beating the system becomes a badge of honour. Therefore retail corruption to us is much more poisonous than wholesale corruption. This wholesale corruption exists in every country. Retail corruption, the insidious kind, corrupts the moral fabric of an entire nation.'

The ipaidabribe website took off swiftly, tapping into some deep sense of shame perhaps that many bribe-givers felt. Indians flocked online to record their experiences of everyday graft: between 100 and 500 rupees ($2 to 8) for a passport to be verified by police; 1,000 rupees ($16) for a gas connection; 6,000 rupees ($100) to register a stolen car; 10,000 rupees ($160) for a birth certificate; 500,000 rupees ($8,500) to enrol in a medical college.

By the middle of 2013, ipaidabribe.com had recorded more than 1.9 million visitors, and received more than 22,000 reports of bribes being given, to a cumulative value of $15.4 million. Some of the biggest bribes were given to officials in the customs department. The most frequent reports of bribe-taking involved the police.

A man from Chennai reported naked extortion: having passed a breathalyser test, he was forced to pay 500 rupees when police threatened to plant a bag of drugs on him. Another was asked for 400 rupees for driving dangerously, then the 'fine' was reduced to 200. No receipt was given. 'I would not have had an issue had I to pay the full 400 bucks [rupees],' he wrote. 'It felt worse to pay the 200 bucks and add to the nexus of bribe givers–bribe takers.'

A minority of people reported having successfully resisted demands for bribes – ididntpayabribe – perhaps by having their paperwork in order and submitted in good time, by gently but firmly insisting they were not paying, or by loudly demanding service, like the man who turned up to pay his property tax only to find a crowded office with most people paying to jump to the front of the line. 'We did not pay a bribe but then we had to wait two hours or so,' he reported to the website. 'It was only when I started screaming "Why is the first-come first-served policy not being followed?" that they took the money from me. When I started to speak other people followed.'

The wealth of crowd-sourced information can help drive down the price of corruption, by allowing people, for example, to shop around for land registry offices that demand lower bribes. Although neither bribe-giver nor bribe-taker is named, the data turns the spotlight on departments where corruption is most rampant, with occasionally positive results: one (honest) transport commissioner, for example, was able to use the data as evidence of corruption within his own department and as a tool to implement a clean-up of procedures.

As well as the raw data comes insight into the psychology of bribe-givers and bribe-takers, and, its founders ultimately hope, a chance to harness the popular mood, to make bribe-giving less socially accepted, and to re-engage the middle class in the re-creation of a functioning state. 'A person who experiences petty corruption every day is broken in spirit,' one of the website's then managers, T. R. Raghunandan, told me when I met him in Bengaluru (Bangalore) in 2011. 'When your spirit is broken, you tend to accept other forms of bad governance also.'

Nearly half of the visitors to the website have come from abroad, many from the United States, UK and, interestingly, Greece. Ipaidabribe.com has spawned copycat sites all over the world in sixteen countries from Kenya to Russia, Sierra Leone to Egypt, including more than ten in China: all of these were soon blocked by the authorities after receiving a massive popular response. Plans for a mobile site and versions in different Indian languages are also well advanced.

There are times when corruption can seem to be almost embedded in the Indian psyche. An Indian friend of mine once told me that the middle class don't really mind corruption, because it allows them, the people with money, to jump to the head of the line. And in a nation of 1.2 billion people, where the bureaucracy often functions at a snail's pace, that line could get very long if there weren't ways around it. Yet my friend was probably being too cynical. As the India Against Corruption movement proved, a rising number of Indians are sick of the way that bribe-giving makes them feel, that they would like to live their lives without needing to pay this demeaning 'tax', if only the systems of governance worked efficiently and coherently, and rules were transparent and fairly applied. Many of these people turned out onto the streets in 2011 – some may have paid bribes since, but I suspect did not feel comfortable in so doing.

A 2010 study by the New Delhi-based research group CMS India showed what it called a 'ray of hope'.[1] Its data, based on surveys of people's perceptions of corruption, and experiences of having paid bribes, showed significant declines since 2005. The proportion of people who felt that corruption had increased fell from 72 per cent in 2005 to 45 per cent in 2010; but the number who actually experienced corruption fell more sharply, from 61 per cent to 28 per cent.

This is a stunning drop, and runs counter to the received wisdom that corruption is rising all the time.

The declines were largest in areas such as phones, where the private sector has displaced the public sector in service provision, or in rail reservations, where computerization has replaced human contact. Where once a landline cost both time and grease money, obtaining a mobile phone today is as quick as walking into a store. Where once it was virtually impossible to buy a railway ticket without paying a tout, now the whole system runs on the Internet, and is completely transparent. When the roots of corruption run so deep, policing human interactions will always be harder than removing humans from the equation entirely. Indeed, the idea of e-governance has grown more and more powerful and popular in India, its uses ranging from land registration to paying property tax online and tendering for government contracts through e-procurement. The Internet can help Indians to help themselves to remove corruption.

At the World Economic Forum meeting, held in the IT city of Gurgaon just outside New Delhi in 2012, ipaidabribe's Ramesh Ramanathan sat on a panel alongside Kris Gopalakrishnan of the leading IT company Infosys, CAG Vinod Rai and several other leading figures from industry and development. In an event where the gloom surrounding the Indian economy cast a pall over proceedings, the panel provided a welcome burst of optimism. India, several of the panellists argued, was reaching a 'tipping point', where public weariness with corruption, combined with the technological solutions to significantly reduce it, could help the nation turn the corner. Ramanathan spoke about how the Caucasus nation of Georgia had turned the corner in the battle against corruption in the past few years, and said India had the potential to follow suit. 'India is at an inflexion point,' he said. 'Citizens are suddenly becoming empowered. There is the same excitement that we saw with the economic reforms twenty years ago. Media and technology are clearly catalysing forces for that.'

While many of the speakers at the Forum were disparaging about the nation's political leadership, one of the most potentially transformative schemes is coming from the government, in the form of a nationwide identity card system that aims to provide every Indian with a unique sixteen-digit identity number. Smart cards that record names as well as biometric data including fingerprints and iris scans are already being produced and distributed across much of India. The project, known as Aadhar (meaning 'support' or 'foundation'), forms the backbone of a scheme to replace the unwieldy and disastrously leaky system of handing out rations and subsidies for food, fuel, scholarship grants to the poor and pensions to the elderly, and replacing them with cash payments that one day can be made directly into the bank accounts of the people for whom they are intended.

Millions of Indians lack the identification papers they need to open a bank account or receive welfare from the system: this system aims to bring them into the fold, and increase financial inclusion for the poor. In a country where lists of welfare recipients are stuffed with fake names, and corrupt officials routinely steal much if not most of the benefits meant for the poor, Aadhar promises a significantly cleaner, more transparent system. In a country that spends some $40 billion on subsidies, it also promises to save the government a considerable sum of money. Nandan Nilekani was a hugely successful software entrepreneur, who co-founded the IT giant Infosys, before joining the government in 2009 to set up the scheme. He calls it the 'essential plumbing' that will enable the government to set up a pipeline directly to the poor.

Some critics fear the beginnings of an Orwellian police state, while others worry that cash transfers will be spent unwisely – on alcohol, for example, rather than food and fuel. A third group fears it will be used to justify an expansion in the welfare state, at a time when the government should instead be concentrating on removing the barriers to free markets and free enterprise. Those fears were only reinforced in 2013 when the government passed a Food Security Bill that aims to provide subsidized food grains to two-thirds of the nation's 1.2

billion people. Yet the Aadhar scheme's supporters see almost immeasurable benefits from this new application of technology.

Technology, of course, has also enabled India's middle classes to be heard more clearly than ever before, as the young take to Facebook and Twitter to express their displeasure with the way the country is governed and, as we have seen, to organize protests. In the Information Age, technology offers India a path to a more transparent future, where information in the hands of citizens gives them real power to choose.

Far from the restaurants and bars of San Francisco's Bay Area, information (and information technology) was also on the minds of millions of people on the teeming northern plains of the Ganges in April and May 2007, as the vast and populous state of Uttar Pradesh (UP) held what some experts have called the first 'mass mobile phone elections' in India's history. The Dalit-based Bahujan Samaj Party, argue Robin Jeffrey of the University of Melbourne and Assa Doran of the Australian National University, used the now almost ubiquitous mobile phone as a 'force multiplier' during the election campaign, helping party workers overcome the hostility of the (middle-class-dominated) mainstream media and contributing to the party's surprise victory – and the installation of its leader, Mayawati, as Chief Minister.[2]

Phone messages helped party workers communicate with each other, organize meetings and activities, and communicate directly with voters, adding a dynamism and zeal to the campaign that 'leapt the obstacles imposed by illiteracy, bad roads, long bus rides, uncertain postal services and hostile neighbours', according to Jeffrey and Doran.[3] There are obvious parallels to the Obama campaign's use of online technology and texts in 2008, but the effects could be more far-reaching in India. Mass dissemination of mobile phones, together with some of the cheapest call and texting rates in the world, have helped subvert the barriers of social hierarchy and discrimination that have held India back – empowering women for example – but they may also have energized the functioning of democracy in UP. They won't win an election on their own but they can foster greater engagement. By 2012, Jeffrey told me, other parties had cottoned on to the tactic: turnout was up but Mayawati's edge was blunted, and she lost power.

Given Mayawati's reputation for corruption and misgovernance during her various terms as Chief Minister of Uttar Pradesh, it might seem to be stretching the argument to claim her victory in 2007 as one step in a democratic information revolution in India. Yet, in a very real sense, that is exactly what is happening in this country. We saw in Chapter 3 how the Association for Democratic Reforms has forced out into the open information about politicians' financial and criminal records, and in Chapter 5 how Anjali Bhardwaj and her Collective of Vigilant Citizens were using the RTI Act to shed new light on the performance of elected representatives. The media, of course, has also played a massively important role. Indeed, the economic reforms of the 1990s, and the media revolution of the 2000s, have not just unleashed huge aspirations among the Indian people for a better life for themselves and their children: they have also given voters much more information about the people who are asking to represent them, in many different ways.

In UP, thanks in part to mobile phones and in part to a massive campaign of voter enrolment and education by the Election Commission targeting young and female voters, turnout in the UP elections rose by a quarter in 2012, to a record 60 per cent. That is a stunning rise in engagement in a democracy that some outside observers wrongly condemn as broken. Democracy in India, insisted then Chief Election Commissioner S. Y. Quraishi to me in 2011, is 'alive and kicking'.

But if the poor have never lost faith in Indian democracy, turnout among India's middle classes has traditionally been lower. Here, though, social media promises to become another important vehicle for voice and empowerment – and not just for organizing protests against corruption and sexual violence.

A 2013 study by the independent IRIS Knowledge Foundation suggested that the fortunes of candidates from more than 150 seats in India's Lok Sabha – more than one in four of those on offer – could be potentially determined by Facebook users in the 2014 elections.[4] In the parliamentary constituency of Thane in Mumbai, the winning candidate in 2009 recorded a margin of just 49,000 votes. In a constituency where 419,000 voters use Facebook, the potential for a concerted social media campaign to swing the vote in someone's favour is obvious. 'Indian democracy is on the cusp of a revolution led by social media,' the report says. 'Facebook users may be the new votebank that Indian politicians have to now worry about.' In 2014, an estimated 100 million young Indians will enter the electorate for the first time, angry and disaffected with the political elite, but more connected than ever before. As a whole, only one in ten of the electorate will be Facebook users – perhaps 80 million out of 800 million – but their potential to affect outcomes will only grow with each passing year. That is not to say that Facebook or even Twitter will be major factors in 2014, but the smart politicians will surely be looking for ways to harness the power of social media. As we will see in the next chapter, some politicians – notably Gujarat's Chief Minister Narendra Modi – already have.

In 2013, the power of information was put to the test in the state elections in Karnataka, home to the nation's IT capital Bengaluru. Turnout was traditionally higher in the countryside than in Bengaluru; the big two parties, Congress and the BJP, were seen as notoriously corrupt and in the thrall of the mining mafia, and young city-dwellers were turned off by the whole process; at the same time, urban governance had been appallingly bad.

Rajya Sabha MP Rajeev Chandrasekhar used social networking and traditional media to try to engage the urban youth and focus the debate on governance rather than on power politics – in other words to inject some meaningful *information* into the campaign. He urged voters to quiz candidates on key issues relating to governance, and even drew up a list of thirteen 'pointed questions on issues taxpayers have a right to know'. At the same time, the small Lok Satta Party fielded candidates who were honest and clean and had real ideas about how to govern. The results were inconclusive – turnout in Bengaluru rose from 48 per cent to 57 per cent, and although Lok Satta failed to convince people that it was a viable alternative to the big two, it picked up a few per cent of the urban vote and one of its candidates picked up 11,000 votes in his constituency. Nevertheless, this is an experiment that will surely be repeated elsewhere as time goes by.

So if more people in India are engaging with politics these days and getting more information about the candidates before them, and if more are turning up to vote on election day, the obvious question is, what are they all voting for? Caste and identity remains a major factor – the old cliché that Indians do not so much cast their vote as vote (for) their caste is still relevant, especially in UP.[5] Nevertheless, and notwithstanding the Karnataka experiment, compelling evidence is emerging that governance matters more than ever before. A study of the results of the 2009 parliamentary elections found a close correlation – at the level of individual states – between economic performance and electoral success. In other words, in states where the ruling party achieved high rates of economic growth, their candidates won 85 per cent of the seats they contested; incumbents in states growing well below the national average won just 30 per cent of the time.[6]

One of the authors of that study was Columbia University's respected economics professor Arvind Panagariya. He says the country has undergone a 'revolution of rising expectations' since the economy was liberalized two decades ago and growth began to take off. 'People at all levels, especially the poor, had discovered that unlike during the first four decades of Independence, rapid improvement in economic fortune was possible,' Panagariya wrote in an op-ed. 'They, therefore, now punished non-performing governments with electoral defeat and rewarded performing ones with victory.'[7]

The caste factor may be lessening in importance, or is perhaps being somewhat negated because everyone is now playing the game of building coalitions of different castes. Corruption can also play a role in determining electoral outcomes, but only when it becomes excessive or brazen. 'In India, the perception is that everybody is corrupt,' Panagariya told me. 'The mere fact of corruption everybody accepts. But if it becomes excessive, if there is nothing covert about it, that hurts you.'[8]

The study is far from conclusive, but its findings have been repeatedly reinforced in elections in individual states across the country in the past decade. From Bihar to Gujarat, Odisha to New Delhi to Chhattisgarh, state governments that have performed reasonably well and delivered rates of economic growth significantly higher than the national average have won re-election to second or even third terms.

The northern state of Bihar, for instance, has been transformed from a symbol of crime, poverty, corruption and caste-based governance – nicknamed the Jungle Raj – to an unlikely symbol of hope in recent years, under the leadership of 62-year-old Nitish Kumar. Ostensibly a socialist from the small Janata Dal (United) Party, Kumar had served as a cabinet minister in coalition governments between 1999 and 2004 before taking over as Bihar's chief minister the following year. Since then, he has cut crime and streamlined government; given bicycles to girls who attend school and employed tens of thousands of new teachers; built roads and improved healthcare. He has also encouraged business and investment, and achieved some of India's highest levels of economic growth of any state over the period. His reward was to be voted back into office in 2011 with an overwhelming mandate.[9]

'India has changed,' wrote Shekhar Gupta, editor of the *Indian Express* newspaper. 'Our voter is no longer confused. Nor is she a prisoner of narrow-focus prejudices and loyalties. She now reads the big picture: agendas, track records and what's-in-it-for-me-and-my-children's-future. That is why verdict after verdict, you get the same message. That our elections are becoming increasingly meritocratic.'[10]

What is true at the state level is also true at the constituency level, Odisha MP Jay Panda told me. Thanks to economic growth, voters are demanding the opportunities that they can see others attaining. At the same time, again thanks to the economic boom of the past two decades, ruling party politicians have the money and means at their disposal to make a difference. 'Economic liberalization and development are empowering the disenfranchised and giving the poor a leg up,' he told me. 'People do indeed benefit, and that forces us as politicians to focus on what people want.'

Panda, who we also met in Chapter 9, is an extraordinary politician, spending huge amounts of his time interacting with his constituents directly, and bringing tarmac roads and bridges even to the remotest parts of his constituency. His Chief Minister Naveen Patnaik, he says, has rejected the old ways of governing, where you only reward those constituencies or communities that voted for you, and as a result has won considerable support in tribal villages that did not count among his initial support base.

The more politicians get the message, the better governance will become and the more democracy will help India grow. Pratap Bhanu Mehta, president of the New Delhi-based Centre for Policy Research, calls it a 'mandate for a dream'. As voters choose empowerment over patronage, he wrote in the *Indian Express*, 'there is almost a social revolution in the making'. Panda said that India is too big and diverse for 'the epiphany' to happen at the same time everywhere. Nevertheless, he said, momentum is building. 'We'll approach a tipping point in the next five years, allowing the country as a whole to shift gears.'[11]

No national government could possibly be expected to solve all the problems and heal all the wounds of so vast and so various a country. Democracy in India will function better the closer government comes to the people, so that decentralization of political power to state, city and local governments is critical – another reason why, in the words of the Carnegie Endowment's Milan Vaishnav, 'India needs more democracy, not less'.[12] It is no coincidence that much of the good news in India at the moment is taking place at the level of individual states, whose governments exercise considerable control over issues ranging from law and order to education, electricity, land, and roads.

Another trend, christened 'competitive liberalization', has seen individual Indian states increasingly competing with each other to attract investment dollars. Capital and labour, say the US-based India scholars Devesh Kapur and Arvind Subramanian, are already flowing to the best-performing states, pushing the laggards to raise their games.[13] Take, for example, the Chief Minister of the southern state of Tamil Nadu, J. Jayalalithaa, a 65-year-old who vented her fury on her own state government bureaucracy in 2011 after the South Korean carmaker Hyundai chose Gujarat as the location for its next plant rather than invest in her state, partly because of Tamil Nadu's unreliable power supplies. Her message was clear – her state must improve its electricity supply if it wanted industry to expand. Or take the poor central state of Chhattisgarh, better known as a hotbed of Maoist insurgency than as an investment destination, but which has now started to parade its attractions at a glitzy annual 'Global Investors Meet'. Chief ministers from individual states have increasingly begun travelling to countries like China and the United States to attract investment (rather than leaving that kind of global business diplomacy to the central government). In terms of ideas on how to govern better, while many are too proud to learn from the success stories of other, rival states, there is evidence that some are gradually picking up ideas on 'best practices'.

The big picture, however, remains less rosy. India's parliament often seems more interested in protecting the vested interests of its members than in cleaning up its act. Neither of the two big parties has been quick to grasp the idea of good governance as good politics, at least not at the national level. Rahul Gandhi does talk the language of clean governance, but the only politician who is offering that kind of national vision today with any real conviction, and with any track record behind him, is Narendra Modi.

15

I'm the Man

Narendra Modi offers himself as India's saviour

'The modern-day Neros [of Modi's government] were looking elsewhere when . . . innocent children and helpless women were burning, and probably deliberating how the perpetrators of the crime can be protected.'
India's Supreme Court, April 2004

'I have not done anything wrong, and I am committed to the human cause.'
Narendra Modi to the author, April 2012

He strode onto the stage just after the sun had set and waved to his adoring fans as they chanted his name, as though he were a rock star. 'Modi, Modi, Modi.' A huge image of Gujarat's chief minister hung down the left-hand side of the stage, with an orange and white scarf neatly draped around his neck. Next to it, a podium and bulletproof-glass screen awaited him. In the centre of the stage, the real Narendra Modi had a golden cloak draped around his shoulders, for just a second, before he cast it aside. 'Bharat Mata Ki Jai [Victory to Mother India],' the crowds chanted, as Modi took the microphone. He avoided the bulletproof podium, calmed the crowd, and launched into a full-throated attack on the Congress, his tone rising and falling from impassioned declaration to low growl, his hands cutting through the night air as he drove home his message.

It was April 2013, and India's most controversial politician was campaigning for the BJP, not on his home turf but way down south, in India's IT capital of Bengaluru, just a week ahead of elections in the state of Karnataka. The BJP was struggling to win re-election in Karnataka, buffeted by a huge corruption scandal and split by the formation of a breakaway party, and Modi was supposed to be riding to the rescue. But this was not just a local affair; it was also part of a national campaign to project Modi as a potential prime minister. Nationally televised, it was part of Modi's assault on the hearts and minds of the entire country. Modi had just swept to a third consecutive election victory for the BJP in his home state of Gujarat. Could 'hat-trick Modi', as his supporters triumphantly dubbed him, make the transition from Gujarat to the national stage; could one of India's most charismatic but divisive politicians be the person to turn India around?

Straightaway, Modi identified his target – the Congress Party's crown prince Rahul Gandhi – referred to not by name but as 'a leader born with a golden spoon in his mouth'. Rahul's coronation as Congress vice-president just three months before was portrayed as yet another set of broken promises, his subsequent attempt to campaign in Karnataka by attacking the corruption within the BJP dismissed as a hypocritical sermon delivered by a leader of a deeply corrupt party. Modi's voice rose and fell, laden with emotion, anger, passion, contempt, each sentence followed by a pregnant pause to drive home its meaning. Rahul's own emotion-laden acceptance speech in Jaipur was scornfully dispatched.

'Brothers and sisters, in the social system we have grown up in, we have our own set of values,' he said, speaking in Hindi. 'Even today in families, if a mother asks her son to do something, the son can never disrespect his mother's word. That is correct, right? Any son, does he disrespect his mother's word? That is the value system in *this* country.'

But the Congress Party, Modi was implicitly reminding his audience, is run not by a real Indian, but by Sonia Gandhi, a woman he often derisively calls 'Italian bhabi-ji' (sister-in-law). In the culture of the Congress Party, Modi continued, 'a mother sobs, and tells her son "Beta [son], power is poison."' He paused, and then his voice grew even more wheedling, his back hunching slightly, the syllables even more drawn out, his contempt for the part he was playing even more evident. '"Be-eta,"' he repeated, '"being in power is poison."

'But within a hundred days,' Modi went on, standing up straight once again, his hands sweeping to right and left again, 'the son goes around Karnataka, and says "Give us political power. Give us the seat of power." So brothers and sisters, these are hypocritical words. This is two-faced politics.' Modi is one of the most charismatic public speakers in Indian politics today, a demagogue who mixes humour with vitriol to captivate his supporters and appal his enemies. He has a following perhaps more devoted than any other Indian politician, particularly among the young, but engenders more hate and fear than anyone else in politics today. He is celebrated as India's most effective administrator, and heralded for ushering in a prolonged economic boom in his home state of Gujarat; he is fawned over by business leaders for cutting red tape, curbing corruption and welcoming industrial investment. But he is hated and mistrusted by his liberal foes, accused of complicity in the mass murder of Muslims during brutal riots shortly after he took office, charged with promoting a culture of prejudice and discrimination against Muslims in Gujarat ever since and of being deeply intolerant of dissent.

At a time of desperately weak and corrupt leadership, Modi is seen by his fans as India's saviour, a strong and decisive man who could rescue its economy and restore its battered national pride. In a country sick of the stale air of dynastic politics, of the self-righteousness and inherited privilege of the Gandhi family, this self-made son of a tea-stall owner represents a dynamic breath of fresh air, a break from the past and a man with a vision for the future.

Yet Modi's brand has been badly sullied by his alleged role in the riots. The United States denied him a B1/B2 entry visa in 2005 on those grounds, and still restricts access to the level of its consul general in Mumbai, rather than at ambassadorial level. His critics say he will polarize the country along religious lines and undermine India's long-cherished secular identity, its tradition of tolerance and free speech, the very fabric that has kept this nation largely peaceful since the horrific violence that accompanied Partition, and that sets it above its Muslim neighbour Pakistan.

Amid the chaos and tumult of Indian democracy, Modi offers the Chinese model: a dictator perhaps, but one who can rule with single-minded focus on promoting economic growth; the champion of a modern India, provided, of course, you don't ask any inconvenient, nay divisive, questions about human rights. In January 2013, 36 per cent of Indians surveyed by Nielsen on behalf of *India Today* said Modi would be the best bet for the prime minister's job. Rahul Gandhi scored a more modest 22 per cent.[1]

In 2002, the western state of Gujarat had erupted into horrific violence. First, fifty-nine Hindus, most of them pilgrims returning from the holy city of Ayodhya, burned to death inside a railway carriage on 27 February after clashing with Muslims on the station at a place called Godhra. The dead included men, women and children. In the three days that followed, Hindu mobs rampaged through the state in an orgy of retribution against Muslims, massacring between 1,000 and 2,000 of them. The police were accused of standing aside and letting the mobs wreak their revenge, or at times of actively encouraging them. Modi was accused of having issued instructions that police should allow 'people to vent their frustration'.

In neighbouring Pakistan, where I lived at the time, the news was greeted with anger and bitterness. Modi, it seemed from across the border, represented the evils of Hindutva, a new narrow casting of Indian identity that saw greatness only in the Hindu aspects of its national culture.

Yet over the years, Modi has forced his critics to constantly re-evaluate and reassess their judgement of him, as he proved himself adept not only at shaping his image but also at developing his state. By 2012, when I profiled Modi for the *Washington Post*,[2] I quoted Ron Somers, the head of the US-India Business Council, calling Modi's government a 'role model' for progressive leadership, and a Congressional Research Service report lauding Gujarat as 'perhaps India's best example of effective governance and impressive development'. Modi, the report said, 'has streamlined economic processes, removing red-tape and curtailing corruption in ways that have made the state a key driver of national economic growth'.

I first travelled to Gujarat in 2007, ahead of state elections there that Modi was destined to win comfortably. Then, I was denied an interview but granted a brief audience in his office, which turned out to be a strange, unsettling encounter. 'I know how fascinated you foreigners are with India,' he said, as we made small talk. 'I have a list,' he continued. 'How many foreigners come here, how many like it here. A lot of them marry Indian women, some even marry their maids.'

But if Modi made no secret of his disdain for foreigners in that first meeting, my next interview with him, some five years later, was very different. This time he seemed keen to impress, to make a case for his international rehabilitation – to smooth the way, perhaps, for an eventual attempt on the Prime Minister's Office. Then, we must have talked for an hour, about investment, about governance, and even, briefly, about the riots and discrimination. He did his best to be charming, to smile and demonstrate a lighter, human side. I have to admit to having found it equally unsettling.

Narendra Damodardas Modi was born on 17 September 1950 in the narrow streets of the Gujarati town of Vadnagar, the third child of a lower-caste family who ran a tea stall and were also, like their fellow caste members, in the business of extracting and selling vegetable oil. Helping out at his father's tea stall, his lifelong hatred for the Congress party apparently began when, as a six-year-old, he was swept up in protests to support Gujarat's claim to become a separate state, distributing badges, shouting slogans, and, a few years later, leading his schoolmates in celebrations when their wishes were finally granted. He is remembered as a devout Hindu, according to Nilanjan Mukhopadhyay's compelling biography, a mediocre student but one who had a flair for debating and theatre, a stubborn, argumentative boy who always cared about his clothes and his

personal grooming. At the tender age of eight, he first started attending meetings of the Rashtriya Swayamsevak Sangh (RSS), the
volunteer body that forms the core of the family of organizations
promoting Hindutva, apparently developing an instant liking for its
culture of discipline and responsibility.[3]

But while these details of Modi's early age can be openly discussed,
his marriage to Jashodaben Chimanlal remains shrouded in mystery
and has become a subject journalists investigate at their peril. Indeed,
Mukhopadhyay says he decided at an early stage of writing his biography that it was simply not worthwhile to try to track down Modi's
estranged wife in the government primary school where she apparently teaches, or even to broach the subject in his interviews with the
Chief Minister himself, for fear of provoking his wrath and seeing
doors closed against him.[4] What is known, according to Vinod Jose,
is simply this: in keeping with the traditions of his Ghanchi caste,
Modi's parents arranged his marriage to a girl from a neighbouring
town who was three years younger than him. Engagement at a very
young age was followed by a religious ceremony at the age of thirteen,
but when the time came for Modi to begin the third stage of his
marriage – cohabitation with Jashodaben – the young man baulked.
Modi disappeared for two years, wandering the Himalayas in a spiritual journey, surviving as a mendicant, pondering whether to follow
a priestly life or a political one. The 'marriage' was never formally
dissolved, nor was Jashodaben formally released from her commitment, but Modi was clear in his mind that it was not going ahead.[5]

Rumours of a relationship with a female minister in Gujarat were
later to surface briefly, but by and large Modi's personal life remains a
remarkably closed book, and one where he seems to deeply resent
intrusion.[6] It has a strange parallel to the way Rahul Gandhi closely
guards the details of his life before and outside politics. Is it because,
in their own very different ways and for different reasons, both men
find close relationships and trust somewhat difficult terrain, or are
they just private men who resent media intrusion? It is striking that
these two rivals, so widely touted as future leaders of India, are both

extremely controlling and guarded in the way they deal with the press, even when it comes to politics. But then, Manmohan Singh is hardly known for giving interviews, nor indeed is Sonia Gandhi.

Modi's rise to political prominence really began during Indira Gandhi's Emergency of 1975–7, when the RSS was banned and its members forced underground. It was a hugely influential period in his life, he told me, when he met many of the leaders of the anti-Congress movement and helped organize many protests against the Emergency. A decade later he crossed over into the BJP, the political front of the Hindutva movement, and worked as the organization secretary for Gujarat as the party quickly gathered strength, helping them to their first election victory in the state in 1986. In the 1990s, the Hindu nationalist project was invigorated by the campaign to tear down a mosque in Ayodhya, said to have been built on Lord Ram's birthplace, and replace it with a Hindu temple. The BJP took power in Gujarat in 1995, and in all of India in 1998 under Atal Bihari Vajpayee. Modi found himself in New Delhi, as the party's national organization secretary, making a name for himself with his jingoistic style when Pakistan sent troops into the mountain heights of Kashmir during the brief Kargil war of 1999. In his profile of Modi for *The Caravan* magazine,[7] Vinod K. Jose records his reaction during one TV debate, when asked how India should respond to Pakistani provocation: 'We won't give them chicken biryani,' he said, 'we will respond to a bullet with a bomb.' It was classic Modi, the Hindu vegetarian deriding any attempt to appease the meat-eating Muslim with a lavishly prepared biryani dish, beating his chest with self-righteous nationalist fervour, declaring that proud India would no longer be taken advantage of.

In October 2001, with the BJP in Gujarat riven by infighting, Modi was returned to the state and was installed by Vajpayee as its Chief Minister. He was still consolidating his position when the riots began in February 2002. It is worth remembering that Gujarat was already perhaps India's most polarized state between Hindus and Muslims, and had already been the scene of some of the country's worst communal riots since Partition, notably in 1969, 1985 and 1992, when hundreds of people died. But it was what happened during what became known as India's first 'televised riots' in 2002 that shook India's secular fabric and blotted the reputation of a state and a politician.

Although some people would tell us that the Muslims of Gujarat should simply 'move on' from that violence, and some Indian readers may feel this is now ancient history, I believe that it is important to remind ourselves of what happened during 2002.

Afroz Bano was fifty-two when the riots began, sitting at home with her son when the sound and fury of the mob began breaking over their neighbourhood. They tried to flee from the back of the house, she said, but soon came up against a police roadblock. 'The police started beating us, to stop us passing,' she told me, a surviving granddaughter at her side. 'Then the mob approached. We were sandwiched. The mob started pelting us with stones, and a big piece of rock hit my son. They took his body, poured kerosene on it and set it alight in front of me.' Bano's daughter-in-law was visiting her family at the time: they too had nowhere to run. The girl's mother was slashed across the face with a sword, Bano said, and died on the spot; her sister was burned alive, her eight-year-old niece likewise thrown onto the fire, along with two nephews of about the same age; her sister-in-law was raped, slashed with a sword and dumped naked in a pool of blood. The family say they can identify many of the perpetrators, but all are still free or have been released on bail.

Farida says she saw entire families burned to death, and some shot by police, before her eyes. Again, she says her appeals to the police for help were rudely rebuffed. 'The policeman hit me with a lathi [cane],' she said. 'He said: "Today you must die. Come hell or high water, we are not going to help you." And then he put a gun to my head.' Farida says two friends pulled her back from the policeman, but even though she has identified him, he has still not been punished. 'I saw a boy pulled from a rickshaw and killed,' she told me. 'I have given the names of thirty guilty people. Four of the thirty are not alive any more, but the other twenty-six have still not been tried and are still free. Meanwhile I have been bullied and blackmailed and threatened. I still get calls saying: "We will kill you if the verdict goes against us."'

In its report on the Gujarat riots,[8] Human Rights Watch says scores of Muslim women and girls were brutally raped before being mutilated and burnt to death. It said the attacks appeared to have been planned in advance. Between 28 February and 2 March thousands of attackers descended on Muslim neighbourhoods, dressed in the Hindu nationalist uniform of saffron scarves and khaki shorts, and carrying swords, tridents, explosives and gas cylinders, as well as computer printouts. They were guided by computer printouts listing the addresses of Muslim families and their properties. The police joined in. 'At best they were passive observers,' the report concluded, 'and at worse they acted in concert with murderous mobs and participated directly in the burning and looting of Muslim shops and homes and the killing and mutilation of Muslims. In many cases, under the guise of offering assistance, the police led the victims into the hands of their killers.' Panicked calls to the police, fire brigades and ambulance services generally proved futile, either left unanswered or met with responses like 'We don't have any orders to save you,' or 'We cannot help you, we have orders from above.' Some lines were eventually cut to make further calls for help impossible.

Ten years later, Human Rights Watch was to issue another damning update on the aftermath of the Gujarat riots.[9] It accused the authorities in Gujarat of subverting justice, protecting the perpetrators of the attacks, and intimidating those who were calling for accountability. The state government, it said, had resisted Supreme Court orders to prosecute those responsible for the carnage, with investigations deliberately stalled or simply not pursued, and evidence that senior BJP leaders led the mobs was ignored by state police. Only when a Supreme Court-appointed Special Investigation Team took over the investigation was BJP lawmaker Maya Kodnani finally convicted in August 2012 of orchestrating the massacre of ninety-five people, after a court heard evidence that she had handed out swords and exhorted the mob to kill Muslims.[10]

Kodnani's conviction was an embarrassment to Modi: despite the accusations against her, he had appointed the former gynaecologist as his minister for Women and Child Development in 2007, although she resigned the post in 2009. But the Special Investigation Team (SIT) also concluded that it had found no 'prosecutable evidence' against Modi, the so-called 'clean chit' that his supporters say now clears his path to the Prime Minister's Office.[11]

Modi has been extremely reluctant to talk about the riots, famously walking out of a television interview with the combative journalist Karan Thapar in 2007 when he launched straight in with an inquisition on the subject.[12] Indeed, my own request for an interview with Modi in 2012 was stalled for several months after I submitted a list of proposed questions, some of which strayed a little too close to the controversy for comfort. It is fairly common practice these days for high-profile interviewees to demand questions from journalists in advance, in order to gauge their intentions and limit the room for aggressive interrogation. It is also fairly common practice for journalists to deviate from the script they have prepared, but it wouldn't have been the first time I had lost an interview by being a little too honest. Finally, though, because I was writing a story about how American carmakers were investing in Gujarat, because I was visiting the state anyway, and because Modi was trying to rebuild his international image, my interview request was granted in March 2012. But as I waited in Modi's anteroom, his assistant pulled me aside for a quiet word. I wouldn't be asking about the riots, he wanted to be sure, because it wasn't on my list. So many people, visiting diplomats and trade delegations, want to talk about the riots, he said, but Modi wanted to talk about governance and development. If I veered from the script, he wouldn't be able to get interviews for any foreign journalists in the future.

There had, fortunately, been some negative comments about Modi coming out of Washington a few days before. I would have to mention this, I said, and needed to give the Chief Minister the chance to reply. We agreed there would be just one question about the riots – in the event I followed up with two more, and everyone seemed happy. In the first place, Modi handed me an eighteen-page deposition he had given to the SIT, in the form of a question-and-answer session.[13] In it, he categorically denied having made comments in the aftermath of the Godhra attack like 'Hindus should wake up now', or 'Every action should have an equal and opposite reaction.' He denied having given the green light for the riots during a meeting of his top officials on the evening of 27 February 2002, and insisted that he had repeatedly called for peace and harmony to be maintained.

Modi told me the accusations were being levelled by 'some vested interest groups' and said there should be a detailed study of conditions in Gujarat. 'A misinformation campaign is going on, allegations are going on,' he said, 'but the reality is totally different.' I was referred to the Sachar Committee report, a 2005/6 study into the social, economic and educational conditions of Muslims in India, and given summaries of some of its findings.[14] It showed that Muslims occupy more government posts in Gujarat than in other states, have higher per capita incomes and much higher literacy rates than the Indian average, and a higher percentage complete their schooling. So was he annoyed by the constant accusations? 'No,' he said. 'Why? Because I have not done anything wrong, and I am committed to the human cause.'

Modi's reluctance to talk about the riots may be partly a legal one, to avoid complicating matters until the investigations are complete and the Supreme Court finally accepts the verdict of its own investigators. But his reluctance to offer any apology or even the mildest regret for the violence seems to me to have deeper roots. In the aftermath of the riots, with elections approaching, Modi campaigned on a macho, chest-thumping assertion of Gujarati Hindu pride, or Asmita. There was nothing to apologize for, he was telling his supporters, portraying his accusers as enemies of the state and of Gujarati people in general. Modi is sometimes nicknamed chhappan, which means

56, for the 56-inch chest of which he boasts. His appeal to the electorate was based on staring his accusers down. It is what his supporters demand, but it is also a fundamental character trait. Those who wait for Modi to back down even slightly, to express the merest hint of contrition, to move even slightly towards the centre, may have to wait for a very long time.

'People are asking how Gujarat has progressed,' he continued in our interview:

> A few said it was because of the chief minister, a few said it was because of policy, a few said it was because the people are entrepreneurs. I want to tell the world what the reality is. The real story is that we could progress because of the unity, peace and harmony there is in our society. That is the real strength. There is no casteism; there is no communalism. Because of that reason Gujarat is prospering. In the history of Gujarat, every year there was communal violence. In the last ten years there has not been a single case of communal violence. It is the most peaceful period in the history of Gujarat. I want to convey to the global world: please try to understand, you appreciate on progress, you appreciate on development, but behind development and progress, the real strength is peace, harmony and unity.

While Modi is right that there have been no incidents of communal riots in Gujarat since 2002, his declaration of perfect brotherly love has an element of Orwellian double-think about it. In the course of my reporting on Gujarat, I strayed as far as possible from the guided tours and the usual suspects. In shopping malls, I talked to middle-class Hindus of all ages, on the streets I found ways to get into quiet conversations with Muslims. There was a remarkable consistency in what I was told. Devina Bhardwaj, who runs a clinical research company, offered a moderate but casual dismissal of the charges against Modi when I met her in 2007. 'Everybody does good and bad things, but the good things he does are so much,' she told me. And the riots? I asked. 'I have not seen him do it,' she said. 'There have always been riots in Ahmedabad.' Hardik Parikh, a 23-year-old student, offered a common refrain – terrorism had been on the rise in India, and Muslims were breeding too fast. 'It was important to teach the Muslims a lesson,' he said. 'They are mushrooming and they will start to kill Hindus. It should not be repeated, but once is OK.'[15]

Kalkit Chaudhury, who was training to be a government teacher, offered a similar justification, in a conversation in another Ahmedabad shopping mall in 2012. 'Whatever happened in 2002, the riots, it was all very right,' he said. 'If Hindus were killed on the train, why shouldn't the same happen to Muslims? Until there is solid evidence against Narendra Modi that he ordered the riots, we shouldn't blame him for it.'

I won't name the Muslims I spoke to, because to do so could complicate their lives in Gujarat, but respectable men and women told me stories of being denied access to bank loans, to higher educational opportunities and to employment. 'My eldest son is a chartered accountant,' said one lady, 'but he is really struggling to get work. There is always an excuse, all slots have been filled, there is no more requirement. They tell us to our face, we need to pay a heavy donation to get a seat in college, or to get a job, just because we are Muslims.' Another woman told me her nephew had been denied a bank loan to study to be a pharmacist, but the family had somehow scraped together the money to pay for his studies. When he qualified, all his (Hindu) classmates had found work easily, but he was left unemployed, she said.

Modi can't be blamed for the discrimination in Gujarat, any more than he can take credit for the findings of the Sachar Committee report. But the divide between Hindus and Muslims certainly widened after the riots, and no attempt seems to have been made to bring the two communities together, or to combat prejudice. Communities live in their own colonies throughout India, but Ahmedabad has surely become India's most divided city since the riots. In the slums of Citizen Nagar on the outskirts of town, Muslims who lost their homes in the riots live in the shadow of a vast, stinking garbage dump. There are scarcely any civic amenities in Citizen Nagar, and a huge well of bitterness against Modi. Many others have sought safety in numbers in Juhapura, a Muslim-only enclave of some half a million people in the southwest that is nicknamed Little Pakistan. The condition of the roads, the reliability of water supplies, all so good elsewhere in the city, all deteriorate sharply when one crosses 'the border' (as it is known) into Juhapura. There are no public toilets in Juhapura and too few schools. Hindus are reluctant or even scared to enter this neighbourhood, Muslims routinely denied access to rent apartments outside it by virtue of their religion alone.[16]

In the idiom of this state, to be 'Gujarati' means to be a Gujarati Hindu; to be a Muslim is to be an outsider. This needs to be understood in terms of Gujarat's history: the state sits on India's western border with Pakistan, and has suffered many waves of Muslim invasion and occupation over many centuries, by Arabs from present-day Pakistan and Mughal rulers from New Delhi. Its iconic Hindu temple at Somnath has been destroyed countless times by those invaders. Yet I still find it disconcerting to sit for evening drinks with a charming, middle-class couple in their back garden in Ahmedabad, and have this history recounted at length to justify modern-day retribution. That Muslims breed faster than Hindus is a refrain I heard countless times in Gujarat, even if the census data shows their share of the population in the state keeping roughly steady at around 9 per cent.[17]

The fact that Modi thrives off these prejudices is not really challenged. In September 2002, just nine months after the riots, he made a public speech asking if the government should really be running relief camps for Muslim riot victims. 'Should we open child-producing centres?' he asked, bemoaning the fact that one religious community was obstructing the state's family planning policy and therefore its progress. 'If Gujarat is to be developed, then an economic system has to be developed where every child born in Gujarat gets education, manners and employment. And for this, those who are multiplying population at a rapid rate will need to learn a lesson,' he said, before bemoaning the education Muslim children received at madrasas. 'Those who have got no education, and have got only religious education, would they not become a burden on Gujarat?'[18] Modi never even visited any of these 'child-producing centres', and when Prime Minister Vajpayee visited the state in 2002, he was taken to a camp for riot-affected Hindus.

The Modi message resonated perfectly with the people of Gujarat, sweeping the BJP towards a resounding victory in state elections held in December 2002. Here was the evidence to support the BJP theory (once voiced by Vajpayee himself) that the party did not need Muslim votes to take power. Nationally, though, it was a different story. The fact that the BJP ultimately backed Modi after the 2002 riots did nothing to help them elsewhere in the country, alienating many moderate Hindus, and may have contributed to their surprise defeat in the 2004 general election.

There were to be no more riots in Gujarat, as Modi was keen to point out, but the portrayal of the Muslim as outsider, as enemy, as potential terrorist, did not abate. Again, it is important to remember why this message gelled with so many Indians, as the country suffered from a wave of terrorist attacks that had spread from Kashmir to other parts of the country. But in Gujarat, the point was driven home with special vehemence, as police concocted supposed plots against the Chief Minister's life and executed innocent Muslims in 'fake encounters'.

In June 2004, the dead bodies of four people, including nineteen-year-old college girl Ishrat Jahan, were displayed to the media as terrorists who had been killed after a car chase. Subsequent judicial inquiries found no evidence of Jahan being linked to any terrorist group, and concluded she had been kidnapped by the police and executed in their custody. In November 2005, a Muslim underworld criminal called Sohrabuddin Sheikh was picked up along with his wife Kauser Bi. While she disappeared, the police claimed he had been killed after a gun battle. The state government's lawyer later admitted the gun battle had been staged, and that Kauser Bi had also

been killed by the police. More than ten police officers were charged
and jailed in relation to the murders. In September 2013 the most
famous of them, Deputy Inspector General D. G. Vanzara, resigned
from the police[19] complaining that he was being unfairly scapegoated
for protecting the state from 'Pakistan-inspired terrorism'. The police,
he said, 'have simply implemented the conscious policy of this government which was inspiring, guiding and monitoring our actions from
very close quarters'.

Sheikh was no angel. Police said dozens of AK-47 assault rifles had
been recovered from his house, and he had many cases pending
against him, including for murder. But Modi positively revelled in his
death. 'What should be done to a man from whom a large number of
AK-47 rifles were recovered, who was on the search list of police from
four states, who attacked the police, who had relations with Pakistan
and wanted to enter Gujarat?' he asked the crowds during his 2007
re-election campaign. When the crowd shouted 'Kill him, kill him,'
Modi replied: 'Does my government need Soniaben's [Sonia Gandhi's]
permission for this?'

I had followed Modi on that campaign and been struck by his ability
to connect with the crowds.[20] In one rally, he had ruthlessly mocked
his opponents' campaign slogan of 'Chak De Congress!' – a reference
to a Bollywood blockbuster film of the same year about a fictional
resurgence of the Indian hockey team *Chak De India!* (loosely meaning 'Come on India!'). Not only was Chak De a Punjabi term, Modi
pointed out, but it is what Punjabis would say when their jeep had
fallen in the ditch and they need to heave it out. With his arms
waving, Modi would have the crowd in stitches as he mimed how
Congress had fallen into the ditch, and everyone was heaving together
('Cha-ak De-eh') to pull it out.

But the humour would soon give way to spite. In Godhra, the
communally polarized town where the Hindu pilgrims had burned to
death on the train, I watched as he accused Sonia Gandhi of protecting terrorists and being scared to hang Afzal Guru, who had been

convicted, some said on sketchy evidence, of involvement in the 2001 attack on India's parliament. 'If you don't have the courage,' he taunted Gandhi, 'send him to Gujarat. We will hang him here.'

Being firm on terrorists – or promoting the idea of a 'war on terror' for political gain – is a strategy popular with politicians throughout the world. Many Hindus have watched with consternation as Congress bent over backwards to practise positive discrimination in favour of Muslims and lower castes in an often cynical ploy to win their votes. When Modi says he stands against appeasement and the 'vote-bank' politics of Congress, his comments accord with a large section of the population. But Modi is more explicit than most in the way he exploits people's prejudice and fear for his own ends.

Muslims will be tolerated in Gujarat only on Modi's terms, provided they bow their heads to India's Hindu culture and accept their place, effectively as second-class citizens. In this worldview, it is those who keep harping on the riots and seeking justice for its victims who are the true dividers of Gujarati society, not the people who encouraged, facilitated or carried out the violence. Yet once that relationship and those rules were established, there has been little need for Modi to remain on the offensive against Muslims during his ten years as Gujarat's chief minister. Prosperity and development were the real priorities of the Gujarati people, and they have been Modi's mantra for many years now. BJP supporters make much of the fact that a small proportion of Muslims may now be voting for Modi, but that is hardly surprising in a democracy based on patronage and that rewards those who choose the winning side. That the BJP did not field any Muslim candidates in the 2012 state elections is also telling.[21]

Modi's supporters have also begun propagating a new argument to undermine those who would bar him from top office on the basis of the riots. Congress, they say quite justifiably, encouraged the 1984 riots in the wake of Indira Gandhi's death that saw thousands of Sikhs mercilessly butchered, and in some cases local leaders even led the mobs in New Delhi. Congress has been just as bad as Modi, they say, so make your political choice on other grounds, on governance and tackling corruption: don't deliver hypocritical lectures on human rights. Congress does not really care about Muslims anyway, they claim, they just treat them as a 'vote bank' to be thrown a few concessions now and then.

There is certainly truth to this argument: Congress politicians were said to be responsible for the deaths of many innocent Sikhs in 1984. Even so, Congress does not have discrimination against the Sikh community in its DNA. In 2005, a Sikh prime minister from the Congress Party, Manmohan Singh, stood up in parliament and offered an apology to the Sikh community and the Indian nation for an act he described as 'the negation of the concept of nationhood enshrined in our constitution'.[22]

In 2012, Modi embarked on a series of day-long 'fasts' around Gujarat, meant to promote the peace, harmony and unity that he talked about and to remind electors of his development record. During these events, Modi generally sat silently and pensively on a stage while sycophants, including several Muslim businessmen, spent hours extolling his virtues in the name of *sadbhavana*, or compassion. He was feted, garlanded and presented with a series of turbans, hats and scarves. But there was one telling reminder that this was harmony on Modi's terms: when one Muslim leader brought a white skullcap out of his pocket to place on the Chief Minister's head, Modi politely but firmly refused. There is to be no bending of Modi's back where Muslims are concerned, and certainly no 'appeasement' or discrimination in their favour. While Muslims in Ahmedabad, recognizing the importance of education, have built their own schools, Modi will not lend a hand, refusing to implement a central government programme that would have provided more than 50,000 scholarships to Muslim students in his state.

Yet Modi is not in the running as a potential prime minister of India on the basis of his treatment of Gujarat's Muslims. He is running as India's most effective administrator, as the only man who can save its economy and restore its battered national pride. As the riots of 2002 recede into past history for most Indians, and a new generation of voters grows up who were not even politically aware when they took place, the question that most people are now asking is how effective he would be as a prime minister.

When it comes to Modi's economic development record, as with everything concerning this man, it is all but impossible to find middle ground. In my enquiries over the years, I was plied with propaganda from both sides that seemed to grant no fallibility from one side, no credit for anything from the other. There is no doubt that Gujarat's economy has grown quickly since Modi became Chief Minister, but critics told me this was more a factor of Gujaratis' natural aptitude for business, of India's boom and the state's long coastline. Growth has been at the expense of the poor, has done nothing to create jobs or improve shocking rates of malnutrition in the state, I was told. Yet those same critics conveniently omitted to tell me that many of their conclusions were drawn from a 2004 Human Development Report, too early in Modi's tenure to be relevant, and without any consideration of whether those numbers had improved at all during the decade since he took office. On the other hand, Modi's fans would seem to portray him as the only man who could save India, someone who has single-handedly turned Gujarat into a shining model of modernity and progress and has the people of his state united behind him.

Columbia University professor Arvind Panagariya, who is one of the smartest economists covering India, says there is 'no denying the major economic advances' the state of Gujarat has made since Narendra Modi came to office in October 2001.[23] In the first place, the Gujarati economy has grown by an average of 10.27 per cent a year in the decade from 1 April 2002 to 31 March 2012. That outstrips India's average growth rate of 7.9 per cent over the same period, and even tops the 9.33 per cent recorded by the economic powerhouse Maharashtra, home to India's financial capital Mumbai, and the thriving southern state Tamil Nadu, which recorded 8.69 per cent growth per year over the same period. It also comfortably outstrips the growth rate of 6.45 per cent that Gujarat recorded in the eight years from March 1994 to April 2002. Real per capita income has more than tripled over the most recent decade.[24] Of course, Modi does not deserve all the credit for this, but in a state where political power is so centralized in his hands, and where economic development has become a clear priority, he surely does deserve a share of the credit.

As the leading economist Bibek Debroy sets out in his book *Gujarat: Governance for Growth and Development*, the state's economic boom has been accompanied by a significant fall in poverty levels, especially in rural areas.[25] In the five years to 2009/10, the percentage of rural Gujaratis below the official poverty line fell from 39.1 to 26.7 per cent, a significantly sharper decline than the national average. Poverty is far from being eliminated in Gujarat, and inequality is as striking here as in all of India, but there is no doubt that progress is being made.

Modi has also worked hard to build the infrastructure that economic growth requires, helping to improve and extend Gujarat's already decent road network. Nearly three-quarters of Gujarati households now enjoy tap-water connections, up from around a quarter in 2002.[26] More significant advances have been made in reforming the electricity sector and extending regular power to its villages. This in itself has helped to sharply lower girls' dropout rates from schools. Farmers were offered rationed, but reliable, electricity for eight hours a day on a separate power line, cutting down on power theft and enabling them to pump the water they needed to support a large expansion in cotton and wheat farming without bankrupting the distribution company. Gujarat also succeeded in cutting down on transmission and distribution losses in the electricity sector, though it has to be said that the decline in the past decade is not as great as in states like Maharashtra or West Bengal, and the overall level of losses in Gujarat remains markedly higher than in states like Andhra Pradesh and Tamil Nadu.

Effective measures to conserve water through check dams and ponds, and to promote micro-irrigation through drips and sprinklers, have helped power semi-arid Gujarat towards steady rates of agricultural growth, and to raise the average groundwater level in the state. Industrialists have been courted assiduously, and in some cases given huge tax breaks and other benefits to encourage them to invest in Gujarat, bolstering the state's reputation as a key manufacturing hub. Ratan Tata relocated here – on extremely favourable terms that involved massive tax concessions and promises of significant state infrastructure investments – when he failed to acquire the land for his Nano car factory at Singur in West Bengal. In 2012, I reported on Ford's plans to open a new car plant here, and on General Motors' plans to expand – both companies praised the stable policy environment, the lack of corruption and the excellent infrastructure.[27] In 2012, reflecting Modi's keen interest in climate change, Gujarat also opened what it proudly declared was Asia's largest solar park.

In its annual survey in 2012, *India Today* magazine rated Gujarat as the most improved large state in India, and the state offering the most attractive investment environment.[28] Modi's state has won a number of awards – both domestically and internationally – for its power-sector reforms, for e-governance and using technology to address citizens' grievances, and for economic freedom.

It is important at this juncture to offer one important caveat. Gujarat is far from being the only state in India that is making progress, and is certainly not the only one where innovative ideas in governance are being recorded, or that has received awards for those ideas. Gujarat still scored relatively modestly on the *India Today* survey in terms of improvements in infrastructure (sixth out of 30), health (ninth), law and order (eleventh) and education (twelfth). This is not to deny Modi's achievements, just to point out that he is not alone in governing effectively or innovatively at the level of India's states.

It is at the annual Vibrant Gujarat business and investment summit that the hype around Modi's achievements gets turned to full volume.

India's leading industrialists line up to shower the Chief Minister with praise, while promising to shower the state with billions of dollars of investment. India's richest man, Mukesh Ambani, calls Modi an inspiring leader who 'has made India and Indians proud by putting Gujarat on the global map'. His brother and business rival Anil Amabi hailed the Chief Minister as 'the next leader of India', while telecom moghul Sunil Mittal was equally effusive: if there is anyone who can run India as a CEO, he said, 'it is Narendra Modi'.[29]

Here, though, the reality does not match the hype, with the flow of actual investments lagging significantly behind the public promises. Ajay Shah of the National Institute of Public Finance and Policy pointed me towards statistics that put Gujarat's investment record in a slightly different light. Looking at data for investment projects actually under implementation (rather than promised), Gujarat's share of the India total dropped sharply between 1995 and 2003, from something over 13 per cent to below 9 per cent, and has only recovered slightly since then. Maharashtra has comfortably outpaced its rival since the late 1990s.[30] Perhaps to talk of an economic miracle in Gujarat under Modi is to overstate the case. Equally, though, his record as a champion of industry cannot be simply brushed aside.

'We make a very simple promise to all who wish to invest in Gujarat,' Modi told me. 'We promise an atmosphere of clean, proactive and responsive government. We promise an environment that minimizes red tape-ism and encourages business.'

Modi keeps that promise through hard work and strength of will. Sleeping just three and a half or four hours a night, he rises by 5 a.m., does some yoga, checks his emails and checks Google Alerts to see what has been written about him and his state.[31] The rest of his day begins by 7.30 a.m. Modi admitted to me to being a 'workaholic', says he has no time to even read books these days, and no pastimes at all apart from that early morning yoga. His personal vices appear to run to a keen sense of clothing and grooming, and a penchant for Montblanc pens, expensive Swiss Movado watches and Bulgari glasses.[32]

He expects a similar dedication from his administration. Bureaucrats are kept on a tight leash and to tight deadlines. Even cabinet ministers clock in and out, and keep him informed if they leave their offices for meetings, a way of working radically different from anything else seen in India. Corruption has certainly not been eliminated in Gujarat under Modi, but it is not the free-for-all one sees in some other states. Bureaucrats won't be punished necessarily for skimming a little off the top, but they will be pulled up if they drag their feet implementing a project that Modi has sanctioned.

Every major decision in Gujarat goes through Modi, with even his ministers reduced to bit-part players. One local journalist recalls being asked by one minister for a copy of the statement that the Chief Minister's office was issuing in his name, so that he would at least be able to answer questions if another reporter called. Words like 'trust' and 'delegation' seem to be missing in Modi's vocabulary. 'There is no room for such things as a team,' said a member of parliament from Gujarat who has known Modi for three decades but asked for his name to be withheld while talking about a party colleague. 'It is not easy to know this person completely. He doesn't trust anybody.'

That individualistic, 'bulldozer' style does not make him popular in the upper reaches of the BJP or necessarily make him well suited to the more consensual style of India's national politics. Would he be able to lead a coalition government? Could he manage a huge, sprawling nation and direct a massive national bureaucracy without a radical change in the way he works? Is he capable of changing, or would India have to adapt to him?

These are questions that may have an answer before long. There are perhaps half a dozen other chief ministers who have shown promise in the way they have governed their states – Nitish Kumar in Bihar, Shivraj Singh Chauhan in Madhya Pradesh, Sheila Dikshit in Delhi and Naveen Patnaik in Odisha spring to mind – but Modi is the only one of them who is so far projecting himself as a national leader, and who is offering solutions to the problems the nation faces. Modi generates fanatical support among the BJP rank and file, and a booming following among India's aspirational middle class. He has mastered the art of self-promotion, saw the importance of social media early, and has a large, growing and vociferous band of supporters who seem to dominate the world of Twitter in India. But is he the answer to India's problems he pretends to be?

Since I arrived in India nine years ago, I have grown immensely frustrated with its chaotic style of government, the inability to take decisions, the rampant corruption and the denial of economic opportunity to so many of its people. But I have also come to love its freedom of speech, its secular DNA, and the checks and balances inherent in its democracy. To deliberately mix a metaphor, it is the glue that keeps India together and the oxygen that keeps me breathing here.

I can understand the frustration in the way that the great secular vision of India's Independence leaders has been debased by today's mediocre politicians into the politics of appeasement and pandering. But the miracle of India, the way that Hindus and Muslims live together largely peacefully as citizens of this great nation, largely immune from the polarizing winds of the 'War on Terror', still inspires me to hope.

While Modi promises to cut through much of the tangled mess of governance and unshackle entrepreneurs, he threatens many of the things I love about India. I find Gujarat under Modi to be stifling, a state where cinema owners dare not show films about the riots for fear of violence, where criticism of Modi is interpreted as disloyalty to the state, where some of the oxygen of democracy has been shut off. A state, in short, that is ruled by fear.

In 2012, I visited a political science professor at Ahmedabad University, a randomly picked interview meant to help me understand the state better. I was hoping for balance, for analysis, for some independent perspective. When we met, the first thing he said was: 'Why have you picked me?', spoken with the terror of someone who really does not want to talk, least of all to a journalist. For a few minutes, obviously nervous, he lauded Modi to the skies. Then, with an already weary heart, I asked about the riots. 'It was started by the Muslims, so in the first place they are responsible,' he told me. 'And within twenty-four hours the state government did control the riots.' That was a blatant lie, but there was no point in arguing with someone who seemed so scared to talk sincerely.

In the aftermath of the riots, the Confederation of Indian Industry had been forced to make an embarrassing apology for comments made by some of its members that had been critical of Modi.[33] But it is not just when it comes to the riots that Modi demands to know who is with him and who against. At the 2009 Vibrant Gujarat Summit, the chairman of the Essar group, Shashi Ruia, dared to deviate from the sycophantic script to offer the mildest criticism of Modi's government. Essar and other long-time investors in Gujarat had been put out by the extremely generous terms offered to Ratan Tata to build his car factory there, terms that were much more generous than they had been offered. 'Ghar ki murgi dal barabar,' Ruia observed, which roughly translates as 'Even a tasty chicken dish, when cooked at home, is like a regular meal of dal [lentils].' It was a fairly anodyne warning not to overlook, or take for granted, the companies with established records in the state. But it was apparently too much for Modi to accept. Essar soon ran into trouble, its applications for land and environmental clearances suddenly stalled, the red carpet dramatically tugged away. Ruia was forced to return to Gujarat and offer Modi an apology, according to a senior local journalist. Even the mildest dissent, from a respected figure and valued investor, had to be ruthlessly crushed.

Modi has been compared to Indira Gandhi's headstrong son Sanjay, who, fortunately for India perhaps, never lived long enough to rule the country.[34] He reminds me a little of Margaret Thatcher on steroids, a man who is definitely not for turning, or compromise, and certainly not for taking criticism on board. He is the champion of India's newly rising lower middle class, just as Thatcher was the champion of England's council house-owning, upwardly mobile aspirants. He is the political equivalent of television's Arnab Goswami: a nationalist, a bully, but an achiever, a messiah for the middle class and the young.

The United States has always tried to tread a fine line with Modi. Unlike Britain, it kept diplomatic channels open, albeit at consular rather than ambassadorial level, and has actively encouraged business ties with the state. 'We believe it would dilute our influence to avoid Modi completely,' the US embassy wrote in a 2006 cable released by WikiLeaks,[35] adding that waiting until Modi 'achieved national stature' to engage with him could be seen as opportunistic and deepen suspicions of the United States among sections of the BJP. In 2012, Assistant Secretary of State Robert Blake wrote to Ron Somers, the President of the US-India Business Council, underlining Gujarat's importance to the American business community and recommending that the council formally sponsor the Vibrant Gujarat Summit. 'Our mandate does not lend itself well to formal governmental partnership in an event promoting investment abroad,' Blake wrote, ignoring broader questions about his government's relations with Modi. 'That said, with USIBC's history of advancing U.S.-India commercial links, I would encourage you to lead U.S. participation in the 2013 Vibrant Gujarat Summit, perhaps along with other business groups.'[36]

By the summer of 2012, it was apparent in my conversations with diplomats that those Europeans who had frozen Modi out were having serious second thoughts, as the chances of him eventually becoming prime minister increased. Britain, with one of the largest Gujarati diaspora populations in the world, and as a significant investor in Gujarat, was clearly growing more and more uneasy with its own isolationist policy. At the end of October 2012, in the middle of the Gujarat election campaign, it announced it was restoring diplomatic ties and sending its High Commissioner to the state to meet Modi. Three months later, High Commissioner Sir James Bevan led representatives from around fifty British companies to the Vibrant Gujarat Summit, the country's largest business delegation there ever.[37]

After his third election victory in Gujarat at the end of 2012, Modi's supporters chanted 'Delhi, Delhi' as they urged their man on for a bid on the prime ministership. 'They used to say good economics does not make good politics,' he told a crowd in Ahmedabad. 'In Gujarat, people have shown that good economics and good governance is possible together, as well as supported. If there is good governance and development, people leave everything else and people support you.'[38] In February 2013 he addressed a packed hall of students at the Shri Ram College of Commerce in Delhi and reinforced his message of politics based on 'good governance' and development, pitching himself as the natural leader of a young, aspirational and tech-savvy India. It was an India where government has no business to be 'in business', which needed better branding as well as a renewed sense of national pride.[39]

He is the champion of the Twitter generation, exploiting the power of social media as effectively as any other Indian politicians and talking excitedly about the power of technology to harness Indian talent and build a brighter future. To his followers on Twitter, he has become NaMo, a name with the feel of a Vedic chant that expresses just the right level of devotion. Unbelievers are rounded on and slain in 140 characters or less. In response, his arch-rival Rahul Gandhi has become RaGa, a melody, or perhaps a musical foundation for improvisation. To the trolls, RaGa becomes Pappu, the simpleton, NaMo becomes Feku, the braggart. Back and forth fly the adulation and the insults, expressing the popular caricatures of these two men who would lead India.

There is still a hard edge to this new, development-focused Modi, and still a few touchstones to remind his audience of what he stands for. In Bengaluru he was still scorning the central government as the 'Delhi Sultanate', an old Modi gag that harked back to the era when Muslim invaders ruled India from the national capital. On foreign policy, Modi offered none of the platitudes of Manmohan Singh, where every country is a strategic ally and the hand of friendship is relentlessly offered to Pakistan. Singh's government was ruthlessly mocked for allowing its neighbours – from China and the Maldives – to walk all over it. In January, as we saw in Chapter 6, the Indian media had erupted in outrage after two soldiers were killed by Pakistani troops on the Line of Control in Kashmir, and one was beheaded. Two months later, Pakistani Prime Minister Raja Pervez Ashraf made a brief visit to a Muslim shrine in India and was given lunch by Foreign Minister Salman Khurshid. 'Pakistan comes and beheads our jawans [troops], and the Delhi Sultanate can do nothing,' Modi said. 'And when they do something, what do they do? They feed the Pakistani Prime Minister with chicken biryani.'

I talked to many young people as they left the National College grounds in Bengaluru at the end of his rally there. Many, like 23-year student Nagarjun Shetty, were fans, arguing that Modi would bring progress and transparency and much-needed change. The riots of 2002, they reminded me, were a far-off memory from a distant place, something as far removed from their consciousness as the anti-Sikh riots in 1984. For them, the certainties of Narendra Modi, his promise of a new era, his record of achievement, were much more compelling than the cautious meanderings of dynastic duffer Rahul Gandhi. 'Modi is the youth icon, he is known for good governance,' said 23-year-old software engineer Satish Batchu. 'Rahul Gandhi says he needs more time, he is not ready – how can he be a youth icon?'

Others, though, were undecided. 'You have to sacrifice a few things if you want a good prime minister, and he is a good candidate,' said twenty-year-old Aishwarya Kirit, arguing that the riots should not be forgotten, but nor should they necessarily stand in his way.

'We should remember both 1984 and 2002,' said her friend and fellow student, nineteen-year-old Shraddha Sharma. 'It plays a part in what we claim from our politicians, that they deliver better and we don't have any more riots.' But while Kirit said she had yet to see any better candidate on the horizon, Shradda was not ready to back Modi as the leader of her huge and diverse nation. 'I personally feel it would send the wrong message, to people like extremists; it might say to them – do whatever you want.'

In his speech to the Confederation of Indian Industry in April 2013, Rahul Gandhi had warned India to give up on the dream of a white knight who will come on a horse, with the sun in the background, and fix everything. 'It's not going to happen,' he said, adding that one man could not solve the problems of a billion people.[40]

A few weeks later in Bengaluru, Modi said his arch-rival had not done his homework or read his Indian history. One man, he said, can make a difference, and often had in the past. By direct implication, this white-bearded knight from Gujarat was saying he could ride in, with the sun behind him, and make everything right. Say what you like about Narendra Modi, but he doesn't lack confidence in his own ability. But in his assault on secularism and the rights of minorities, in his autocratic style, does Narendra Modi threaten the very essence of what makes India great?

16

Hell is for Children

Efforts to protect India's women and children intensify after the Delhi gang-rape

'During our deliberations we have seen there is a large-scale trafficking of women and children in India. We have also noted the involvement of various elements of the police force in the propagation of such a heinous crime . . . It is clear that this institutional bias against the weaker sections of our society has resulted in women and children being contained and managed like chattels, due to the apathy of the state.'
Justice Leila Seth, member of the committee asked to look at ways to protect women in the wake of the Delhi gang-rape, January 2013

She was just eleven years old when she first moved to New Delhi, a small, shy, dark-skinned 'tribal' girl who had never been outside the remote village in eastern India she called home. A cousin had convinced her to come, saying she wasn't contributing enough to the family's income, and wasn't doing well enough at school to make it worth staying on. Finding household work wouldn't be hard, the cousin said, and so it proved. For fifteen months, the young girl worked as a maid on the outskirts of New Delhi, seven days a week, and took the train home at the end of her contract with her entire wages of 10,000 rupees ($180) in her pocket. It might not seem like much money, but she was proud and happy.

The girl, who we may as well call Mary since she has asked for her real name to be concealed, stayed at home with her parents for a while, until an older man called Vikram turned up at the family's door. He was from the same sub-caste, virtually a relative in these small rural communities. Vikram beguiled her with tales of even better wages to be had in Delhi, money that would help support her eight brothers and sisters through school. His patter was good, honed through constant practice, but in truth she and her parents didn't need much convincing. Off they went together on the train, to the bright lights and teeming crowds of New Delhi.

What she didn't know at the time was that Vikram was not exactly the well-meaning relative he claimed to be. He was a trafficker in young girls, a 'placement agent' who made his living supplying under-age maids to Delhi households. Mary, as it turned out, was completely out of her depth, vulnerable, and at his mercy.

Her first job was in a wealthy middle-class household in the New Delhi suburb of Saket, near the gleaming shopping malls where J went to hang out with her friend many years later. Set to work in a large four-storey house, she was given a small single room on the top floor, but was constantly up and down the stairs, ferrying cups of tea back and forth to the clothes shop that her employer owned a few doors away. Every night she was locked in, every morning at around six o'clock the house owner would let his three dogs out onto the roof, and let her into the house to start preparing breakfast. She hated it, and after just over a week, she ran away.

On the streets, she called Vikram, and he picked her up. Almost at once he found her another job further south in Gurgaon, the capital's fast-expanding satellite city, home to IT companies in gleaming skyscrapers, and more shopping malls. But she never left the house; nor could she dream about window-shopping. Instead, she was set to work 'dusting, sweeping, mopping and washing the clothes' from 7.30 in the morning until at least 11 at night, seven days a week. She ate sitting on the floor in the kitchen, slept on the floor in the lounge. Every few months, Vikram would come and pick up her wages. She was given food and lodging, but they didn't trust her enough to put the money in her hands. 'They didn't give me a single penny,' she said. 'Madam used to say that she was scared I would run away if she paid me directly.'

After a year, the period she had agreed to work, she returned to Vikram. It was time to go home, she said, and she wanted her wages. But Vikram was evasive. He promised her all the money she was owed: they would go back home together, but first he had one more job for her. Reluctantly, because she saw no other choice, Mary agreed.

Vikram's brother, who worked together with him in the trafficking trade, took Mary on a train to a small village on the outskirts of the northern Indian town of Jallander, a journey of about eight hours. When they arrived, it was already late. 'Darkness fell and he made me sleep in the forest,' she said. There, he raped her. The following day, he took her to Jallander, where he put her to work as a maid. But Vikram did not come to collect her after a month, as he had promised, but only after a year. Before her eyes, Mary's employer, a man she calls Sahib, boss, handed over to Vikram her entire twelve months' wages. Quietly, he slipped her 6,000 rupees ($110) himself. 'Sahib told me he wasn't sure if this man would pay me or not, so he said: "You keep this money, for two months' work, in your hands, and don't tell him you have it."' It was the only money she was to receive, for two years' work.

Vikram and his brother took her back to their home in Gurgaon, at a time when their wives and children were away, she says. 'I was in their home for seventeen days, and ten days out of those seventeen, they did the wrong thing with me,' she said. She was regularly beaten, and threatened. Vikram claimed he was a member of a Maoist insurgent group active in the impoverished state of Jharkhand where her parents lived. 'He said if I ever tried to run away, he would kill off my family and burn down my house.' He never left her alone, she says, even waiting outside the toilet for her. He took her to a park several times and made her drink alcohol. Once, she was sitting on a small wall on the edge of the roof, crying her heart out; he came up; she told him she would rather die. He gave her a half-push, and threatened to throw her off the roof then and there.

Every year, hundreds of thousands of girls are trafficked from rural India to work as domestic servants in middle-class urban homes. They are expected to work almost every hour of the day, for salaries of as low as 20 or 30 dollars a month. Many are given clothes, money for medical care, and perhaps some cash for an occasional trip home every few years. But many others end up cut off from their families, abused and treated like slaves. Often they are sexually assaulted. Despite the outrage over the gang-rape and murder of J in December 2012, a vast network of child-trafficking and abuse operates in the same city with society's implicit sanction, and under the cover of vast official apathy and societal connivance.[1] It is not only a reminder of the way that a vast section of India's population is excluded from the benefits of the nation's economic rise; it also underlines the broad indifference of many middle-class Indians to the rights of the poor. It highlights just how hard it will be to turn the anger felt over the gang-rape into a broader transformation of Indian society, to turn the anguish over one woman's suffering into a movement to improve women's rights more generally or to protect the most vulnerable members of society.

For years, I have been treated for a succession of football injuries by a witty and sharp Sikh called Sukhvinder Singh. As I lay on his treatment table getting ultrasound for my various pulls and sprains, we would argue about anything and everything under the Indian sun – from Kashmir to politics to what ails Indian society. The nurses at the British High Commission could always tell when I was seeing Sukhvinder, because my booming laugh would echo down the corridors of the Medical Centre. Sukhvinder told great jokes, but was also remarkably well informed. He always made me think twice about my assumptions about this country, and work hard to defend my opinions. So when I started telling him about my trafficking stories, it was not a huge surprise to me when he suggested I might be exaggerating the scale of the problem. All his friends treated their maids very well, he said, and often paid for them to have trips home to see their families. They cared about their servants, he insisted, and the girls were better off in New Delhi than they would be in their home villages. In short, the middle class was helping poor families by giving their children work. Indeed, it is getting harder and harder to find willing workers at an affordable wage, he said.

Nevertheless, the fact remains that families who employ children in India are not just benefiting from cheap child labour, they are supporting a vast and hugely exploitative industry, an organized criminal network of traffickers. By the terms of local law in New Delhi, which has enacted some of India's strictest child labour laws, many ordinary middle-class residents of the capital who employ children should be jailed, activists say. Employing people younger than eighteen in a hazardous job, as domestic service is defined, keeping that person in confinement and withholding wages, has been a 'non-bailable' offence since 2009 – in other words you should be locked up unless a judge says otherwise. Of course, that never happens – the law is widely flouted, and police carry out rescue operations very rarely, only after specific complaints from parents or activists.

Although I am sure Sukhvinder's friends treat their maids reasonably well, the system is set up to exploit and not protect these vulnerable girls. Sometimes, placement agencies demand a one-time fee for supplying servants, a sum often docked from the girls' wages by their employers. At other times, the employer pays the wages directly to the placement agency, which might give a portion of that money, or none at all, to the girl. Some Indians have told me that poor families would only suffer if child labour was properly banned, and it is true that, in the short term, some would. But how much better would life be in rural northern India if girls had to wait until they were eighteen until they could move to Delhi in search of work, instead of leaving home at the age of eleven or twelve? How much more likely they would be to complete their education, and perhaps even get married at a later age? How much higher wages might they command, and how much safer might they be? The jobs would, after all, still be there – it is impossible to imagine the Indian middle class living without maids. But how much better to have those jobs filled by adults (perhaps even by those girls' mothers), on at least the minimum wage, and with at least some possibility of standing up for their basic rights.

There has never been a systematic attempt to determine the scale of child labour in India's homes. The government says 5 million children are employed in India, but activists say the real number could be ten times that. A senior official in the home affairs ministry, which oversees the police, told me that as many as 4 million children work in domestic service nationwide and that up to 4,000 placement agencies operate in New Delhi and its suburbs alone. But the official said it was often hard to get his fellow bureaucrats to take the issue seriously, because so many of them employ children at home.

I first met Mary in the cramped headquarters of Bachpan Bachao Andolan (BBA, or Save the Childhood Movement), a small but influential group of activists who have been campaigning for more than three decades to end bonded labour and trafficking and have rescued more than 80,000 children. There, in the basement meeting room that also doubles as an office for lawyer and activist Bhuwan Ribhu, she had sat patiently, looking down without expression as another girl recounted her tale of working unpaid for four years for two families of doctors and business people in Delhi. Still just seventeen years old, Mary was still small and shy. She had her hair tied back in a bun and covered in a patterned scarf. I wondered how easy it would be to get her to talk, but when we turned to hear her story, she looked up and her face came alive. She smiled shyly as she told her story, hiding a nervous laugh behind her painted fingernails, as she recalled how she had run away from the house in Saket. But she also revealed a determination I had not expected to encounter. 'The first thing I want is that man should be punished for what he did to me,' she told me. 'Then I want to see the money I am owed, in my hands. The third thing is to go back home safe and sound.'

One of Ribhu's colleagues told us how he had rescued Mary at New Delhi's railway station in 2011. He was working as part of a network of undercover activists BBA uses to nab traffickers and expose sweatshop owners. Mary was there because Vikram had once again promised to take her home, but the activist had spotted the timid, lost-looking girl at the crowded railway station and sensed something was amiss. Befriending both of them, the activist soon discovered the vital discrepancy in their stories: while Mary was expecting to be taken home, Vikram quietly admitted that he was intent on taking the girl to India's teeming commercial capital, Mumbai, where he presumably intended to sell her off into a life of further slavery or prostitution. The activist told Mary about the ruse; together they fled from Vikram's clutches. Today she lives in Delhi, hiding from Vikram and his threats, changing her SIM card every month so that he can't track her down, but determined not to return home until she gets what she deserves.

Ribhu, a genial but very smart and resolute man, bespectacled, with close-cropped black hair and an equally close-cropped black beard, describes the trafficking of young children through placement agencies as the biggest form of organized crime in India today. 'And the worst part is, it is right there in the open, in our homes, and yet invisible,' he told me. Traffickers often use rape – which can ruin a young woman's marriage prospects by robbing her of her 'honour' – as an instrument of control, he said.

Ribhu had joined BBA as a volunteer fresh out of law school in 2002, launching himself into a campaign to rescue Nepali children who had been trafficked to work in Indian circuses. It was dangerous work. On one early raid on an outfit called The Great Roman Circus in June 2004 in a town in the northern Indian state of Uttar Pradesh, Ribhu, his fellow activists and journalists accompanying them were badly beaten up, while police officers stood by and watched.

Unable to free the girls, BBA sought the help of local politicians, but the circus owner clearly had connections, and stymied their efforts. It was only after more than a month of High Court hearings that the girls were finally freed.

That court decision was to set an important trend in the battle against trafficking of children and bonded labour in India. Again and again, activists have met with apathy from politicians and police, often with downright resistance. Only through the courts have they made progress, with a string of important victories over the past decade that have forced reluctant authorities to act. The judiciary, says Ribhu, should be the last resort, but in India 'it has become the first resort'.

It is not just in the field of trafficking that courts in India have played an active role, wading into areas that might in other countries be seen as the duty of government. In 1995, for example, in response to a Public Interest Litigation, the Supreme Court ruled that all cars in New Delhi would have to run on unleaded fuel. In 1998, in response to the capital's worsening levels of air pollution, it gave all buses, taxis and three-wheeler auto-rickshaws three years to convert to CNG.

More recently, the Supreme Court criticized the Manmohan Singh government over the 2G telecoms scandal and forced police to deepen their probe, leading to the arrest of the Telecoms Minister A. Raja in 2011. It later ruled that all the licences issued by him in 2008 should be revoked, and ordered the government to switch to an auction system to award licences in the future. In 2011 it forced the government to rescind the appointment of P. J. Thomas to head the Central Vigilance Commission, a government anti-corruption body, because he had charges pending against him. In 2013, as we have seen, it took a significant step to make it harder for criminals to remain in parliament.

Many of the Supreme Court's most activist moves have been popular with the general public, but many experts worry that the courts are overstepping the mark, assuming powers that should not be theirs in a fully functional democracy. Ribhu at BBA would prefer elected politicians to be taking the lead, but says he often has no choice but to turn to the courts to force reform.

'It has become the only resort through which change will happen,' he said, 'because politicians are not taking any decision whatsoever. They are afraid of a certain section of society, or of another sector – especially when it comes to children, because children do not vote, so they are never top of the agenda.' What he meant, but could not quite bring himself to say, was that the politicians were in league with the vast and immensely profitable trafficking industry.

After the victory over the circus mafia, the BBA office in the state capital Lucknow was broken into and vandalized, and employees in New Delhi repeatedly threatened. Ribhu was advised to leave the country, and settled in Washington, D.C., for a while to continue his advocacy work. But at the end of 2004 he was back, pursuing case after case across the country. Not every judge was sympathetic, but in July 2009 the tide finally turned. The Delhi High Court made a historic judgement clearly setting out the responsibilities of the police and the government in combating child labour.[2] In April 2011 they won another big victory against the trade in children for circus work, the first time the crime of 'trafficking' had been explicitly established in a legal judgement.[3]

In the 1990s, child labour was seen by some as a social problem but was not considered a crime, and even a decade ago awareness about the issue was appallingly low. In 2006, Ribhu was approached by a journalist for an interview about trafficking. It was not until the two had been chatting for a while that he realized the reporter was actually interested in traffic, in the light of the government's decision to ban rickshaw pullers from the narrow streets of old Delhi. Even today, far too few Indians would cite the trafficking of children as an important problem for the country, or set its eradication as a priority for the government.

But if court victories have been important in prodding Indian authorities into action, there was one case that woke India's middle classes up to the particular hell that is reserved for many of the nation's children. This was the Nithari murders, the shocking discovery of the skulls and bones of seventeen murdered girls and young women around a businessman's home just outside New Delhi in 2006. Nithari had once been a village but had gradually been absorbed into the satellite city of Noida on the outskirts of the capital, and become home to IT and outsourcing firms, manufacturers, and the film and

EFFORTS TO PROTECT INDIA'S WOMEN AND CHILDREN

media industry. Here, just a stone's throw from national television studios, the children of poor migrant workers had been disappearing for months. When they went to the police, their complaints were brushed aside. Talk of missing children in the area had seeped into the nearby TV newsrooms, but no one had taken much notice. That is, until the chopped-up remains were dug up from the backyard and drain of what the media soon dubbed 'The House of Death'.

I went to Nithari in 2006, and spoke to parents in the narrow, muddy streets around the businessman's house, where domestic servants and stall owners eked out a precarious living in the shadows of the rich. Over and over, they told me of how their attempts to find their children had been frustrated, rebuffed by policemen who had no interest in protecting the poor. 'Police said your daughter is beautiful, she might have run away with a man,' Bandana Sarkar told me, in a small single room crowded with plastic jars and a few cheap music cassettes. Sarkar had eventually been forced to identify her twenty-year-old daughter Pinky's bloodstained clothes and scarf. As we talked, her eighteen-month-old grandson – Pinky's son – slept under a blanket. 'Her child cries for his mummy,' she said. 'He wants her but he doesn't know his mother will never come back to him.'[4]

Belatedly, because the case was so gruesome, and so close to the capital, the Nithari case dominated the airwaves and headlines for weeks. It was a media feeding frenzy. Rumours of child pornography and the organ trade were eagerly seized on, even if they were never substantiated. The owner of the house, a bespectacled doctor with a handlebar moustache and a salt-and-pepper beard named Moninder Singh Pandher, was branded a 'psychopath': his servant Surinder Koli was a 'cannibal'. The pair were 'diabolical maniacs' before they had ever been tried, and the lawyers from the local Noida Bar Association refused to represent them. Injected with a controversial 'truth serum', their juicy confessions were leaked to the media to turn up the hysteria one more notch.[5] (Both were later to be sentenced to death, although Pandher is still trying to clear his name, and has so far been acquitted on appeal of some of the murders.)

The episode had nothing pleasant about it, but there was one positive fallout: it woke up the country at last to the long-ignored problem of missing children. The media frenzy surrounding the Nithari killings was a watershed, reminiscent for Americans of the way the disappearance of six-year-old Etan Patz in Manhattan in 1979 helped spark the missing-children's movement in the United States. (Patz was the first child whose face was featured on milk cartons in that country; his body was never found, nor his killer yet prosecuted.) Thanks to the Nithari case, the issue of missing children finally won some attention, and became a story worthy of sporadic media attention.

More than five years later, after the Nithari murders, I was again on the track of missing children when I first met Ribhu. It was the summer of 2012. In the previous few weeks, another mini-epidemic of missing children seemed to have caught the attention of the media, as footage from surveillance cameras – a new phenomenon in modern India – was being repeatedly broadcast on television, showing infants being brazenly snatched from train stations and hospital lobbies as parents slept nearby. But it quickly emerged that the cases highlighted on television were only the tip of the iceberg. The previous year BBA had released a study showing that more than 90,000 children were reported missing in India every year – one every six minutes, a much higher number than anyone had previously believed.[6]

Usually, as we have heard, trafficked children are bought from their parents, or lured away with the promise of a living wage and a better life in the big city, only to be forced to work in farms, factories and homes, or sold for sex and marriage, never to see their families again. But sometimes the traffickers can't even be bothered with that formality – they simply kidnap children off the streets.

Ribhu pointed me towards the tale of Irfan. He was drugged and abducted at the age of eleven by two men on a motorbike as he walked home one day after playing with friends. I met his parents in their modest home in west Delhi in the middle of 2011. 'It was living hell these past two years, trying to figure out where we could find him,' his father, Iqbal Ali, told me. 'I used to run a biscuit bakery, but from the day he disappeared, I got so caught up trying to meet politicians, police – and people who claim to do magic to get children back – that I had to shut down my bakery. I had no time for it.'[7]

The family had celebrated no weddings, no festivals, nor attended parties of any kind. 'We never even went to the tailor for new clothes, there was no zest in us to celebrate,' he said. They had another child, a girl called Kehkashan, 'because we were so lonely,' his mother Shabnam told me.

But Ali did not give up the search for his only son. He joined forces with other parents who had lost their children, put up posters, badgered the media to take up their cases. As we chatted, he dug out one of the posters, holding it up proudly, pointing out his son's face.

Remarkably, and rarely, it all paid off. Just a month before I met his parents, two years after he had been abducted, Irfan had finally made it home. He emerged from the other room to tell me his story. 'I was walking home from school when I saw two men on a motorcycle, with helmets. One got down and stood in front of me, and put a hanky over my nose and mouth, and I fainted. When I woke up, I found myself in this really big house; my hands and feet had been tied, and my mouth was covered so I could not cry out.'

Irfan had suffered perhaps the most common fate – kidnapped to satisfy India's insatiable demand for cheap agricultural labour, imprisoned in virtual solitary confinement in a room adjoining a buffalo shed outside the town of Mullanpur, some 200 miles northwest of his home in Delhi. 'I was supposed to bathe the buffalo, to feed them, to pick up the dung,' he said. 'I was fed just once a day, just leftovers. When I used to shriek and make a fuss, they would tie my hands and feet again at night.'

One day, though, the man who brought Irfan his food failed to show up. The young boy saw his chance, climbed on a chair in the shed where he was held and smashed a window with an earthen vase. But there was one small problem. Irfan had no idea where he was. He walked a mile or so to the nearest road, and then he just started walking down it. A car passed, but did not stop to give him a lift. 'I kept walking, walking and walking, until dawn,' he said.

Then he came across a small factory making fodder for cows and buffalos. The labourers there were amazed to see such a young child on his own, and took him to the factory owner, who had a computer and access to the Internet. Together they searched the Web, but couldn't find his family's address. He decided to stay.

For several months, he took shelter with the factory owner's family, running errands for their shop in return for food and lodging. They treated him well, he said. But then, one day, as the media storm about missing children reached its peak, he saw photographs of his parents and himself on a TV show. His father's relentless campaign had paid off, and the media attention had yielded results. Irfan knew it was time to go home. With a few hundred rupees in his pocket, a gift (in lieu of wages) from the family who had sheltered him, he took the train back to New Delhi, and a bus to the suburb of Nangloi, the only address he had in his memory.

'But when I arrived it had all changed,' he said. 'Before, there was no overpass, no Metro. Now, it looked like a completely different place to me.' Yet Irfan's new-found luck had not run out. After half an hour of wandering, he bumped into a friend, who took him home.

'We were just overwhelmed with happiness,' said his mother, Shabnam, as the family sat proudly together on their small bed, an old grey television on a shelf above their heads. Irfan, with his black hair spiked up on end, was dressed in a purple V-neck sweater, with a white laurel wreath embroidered on the chest, above the words 'Live It'. As his parents talked, he played easily with his five-month-old baby sister, a girl whom he had not even known existed until a month before. He looked like a typical young teenage boy, with a shadow of hair on his upper lip and a shyness that could easily be mistaken for sullenness: my photographs show him dropping his chin and gazing up at the camera from beneath his brow.

'We went and got new clothes made for all of us,' his mother said, repeating several times a sentence that seemed to sum up her disbelief and pride in her lost son's return: 'All his old clothes were too small, because he had grown so tall.'

Something might just have changed in India because of the gang-rape and murder of J and the outrage that surrounded it. On the afternoon of 23 December 2012, with calls resounding for the death penalty to be extended to rapists, India's forceful Finance Minister Palaniappan Chidambaram telephoned 79-year-old Jagdish Sharan Verma, who had retired as Chief Justice of India nearly fifteen years before, and asked him to take on an important new role. Chidambaram, apparently acting on the instructions of Prime Minister Manmohan Singh, wanted Verma to head up a three-member committee to look into any legal changes that might be required to protect India's women more effectively. The other two members were to be Gopal Subramaniam, a former Solicitor General of India who was still a practising senior Supreme Court advocate, and Leila Seth, another respected retired judge who also happens to be the mother of author Vikram Seth.

The Indian government loves to deflect public pressure by setting up a committee and shelving its eventual report. On this occasion, it may have been wary of caving into public pressure to introduce the death penalty for rape, and wanted the committee's recommendations as cover. In any case, it did not appear to take the committee led by this elderly man very seriously. The government gave the Verma Committee just a couple of months to submit its report, and hardly went out of its way to offer advice or logistical support. The team was given the use of a couple of government rooms, and a car to bring Verma and Seth to work in the morning, but ended up functioning almost entirely out of Subramaniam's private office. Astoundingly, the nation's Home Minister Sushilkumar Shinde did not once interact with the committee during its deliberations – although knowing 72-year-old Shinde's appalling track record of gaffes and banal public comments, one has to wonder if this was much of a loss. But to Verma's consternation, neither did most of the country's police chiefs. Nevertheless, the government got a whole lot more than it bargained for.

The committee started by inviting suggestions from the general public. It received an incredible 80,000 of them, and, thanks to a team of young volunteers, read every single one. Faced with universal opposition from women's groups, it did not recommend the death penalty for rape, but what it did recommend resounded far more widely and deeply than anyone could have imagined.

Expectations had not been especially high as they held the press conference to release their 657-page report, which incidentally the team had completed in just twenty-nine days. Verma began by quoting Aristotle and Mahatma Gandhi, his neck wrapped in a scarf against the cold. 'More platitudes,' tweeted someone on my timeline. But what followed surpassed almost everyone's expectations. The Verma Committee had not just confined itself to a cursory examination of the laws – its members had looked at the entire structure of governance that surrounds the protection of women in India, and found it deeply wanting. Police, politicians and even the army were castigated for being incompetent, apathetic and even criminal in their disregard for women.

Murderers, thieves and rapists were sitting in India's parliament making laws affecting women, the report pointed out. The police were not only failing to report and investigate allegations of rape, but were actually involved in the large-scale trafficking of women and children. Even though the police establishment has been aware of the problem for years, nothing had been done to address it, Verma said. At the same time, with total impunity, members of the army and security forces were raping women in conflict zones within India. All this must change, the committee insisted.[8]

It was the failure of governance that was the 'obvious root cause' of the dangers India's women faced, not the want of a few laws here and there, they said. The younger generation, Verma said, had taught their elders something in the way they came out in large numbers to protest peacefully, and resisted provocation by the police. The protests, in the view of Subramaniam, were 'clearly a call to modern India to renounce old ways of looking, thinking and acting towards women, and are a strong positive move towards their empowerment'.

No one was spared. Verma, clearly still sharp as a tack despite his advanced years, said the lack of cooperation he had received from police chiefs was 'laughable', and the way they were appointed had to be re-examined. 'If they considered this [committee] to be irrelevant, that shows the sense of responsibility they have toward the discharge of their statutory and constitutional duty,' he told the CNN-IBN television channel directly after his news conference. He said he had been 'shocked' at the way the country's Home Secretary had congratulated Delhi's police chief for his supposedly swift response to the Delhi rape, but also shocked by the apathy within society that had let passersby ignore the plight of the victims lying by the roadside for so long after the rape.

But the committee did much more than apportion blame. It laid out a comprehensive and far-reaching blueprint for reform in the way India is governed. The report told the government to shake off its apathy towards the problem of missing children, to register and investigate all cases of missing children, and to pass much stricter laws on child-trafficking. It recommended that marital rape be criminalized and that India's outdated rape laws be overhauled, so that sexual assault falling short of penetration would be subject to much stronger penalties. The committee also recommended that the law be changed to make the sexual assault of men a crime, as well as to recognize gay, transgender and transsexual rape. Politicians facing serious criminal charges like rape and murder should resign from parliament, Verma said, while a controversial law granting the army virtual impunity from prosecution in conflict zones within India should be urgently re-examined. Indeed, members of the armed forces who are accused of rape should be tried under civilian rather than military law, it reasonably argued. The panel had also recommended that members of parliament charged with rape and other serious crimes be forced to resign their posts and that marital rape be outlawed.

Throwing down the gauntlet, Verma said the report had been completed in double-quick time so as to be ready before the next session of parliament, and challenged the government to show the same urgency in passing and implementing its recommendations.

The first response from civil society was enthusiastic, but there was immediate scepticism about how far its recommendations would be followed. Kiran Bedi, once India's most senior female police officer and now a leader of the anti-corruption movement, tweeted that the report had exposed the 'arrears of 64 years of apathy in the criminal justice system, people, police, laws, prosecution on several counts'. The author Nilanjana Roy called it a 'hope, a blueprint, and a road map', and added: 'We have to keep this going.'

Just nine days after the Verma Committee submitted its report, the government sprang another surprise, dramatically picking up the gauntlet that Verma had thrown down. Instead of waiting for parliament to come back from its winter recess, the cabinet pushed through an emergency ordinance at the beginning of February 2013 that dramatically tightened the country's law on sexual assault and trafficking.[9] It was an obvious bid to satisfy public opinion, and drain some heat out of the anger that was still simmering after the rape.

Accepting many of Verma's recommendations, the new ordinance changed India's rape law to allow for tough penalties for all types of sexual assault. In the past, rape had been defined as sexual intercourse involving penetration only, and anything short of that fell under the ambit of criminal assault on a woman with 'intent to outrage her modesty', an offence that carried a light penalty. That provision was almost never enforced, leaving women vulnerable to, for example, groping on public transportation by men who knew they were unlikely to be prosecuted.

Separate offences with strict punishments were introduced for stalking, voyeurism, stripping a woman or carrying out an acid attack. Astonishingly, for the first time in India trafficking was outlawed in all its forms, with stiff penalties for the trafficker and for those employing people who had been trafficked.

In effect, that meant that anyone employing children like Mary as maids – a sizeable proportion of the Indian population – could be jailed for at least five years. The vast network of 'placement agents' like Vikram, who had been very tough to prosecute effectively unless it could be proved they had engaged in kidnapping or used force, could be put away for at least fourteen years. A police officer or other public servant found to have been involved in trafficking would be automatically jailed for life.

The ordinance exceeded Verma's recommendations in one important area: the government bowed to popular pressure to allow the death penalty in cases in which a rape leaves a woman in a persistent vegetative state.

It amounted to potentially one of the most significant changes to India's laws to protect women since the British laid out the country's penal code in 1862, potentially ranking with bills to outlaw the payment of dowry when women are married, first introduced in 1961, and a 2006 Bill outlawing domestic violence. The new Bill came into force as an ordinance the moment the President signed it into law, which happened after a further two days, but would have to be ratified during the next session of parliament.

Women's rights activists reacted with anger at first. They were furious that the government had not gone far enough by failing to outlaw marital rape, or to deal with the legal impunity enjoyed by members of the country's armed forces in conflict zones. The new law had also made rape gender-neutral, something that hardly seemed to them like a progressive step (although that provision was later changed by parliament).

'The ordinance is a complete betrayal of the faith that people had put in the government – that they will carry forward the demand from the street, the demand from the women's movement and what was reflected in the Verma Committee report,' activist and lawyer Vrinda Grover said at a news conference, flanked by several other leading women's rights activists. 'This is an act of bad faith. It is the most horrible form of politics this government could have played on us.'

Ribhu, however, was ecstatic. After a decade of painful legal struggle and painstaking progress, he had suddenly achieved his wildest dreams almost overnight. Traffickers of children and women were no longer above and beyond the law, and could finally be brought to book. A huge and many-tentacled industry of child servitude was suddenly threatened – provided, of course, that the police could be prodded into actually implementing the law. 'My wife keeps telling me I can retire now,' he told me over the phone, his broad smile beaming down the line. He had been called to the committee in January for what was supposed to be a brief chat about missing children and the trafficking industry. He had ended up returning to Subramaniam's office night after night and giving a detailed account of the scale of the problem. It had paid huge dividends.

Two of my stories – on missing children and the trafficking of children for domestic service – had even been submitted by him to the Verma panel in evidence. It was a tiny contribution, along with 80,000 other submissions, but it was satisfying to have been involved even in so marginal a way. True, the government had avoided some of the most controversial issues, but that was perhaps understandable in an emergency ordinance. There would, after all, be time to discuss those later in parliament – for now, the bar in the battle to protect women had been significantly raised.

'Parliamentary debate can wait, public opinion can wait, but women need to be protected now,' Ribhu told me. 'Every single hour, a woman is getting raped in India. Eighteen children get raped in a single day on average in India, and every single day, hundreds of thousands of women are assaulted, groped, stalked and trafficked.'

Laws don't change society on their own, but they do have a role to play, especially when people like Ribhu are there to push for their enforcement. For the first time, I could really imagine a situation, perhaps a decade from now, where employing children as maids in New Delhi was no longer socially acceptable.

Just to put the icing on the cake, it turned out that Ribhu had brought Mary along to one of his briefing sessions with the Verma Committee. There, the three committee members had been so moved by what she told them that they included a transcript of the story in their report. What is more, on behalf of the committee, Gopal Subramaniam decided to give her the equivalent of $2,750 out of his own pocket to make up for unpaid wages. He also offered to pay for psychological counselling and to finance her education.

The girl, Subramaniam later told me, had been bashful at first while she related her tale, then later, over tea and biscuits, she had started to relax. 'I asked her: "Don't you want to study and become a rocket scientist?" The smile we saw was extremely emotional for us.' The money, he said, was 'a small token of our respect' for the girl. 'It was not based on charity; it was based on the principle of reparation. We have taken away her rights and society has to repay her.'[10]

The ordinance was duly passed into law in the next session of parliament, although with some changes. In the end, it did not quite deliver what Ribhu had hoped for. At the last minute, the parliamentary committee drawing up the Bill had changed the wording – trafficking would only be covered by the new law if prosecutors could prove the perpetrator intended to physically or sexually exploit the child, was engaged in slavery or had removed the child's organs. Employment of trafficked children for labour, included in the ordinance, was excluded from the Bill – sparing those who employ children as maids – and Ribhu was worried that a historic opportunity had been lost.

Yet once again, judicial activism helped temper the disappointment for this activist and gave a ray of hope for the many children he tries to protect. In May, the Supreme Court passed a landmark judgement forcing police to register all cases of missing children as offences that required investigation. There would be a presumption of the crime of kidnapping or trafficking in each case, unless and until the police could prove otherwise through their investigation. Each police station would be manned around the clock by an officer with specific training in juvenile welfare, and would also be assigned a paralegal volunteer who would help parents register and follow up on cases. The casual way that police had dismissed the parents of the Noida murder victims – your daughter is pretty and must have run off – would no longer be so easy to maintain. Finally, every case of an untraced child – more than 100,000 for the last four years alone – would have to be registered and an investigation opened.[11] An imperfect parliamentary Bill would be significantly strengthened by these new provisions, giving Ribhu fresh hope that the corner was at last being turned in the battle against child labour and trafficking.

When it came to protecting women, the Bill that followed J's rape and murder had other lacunae. It declined to follow Verma's sugges- tion and ban politicians from parliament if they had been charged with rape. The punishment for acid attacks was, in the end, not raised, but left at seven years.

Yet, in the end, women's activists seemed satisfied, their initial fury dissipating as the dust settled. Measures were upheld that dramati- cally toughened penalties for rape, whose definition now extended beyond just penetrative sex. Separate offences for voyeurism and stalking were duly introduced. Anyone convicted of gang-rape would face a minimum of twenty years in jail. The same punishment was imposed for rape of a minor, or for any police officer or public official convicted of rape. From now on, government approval would no longer be required to prosecute officials or politicians, as it had been previously. And finally, any police officer who failed to register a complaint would face up to two years in jail, a potentially significant step that could have lasting consequences.

'This law is a major gain for us. There are many firsts in this,' the activist Kavita Krishnan told my colleague Rama. 'It does not address 100 per cent of what we demanded, but we don't want to delay or deny what we have got in order to wait for that perfect law.'[12]

In the months that followed the Delhi gang-rape and the Verma

Committee report, the horrific sexual abuse of women in India continued unabated. Police statistics showed incidences of rape and molestation actually rose sharply in Delhi in 2013, despite all the publicity and anger surrounding the previous gang-rape. Every two hours, a woman in Delhi is molested or raped, the *Hindustan Times* reported in March, recording some of the victims during one two-day period:[13] a young woman working in a pub, a domestic help, a housewife, a jobseeker and an eight-year-old girl. Outside the capital, a teenage girl in Gurgaon was repeatedly raped by her father over a three-year-period; a ten-year-old Dalit girl was raped in Bulandshahr, and her family ostracized and persecuted in her village by higher-caste neighbours; a Swiss tourist was gang-raped while camping with her husband, an American woman gang-raped after accepting a lift late at night. Six fast-track courts were set up in New Delhi in an attempt to bring speedier justice, but were soon overwhelmed, and the backlog of cases only grew.[14]

In April, a five-year-old girl was raped and brutally tortured by a neighbour and left to die in a locked room in east Delhi. Her parents, frantic with worry, were dismissed by the police. Only when local members of Kejriwal's Aam Admi Party intervened did they even register a case. When the young girl was finally found, lying in a pool of her own blood, the same police station allegedly offered the parents 2,000 rupees ($32) to hush the matter up.

Some incidents, in particular the gang-rape of a 22-year-old photo-journalist in Mumbai on 22 August 2013, commanded the nation's attention and provoked fresh bouts of national soul-searching. Others, like the gang-rape of a nineteen-year-old girl in New Delhi, who was dragged from her shack at knife-point on the same night as the incident in Mumbai, barely merited a mention in the papers. Amanda Hodge of the *Australian* newspaper took up the story of that girl, five of whose six attackers were eventually arrested but whose own suffering commanded no national sympathy. 'It is hard to escape the conclusion this middle-class soul-searching is preoccupied with its own welfare, and that concern for the safety of the women of the country's vast underclass comes a distant second,' she wrote. 'That is not to say that people such as Pooja have not benefited from India's heightened focus on violence against women. A year ago, it is difficult to imagine that the gang-rape of a low-caste Bengali woman would have stirred too many Delhi police officers into action.'[15]

Meanwhile, Indian women like the BBC correspondent Rupa Jha came forward in growing numbers to movingly describe their own experiences of childhood sexual abuse at the hands of family members, in an attempt to tear down India's 'code of silence over sexual abuse'.[16] Yet there was little hope that promised gender-sensitivity training of the Indian police force would bring any dramatic improvements in attitudes any time soon, and in rural India there was no sign of progress.

On 13 September 2013 one of those fast-track courts sentenced four men to death by hanging for the rape of J. The ringleader of the group, Ram Singh, had hanged himself in his jail cell back in March, while the boy, nicknamed Bhura, had been sent to juvenile reform home for three years. Yet just two weeks later, a small item in the *Times of India* newspaper showed how shallow a victory that was. It recorded the case of a woman just outside the western city of Pune, who had reacted to the rape of her own daughter by selling the twelve-year-old girl to the same man who had raped her. The girl had then been sold on again, to a brothel, before finally escaping after four months of confinement, rape and torture.[17]

And the 'god-man' who had condemned J for being 'as guilty as her rapists', who had suggested she could have escaped the entire ordeal by taking God's name and appealing to her attackers as her 'religious brothers'? In August, 72-year-old Asaram Bapu was accused of having sexually assaulted a sixteen-year-old girl at his ashram in the city of Jodhpur in Rajasthan. After initially avoiding arrest, and following a violent stand-off between his supporters and police outside another of his ashrams in the city of Indore, the 72-year-old was taken into custody by the Indian police.[18]

There is little doubt that the news that will emerge from India in the coming years will be nothing if not confusing, constantly raising and then dashing hopes that far-reaching progress is at last being made in protecting the society's most vulnerable members, women and children. Some will despair of progress in fighting centuries of oppressive tradition; others will argue that the convulsive changes brought about by India's rapid modernization are making matters worse.[19] Yet like the man we met at the end of chapter 1 holding up a placard during the rape protests at Jantar Mantar, some will argue that now is the first time they have felt hopeful in a very long time. India is at least waking up to the scale of the challenges it faces, and that has to be a good thing.

Afterword

'This is a chance for a psychological transformation of society. The peaceful protests expressed a desire for change, as wanting a new order, wanting a new dispensation.'
Gopal Subramaniam, member of the Justice Verma Committee set up in the wake of the Delhi gang-rape, speaking to the author,
January 2012

At 2.33 and 11 seconds in the morning on Monday 30 July 2012, a power line between two fast-growing cities in northern India tripped, overloaded by excessive demand.[1]

In the twenty-five seconds that followed, the failure cascaded from one transmission station to another across northwestern India, until some 300 million people were left in the dark. Engineers worked to repair the damage, but it was slow going. In the midst of a long, baking hot summer, Indians woke up sweating, as fans and air conditioners failed. Some emerged from their homes in the dark. As dawn broke, many went without showers as electric water pumps failed. The morning commute in the capital turned to gridlock as traffic lights stayed dark, while the gleaming new Metro system, a symbol of India's modernity, was stalled for hours. Call centres and back office operations on the outskirts of New Delhi closed their doors and sent their employees home. It took fifteen hours to restore 80 per cent of electrical service.[2]

Then, on the 31st, the same line, between Bina and the bigger city of Gwalior, tripped again, at 1 p.m. and 13 seconds exactly. This time the failure had an even more dramatic cascading effect, as power swung through the system looking for a way out. In the next three minutes and five seconds, the official report says, a further sixty-six major power lines tripped. By three and a half minutes past one, the whole of northern India, a vast area ranging some 3,000 km from the Burmese border in the east to the Pakistani border in the west, was without electrical power, with 600 million people cut off. More than 500 trains were brought to a halt, while more than 200 miners were trapped underground for hours. This was the largest blackout in global history.[3]

As the news broke, there was consternation abroad, and not a little amazement. This was supposed to be an emerging Asian power – not in the same league as China, perhaps, but the up-and-coming destination of so many Western jobs. India was supposed to be 'shining', not dark. American business people emailed their Indian counterparts to ask how they were coping. Security consultants in faraway head offices were roused to offer advice to distant countrymen and women in India on how to survive should law and order begin to break down. But this was not New York in 1977, where a blackout in the midst of an economic crisis caused widespread looting, saw thirty-five blocks of Broadway destroyed and thousands of people arrested. This was India in 2012, where people were used to muddling through when the government let them down. There were no protests, no riots, just a weary shrug.

Factory owners, hospitals and middle-class householders are so inured to intermittent grid failure that most run backup generators or batteries. More than 300 million Indians are not even connected to the national grid, and rely on candles, kerosene lamps or torches at night. Huge swathes of rural India were not even aware there had been a power cut.

Nor did the government seem to feel much pressure. As luck would have it, the Power Minister was about to be replaced anyway, in a cabinet reshuffle. In the midst of the second blackout, Sushilkumar Shinde was duly promoted to the more prestigious role of Home Minister. With an emphatic wave of his hand, he rated his performance as Power

Minister as 'excellent'. Nor was his replacement a thrusting young tech-
nocrat determined to set things right. He was a 72-year-old ruling party
loyalist who wasted no time, not in apologizing for the mess, but in
congratulating his own predecessor for a job well done. 'We are very
proud. We have an excellent system,' Veerappa Moily told a crowd of
disbelieving reporters on the day he took office. Perhaps, he added,
there were certain 'localized' failures.

But the self-satisfaction of India's government was grotesquely
misplaced, for the blackouts of 2012 revealed deep-rooted problems
in India's power sector, and in its governance. Put simply, electricity
generation is already failing miserably to keep pace with demand. As
India grows, modernizes, industrializes and urbanizes, as every person
in this country demands regular electricity supplies as their right, the
demand for power is set to grow exponentially. It is far from clear that
the power sector can keep up.

From coal mining to electricity generation and distribution, the
sorry tale of India's power sector exposes a deep malaise in the country's governance. It is a malaise that reflects many of the country's
weaknesses: the corruption of its politicians, the bankrupting of its
nationalized industries by political populism, the failure of its infrastructure to keep pace with economic growth, the stark disregard for
equality inherent in the fact that nearly one third of the population
still lack electricity in their homes. More fundamentally it is rooted in
the failure of India's politicians and institutions to keep pace with
their people's rising expectations. As parts of India's private sector
forged ahead into the twenty-first century, as a nation of 1.2 billion
people dreamed of a land of aspiration and opportunity, India's politicians and many of its bureaucrats seemed stuck in the nineteenth
century. The blackout destroyed any lingering hope that India's entrepreneurial spirit could somehow deliver a significantly brighter future
without a dramatic improvement in the way the country is governed.

India's scientists, software engineers and entrepreneurs stand at the
cutting edge of modern progress; in November 2013, it launched an
unmanned orbiter destined to travel 140 million miles towards the

frozen planet of Mars, a space mission developed at a fraction of the cost of similar programmes elsewhere in the world. In healthcare, India has an unmatched reputation for affordable innovation that could revolutionize medical care in developing countries. India has ambition and aspiration and the talent to deliver; yet it cannot grant hundreds of millions of its own people the simple gift of electric light.

It has the fifth-largest coal reserves in the world, but is forced to ration power through regular outages; it has a young population desperate to learn and get ahead in the world, but too many of them are growing up without any electricity in their own homes; it dreams of harnessing the potential of its vibrant private sector to become a global leader, but can't even supply reliable power to industry. Tens of thousands of Indians die prematurely every year because of the failure to enforce pollution standards at the country's coal-fired power stations,[4] while the entire nation stands to suffer more than most peoples around the world from the harmful effects of climate change; yet the government lacks a plan to deal with the environmental mess created by its coal industry, let alone a coherent long-term strategy to develop renewable fuels on anything like the scale that it requires. Nothing symbolizes the need for India to be governed properly more conspicuously than the power sector, because the entire nation's future depends on electricity – and because it shows in stark terms how inequality, corruption, populism and poor governance have real outcomes for India's future.

Two decades after India embarked on reforms meant to liberalize its economy, the country's power sector is still crippled by a maze of regulations, by disjointed government and weak leadership, by bureaucratic inertia and by ineffective regulation. Corruption stretches from the widespread theft of electricity to the rampant loot-ing of natural resources by politicians, bureaucrats and industrialists, while populism is undermining the economy and leaving the poor worse off. The lack of investment in infrastructure is so serious that coal lies un-mined because there are no railway lines to transport it to market. The World Bank says the lack of reliable electric power is the biggest barrier to jobs growth and investment in India today.[5] The contrast with China, where the infrastructure needed to support a modern economy is built in anticipation of future economic growth, could hardly be starker.

While the underlying cause of July's blackout was the yawning gap between the demand for electricity and its supply, the overload itself was blamed on individual states drawing too much power from the grid, in defiance of regulations. But the bigger question is why democracy is leaving so much of India in the dark.

The biggest offender in 2012, perhaps predictably, was the unruly state of Uttar Pradesh, whose consumers and industry suffer constant rationing of electricity. Its Chief Minister, Akhilesh Yadav, was swift to blame a previous state government for failing to set up enough power plants. But insiders said Yadav had compounded the problem by pushing the state power-distribution company to provide twenty-four-hour power to four districts politically important to him, his relatives or close allies. 'This led other politicians to start putting enormous pressure on the power corporation to supply more electricity in their areas as well,' said Shailendra Dubey, secretary general of the All India Power Engineers Federation. Among them, allegedly, was Bhagwan Sharma, the strongman we met in Chapter 3, who made it a point of pride to defend his constituents' interests and ensure they got enough power. 'The power corporation had no choice but to overdraw from the grid to satisfy these elected politicians,' said Dubey. 'They could not say no to their political bosses.'

Underlying this problem, though, was the central government's failure to exert any discipline in its management of the power grid, to enforce existing rules or punish states that cheat. With a national coalition government dependent on regional parties to survive in office, the glue that holds the Indian government together is a complex interplay of bribery and blackmail, coupled with occasionally intersecting self-interest. Chief ministers were exploiting the weakness of the central government led by Manmohan Singh, extracting electric power in return for political support. In short, Singh's government was unable to call governments like Yadav's to account, because it needed his party's backing in New Delhi's parliament.

'It is open lawbreaking that goes on all the time in India,' one power ministry official said. 'This time it went beyond limits. We are powerless to enforce grid discipline like they do in developed countries of the world. There are political constraints. We are even afraid to name the [offending] states.'[6]

It is hard to understate just how important it is for India to get its power sector right. Like China two decades ago and the United States in 1950, the nation stands on the cusp of transformational economic and social change that will see its demand for electricity explode.[7] Whether India succeeds in meeting that demand could be the single most important factor determining its economic prospects over the next two decades, and could have a major impact on whether it succeeds in pulling hundreds of millions of people out of poverty. But does anyone in the government have a vision of how to meet that challenge, and the will to implement that vision? Around a quarter of the power that India generates is either stolen or leaks away from poorly insulated lines, because of decades of underinvestment in the grid. That is roughly five times the corresponding figure for China. It represents a criminal waste of precious resources that the country can ill afford. In order to buy votes, Indian politicians give away another huge chunk of the nation's electrical power either free or at heavily subsidized rates to farmers, while still more is supplied to consumers at a loss. It is naked populism that is destroying the environment and the economy.

Farmers use their free power to run water pumps around the clock to irrigate their land, depleting groundwater levels to a dangerous degree. The 2012 blackout was partly blamed on the late arrival of the monsoon that year, causing a spike in power use by farmers.

The great Indian power giveaway – free power given by politicians to buy votes – is also bankrupting state electricity-distribution companies. By the middle of 2012 they had run up losses of some $46 billion, or 2 per cent of national income, largely financed by public-sector banks – a debt that was straining India's financial system. As a result, they have little money to invest in equipment or pay salaries, or even to pay for the electricity that is being generated by newly built power plants. Indeed, every unit of power they supply to rural India pushes the distribution companies four rupees deeper into the red – a simple reason why they ration power and why so many of the nation's homes are still in the dark, either constantly or intermittently.

The cost of electricity purchases is rising sharply, partly because India's state-dominated coal industry is stagnating and power stations are forced to import increasing amounts of costly foreign coal. But politicians prevent the state distribution company from raising tariffs for political reasons, senior official R. S. Pandey told me in frustration – almost every year there are local, state or national elections to contend with. As a result, the power corporation has not recruited any staff for the past thirty years. Decades-old transformers frequently burn out. Most overhead electrical wires are not insulated, making theft as easy as hooking a pole onto them, and law enforcement is virtually non-existent.

But it is in the villages that stretch across the vast plains of northern India that the extent of the power crisis really hits home. Here, many people were unaware that a blackout had hit half the country only a few days before. So few homes have electricity here, and those that are connected receive power so intermittently, that the largest power failure in world history was a non-event. Health clinics cannot operate effectively without power or refrigeration for medicines; children cannot study in the dark. The lack of power helps explain India's low standings on human development indices, as well as the smog that hangs over these northern plains – thought to be contributing to the melting of the Himalayan glaciers – from the widespread use of firewood and dung for cooking.

The village of Kataiyan is completely without electricity. There, my colleague Rama Lakshmi spoke to 35-year-old Gulabi Amarikan, who described the darkness as a source of shame. 'I have three children, but will they do anything better in their lives?' she said, while preparing to cook lunch on a wood stove in her cramped, dingy kitchen. The floor was swept clean and her children were also clean and smart, but her ambition for them was being thwarted. 'They can't watch TV to learn anything like other children do. They can't read at home,' she said. 'We have to live in the dark and in ignorance.'[8]

Prahalad Yadav, a 45-year-old farmer, has tried to put pressure on politicians to help them. But here, democracy isn't much help. 'This time we went around telling all the villagers not to vote. "No electricity, no vote," we shouted. Each time the candidates come and promise; each time we trust; each time we get fooled.' But Prahalad's attempts to organize a boycott eventually foundered on election day: the village is dominated by the Yadav caste, and voted for the Yadav-led Samajwadi Party. 'Everybody votes on caste,' he said. 'They are from our caste and they come and beg for votes with folded hands. It is hard to say no.'

In the village of Kenwasia, only those who bribe the power engineers have electricity; the poor part of the village, inhabited by Dalits, is completely dark. Vinod Gupta, a 20-year-old small farmer, lamented politicians' broken promises: '"Whatever your problem is, we will solve it," the politicians say during election time. When they win, they never come back.'

The darkness here is a physical manifestation between the empowered and the disempowered in today's India, a dividing line that cuts off the poor from any part in the nation's progress. 'If there is light, children can study in the evening,' said 66-year-old Raja Ram, with a walking stick, and a memory almost as long as independent India. 'But now the children just play in the mud and waste their time. My life has been spent in darkness. At least my grandchildren's lives should have all the good things electricity brings.'

Those who can, steal it. Every few miles here, sunset brings young men out to stand on roofs or street corners, using long bamboo poles to tug at the overhead power lines. Once they hook their wires to the cable, they light a bulb in their tiny shops or a fan in their homes. By

morning, the illegal hook-ups have been removed so that police officers don't spot them. Businesses are also tapping into power lines
illegally or bypassing meters, but vote-hungry local politicians protect
the thieves. For the lonely power engineer, any attempt to inspect
lines and punish thieves is a dangerous game. 'There is a lot of political interference,' one inspector told me as we travelled by car to meet
up with local police for a series of raids around the town of Modina-
gar. 'The local politicians say: "I will have you killed, I will have you
suspended. I will have you transferred." They complain to our higher-
ups. It is very difficult.'

Another engineer acknowledged avoiding many villages because
screaming people surround him demanding electricity. 'I know that
more than 30 per cent of our electricity is lost to illegal tapping by
people. But we cannot arrest them because our politicians get angry
and transfer us to difficult postings,' he said. 'All these people have
political connections. The politicians do not want us to harass the
poor either. They are more interested in getting votes than getting
payment for electricity.'⁹

The power sector is, in a sense, one of the most visible manifesta-
tions of the fundamental breakdown in the rule of law in India. But
it is also a symbol of the triumph of populism over sound economics.
'Successive governments in India at the central and state levels have
considered populism – the promise of cheap or subsidized power – an
effective strategy,' wrote Arvind Subramanian of the Peterson Institute of International Economics in Washington. 'But the consequence
has been either no power or highly interrupted power for a vast majority of Indians.'¹⁰

Power symbolizes the way Indian democracy often fails to meet the
most basic aspirations of voters, for transparent government, jobs,
empowerment and opportunity – the politics of patronage trumping
the politics of aspiration. Yet, even in the gloom of India's power politics, there is still a ray of hope. As we saw in Chapter 14, that hope
principally lies at the level of individual states.

In recent years, Delhi has made significant improvements in its power-sector performance by privatizing much of the distribution. Gujarat is experimenting with charging consumers more for steady, reliable power, and less for standard connections. West Bengal has made progress in reducing losses by cutting political interference in the power sector, and sending a clear signal that theft will not be tolerated.

Subramanian sees these as hopeful signs that some states are finding their own way forward, seeking to reap electoral rewards not through populist giveaways but through good governance. Instead of offering voters sops like free power – which ultimately bankrupt the government and undermine the local economy – some state governments recognize that getting the economy right can be the most powerful vote-getter of all. Only by charging people for the electricity they consume can the government afford to supply reliable, uninterrupted power to all, and so drive rapid growth in their local economy. 'If India could "crack" power,' he wrote, 'it would address the bigger problem of severing the link – actual and perceived – between [costly] populism and electoral success.'

Back in Uttar Pradesh, though, the idea that the system will change – and that democracy will work in favour of sound economics – still seems fanciful. 'The politicians and the judiciary we have, it is very difficult to prosecute anybody for the theft of electricity, because the fear of the law is not there,' said Pandey of the state distribution company. 'This is the dark side of Indian democracy. Hooliganism and vandalism is always there.'

As we saw at the beginning of this book, democracy has arguably been India's most cohesive force, saving this vast nation from violence and disintegration. But it should be clear by now that merely keeping the nation together is no longer nearly enough. As the cancer of corruption has eaten away at Indian democracy, cynicism has grown – polls show a majority of middle-class respondents feel it is an obstacle to the country's economic progress, and many express a not-so-secret yearning for a short dose of Chinese-style dictatorship. The protests that swept India in the past few years, especially the anti-corruption movement, expressed contempt for the state and rejected the idea that politicians and parliament were the ultimate arbiters of popular will.

As India has entered the information age, as economic reforms, media freedoms and connectivity have opened people's eyes, so likewise have expectations and aspirations risen dramatically, not just among the middle class but among the poor also. The demands on the state to deliver have grown exponentially too, not for handouts so much as for it to provide the solid foundation upon which economic opportunity can be built. But when it comes to law and order, healthcare, education and coherent decision-making, the state has largely failed to fulfil the tasks allotted to it. The risk is clear, that unsatisfied expectations lead to frustration, and that frustration leads in turn to crime and violence. The apparent rise in incidences of rape, including gang-rape, shows this risk cannot be easily dismissed. Democracy, in short, has to deliver more than a nation; it has to satisfy fast-rising aspirations for equal citizenship, and for opportunity. So far, its record on that score remains patchy at best.

Yet out of this chaos I find considerable reason for optimism. Aspirations and frustrations can also be channelled into pressure for change, and indeed are already working in that direction. Economic growth has produced a dramatic enlargement of the middle class. Traditionally seen as a mute spectator to Indian democracy, India's middle class used to be all but ignored by politicians, who preferred to woo the far more numerous ranks of the poor. As a result, many middle-class Indians were too disillusioned with politics to even cast a vote. But the idea that they are irrelevant spectators to the great game of Indian democracy is outdated, if it was ever really true. Their votes may not yet be the largest in number, but their voices are being carried loud and clear through the medium of television, and through people like Arnab Goswami. They are getting up off their backsides and coming out on the streets in hundreds of thousands to express their frustrations. It is possible to be hugely encouraged by that fact without necessarily subscribing to Anna Hazare's worldview or wanting every rapist to be hanged forthwith. Protests are often led by radical figures, but supported by a more moderate, peace-loving mass of citizens who want to see the system shaken up. The end result often comes closer to the moderate position than to the desires of the radicals. In other words, the protests act as much-needed correctives, while the consultative process that follows in their wake sometimes produces a decent compromise. Hazare and Kejriwal's vision of an all-encompassing Jan Lokpal will probably never be implemented, but India might end up with a more robust set of anti-corruption laws and bodies. Rape laws have already been tightened, without anyone being lynched just yet. In the same way, it is also possible to like the way Arnab Goswami has shaken up the existing power structures without necessarily agreeing with his vision for India and its relations with neighbouring countries.

Social media has played its role too in India's awakening. There may only be 13 million Indians on Twitter, or around 1 per cent of the population, but they are sufficiently vocal to annoy the established powers that be. Much of what passes for comment on Twitter is superficial, but there is no doubt that it allows its users to feel that their voices are being heard, and that they can speak truth directly to power. Facebook and Twitter allow them to locate those who think the same way, and draw confidence from their support before taking to the streets.

The government, meanwhile, looked out of its depth when dealing with the rape protests of 2012/13. In the past, instead of engaging in a battle of ideas, the conventional official response to a protest has been to deal only with the protest leaders; to cajole, co-opt or discredit them; to engage the communities they represent by offering them sops. Today, in an era of leaderless protests, where protesters are no longer bussed in by political parties but gather of their own accord, transcending both caste and community, the old approach becomes impossible. As 2013 dawned, faced with a leaderless protest, the authorities looked unsettled and out of touch. The protesters were asking to be heard and to be engaged, not to be bought off. Afterwards, there was a great deal of talk within the government of a new strategy to deal with 'flash mobs', but the fundamental problem – the fact that India's leaders are unable or unwilling to articulate their positions, or engage in a battle of ideas – was ignored. It cannot be ignored for ever.

Of course, progress will not occur in a straight line, nor will the influence of the media and the social media be entirely benign. The middle class only protests when its self-interest is threatened: the rape of 'a girl like us' elicited a national outpouring of anger, but the routine rape and murder of Dalit and tribal girls continues without anyone batting an eyelid – indeed, the middle-class practice of employing child maids arguably fuels this abuse by putting girls in positions of extreme vulnerability. The best-selling author Chetan Bhagat argues that the failure of the middle class to 'lend its media power' to protect the interests of the poor, its failure to use that power for anything other than self-serving purposes, is a fundamental flaw in its agenda for change.[11] The exclusion of the poor from that change agenda leaves them alienated and open to exploitation by the country's politicians, who speak their language and throw them scraps from the top table. In return, the poor ignore politicians' misdeeds and vote them back into power, he argues.

Bhagat makes a perceptive point, but his conclusions seem to me too gloomy. The voice of the new middle class may be strident and jingoistic at times, and at others liberal and patronizing: it is almost always loudest in defence of its own interests, and it often has a tendency to see messiahs in the distinctly flawed forms of Narendra Modi or Arvind Kejriwal, or to be attracted to fiery preachers like Arnab Goswami; but I firmly believe it will be a force for positive change. In the end, what middle-class people in India need above all else are equality of opportunity and treatment, the rule of law and the certainty of functioning institutions. They want politicians to perform, not to distribute sops to particular communities. Their influence is already substantial through the media, and the potential for their votes to swing elections is growing with every passing year. Their demands could be exactly what India needs.

Corruption may still be part of almost every Indian's life in one way or another, but it seems to me that it is being squeezed. The high-profile scandals of the past few years may have involved mind-boggling sums of money, but the opportunity for such brazen theft has surely been narrowed, with a vigilant Comptroller and Auditor General and an aggressive media potentially looking over the politician or bureaucrat's shoulder. Many middle-class people still use corruption as a vehicle to jump what would otherwise be a very long queue, but the Right to Information Act at least gives the poor an alternative form of bargaining power.

But the final reason that Bhagat is too gloomy in his assessment is that the poor are also embracing an agenda for change and for good governance. As we saw in Chapter 14, voters in some parts of the country are thinking beyond caste and communal identities and returning to power only those politicians who govern them with a reasonable degree of efficiency.

One worrying aspect of Indian politics is that even though economic reforms have transformed the country in the past two decades, very few politicians actually defend those reforms or advocate more of the same. Reform, when it happens, is carried out under duress – during a balance of payments crisis in 1991 for example – or by stealth. There is no national political mandate for liberalizing the economy and freeing up the nation's undoubted economic potential. It is almost as though Indians don't quite trust their success, and their ability to compete on the world stage – we can't let foreign supermarkets in, they say, because it will destroy our local stores, without for a minute appreciating the fantastic levels of convenience and customer service those local stores provide. It is also, of course, because politicians are still stuck ideologically in a bygone age; because lazy populism, victimhood and status quo-ism seem like easier cards to play than appeals to bravery and change; and because those reforms are seen as having disproportionately benefited a handful of crony capitalists – which is true, except for the fact that they have also lifted hundreds of millions of people out of poverty and helped to elide caste divisions.

Yet perhaps a leader will emerge some day who can truly sell India on the power of its private sector, on the idea of this nation as modern, well-governed, equitable but also aspirational.

Some days, one wakes up in India feeling despair. The problems are so great, so insurmountable, it is easy to imagine that nothing will ever change. Yet on others – and these are the days that matter – the energy, the ambition, the desire of this country are infectious: yes, change is possible, and it has to come.

India was never the shining soon-to-be superpower that its enthusiasts suggested in 2004. Even its economic 'miracle' of the past two decades looks slightly less impressive with the benefit of hindsight, carried as it was on a wave of global liquidity and a wider emerging market boom. But the gloom that has now enveloped the country looks equally exaggerated. Complacency was always the easiest trap for India's elite to fall into, their sense of entitlement and indifference to others' suffering their greatest sin. Today, when a middle-class Indian friend tells me she has never felt so pessimistic about the nation's future, I am perversely encouraged. The first step towards recovery is to realize one has a problem. The gloom that envelops India today tells me the nation has been shaken out of its complacency and is waking up to the scale of the challenge ahead, to fulfil its potential and take its rightful place on the world stage.

Those who are jealous of China's economic success – those who yearn for some kind of business-friendly dictatorship rather than India's unruly democracy – often have a tendency to overlook the appalling suffering that hundreds of millions of people endured in the years of Mao's Great Famine or the Cultural Revolution. In the end, comparisons between India and China are facile, since they are such different countries with such different cultures and histories. But in the great democracy–dictatorship debate, I would say only this: dictatorships can sometimes produce coherent, decisive governance, but they are also capable of horrific evil; they almost always end in upheaval, which often destroys many of the accomplishments they might have made; and they are extremely bad at incorporating the voices of minority groups, of the disadvantaged or the marginalized. Whatever system is best for China, I have no doubt that in a nation like India, of almost unimaginable diversity and crippling hierarchy, dictatorship would have been a disaster – even more than it has been in neighbouring Pakistan. Democracy has not only held India together against all the odds; it has also given voice to the voiceless, and allowed the underprivileged to begin raising their bowed heads and asking questions of their supposed superiors. Democracy is always a hard slog, and progress will always be uneven and halting, but India stands much better prepared to confront her challenges today than she did a decade ago.

The battle ahead is to build a new India, where women are safe and opportunity is more equally distributed, where the poor are protected but enterprise is rewarded, where investment is encouraged but corruption reined in, where the bureaucracy is invigorated and politics disinfected, where the old hierarchies are broken down and replaced by modern institutions, where the rule of law replaces the rule of patronage and influence. The battle will not simply be about voting every few years, but will involve a constant struggle to build a better nation, through protest, through voluntary work and advocacy, through the media and social media. It is a battle that must be joined, for India's future hangs in the balance. The old India, of patriarchy and caste, of venal politicians and corrupt business leaders, will not willingly move aside, but the force of history is not on its side.

There are undoubtedly pockets of darkness in India, but there are also rays of hope. For all its problems, India remains a beacon of promise in a deeply troubled region. It is time now for a reinvigorated, reawakened democracy to deliver. India's future will only shine if its people take up the challenge, and join the struggle for a better society.

Notes

INTRODUCTION

1 *The Times of India* crowed about India's new status as a rich country, after four billionaires – Lakshmi Mittal, Mukesh Ambani, Anil Ambani and K. P. Singh – made it into the global top 10 in the 2008 *Forbes* list.

2 Alistair Scrutton. 'A cocky India enjoys global economic limelight', Reuters, 3 Dec 2007.

3 'Commonwealth games athletes' village is "unfit for human habitation"', Press Association, 21 Sept 2010; Andrew Buncombe, 'India's games stink', *Independent,* 22 Sept 2010.

4 *Report of the Comptroller and Auditor General Report of India for the year ended 31 March 2011 on XIX Commonwealth Games,* 2010.

5 *Report of the Comptroller and Auditor General Report of India on Issue of Licences and Allocation of 2G Spectrum by the Department of Telecommunications (Ministry of Telecommunications and Information Technology).*

6 In a December 2011 poll on the Churumuri website, more than 56 per cent of respondents agreed that democracy had become a hindrance to India's growth and development, against 35 per cent who disagreed.

7 Ashutosh Varshney persuasively makes the case for Nehru as the father of Indian democracy in 'Raising democracy', *Indian Express,* 30 Nov 2012. See also Ramachandra Guha, *Patriots and Partisans*, Penguin India, 2012, ch. 7, 'Verdicts on Nehru: the rise and fall of a reputation'.

8 Ramachandra Guha, *India After Gandhi*, Picador India, 2007, ch. 3, 'Apples in the Basket', pp. 35–58.

9 ibid., ch. 6, 'Ideas of India', pp. 103–23.

10 Katherine Frank, *Indira. The Life of Indira Nehru Gandhi*, HarperCollins, 2001, pp. 289–324, covers her ascent to PM.

11 Keith Bradsher, 'Falling Economic Tide in India Is Exposing Its Chronic Troubles', *New York Times*, 4 Sept 2013.

I: ASKING FOR IT

1 Author's interviews, except detail on smartphone and Chetan Bhagat novel,

from Krishna Pokharel, Saurabh Chaturvedi, Vibhuti Agarwal, Tripti Lahiri, 'New Delhi Attack: The Victim's Story', *Wall Street Journal*, 8 Jan 2013.

2   Bhura's tale is well told by Andrew Buncombe in 'A mother's story of the teenager India wants to hang after a gang rape that shocked a nation', *Independent*, 12 Jan 2013.

3   Kumari quote from Rama Lakshmi, 'India moves to curb anti-rape protests', *Washington Post*, 24 Dec 2012.

4   The best real-time account of the protests in New Delhi can be found in Nilanjana Roy's blog, Notes from Raisina Hill, 22 Dec 2012.

5   Javed Anwer and Rukmini Shrinivasan, 'The year social media came of age in India', *Times of India*, 31 Dec 2012.

6   Rama Lakshmi, 'India women alter Slutwalk to better match country's conservatism', *Washington Post*, 22 July 2011.

7   Olga Khazan and Rama Lakshmi, '10 reasons why India has a sexual violence problem', *Washington Post*, 29 Dec 2012.

8   Data on underage marriage from United Nations Population Fund, 'Motherhood in Childhood, Facing the challenge of underage pregnancy. The State of World Population 2013'. Attitudes to wife-beating from Unicef, 'Progress for Children. A Report Card on Adolescents. Number 10,' April 2012

9   For a collection of some of the worst remarks see Rama Lakshmi, 'Amid rape fiasco, India's leaders keep up insensitive remarks', *Washington Post*, 4 Jan 2013.

10 Rama Lakshmi, 'India struggles with social media following rape uproar', *Washington Post*, 5 Jan 2012.

11 Simon Denyer, 'Indian village proud after double "honour killing"', Reuters, 16 May 2008.

12 Simon Denyer, 'In rural India, rapes met with silence', *Washington Post*, 9 Jan 2012.

13 Sai Manish and Priyanka Dubey, 'Haryana's Bestial Rape Chronicles', *Tehelka*, 27 Oct 2012.

14 Rama Lakshmi, 'A day in the life of a young New Delhi woman', 9 Jan 2013, reprinted by permission of *The Washington Post*.

15 Email from M. Rajshekhar of the *Economic Times*.

2: MAN OUT OF TIME

1   Simon Denyer, 'Indian leader's legacy is fading', *Washington Post*, 5 Sept 2012.

2   The description of Singh as a 'tragic' figure was coined by the historian Ramachandra Guha, who had persuasively argued that the Prime Minister would have gone down in history with his reputation largely intact if he had only known when to resign – after one term in office.

3   'Angry govt for "strong action" against article slamming PM', *Hindustan Times*, 6 Sept 2012.

4   M. J. Akbar, 'A perfect storm of stupidity', *Sunday Guardian*, 9 Sept 2012.

5   Vinod K. Jose, 'Falling Man', *The Caravan* magazine, Oct 2011.

6   Ramachandra Guha, *Patriots and Partisans*, Penguin, Allen Lane, 2012, ch. 5, 'The Professor and the Protester', p. 105.

7   PM's reply to the debate on the Motion of Confidence in the Lok Sabha, 22 July 2008. Further details on his childhood from Vinod K. Jose, 'Falling Man', *The Caravan* magazine, Oct 2011.

8   Manmohan Singh interview by Charlie Rose, 27 Feb 2006, Prime Minister's Office (PMO) website.

9   Ajith Pillai, 'Why nice guys finish last', *Outlook* magazine, 25 Oct 1999.

10 Sonia Gandhi, *Rajiv*, Viking, Penguin India, 1992, p. 6.

11 Manmohan Singh interview by Charlie Rose, 27 Feb 2006, Prime Minister's Office (PMO) website.

12 Surjit S. Bhalla, 'Message to Sonia: reform or perish', *Indian Express*, 30 Mar 2013.

13 Barkha Dutt, 'Introspect, and act', *Hindustan Times*, 8 June 2012.

14 'India's telecoms scandal; Megahurts', *Economist*, 11 Feb 2012.

15 Supreme Court judgement on spectrum allocation, 2 Feb 2011.

16 *Report of the Comptroller and Auditor General Report of India on Issue of Licences and Allocation of 2G Spectrum by the Department of Telecommunications (Ministry of Telecommunications and Information Technology).*

17 Statement by A. Raja, Minister of Communication & Information Technology, to Joint Parliamentary Committee to examine matters relating to allocation and pricing of telecom licences and spectrum from 1998 to 2009, pp. 56, 83–4.

18 Shalini Singh, 'Within two weeks of the 2G scam, PM wanted "arms length" from Raja'; 'New papers show PMO analysed and agreed with Raja's actions before 2G scam'; both stories, *The Hindu*, 18 Mar 2013.

19 'Sukh Ram sentenced to 5 years jail in 1996 telecom scam case', Press Trust of India (PTI), 19 Nov 2011.

20 Simon Denyer, 'India's telecoms revolution hits a snag', *Washington Post*, 2 June 2012.

21 'Sheer ecstasy greets A. Raja at Chennai airport', *Headlines Today*, 8 June 2012.

22 'How India is losing its magic', *Economist*, 24 Mar 2012.

23 Standard & Poor's, 'Will India be the first BRIC fallen angel?', 8 June 2012.

24 *Report of the Comptroller and Auditor General Report of India on Allocation of Coal Blocks and Augmentation of Coal Production, for the year ended March 2012.* Tabled in Lok Sabha, 17 Aug 2012.

25 Ashish Khetan, 'Corruption by Weakness', *Tehelka*, 11 Aug 2012.

26 Corrected transcript of the interaction between the PM and Newspaper Editors, PMO website, 29 June 2011.

27 'Congress leader Digvijay Singh targets CAG Vinod Rai', PTI, 31 Aug 2012.

28 'Global peer review lauds CAG's findings', *Times of India*, 2 Dec 2012.

29 Simon Denyer, 'Indian leader's legacy is fading', *Washington Post*, 5 Sept 2012.

30 Sanjaya Baru, 'Decoding Manmohan Singh's red lines', *The Hindu*, 23 Jan 2013.

31 Simon Denyer, 'Musharraf ready to meet India halfway on Kashmir', Reuters, 18 Dec 2003.

32 Simon Denyer, 'India mood darkens as corruption undermines nation's self-confidence', *Washington Post*, 20 Mar 2011.

33 PM's Interaction Editors of the Electronic Media, PMO website, 16 Feb 2011.

34 Corrected transcript of the interaction between the PM and Newspaper Editors, PMO website, 29 June 2011.

35 PM's address to Biennial Conference of CBI and state anti-corruption bureaux, 21 Oct 2011.

36 'India's Scholar-Prime Minister Aims For Inclusive Development', Q&A with *Science* magazine, 24 Feb 2012.

37 Anil Chaudhary, a member of the Indian Social Action Forum, quoted in Rama Lakshmi, 'Activists bristle as India cracks down on foreign funding of NGOs', *Washington Post*, 20 May 2013. The same argument was made by Pratap Bhanu Mehta in the *Indian Express* on 29 February in an op-ed headed 'Do Not Disagree'. Mehta argued that the real reason for the impasse over Kudankulam was the state's lack of credibility, which stemmed from its own secrecy. 'The prime minister unwittingly showed what a banana republic India can be,' he wrote. 'If a few crores here and there, given to NGOs which have instruments of power other than their ability to mobilize, can bring this country to a standstill, then we are indeed in deep trouble. Banana republics are more paranoid about dissent than self-confident democracies.'

38 'If we have to go down, let us go down fighting: PM', Indo-Asian News Service, 14 Sept 2012.

39 'India's prime minister faces defining moment on economy', *Washington Post*, 3 July 2012.

3: MONEY (THAT'S WHAT I WANT)

1 Data on Bhagwan Sharma from Association for Democratic Reforms. Myneta.info

2 *Lok Sabha Election Watch 2009*, published by National Election Watch and the Association for Democratic Reforms.

3 Simon Denyer, 'In Indian politics, criminals thrive', *Washington Post*, 6 Mar 2012.

4 Milan Vaishnav, 'Money, Muscle and the Market for India's Criminal Politicians', Center for Advanced Study of India, University of Pennsylvania, 13 Feb 2012.

5 'BSP MLA held on charges of rape', *The Hindu*, 30 June 2008.

6 Prem Shankar Jha, 'Getting the Vote Right', *Tehelka*, 10 Sept 2011.

7 Vinod K. Jose, 'Falling Man', *The Caravan* magazine, Oct 2011.

8 KPMG, *Global Anti-Bribery and Corruption Survey*, 14 Mar 2011.

9   World Bank, *Doing Business*, 2013.

10 Devesh Kapur and Milan Vaishnav, 'Builders, politicians, friends forever?', *Business Standard*, 29 Oct 2012.

11 Seshan's later attempts to capitalize on his popularity and credibility by standing for elections ended in failure, with two heavy defeats at the polls. Some commentators have argued that this experience should serve as a warning for the founder of the India Against Corruption movement, Arvind Kejriwal, who went on to set up his own political party in 2012.

12 Nidhi Dutt, 'Free TVs and laptops for voters in Tamil Nadu election', BBC News website, 12 May 2011.

13 Sarah Hiddleston, 'Cash for votes a way of political life in South India', *The Hindu*, 16 Mar 2011. From: WikiLeaks cable 206688: cash for votes in South India. Sent by Acting Principal Officer J. Frederick Kaplan, Chennai, 13 May 2009.

14 Association for Democratic Reforms, *Crimes against women including rape cases declared by MPs, MLAs and candidates*, 20 Dec 2012.

15 Association for Democratic Reforms and National Election Watch, *Analysis of Income Tax Returns Filed and Donations Received by Political Parties. (Fiscal years 2004/5 to 2010/11)*. Released 10 September, 2012

16 '98% Indians want criminals to stay out of Parliament; Avaaz survey', *The Hindu Business Line*, 6 Sept 2013.

17 John Chalmers, 'Rahul slams move to shield convicted politicians', Reuters 27 Sept 2013; Hari Kumar, 'Rahul Gandhi Opposes Ordinance Seeking to Protect Convicted Lawmakers', *New York Times* India Ink blog, 27 Sept 2013.

18 'Middle-class makes its voice heard', *Times of India* editorial, 3 Oct 2013.

19 S.Y. Quraishi, 'Pressure of a Button', *Indian Express*, 3 Oct 2013.

20 The Political Parties (Registration and Regulation of Affairs, etc.), Draft Bill 2011, Association for Democratic Reforms.

4: IT'S A FAMILY AFFAIR

1   Simon Denyer, 'Rahul Gandhi discovers the limits of Indian politics', Reuters, 6 Aug 2004.

2   Rahul has repeatedly tried to dampen speculation that he was prime minister in waiting, arguing that the top post was not his 'priority', and berating reporters who asked about the issue for posing 'a wrong question'.

3   'Indira's Gandhi's death remembered', BBC news website, 1 Nov 2009. http://news.bbc.co.uk/2/hi/south_asia/8306420.stm. Human Rights Watch, 'India: Bring Charges for Newly Discovered Massacre of Sikhs', 25 Apr 2011.

4   Ramachandra Guha, *India After Gandhi. The history of the world's largest democracy*, Picador India , ch. 25, 'This son also rises', pp. 575–602.

5   Aarthi Ramachandran, *Decoding Rahul Gandhi*, Tranquebar, 2012, p. 31.

6   Sonia Gandhi, *Rajiv*, Viking, Penguin India, 1992, p. 71. Cited in Ramachandran's book.

7   Sonia Gandhi, *Rajiv*, cited in Ramachandran's book.

8 Ramachandran, *Decoding Rahul Gandhi*, ch. 2, 'Education and Work', pp. 27–52.

9 Interview transcript, *Tehelka*, 24 Sept 2005.

10 *India's Elected. Our MPs: A report card, 14th Lok Sabha 2004–2009*, published by The Express Group in association with PRS Legislative Research, Indicus Analytics, Liberty Institute, p. 325. More recent data was supplied to the author directly by PRS.

11 Desai made this comparison at Ramachandran's book launch in New Delhi.

12 Aarthi Ramachandran, *Decoding Rahul Gandhi*, Tranquebar, 2012, p. 48.

13 ibid., pp. 36–8.

14 Saba Naqvi, 'Rahul Gandhi: Zero Worship?', *Outlook* magazine, 11 Mar 2012.

15 Simon Denyer, 'The new face of the Gandhi dynasty', *Washington Post*, 3 Dec 2011.

16 Santosh Desai, 'An absence called Rahul Gandhi', *Times of India*, 20 Jan 2013.

17 Ramachandra Guha, 'The nervous soldier', *Telegraph*, 26 Jan 2013.

18 Chetan Bhagat, 'Silence of the Gandhis', *Times of India*, 29 Dec 2012.

19 *India Today*-Nielsen Mood of the Nation Polls.

20 Patrick French, *India: A portrait*, Penguin Books India, ch. 4, 'Family Politics', pp. 91–123.

21 Prem Shankar Jha, 'Getting the Vote Right. How our electoral system has been made ineffective over the decades. And how we can fix it', *Tehelka*, vol. 8, issue 36, 10 Sept 2011.

22 Shankar Raghuraman, 'Republic of Hope', Survey by Ipsos of 18–35-year-olds in eight major cities, *Times of India*, 25 Jan 2012.

23 Simon Denyer, 'Gandhi still confident in "fight for India's soul"', Reuters, 22 Apr 2004.

24 Tavleen Singh, 'Please no more purdah politics', *Indian Express*, 17 June 2012.

25 Simon Denyer, 'Priyanka sprinkles Gandhi magic on Indian campaign', Reuters, 25 Apr 2004.

26 NDTV, In conversation with Priyanka Gandhi, 24 Apr 2009.

27 Speech by Rahul Gandhi, All India Congress Committee Session, Jaipur, Indian National Congress website.

28 Meghnad Desai, 'Bharat versus Hindustan', *Indian Express*, 27 Jan 2013.

5: IS THERE SOMETHING I SHOULD KNOW?

1 Shankkar Aiyar, *Accidental India. A History of the Nation's Passage through Crisis and Change*, Aleph, 2012, pp. 261–2.

2 US Freedom of Information Act website. Freedom of Information: statistics on implementation in central government; UK Ministry of Justice. 12 Dec 2012, implementation India data from Shailesh Gandhi in interview with author.

3 'CWG scam: CIC notice to CBI on delay in giving information', *Times of*

India, 11 Jan 2013; 'Bid for CWG was secretive, hasty: RTI query', Indo Asian News Service, 2 Nov 2010.

4   Vidya Subrahmaniam, 'When the RTI "Basmasura" chased the government', *The Hindu*, 26 Sept 2011; 'The Power of RTI', *The Hindu* editorial, 5 Nov 2012.

5   List of RTI Activists Killed. NCPRI – National Campaign for People's Right to Information.

6   *Central Information Commission Annual Report 2011–12*

7   Janani Ganesan, 'Has curiosity killed the RTI cat?', *Tehelka*, 26 Feb 2012.

8   The broader problem of 'golden parachutes' has been well highlighted by Devesh Kapur, of the Center for the Advanced Study of India at the University of Pennsylvania ('Golden parachutes, leaden results', *Business Standard*, 17 Mar 2013). He argues that former bureaucrats and former judges are packing appointments to regulatory bodies, stymieing the introduction of professionals and expertise into these areas, and making senior bureaucrats even more determined to please their political masters towards the end of their careers in order to get such a 'golden parachute'.

9   'RTI Act can't violate personal privacy, says PM Manmohan Singh', *Economic Times*, 13 Oct 2012. 'RTI Act needs a critical review, Manmohan Singh', *India Today*, 14 Oct 2012.

10 *Safeguarding the Right to Information. Report of the People's RTI Assessment 2008*, RTI Assessment & Analysis Group (RaaG) and National Campaign for People's Right to Information (NCPRI).

11 Rukmini Shrinivasan, 'Don't pay a bribe, file an RTI application', *Times of India*, 2 May 2011.

12 For a good analysis of the importance of a Whistleblowers Bill, see Shekhar Singh and Anjali Bhardwaj, 'The responsibility to protect', *Indian Express*, 6 May 2013.

13 Abhijit V. Banerjee, Selvan Kumar, Rohini Pande and Felix Su, 'Do Informed Voters Make Better Choices? Experimental Evidence from Urban India', 1 Mar 2010.

6: HEADLINE HUSTLER

1   Rahul Bhatia, 'Fast and Furious. The turbulent reign of Arnab Goswami', *The Caravan*, 1 Dec 2012.

2   Goswami no longer gives interviews, pleading corporate policy and too much attention on himself.

3   Lydia Polgreen, 'A journalist in India Ends up in the Headlines', *New York Times*, 3 Dec 2010.

4   Hartosh Singh Bal, 'This is not journalism as we know it', *Open* magazine, 27 Nov 2010.

5   Bhatia, 'Fast and Furious'.

6   Newslaundry, 'Can You Take It Barkha Dutt' (interview with Madhu Trehan, uploaded 6 Feb 2012).

7 'Army readies tough reply to Pak butchery', *Mail Today*, 10 Jan 2013.

8 Praveen Swami on CNN-IBN's *The Last Word*: 'Indian media's response to soldiers' killing jingoistic?', 10 Jan 2013.

9 Praveen Swami, 'Runaway grandmother sparked savage skirmish on LoC', *The Hindu*, 10 Jan 2013.

10 Praveen Swami, 'Locked in U.N. files, 15 years of bloodletting at the LoC', *The Hindu*, 30 Jan 2013.

11 Barkha Dutt, 'Confessions of a War Reporter', *Himal Southasian*, June 2001.

12 'We reserve the right to retaliate, says Army Chief', *The Hindu*, 14 Jan 2013; 'Theatre fest takes hit, plays by two Pakistani groups cancelled', *Indian Express*, 17 Jan 2013; 'PM rules out business as usual, as India turns up heat on Pak', *Hindustan Times*, 15 Jan 2013.

13 Mani Shankar Aiyar, 'The hostility industry', *Indian Express*, 16 Jan 2013.

14 NDTV lost the first round of that battle in 2013 when a court in New York dismissed the case against Nielsen on the grounds of lack of jurisdiction. NDTV has appealed, however, arguing that although the alleged wrongdoing occurred in India, their allegations were actually against Nielsen in New York.

15 Tharoor anecdote quoted in Bhatia, 'Fast and Furious', *Caravan* profile, 1 Dec 2012

16 Indiantelevision.com interview with Goswami, posted 18 Feb 2010.

17 'The bullet bites you', column by Arnab Goswami in *Outlook* magazine, 22 Aug 2011.

18 Robin Jeffrey, 'Missing from the Indian newsroom', *The Hindu*, 9 Apr 2012.

19 A study by Vinod Mudgal, of the Centre for the Study of Developing Societies, found that the country's leading English and Hindi newspapers devoted only 2 per cent of their coverage to rural issues. 'Rural Coverage in the Hindi and English Dailies', *Economic and Political Weekly*, 27 Aug 2011.

20 India ranked 141 out of 179 nations in the Reporters Without Borders 2013 Press Freedom Index, and equal 79 out of 193 in the 2012 index produced by Freedom House.

21 Interview with the author.

22 Standing Committee on Information Technology (2012–13), Fifteenth Lok Sabha, *Ministry of Information and Broadcasting. Issues Related to Paid News*, May 2013. The Bollywood movie mentioned was *Bunty aur Babli*.

23 'Press Council chairman Justice Katju slams media for dumbing down', interview with Damayanti Datta, *India Today*, 27 Jan 2012.

24 An annual report by the CMS Media Lab in New Delhi found that coverage of corruption had risen sharply between 2008 and 2011 (from 0.29 per cent of airtime in prime-time bulletins by the six main TV channels, to 8.11 per cent). Coverage was dominated by corruption among government bodies and services, but coverage of private-sector corruption rose from 4.6 per cent of airtime in 2010 to 15.3 per cent in 2011.

7: THIS LAND IS YOUR LAND

1   Simon Denyer, 'Indian communists turn sickles into hammers', Reuters, 5 Feb 2007.

2   Simon Denyer, 'Flagship India car plant bulldozes farmers' hopes', Reuters, 2 Feb 2007.

3   Critics argue that Banerjee's Trinamool Congress have adopted the violent tactics of the Communists since she took over as West Bengal's chief minister in 2011. For my own profile of Banerjee, see: Simon Denyer, 'Mamata Banerjee personifies populist force in Indian politics', *Washington Post*, 20 May. 2012.

4   Simon Denyer, 'Industry is the enemy for barricaded India farmers', Reuters, 5 Feb 2007.

5   Simon Denyer, 'Farm, factory row leaves communists red-faced', Reuters, 6 Feb 2007.

6   Simon Denyer, 'India Maoists exploit anger over land seizures', Reuters, 16 Mar 2007.

7   Banerjee's campaign slogan was 'Ma-Mati-Manush', Mother-Land-People.

8   Simon Denyer, 'Land battles threaten POSCO's Indian steel project', Reuters, 19 Mar 2007.

9   Rama Lakshmi, 'In India, Old Land Records Go Digital', *Washington Post*, 17 July 2009.

10 *Crime in India 2012*, National Crime Records Bureau, Table 3.2 http://ncrb. nic.in/

11 The Gazette of India. '*The Right to Fair Compensation and Transparency in Land Acquisition, Rehabilitation and Resettlement Act, 2013*'. Published on behalf of the Ministry of Law and Justice, 27 Sept 2013.

12 FICCI statement on Land Acquisition, 29 Aug 2013. Assocham statement quoted by Reuters, 'India's parliament passes land acquisition bill', 29 Aug 2013.

13 KPMG, *Global Anti-Bribery and Corruption Survey*, 14 Mar 2011.

14 Barun Mitra. 'Land Wars: People's aspirations confront with archaic legislation', *Liberty Institute*, 28 June 2011.

15 Liberty Institute, 'A grassroots initiative to document village land rights', Jan 2013.

16 Vasundhara Sanger, 'A mother speaks: I worry for her but I know Medha is right', *Times of India*, 19 Apr 2006.

17 Arundhati Roy, 'The Road To Harsud', *Outlook* magazine, 26 July 2004.

18 Simon Denyer, 'Passions rise as flagship India dam fills', Reuters, 7 Aug 2006.

19 Simon Denyer, 'Indian tribe defends "hill god" from foreign miner', Reuters, 30 Mar 2007.

8: GET UP, STAND UP

1   Simon Denyer and Rama Lakshmi, 'Anna Hazare inspires young, middle-class awakening in India', *Washington Post*, 19 August 2011.

2   Henry Foy, 'FACTBOX – Swami Ramdev, India's most popular yoga guru'.

3   Tinku Ray, 'First female police officer quits', BBC News website. 27 Nov 2007.

4   'The most powerful Indians in 2009: 70–74', *Indian Express*, 29 Mar 2009. 'Court to hear cola case after six weeks', *Times of India*, 5 Aug 2006. 'The House of Bhushan', *Tehelka*, 6 Sept 2008.

5   Rahul Bhatia, 'Fast and Furious. The turbulent reign of Arnab Goswami', *The Caravan*, 1 Dec 2012. The profile also provides an interesting account of how Goswami changed his mind over coverage of Hazare.

6   Rajeev Chandrasekhar, 'History will show that Jantar Mantar was the moment that triggered change', *New Indian Express*, 17 April 2011.

7   'Team Anna Hazare consists of Maoists, fascists & anarchists: Congress', *Economic Times*, 15 Aug 2011.

8   The historian Ramachandra Guha says he tried to advise Kejriwal at the time to stay away from the cameras, and not to respond to the provocations that came from the other side, but the advice clearly fell on deaf ears.

9   'The third flight path. Aruna Roy interviewed by Shoma Chaudhury', *Tehelka* vol 8 issue 32, 13 Aug 2011.

10 Rama Lakshmi, 'India's Baba Ramdev is guru, TV star and source of contro-versy', *Washington Post*, 24 Dec 2009; Damayanti Datta, with Piyush Babele, 'Billionaire Baba', *India Today*, 20 June 2011; Pradeep Thakur, 'Remittances by Ramdev under Ed scanner', *Times of India*, 14 Aug 2011.

11 Manoj Rawat and Mahipal Kunwar, 'Baba Ramdev's epic swindle', *Tehelka*, 19 Mar 2012.

12 'Rs 5 crore demand on Ramdev's trusts for alleged tax evasion', Press Trust of India, 11 Nov 2012.

13 'Corrupt, repressive and stupid', editorial, *The Hindu*, 17 Aug 2011.

14 Simon Denyer and Rama Lakshmi, 'Anna Hazare, India's leading anti-corrup-tion activist, refuses to leave Delhi jail', *Washington Post*, 16 Aug 2011.

15 Simon Denyer and Rama Lakshmi, 'Indian PM slams anti-corruption activist as protests over arrest spread', *Washington Post*, 17 Aug 2011.

16 Simon Denyer and Rama Lakshmi, 'Indian activist wins right to fast in public, prepares to leave jail', *Washington Post*, 18 Aug 2011.

17 Simon Denyer, 'India anti-corruption movement loses steam', *Washington Post*, 3 Jan 2012.

18 Anna Hazare with *Indian Express* Editor-in-Chief Shekhar Gupta on NDTV 24x7's *Walk The Talk*, transcript published in *Indian Express*, 6 Nov 2012.

9: HOW CAN YOU MEND A BROKEN HEART?

1   *Indian Express*, transcript of Arun Shourie's interview with Shekhar Gupta on NDTV's *Walk The Talk*, 18 Sept 2011.

2   Rajya Sabha website, Official debates. Government Bill. The Lokpal and Lokayutas Bill, 2011. 29/12/2011.

3   'Parliament's most shameful hour', Headlines Today, 30 Dec 2011.

4   Ramachandra Guha, *India After Gandhi*, Picador India, 2007, pp. 146–50.

5   PRS Legislative Research, *Vital Stats. 60 Years of Parliament*.

6   Nehru's speech to the Lok Sabha was itself extensively cited by former President R. Venkataraman at a seminar on Nehru and Parliament, held in New Delhi on 14 Nov 1985. Reproduced in *Mainstream Weekly*, 5 May 2009.

7   'Quiet rehabilitation? UPA sends out the wrong signals by inducting tainted leaders in House panels', *Times of India*, 5 Oct 2012.

8   PRS Legislative Research, *Vital Stats. 60 Years of Parliament*.

9   Perhaps the most controversial judgement of recent years was the Supreme Court's 2012 decision to cancel 122 telecom spectrum licences in the wake of the 2G scandal, and to rule that spectrum should be considered a natural resource, and sold only via a competitive auction process. In the process, the court moved into areas of policymaking normally reserved for the executive.

10   'Will the honest netas please stand up?', *Hindustan Times*, 28 Nov 2011.

11   PRS Legislative Research, *Vital Stats. Working of State Assemblies*.

12   Shashi Tharoor, 'Shall we call the president?', *Tehelka*, 17 Dec 2011.

13   Baijayant 'Jay' Panda, 'Choosing between reform and referendum', *The Hindu*, 11 Jan 2012.

14   Baijayant 'Jay' Panda, 'House of opportunity', *Indian Express*, 22 Nov 2012.

15   K. Srinivasan, 'MPs score card till winter session 2012 of 15th Lok Sabha – interesting facts', India Vision 2020 Yahoo group.

16   Ramachandra Guha, 'Degrading democracy', *The Telegraph* (Calcutta), 3 Dec 2011.

17   NDTV, *The Big Fight*, 'Weak government, disruptive opposition?', 4 May 2013.

10: FIGHT THE POWER

1   Simon Denyer, 'The angry face of India's anti-corruption battle', *Washington Post* World Views blog, 9 Nov 2012.

2   Rama Lakshmi, 'India's anti-corruption activists are back on the scene', *Washington Post*, 19 Oct 2012.

3   Saba Naqvi, 'Robert Vadra: His Royal Son-In-Lawlessness', *Outlook*, 22 Oct 2012.

4   Sunetra Choudhury and Abhinav Bhatt, 'Never attack family: Digvijaya Singh's lesson on political ethics to Arvind Kejriwal', NDTV, 16 Oct, 2012.

5   Lakshmi, 'India's anti-corruption activists are back on the scene'.

6   Shekhar Gupta, 'First family, second nature', *Indian Express*, 13 Oct 2012.

7   Sagarika Ghose, 'Robert Vadra vs Arvind Kejriwal: this is also a class war', CNN-IBN website, 11 Oct 2012.

8   'Salman Khurshid calls Kejriwal a "guttersnipe"', India TV news, 14 Oct 2013; 'Angry Salman Khurshid's words kick up storm', *Hindustan Times*, 17 Oct 2012.

9   'Kejriwal has a streak of Hitler in him: Digvijaya', *Hindustan Times*, 19 Oct

2012. 'Salman Khurshid will not do a scam for Rs.71 lakh, says Beni Prasad Verma', Headlines Today/*India Today* website, 15 Oct 2012.

10   Simon Denyer and Rama Lakshmi, 'India anti-corruption crusader ups ante', *Washington Post*, 10 Nov 2012.

11   Ramachandra Guha, *India after Gandhi*, Picador India, 2007, pp. 483–8.

12   ibid., p. 597.

13   'Corrupt ministers will be jailed six months of AAP coming to power: Kejriwal', Zee News, 26 Nov 2012.

14   A popular street snack which consists of a round, hollow crisp fried Indian bread, filled with a potato-based stuffing and dipped in spicy masala water.

15   Rahul Gandhi address to Confederation of Indian Industry in New Delhi, 4 Apr 2013

16   Pratap Bhanu Mehta, 'Left Behind', *Indian Express*, 9 Dec 2013.

17   In September 2013, in what one independent Rajya Sabha member Rajeev Chandrasekhar announced that he had donated 500,000 rupees ($8,000) to the Aam Admi Party for its Delhi campaign, saying its views on transparency and corruption-free government "resonate closely" with his beliefs.

11: HARD TIMES FOR AN HONEST MAN

1   Parakram Rautela, 'Going on 41', *Times of India*, 21 Oct 2012.

2   Letter from Khemka (Inspector-General of Registration, Haryana) to All Deputy Commissioners-cum-Registrars in State of Haryana, dated 11 Oct 2012. Notes on internal memo, signed by Khemka, dated 12 Oct 2012.

3   Vadra is certainly not alone in using family connections to make money in India, and he may not have been the first to use the Gandhi name in this regard. In 2013, a series of US embassy cables released by WikiLeaks reported that Rajiv Gandhi, before entering politics, had acted as a middleman for a Swedish company looking to tie up a fighter aircraft deal, and that Sanjay Gandhi's company Maruti had sought a similar role for the British Aircraft Corporation in the 1970s. (Murali N. Krishnaswamy, 'Rajiv Gandhi was "entrepreneur" for Swedish jet, U.S cable says', *The Hindu*, 8 Apr 2013; P. J. George, 'Sanjay Gandhi's Maruti sought to bat for British plane', *The Hindu*, 9 Apr 2013.)

4   Letter from Khemka to Chief Secretary, Government of Haryana, dated 12 Oct 2012. Order from Khemka revoking mutation of land, 12 Oct 2012.

5   The Sitaram Jindal Foundation recognized Khemka in 2011 as joint winner in the category 'Crusade Against Corruption'.

6   Simon Denyer, 'Rule-following official in India gains notoriety', *Washington Post*, 23 Oct 2012.

7   Shalini Singh, 'Behind realty rush in Haryana, a gilt-edged licence raj', *The Hindu*, 4 Feb 2013.

8   'Indian bureaucracy rated worst in Asia', Press Trust of India, 11 Jan 2012, via *India Today*.

9   Inflation-linked pensions for civil servants do help to redress the balance vis-à-vis private sector employees over their lifetimes.

10 Chetan Bhagat, 'Rescue the Nation', *Times of India*, 19 May 2012. As Milan Vaishnav of the Carnegie Endowment for International Peace in Washington, D.C. has noted, India is often seen as a country overburdened by a massive and overbearing bureaucracy, but the reality is somewhat different. In fact, the bureaucracy, like the police and judiciary, is often seriously understaffed. India has one of the lowest rates of per capita public-sector employment of any G20 country, and government employment in India as a whole is on the decline.

11 For a full set of the Administrative Reform Commission's reports see http://arc.gov.in/

12 Shailaja Chandra, 'A better bureaucrat', *Indian Express*, 24 Apr 2012.

13 Letter of 3 Jan 2008, from Sudhir Mittal, Joint Secretary, Ministry of Environment and Forests, to Sanjiv Chaturvedi.

14 Letter dated 19 Jan 2011, from R. R. Rashmi, Joint Secretary to Government of India and Chief Vigilance Officer, Ministry of Environment and Forests (on behalf of president), to Chief Secretary, Government of Haryana, Chandigarh.

15 See letter from Jairam Ramesh, Minister of State (Independent Charge), MoEF, 20 June 2011, to Captain Ajay Singh Yadav, Minister of Environment, Forests, Power and Planning, GoH, Chandigarh. Says evidence supplied by Chaturvedi is robust and referring case to Central Vigilance Commission. Says no cause to review earlier decision revoking charges against him.

16 Jyotsna Singh, 'Controversial AIIMS director transferred out after seven years', *Deccan Herald*, 16 Nov 2012.

17 Astonishingly, the Haryana state government brought fresh charges against Chaturvedi even after he was transferred to Delhi, relating to the very Jhajjar scam he had exposed. These charges were again quashed by the President, on behalf of the Ministry of Environment and Forests in October 2013. See 'Centre Rescues Whistleblower Again', *The Hindu*, 5 Oct 2013.

18 Reddy's son Jagan Mohan Reddy was arrested in 2012 and charged with amassing vast wealth that was disproportionate to his income. Reddy had previously resigned from Congress after being sidelined for the party leadership, and says the charges are politically motivated.

19 In the summer of 2013, another honest bureaucrat captured the nation's imagination. Durga Shakti Nagpal launched a drive against corruption and illegal sand mining in western Uttar Pradesh, only to be suspended by the state government on what was widely seen as a flimsy excuse. After a national outcry, her suspension was revoked.

12: ISOLATION

1 Human Rights Watch, '"These Fellows Must Be Eliminated." Relentless Violence and Impunity in Manipur', 29 Sept 2008.

2 *Report of the Committee on Amendments to Criminal Law*, Justice J. S. Verma (retd), chairman; Justice Leila Seth (retd), member; Gopal Subramaniam, member. 23 Jan 2013.

3 Simon Denyer, 'Indians in remote state plead for curbs on army', Reuters, 21 Aug 2005.

4 Simon Denyer, 'Alienation breeds insurgency in Manipur', Reuters, 31 Aug 2005.

5 Amnesty International, 'Manipur: The silencing of youth', May 1998.

6 The British government had used even more cruel tactics against the Suffragettes who were campaigning for women's right to vote at the beginning of the twentieth century. Suffragettes on hunger strike in prison would not be force-fed, but instead allowed to grow weaker and weaker. When they were finally released, they were too weak to rejoin the struggle; as soon as their strength returned, they would be re-arrested. As a result, the movement was forced to adopt more extreme tactics.

7 Simon Denyer, 'Manipuri woman shifts protest to Delhi', Reuters, 4 Oct 2006.

8 Report of the Committee, headed by Justice (Retd) B. P. Jeevan Reddy, to Review the Armed Forces (Special Powers) Act 1958. Submitted to the Government of India in June 2005. Published by *The Hindu*.

9 Simon Denyer, 'In Kashmir, Indian army's grip still tight', *Washington Post*, 8 Dec 2011.

10 Aditya Menon, 'Omar says Kashmiris are normal people too', *Mail Today*, 7 Apr 2013.

11 Sanjoy Hazarika, 'An abomination called AFSPA', *The Hindu*, 12 Feb 2013.

12 Manipur. A memorandum on Extrajudicial, Arbitrary or Summary Executions Submitted by Civil Society Coalition on Human Rights in Manipur and the UN (CSCHR) to Christof Heyns, UN Special Rapporteur on extrajudicial, summary or arbitrary executions. Mission to India 19–30 Mar 2012.

13 For the stories of Neena and the other women of EEVFAM see Frank van Lierde, *We, Widows of the Gun*, joint publication of Manipuri NGOs and the Dutch international development organization Cordaid, 2011.

14 *Look East Policy and the Northeastern States*, Government of India, Ministry of Development of North Eastern Region, 15 Feb 2011.

15 Simon Denyer, 'As Burma opens, India hopes to turn eastern promise into reality', *Washington Post*, 22 Feb 2013.

16 Simon Denyer, 'In India's remote northeast, civilians challenge rape, killing by security forces', *Washington Post*, 18 Feb 2013.

17 Andrew Buncombe, 'One woman's silent quest for peace on India's wild frontier', *Independent*, 5 May 2010.

18 *Report of Commission of Inquiry, constituted by the Supreme Court of India, in Writ Petition (Criminal) 129 of 2012 [Extra Judicial Execution Victims' Families Association and Another (petitioners) Against Union of India and Others (respondents)], and Writ Petition (Civil) 445 of 2012 [Suresh Singh (petitioner) Against Union of India and Others (respondents)]*, 30 Mar 2013.

19 Christof Heyns, *Report of the Special Rapporteur on extrajudicial, summary or arbitrary executions*, 26 Apr 2013.

20 'Manipur, in focus', *Indian Express*, 8 Apr 2013.

13: I WANT TO BREAK FREE

1 United States Census Bureau.

2 *Annual Status of Education Report (Rural) 2012. Provisional*, 17 Jan 2013, pp. 47–53. Page 55 breaks it down by states.

3 Simon Denyer, 'Amid population boom, India hopes for "demographic dividend" but fears disaster', *Washington Post*, 15 Oct 2011.

4 *Times Higher Education, The World Rankings 2012–2013*.

5 World Bank news release, 'Vibrant cities and flexible labor laws critical for India's employment growth, says World Development Report 2013', 5 Nov 2012.

6 Columbia University's Arvind Panagariya makes a persuasive case that India's child malnutrition statistics exaggerate the scale of the problem. But that there is malnutrition no one denies. For more, read Panagariya, 'Does India Really Suffer from Worse Child Malnutrition Than Sub-Saharan Africa?', *Economic and Political Weekly*, 4 May 2013. For the counterargument, see Angus Deaton, Jean Dreze, 'Food and Nutrition in India: Facts and Interpretations', *Economic and Political Weekly*, 14 Feb 2009.

7 Dilip Chenoy, *India Infrastructure Report 2012*, ch. 18, 'Skill Development in India' National Skills Development Corporation, pp. 199–207.

8 Rama Lakshmi, 'In India, students' aspirations are misaligned with the job market', *Washington Post*, 18 Mar 2013.

9 Anu Madgavkar, senior fellow, McKinsey Global Institute, 'India's missing women workforce', *Mint*, 31 Dec 2012.

10 Jayan Jose Thomas, 'A woman-shaped gap in the Indian workforce', *The Hindu*, 9 Jan 2013.

11 Simon Denyer, 'Drug epidemic grips India's Punjab state', *Washington Post*, 1 Jan 2013.

12 Ranvinder Singh Sandhu, *Drug addiction in Punjab. A sociological study*, published by Guru Nanak Dev University, Amritsar, 2009.

13 Kaushik Basu, 'India's Demographic Dividend', BBC News website, 25 July 2007.

14 Daniela Yu and Linda Lyons, 'Nearly One-Third of Indians Are "Suffering"' Gallup.com', 30 Apr 2012. Data from the Pew Research Center Global Attitudes Project tend to give higher readings for Indians' optimism relative to other countries, but agree the mood has deteriorated sharply of late. 'The economic euphoria in India over the last few years, inspired by the country's seemingly inevitable march toward double-digit growth, has suddenly soured,' it wrote on 10 Sept 2012. 'Although still relatively upbeat compared with many other countries, the Indian public's confidence in their country's direction and future economic growth has declined significantly compared with just a year ago.'

15 Simon Denyer, 'Indians say their lives are getting worse, despite fast economic growth', *Washington Post*, 1 May 2012.

16 Ramachandra Guha. *India After Gandhi*, Prologue, 'Unnatural Nation', pp. xi–xxvi.

17 Ghanshyam Shah, Harsh Mander, Sukhadeo Thorat, Satish Deshpande, Amita Baviskar, *Untouchability in Rural India*, Sage Publications India, 2006, Table 2.9, p. 103.

18 Devesh Kapur, Chandra Bhan Prasad, Lant Pritchett, D. Shyam Babu, 'Rethinking Inequality: Dalits in Uttar Pradesh in the Market Reform Era', *Economic & Political Weekly*, 28 Aug 2010.

19 Hugo Gorringe, 'When development triggers caste violence', *The Hindu*, 8 May 2013.

14: THE AGE OF INFORMATION

1   *India Corruption Study 2010*, CMS India and Transparency International India.

2   Robin Jeffrey and Assa Doran, 'Mobile-izing: Democracy, Organization and India's First "Mass Mobile Phone" Elections', *Journal of Asian Studies*, vol 71, no. 1, Feb 2012.

3   Mobile phones also helped the BSP explain to their voters their unlikely partnership with the highest caste in India, the Brahmins – a partnership that was crucial in the party's victory.

4   *Social media and Lok Sabha Elections*, a study by IRIS Knowledge Foundation, supported by the Internet and Mobile Association of India, released in 2013.

5   A study of election results in Uttar Pradesh by Abhijit V. Banerjee of MIT and Rohini Pande of Harvard (*Parochial Politics; Ethnic Preferences and Politician Corruption*) found that the more people voted along caste lines, the more corrupt were the politicians they elected.

6   Poonam Gupta of the Indian Council of Research in International Economic Relations and Arvind Panagariya of Columbia University, *India: Election Outcomes and Economic Performance*, SIPA working paper, Columbia University, 2011.

7   Arvind Panagariya, 'Is anti-incumbency really pass?', *Economic Times*, 28 May 2009.

8   In aspiring India, voters demand growth', *Washington Post*, 14 Mar 2012.

9   Simon Denyer, 'In India, letting states lead the way', *Washington Post*, 24 Oct 2012.

10 Shekhar Gupta, 'They just didn't get it', *Indian Express*, 7 Mar 2012.

11 Pratap Bhanu Mehta, 'Mandate for a Dream', *Indian Express*, 7 Mar 2012.

12 Milan Vaishnav, 'India Needs More Democracy Not Less', *Foreign Affairs*, 11 Apr 2013.

13 Devesh Kapur and Arvind Subramanian, 'India must look to the states for salvation', *Financial Times* op-ed, 11 June 2012.

15: I'M THE MAN

1   *India Today*-Nielsen Mood of the Nation Poll.

2   Simon Denyer, 'The Two Views on Narendra Modi', *Washington Post*, 5 Apr 2012.

3   Nilanjan Mukhopadhyay, *Narendra Modi. The Man. The Times*, Tranquebar Press, 2013, pp. 28, 31, 56–7, 63.

4   ibid., p. 69.

5   Vinod K. Jose, 'The Emperor Uncrowned. The rise of Narendra Modi', *The Caravan*, Mar 2012.

6   Mukhopadhyay, *Narendra Modi*, pp. 66–9, offers a detailed account of the secrecy surrounding Modi's marriage and the hostility directed towards one journalist who tried to seek out Jashodaben.

7   Jose, 'The Emperor Uncrowned'.

8   Human Rights Watch, *We have No Orders to Save You. State Participation and Complicity in Communal Violence in Gujarat*, 30 Apr 2002.

9   Human Rights Watch, *A Decade On, Gujarat Justice Incomplete*, 24 Feb 2012.

10 Annie Banerji, 'Indian nationalist lawmaker gets 28 years for 2002 massacre', Reuters, 31 Aug 2012.

11 Jason Overdorf, 'India: Modi "not prosecutable" for Gujarat riots', *Global Post*, 10 Feb 2012.

12 Karan Thapar interview with Narendra Modi on CNN-IBN's *Devil's Advocate* programme, IBN live website, 19 Oct 2007.

13 Statement of Shri Narendra Modi to Special Investigation Team, 27–28/3/10.

14 *Social, Economic and Educational Status of the Muslim Community of India. A Report*, Prime Minister's High-Level Committee, Cabinet Secretariat, Government of India, November 2006.

15 Simon Denyer, 'Tale of two cities as Gujarat goes to the polls', Reuters, 7 Dec 2007.

16 Zahir Janmohamed writes eloquently about life in Juhapura. See 'Life After The Riots – Education, Employment, Empowerment', *Outlook* magazine, 8 Apr 2013. For his experiences during the riots, see 'Sanjay and me; Zahir Janmohamed', Kafila.org 24 Feb 2013.

17 Mukhopadhyay, *Narendra Modi*, p. 320.

18 'Should We Run Relief Camps? Open Child Producing Centres?' *Outlook India*, 30 Sep 2002.

19 Letter from Deputy Inspector General D. G. Vanzara (from Sabarmati Central Prison, Ahmedabad) to Additional Chief Secretary, Home Department, Government of Gujarat, dated 1 Sept 2013, reproduced by *International Business Times*.

20 Simon Denyer, 'Modi plays Hindu card in tight Gujarat poll', Reuters, 6 Dec 2007.

21 Hartosh Singh Bal, 'Modi and the Muslims' Malaise', Latitude blog. *New York Times*, 3 Jan 2013.

22 Hasan Suroor, 'Manmohan Singh's apology for Anti-Sikh riots a "Gandhian moment of moral clarity," says 2005 cable', *The Hindu*, 22 Apr 2011.

23 Arvind Panagariya, 'The Gujarat miracle', *Times of India*, 22 Sept 2012.

24 Planning Commission data on growth (Table 91), per capita income (Table 97) and transmission and distribution losses (Table 84).

25 Bibek Debroy, *Gujarat: Governance for Growth and Development*, Academic Foundation, 2012, p. 20.

26 Debroy, *Gujarat*, p. 57.

27 Simon Denyer, 'U.S. Automakers in Race for Indian Market', *Washington Post*, 18 Mar 2012.

28 *India Today* State of the States Survey 2012.

29 Saba Naqvi, 'Narendra Modi. On Clout Nine', *Outlook*, 11 June 2012.

30 Centre for Monitoring Indian Economy, CapEx database.

31 Mukhopadhyay, *Narendra Modi,* p. 288.

32 Ibid., p. 286.

33 Vinod K. Jose, 'The Emperor Uncrowned: The rise of Narendra Modi', *The Caravan*, Mar 2012.

34 Ramachandra Guha compares Modi to Indira Gandhi beween 1971 and 1977 'with a touch of Sanjay Gandhi' in 'The Man Who Would Rule India', *The Hindu*, 8 Feb 2013. A more direct comparison with Sanjay is made by Vinod Mehta in an interview with rediff.com's Saisuresh Sivaswami on 7 Mar 2013, 'Is Narendra Modi Another Sanjay Gandhi?'

35 US Embassy Cable dated 2 Nov 2006, #84043, signed by Consul General in Mumbai, Michael S. Owen, reprinted by *The Hindu*, via WikiLeaks.

36 Letter from US Assistant Secretary of State Robert O. Blake to Ron Somers, 27 Jan 2012.

37 'There are close links between Britain and Gujarat', speech by British High Commissioner to India Sir James Bevan to the Vibrant Gujarat Global Investors Summit, 11 Jan 2013.

38 IBN Live, 'Narendra Modi's victory speech after a hat-trick in Gujarat elections', 21 Dec 2012.

39 'Mr Modi has capital ideas', *Hindustan Times* editorial, 7 Feb 2013.

40 Rahul Gandhi address to Confederation of Indian Industry in New Delhi, 4 Apr 2013.

16: HELL IS FOR CHILDREN

1 Simon Denyer, 'India child maids face slavery, abuse and sometimes rape', *Washington Post*, 19 Jan 2013.

2 High Court of Delhi Judgement, 15 July 2009: Save the Childhood Foundation & others versus Union of India & others.

3 Supreme Court of India, 18 Apr 2011: Bachpan Bachao Andolan versus Union of India & others.

4 Simon Denyer, 'Child murders show India's poor live below justice', Reuters, 11 Jan 2007.

5 Simon Denyer, 'India uses "truth serum" as media bays for blood', Reuters, 12 Jan 2007.

6 Bachpan Bachao Andolan (BBA), *Missing Children of India*, a research study, Vitasta, 2011.

7 Simon Denyer, 'India slowly confronts epidemic of missing children', *Washington Post*, 23 Sept 2012.

8 *Report of the Committee on Amendments to Criminal Law*, Justice J. S. Verma

(retd), chairman; Justice Leila Seth (retd), member; Gopal Subramaniam, member, 23 Jan 2013.

9 'India dramatically tightens laws on sexual assault, trafficking after gang rape', *Washington Post*, 3 Feb 2013.

10 Simon Denyer, 'A young rape victim's story moves India's official panelists to give', *Washington Post* World Views blog, 24 Jan 2013.

11 Supreme Court verdict in case of Bachpan Bachao Andolan versus Union of India & others, 10 May 2013.

12 Rama Lakshmi, 'India legislators pass strict anti-rape law', *Washington Post*, 19 Mar 2013.

13 Dwapayan Ghosh, 'Delhi reels under surge in major crimes since Jan 1', *Times of India*, 30 Mar 2013; 'Every 2 hours, a woman in Delhi is molested or raped', *Hindustan Times*, 8 Mar 2013.

14 Preetika Rana and Tripti Lahiri, 'The Verdict on Fast-Track Trials', *Wall Street Journal*, 11 Sept 2013.

15 Amanda Hodge, 'Caste skews India's view of rape', *The Australian*, 30 Aug 2013.

16 Rupa Jha, 'India's code of silence over sexual abuse', BBC news website, 14 Sept 2013.

17 'Woman sells 12-yr-old daughter for Rs 1 lakh to man who raped her', *Times of India*, 1 Oct 2013.

18 Priyanka Dubey, 'If My Wife And I Had Not Been Present There, We Would Never Have Believed Our Own Daughter', *Tehelka*, 2 Sept 2013.

19 Jason Burke, 'Delhi rape: how India's other half lives', *Guardian*, 10 Sept 2013.

AFTERWORD

1 *Report of the Enquiry Committee on Grid Disturbance in Northern Region on 30th July 2012 and in Northern, Eastern and North-Eastern Region on 31st July 2012*, issued 16 Aug 2012.

2 Simon Denyer, 'India hit by largest blackout in a decade', *Washington Post*, 31 July 2012.

3 Simon Denyer and Rama Lakshmi, 'Power fails in half of India', *Washington Post*, 1 Aug 2012.

4 Debi Goenka and Sarath Guttikunda, 'Coal Kills: An Assessment of Death and Disease Caused by India's Dirtiest Energy Source', Conservation Action Trust, Urban Emissions and Greenpeace India, 11 March 2013. The study suggested that emissions from coal-fired power stations caused between 80,000 and 115,000 premature deaths a year, as well as more than 20 million asthma cases. Another study by Maureen Cropper, Shama Gamkhar, Kabir Malik, Alex Limonov and Ian Partridge published by Resources for the Future in June 2012 surveyed 63 of India's major power plants and estimated 650 deaths per power plant per year. Part of the reason is the high ash content of Indian coal – the University of Maryland's Maureen Cropper says that simply

washing the coal would reduce deaths by 20 per cent. Currently only 4 per cent of Indian coal is washed. See also Muthukumara Mani, 'Washing coal could save lives in India', on the World Bank blog, End Poverty in South Asia, 29 Apr 2013.

5   World Bank, *More and Better Jobs in South Asia*, Apr 2012.

6   Simon Denyer and Rama Lakshmi, 'Historic blackout fuels doubts about India's ambitions', *Washington Post*, 2 Aug 2012.

7   Simon Denyer and Rama Lakshmi, 'In India, satisfying thirst for energy is key to future', *Washington Post*, 23 Aug 2012.

8   Rama Lakshmi and Simon Denyer, 'What blackout? Many Indian villagers live in the dark', *Washington Post*, 7 Aug 2012.

9   Simon Denyer and Rama Lakshmi, 'In India, power corrupts', *Washington Post*, 4 Oct 2012.

10 Arvind Subramanian, 'Can India's Power Problems Be Solved?', Peterson Institute for International Economics, Real Time Economic Issues Watch, 2 Aug 2012.

11 Chetan Bhagat, 'Open letter to the Indian Change Seekers', *The Times of India,* 13 Jan 2013.

Acknowledgements

Inevitably, a book of this nature draws upon the expertise and insight of very many people. The first person I have to thank is my fantastic *Washington Post* colleague Rama Lakshmi, whose reporting I draw on extensively in this book. Rama's knowledge and advice were invaluable throughout my second stint in New Delhi, and we spent many hours discussing India and the issues raised here. She also gave me excellent feedback on the first draft of this book. I am grateful to my foreign editor, Douglas Jehl, for giving me time to write while I was also in the process of moving from India to China, and to the entire foreign desk at the *Post* in DC who helped improve my stories on innumerable occasions. At the *Washington Post* in India, my researcher and translator Suhasini Raj, office manager Pavitra Gulati, and driver Ashok Pandey were a support team *par excellence*, while I could never have written this book without our lovely housekeeper Amuda Prakash bringing me endless cups of tea. At Reuters, I want to thank my former assistant Kriti Anand and the entire New Delhi bureau, whose members included some great journalists and very good friends, as well as a team of reporters around the country who accompanied me on many of my trips and provided useful local insight.

This book would never have happened without my agent Patrick Walsh, whose advice, encouragement and good humour helped me turn an initial set of ideas into a coherent proposal. My fabulous editors at Bloomsbury, Bill Swainson and Diya Kar Hazra, then did a first-class job helping me turn a rough-hewn first draft into what I hope is a more polished final product.

I would like to thank everyone who I interviewed in the course of researching this book and during my seven years reporting in India, and who generously welcomed me into their homes and their lives. Some are named in this book, many are not, but to all of them I am grateful.

I have deep admiration for the work of activists whose lives are dedicated to helping the most vulnerable members of Indian society, and I am proud to count some of them as friends. In particular I want to thank and pay tribute to Babloo Loitongbam of Manipur Human Rights Alert, Bhuwan Ribhu of Bachpan Bachao Andolan, and Anjali Gupta, Nikhil Dey and Shekhar Singh of the National Campaign for People's Right to Information.

Many others spent considerable time with me over the course my stay in India and to them I owe many of the ideas in this book. There is no room to mention everyone here, but for their time, feedback and thoughts I am especially indebted to: Barun Mitra of the Liberty Institute; M. R. Madhavan and Chakshu Roy at PRS Legislative Research as well as Jagdeep Chhokar and Anil Bairwal of the Alliance for Democratic Reforms, who are all doing fine work to deepen Indian democracy; Zahir Janmohamed, whose own book on Gujarat I am looking forward to; Rajya Sabha member Rajeev Chandrasekhar and Lok Sabha member Baijayant 'Jay' Panda, who are among the most interesting thinkers about Indian democracy operating within the system; Arvind Kejriwal, who is attempting to break in from outside; Ashok Khemka and Sanjeev Chaturvedi, who risked their careers to force through change; Suneeta Tyagi, who welcomed us in Haryana; Arvind Panagariya of Columbia University, Arvind Subramanian of the Peterson Institute for International Economics and Milan Vaishnav of the Carnegie Endowment for International Peace, who are among my favourite observers of India in the United States; historian Ramachandra Guha, whose ideas on democracy inspired me; and *Indian Express* editor-in-chief Shekhar

Gupta and NDTV's Managing Editor Vikram Chandra. I must also mention my debt to the ideas of Pratap Bhanu Mehta of the Centre for Policy Research and to the research of Human Rights Watch, to books by Aarthi Ramachandran, Nilanjan Mukhopadhyay and Patrick French, and to some excellent journalism by reporters at magazines *The Caravan* and *Tehelka*.

In particular, I want to thank those people who took the time to tell me their life stories, sometimes dredging up painful memories at considerable emotional cost. Among them were J's father B and her friend Awindra Pandey; Irom Sharmila and her family; Neena Ningombam and the women of EEVFAM in Manipur; Manorama Devi's mother Shakhi; Mary (whose real name I have concealed in this book); the women of Haryana; farmers who lost their land; and mothers who lost their children.

My friends Kim Barker, Alex Perry, Gareth Conde, Mark Milton and James Tapper gave me useful help and encouragement at various stages in this book's development.

But above all, I want to thank my family, starting with my mum and dad, who are sadly no longer around to see this book but sacrificed a tremendous amount to give me an excellent education and upbringing.

Finally I want to thank my wonderful wife Sarah and lovely daughter Molly, whose love, support and laughter really made this book possible. Without their encouragement and their belief in me, without their patience and understanding, I would have never made it to this point.

Thank you all.

Index